# The Art of Caregiving in Fiction, Film, and Memoir

Also by Jeffrey Berman

*Joseph Conrad: Writing as Rescue*
*The Talking Cure: Literary Representations of Psychoanalysis*
*Narcissism and the Novel*
*Diaries to an English Professor: Pain and Growth in the Classroom*
*Surviving Literary Suicide*
*Risky Writing: Self-Disclosure and Self-Transformation in the Classroom*
*Empathic Teaching: Education for Life*
*Dying to Teach: A Memoir of Love, Loss, and Learning*
*Cutting and the Pedagogy of Self-Disclosure* (with Patricia Hatch Wallace)
*Death in the Classroom: Writing about Love and Loss*
*Companionship in Grief: Love and Loss in the Memoirs of C.S. Lewis, John Bayley, Donald Hall, Joan Didion, and Calvin Trillin*
*Death Education in the Writing Classroom*
*Dying in Character: Memoirs on the End of Life*
*Confidentiality and Its Discontents: Dilemmas of Privacy in Psychotherapy* (with Paul W. Mosher)
*Writing Widowhood: The Landscapes of Bereavement*
*Writing the Talking Cure: Irvin D. Yalom and the Literature of Psychotherapy*
*Off the Tracks: Cautionary Tales about the Derailing of Mental Health Care* (with Paul W. Mosher): Vol. 1: *Sexual and Nonsexual Boundary Violations*; Vol. 2: *Scientology, Psychoanalyst Meets Aliens, False Memories, The Scopes Trial of Psychoanalysis, Bizarre Surgery, Lobotomy, and the Siren Call of Psychopharmacology*
*Mad Muse: The Mental Illness Memoir in a Writer's Life and Work*

# The Art of Caregiving in Fiction, Film, and Memoir

Jeffrey Berman

BLOOMSBURY ACADEMIC
LONDON • NEW YORK • OXFORD • NEW DELHI • SYDNEY

BLOOMSBURY ACADEMIC
Bloomsbury Publishing Plc
50 Bedford Square, London, WC1B 3DP, UK
1385 Broadway, New York, NY 10018, USA

BLOOMSBURY, BLOOMSBURY ACADEMIC and the Diana logo are trademarks of
Bloomsbury Publishing Plc

First published in Great Britain 2021

Paperback edition published 2022

Copyright © Jeffrey Berman, 2021, 2022

Jeffrey Berman has asserted his right under the Copyright, Designs and Patents Act, 1988, to be identified as Author of this work.

For legal purposes the Acknowledgments on p. viii constitute an extension of this copyright page.

Cover design: Namkwan Cho
Cover image © iStock.com/Pobytov

All rights reserved. No part of this publication may be reproduced or transmitted in any form or by any means, electronic or mechanical, including photocopying, recording, or any information storage or retrieval system, without prior permission in writing from the publishers.

Bloomsbury Publishing Plc does not have any control over, or responsibility for, any third-party websites referred to or in this book. All internet addresses given in this book were correct at the time of going to press. The author and publisher regret any inconvenience caused if addresses have changed or sites have ceased to exist, but can accept no responsibility for any such changes.

A catalogue record for this book is available from the British Library.

A catalog record for this book is available from the Library of Congress.

ISBN: HB: 978-1-3501-6657-8
PB: 978-1-3501-8536-4
ePDF: 978-1-3501-6658-5
eBook: 978-1-3501-6659-2

Typeset by Deanta Global Publishing Services, Chennai, India

To find out more about our authors and books visit www.bloomsbury.com and sign up for our newsletters.

*For Julie, Again and Again*

# Contents

| | |
|---|---|
| Acknowledgments | viii |
| Introduction | 1 |
| 1  The Idealized Caregiver in Tolstoy's *The Death of Ivan Ilych* | 19 |
| 2  Caregivers as Prisoners for Life in Edith Wharton's *Ethan Frome* | 31 |
| 3  Unmasking the Caregiver in Ingmar Bergman's *Persona* | 53 |
| 4  The Caregiver as Matchmaker in Alice Munro's "The Bear Came Over the Mountain" and Sarah Polley's *Away from Her* | 73 |
| 5  Caregiving Strategies for Survival in John Bayley's *Elegy for Iris*, *Iris and Her Friends*, and *Widower's House* | 95 |
| 6  A Few True Things about Caregiving in Anna Quindlen's *One True Thing* | 123 |
| 7  The Avenging Caregiver in Mary Gordon's *Circling My Mother* | 147 |
| 8  Murderous Caregiving in Michael Haneke's *Amour* | 171 |
| 9  The Divine Gift of Caregiving in Walter Mosley's *The Last Days of Ptolemy Grey* | 193 |
| 10 Caregiving as a Progress Narrative in Margaret Morganroth Gullette's Writings | 207 |
| 11 Caregivers Struggling to Make the Right Decisions in Atul Gawande's *Being Mortal* | 233 |
| Conclusion: Caregiving—A Beautiful Story? | 255 |
| Works Cited | 263 |
| Index | 280 |

# Acknowledgments

A small section of my discussion of *One True Thing* first appeared in *Dying to Teach: A Memoir of Love, Loss, and Learning* (Albany: State University of New York Press, 2007). A longer and slightly different version of chapter 5 appeared in *Companionship in Grief: Love and Loss in the Memoirs of C. S. Lewis, John Bayley, Donald Hall, Joan Didion, and Calvin Trilling* (Amherst: University of Massachusetts Press, 2010).

I am deeply grateful to Ben Doyle, publisher for Literary Studies at Bloomsbury Academic Books, for his enthusiasm and expertise. To paraphrase Henry James, Ben is one of the people on whom nothing is lost. Special thanks to Lucy Brown, assistant editor for Literary Studies at Bloomsbury Academic, for patiently answering my questions and helping me prepare the manuscript for publication. I am grateful to the two anonymous reviewers for their many helpful suggestions for revision. I alone am responsible for whatever lingering weaknesses that remain.

I would not have been able to conduct the research for this book without the invaluable help of the Interlibrary Loan staff at the University at Albany. Thanks to Timothy Jackson, Angela Persico, and Glen Benedict for fulfilling scores of interlibrary loan requests.

# Introduction

"There are only four kinds of people in this world," Rosalynn Carter remarks at the beginning of her 1994 book *Helping Yourself Help Others*: "Those who have been caregivers; those who currently are caregivers; those who will be caregivers; and those who will need caregivers." Adds the former American First Lady, lest we fail to appreciate the meaning of her words, "That pretty much covers all of us!" (3). Carter, a lifelong caregiver, mental health advocate, and honorary chair of the Rosalynn Carter Institute for Human Development at Georgia Southwestern College in Americus, Georgia, doesn't take credit for this comment, which she attributes it to an unnamed colleague. Quoting these words in her 2012 interview with Carter, Sherri Snelling notes that there are 65 million American caregivers, a figure that continues to grow as the population expands and baby boomers age. Snelling, former chair of the National Alliance for Caregiving, points out in her 2013 book *A Cast of Characters* that as a result of increased longevity and a growing older population, we are creating a "new class in society called caregivers who face a potentially later lifelong commitment to care for a loved one" (122).

The growing importance of caregiving may also be seen in the arts. One can't pick up an issue of *AARP Bulletin, AARP The Magazine, Parade*, or *Reader's Digest*, not to mention more specialized print and online publications such as *Today's Caregiver, Caregiver Solutions*, or *Provider*, without reading about the latest novel, film, or memoir about caregiving. Bestselling films like *Away from Her*, starring a ravishing Julie Christie, and *Still Alice*, starring a radiant Julianne Moore, depict the caregiver's struggle with a spouse suffering from Alzheimer's disease. John Bayley penned three memoirs, including *Elegy for Iris*, about caring for his wife, the distinguished British novelist Iris Murdoch, who suffered from Alzheimer's. Anna Quindlen's bestselling novel *One True Thing* is a fictionalized account of her experience caring for her mother, who died of ovarian cancer. Each year a spate of how-to books on caregiving appears, offering much-needed advice to millions of people.

The art of caregiving is a challenging one, perhaps the hardest role in life, one for which most people are not prepared. The subtitle of Snelling's 2013 book,

*Celebrity Stories to Help You Prepare to Care*, conveys her effort to show how the rich-and-famous grapple with the same caregiving problem as everyone else. Snelling shines the best possible light on the subject, as her statement in the preface suggests. "Caregiving is a role which most of us will star or at least be a co-star. It is up to us whether we triumph or flop. When you become a caregiver, you have stepped into the spotlight" (xii).

The spotlight, however, has not yet turned to the image of caregiving in the arts. Despite the explosive growth in the number of caregivers and the increasing depiction of caregiving in literature and films, there have been, to date, no book-length literary or cultural studies of the caregiver. How do we explain this curious scholarly neglect? To begin with, most people are too physically and emotionally exhausted and stressed to write about their experiences while they are still caregiving. According to *Family Caregiver Basics: A Practical Guide*, "More than two-thirds of individuals said caregiving had a negative impact on their career, and almost 80 percent said they missed work during the year to meet caregiving obligations." For many people, fatigue, exhaustion, isolation, and stress are an inevitable part of caregiving, along with depression and despair, but these factors alone do not explain entirely the scholarly neglect of the caregiver in the arts.

Another explanation is resistance, the same phenomenon Kathleen Woodward observes in *Aging and Its Discontents* (1991). "Over the past years I often found myself met by silence when I told people that I was working on a book on aging." Woodward interprets this response as a sign of puzzlement over the paucity of scholarly books on the subject. She remains convinced, however, that this silence "all too often speaks of a suspicion that the subject of aging is, simply, morbid" (21). Woodward then offers two personal examples of this resistance. The first involved a fellow literary scholar, Mary Russo, who mentioned to a colleague that she was part of a Modern Language Association panel on "Feminist Approaches to Aging" in 1988. "How depressing," the colleague commiserated, squeezing Russo's arm "in a gesture of wordless and sympathetic consolation." The second example involved Woodward herself. Explaining the topic of the present book to an "accomplished scholar of American literature," Woodward was told that she must be "obsessed" with aging. "I took her reaction," Woodward wryly reports, "as an index of *her* uneasiness with the subject" (22). Caregiving evokes the same anxiety as aging and death, partly because most caregivers care for elderly, infirm people, and partly because caregiving often involves end-of-life issues for those who will never reach old age.

Still another explanation is that caregiving commands little respect, as Emily K. Abel suggests in *Hearts of Wisdom: American Women Caring for*

Kin, 1850-1940 (2000). "Despite its central place in all of our lives, caregiving receives little social recognition. The dominant culture extols the virtues of independence, seeks distance from such basic life experiences as birth, illness, and death, and trivializes most unpaid work done by women in the home. The history of this activity remains almost completely hidden" (2).

## A Dangerous Activity

Roslyn Carter's definition of a caregiver is as good as any:

> A caregiver, in general, is one who provides assistance to a person to help him/her feel better about, cope with, or cure a physical or mental health problem. Financial remuneration for the assistance, although sometimes necessary to the health-care provider, is not the prime motivation of the true care*giver*. Rather, his or her desire to help a loved one with a critical health problem is a defining quality. (207)

There's nothing in this definition that suggests caregiving is a dangerous activity, but it is, one of the most dangerous, precisely because it is protracted, isolating, and exhausting. Sometimes a caregiver has no relief or respite. Often, caregiving is all-consuming. Speaking from personal experience, Rosalynn Carter, who for many years was the caregiver for her grandfather, father, and mother, as well as for her husband's three younger siblings, who all succumbed to cancer, admitted that caregiving can be extremely lonely, stressful, and frustrating—a traumatic activity.

> The emotional costs of caregiving can be high. According to a national survey published in 1987, by the Select Committee on Aging, many caregivers experience a limited social life, infringement of privacy, and sleep deprivation as a result of providing care. Indeed, many found the task physically and emotionally taxing, especially when they had to lift their loved one or endure his or her agitation, confusion, or dementia-related behavior. (28)

In a 2004 book chapter aptly called "Relentless Self-Care," Irene Renzenbrink likens the caregiver to a "wounded healer," a term coined by the Catholic priest Henri Nouwen. Renzenbrink quotes a comment expressed in 1987 by Robert Fulton, the founder of the Center for Death Education and Counseling at the University of Minnesota. "The time might not be too far distant when signs are posted over the entrance to terminal care wards that read, The Surgeon General of the United States has determined that the care of the terminally ill may be detrimental to your health" (848).

Two closely related phenomena—burn-out, the loss of ability to empathize as a result of caregiving, and compassion fatigue, the feeling of being overwhelmed by caring—are common, as is survivor guilt after the death of a loved one. When compared with the general population, Carter writes, "caregivers were three times more likely to be depressed, two to three times more likely to take psychotropic drugs (such as tranquilizers), and 12 percent more likely to use alcohol as a way to cope with stress" (29). The burden of caregiving usually falls on mothers and daughters: 80 percent of caregivers are women (136–7). Carter cites a survey conducted by Travelers Insurance Company of its own employees indicating that the typical working female caregiver devotes fifteen hours a week to caregiving, while the typical working male caregiver devotes only five hours (139).

*The Commonwealth Fund 1998 Survey of Women's Health* reviewed the impact of caregiving on health and access to health care and found that caregivers are often in need of care.

> One-quarter (25%) of women caring for a sick or disabled family member rate their own health as fair or poor, compared with one-sixth (17%) of other women. More than half (54%) of women caregivers have one or more chronic health conditions, compared with two-fifths (41%) of other women. In addition, half (51%) of all caregivers exhibit high depressive symptoms, while 38 percent of other women do so.

Scientific studies confirm that caregiving contributes to psychiatric morbidity. A 1999 study conducted by Richard Schulz and Scott Beach concluded that elderly spousal caregivers had morbidity risks that were 63 percent higher than noncarers. In 2010, Katy Butler reported in the *New York Times Magazine* a 2007 Ohio State University study of the DNA of family caregivers of people with Alzheimer's disease. The study showed that the end of their chromosomes "had degraded enough to reflect a four-to-eight year shortening of lifespan."

Sherri Snelling points out in *A Cast of Characters* that almost one in three US households have at least one person who is a caregiver (121). Caregivers devote an average of 4.6 years caring for a loved one, but often they spend far longer, sometimes even decades (xx). Caregivers, Snelling reminds us, are the "first responders in our health care crisis" (xii). Tellingly, most people believe they cannot refuse to be a caregiver when the need arises. "Studies by the National Alliance for Caregiving show 75 percent of all caregivers felt they did not have a choice to provide the care their loved one needed and most of us do not think about caregiving until a crisis forces us into service" (124).

## The Personal Element Behind Scholarship

That was certainly true in my case. The greatest shock in my life occurred when my wife Barbara was diagnosed with terminal pancreatic cancer—a redundancy because pancreatic cancer is almost always fatal, usually within a few months of diagnosis. Barbara's diagnosis, on August 12, 2002, one day after our thirty-fourth wedding anniversary, shattered our assumptive world, which the British psychiatrist Colin Murray Parkes defines as a "strongly held set of assumptions about the world and the self which is confidently maintained and used as a means of recognizing, planning and acting" ("What Becomes" 132). I had always assumed that Barbara would outlive me by twenty years. Unlike those in my immediate and extended family, who usually die young, of cancer, nearly all of Barbara's relatives lived to be in their nineties, including her parents and grandparents, with no history of cancer on either side of her family. She could have been a poster child for living a healthy, balanced life. I was Barbara's caregiver for close to twenty months: she died on April 5, 2004, at age fifty-seven. I cared for her at home, mostly by myself, but for the last few months of her life, a hospice aide came twice a week, each time for two and one-half hours, offering invaluable help. If there are angels on earth, they work for hospice.

I continued teaching while Barbara was ill, never missing a single class. Near the end of her life, one of my doctoral students, a former nurse, stayed with Barbara when I taught my classes. Teaching was one of my lifelines: the only time I felt like I was in control of my world was when I was in the classroom. Writing was another lifeline and, because I am a disbeliever, my most sacred death ritual. After Barbara's death, I penned a book about our life together, *Dying to Teach: A Memoir of Love, Loss, and Learning* (2007). In her 2014 memoir *No Saints Around Here: A Caregiver's Days*, Susan Allen Toth observes that she did not begin writing about her husband, James, who struggled for years with Alzheimer's disease and dementia, until eighteen months after his death. Toth needed time to confront her "conflicting feelings, including terror, sorrow, anger, despair, and a love that made the thought of losing James unimaginable" (13–14). By contrast, I needed to confront these feelings immediately. Immersed in writing about grief, I discovered hours going by in a flash, a phenomenon the University of Chicago psychologist Mihaly Csikszentmihalyi calls "flow," in which we lose all sense of time. After completing *Dying to Teach*, I wrote other books about love and loss, spousal loss memoirs, end-of-life memoirs, and death education.

I never imagined while caring for Barbara that I would begin writing a book about her. She was a private person, not given to self-disclosure, and I don't know how she would have responded to a question about whether she would have wanted me to write a book about her. Modesty might have compelled her to wonder why anyone would be interested in reading about her life. She was an inspirational person to all who knew her, and she did everything possible to ease the burden of suffering of her family and friends.

Before submitting the manuscript for publication, I asked my daughters, Arielle and Jillian, both of whom were newly married, to read the manuscript to make sure they were comfortable with the way I wrote about them and their mother. They gave me their approval, but I don't think they were able to read the entire manuscript. Their own grief was still too raw at the time, and reading about their mother's death reopened too many wounds. Nor did they understand why I felt the need to write about Barbara. The short answer, I told them ruefully, is that writers need to write. They still don't understand why I wrote a story that seeks to capture the heartbreaking nature of loss, as well as our joy and gratitude for having been together our entire adult lives. To write an authentic book, I explained to them, I had to show not only the beauty of Barbara's life but also the pain of her protracted suffering, even if it meant making the reader suffer. This is what writers do. Fiercely protective mothers, like their own mother, Arielle and Jillian understandably wanted to spare their young children from the disturbing details of Barbara's death. I assumed that our six grandchildren wouldn't read *Dying to Teach* until they were adults. Imagine my surprise, then, when I learned that my then ten-year-old granddaughter Talia, asked by her teacher to identify her favorite book, brought to school her Baba's memoir about Grandma Barbara.

Writing exposes both caregiver and care-receiver to public scrutiny. This remains one of the most complicated challenges of conveying the reality of caregiving: balancing truth with discretion. I suspect that many, perhaps most caregivers, do not ask permission to write about care-receivers. Sometimes caregivers write with the recognition that care-receivers remain highly ambivalent or distressed about the possibility of being a character in a book, even if the character is portrayed lovingly. Because care-receivers are vulnerable subjects, usually unable to respond to verbal portraits of themselves, writing about them raises ethical questions. These ethical questions do not disappear when a care-receiver dies; if anything, the questions become more urgent.

For example, in her 2012 graphic memoir *Tangles: A Story about Alzheimer's, My Mother, and Me*, Sarah Leavitt admits her hesitation in exposing her mother's privacy. "I often felt like Harriet the Spy, or, in darker moments, like a vulture hovering and waiting for Mom to say or do something that I could record and preserve, even as she slipped away from me." Sometimes Leavitt's mother would pull on the page or try to grab her daughter's pen as she wrote. "The pen would skid and make a mark and I'd label the mark: 'Mom moved my pen.' I wanted to keep every trace of her" (8). Leavitt spent four years writing and drawing the book, pursuing an MFA in creative writing at the University of British Columbia in the process, but her mother began to cry when she read a page or two. "I'm not a real person," Midge Leavitt lamented, "the scariest thing is the things I don't know." Remarks her daughter, sadly, "I didn't try that again" (89). Yet readers are grateful for Leavitt's book, "an extraordinarily moving and vivid account, in text and cartoon-style pictures, of the life and death of an Alzheimer's patient," as John Bayley wrote in the blurb.

## Continuing Bonds

My experience of mourning differs from the classic psychoanalytic view. Freud theorizes in his 1917 essay "Mourning and Melancholia" that "mourning impels the ego to give up the object by declaring the object to be dead and offering the ego the inducement for continuing to live" (*SE*, vol. 14, 257). Freud's failure to theorize the importance of grief and bereavement, Madelon Sprengnether contends in her 2018 book *Mourning Freud*, allowed him to escape from a recognition of his painful early childhood losses. For nearly a century Freud's influential view of mourning held sway over clinicians, but a new theory of bereavement, formulated by Dennis Klass, Phyllis R. Silverman, and Steven L. Nickman in their 1996 book *Continuing Bonds: New Understandings of Grief*, suggests that contrary to conventional wisdom, the bereaved can maintain a relational bond with the deceased while forming new bonds with the living. The authors quote a statement by the playwright Robert Anderson, following his wife's death, with which I continue to identify: "death ends a life, but it does not end a relationship, which struggles on in the survivor's mind toward some resolution which it never finds" (17).

Regrettably, psychoanalysis remains unaware of the theory of continuing bonds. PEP-Web, a database of seventy-two psychoanalytic journals, lists only one reference published in English. In her article "Treating Mourning—Knowing Loss," published in *Contemporary Psychoanalysis* in 2008, Karol Marshall devotes only one sentence to the theory: "We maintain our ties to the dead" (229), which hardly does justice to the complexity of the subject. The theory of continuing bonds resonates deeply in me, for by writing about my experience of love and loss, I maintain a bond with Barbara and help to keep her memory alive. I don't think I'm stuck on past grief. I remarried in 2011; Julie continues to bring delight to my life. We call one of the rooms in our home the "shrine," where we have photographs of Barbara and Julie's deceased parents.

Caring for Barbara was the best of times and the worst of times. I remember during the early months of her illness a colleague asserting that I would be "tested," and throughout her ordeal the word reverberated within me. Our love and devotion were never more intense, our sorrow, never deeper. I couldn't imagine, at the beginning of Barbara's illness, that our children and I would wish for her death, but during the last weeks, when she lay in bed at home in a coma, completely wasted away from the ravages of the disease, unable to eat or drink, we wished for her suffering to end.

Experience has given me a greater understanding of caregiving—and a greater sense of its urgency. Emily K. Abel, the author of several books on the history of caregiving, reaches the same conclusion about how her own life experience influenced her scholarship. She begins *Hearts of Wisdom* by revealing that during the time she was studying family caregiving, her mother was diagnosed with lymphoma and relied on her children for support during the five months she battled the disease. After her mother's death, Abel herself was diagnosed with cancer and turned to others for support. Abel never sugarcoats the reality of caregiving, noting throughout her book that it forces women, in particular, to reexperience losses, but she acknowledges gaining a "deeper appreciation of caregiving as a transformative experience, introducing us to new forms of human connectedness" (1).

To my knowledge, apart from the opening paragraph in *Hearts of Wisdom*, Abel has never written specifically about how her experience as a caregiver or care-receiver has informed her scholarship. Most academics are not self-disclosing. By contrast, I have long been interested in the extent to which personal experiences shape, indeed, catalyze, scholarship, particularly my own. As I remark in *Diaries to an English Professor* (1994) and *Surviving Literary Suicide* (1999), my interest in teaching and writing on suicide may be traced to my mentor's suicide on Labor Day, 1968, an event that forever changed my life, just as Barbara's death later did. I don't regard my lifelong interest in dying, death—and now caregiving—as morbid or depressing; on the contrary, I find these subjects endlessly life-affirming.

My students do too. In the last fifteen years, I have taught three different personal writing courses: "Writing About Illness, Injury, and Infirmity";

"Writing About the Debts and Gifts of Gratitude"; and "Writing About Love and Loss." I give students the opportunity to write about their own experiences with these subjects. Many of my students have suffered traumatic losses far earlier in life than I have. We all become students of love and loss—and recovery. As one of my undergraduates recently wrote, "Forgetting, for me, is the hardest part of my grief." And for me. Writing is a way to memorialize loss; to bring the dead back to life, verbally; and to confront and work through future losses. Unlike Emily Abel, I have not yet needed a caregiver, but, as a mid-septuagenarian—I was among the first of the baby boomers, born in 1945—I probably will. Hence, another reason for my personal interest in this scholarly topic.

## Lived Experience

There is an explosion of self-help books on caregiving, and they serve a useful purpose in offering caregiving tips on the short- and long-term experience of caring for another person. Ann Jurecic's observation about the proliferation of illness narratives in the second half of the twentieth century also applies to caregiving self-help books: "The profound need people have to tell these stories in an era when religious and folk explanations no longer give a satisfying and complete meaning to their experiences, and when biomedicine largely excludes the personal story" (9).

Sometimes self-help books on caregiving may be too depressing to read, as Toth admits. After her husband's diagnosis, she began buying books with titles "like—not exactly—*The Rewards of Caregiving, A New Commitment, Love All the Way*, and *How Caregiving Made Me a Better Person*." She stopped reading these books because it seemed as if the authors were determined to remind her of her flaws. Toth is not opposed to all self-help books, however; she praises *The Selfish Pig's Guide to Caring*, by the British writer Hugh Marriott, for helping her to feel "normal" (31). After his wife, Cathie, was diagnosed with the symptoms of Huntington's disease, Marriott sold their home, bought a sailing boat, and embarked on what was to become a nine-year voyage in which they visited forty countries and sailed almost half way around the world. When his wife's illness became disabling, they returned ashore, and Marriott wrote his irreverent book dedicated to people who felt like "selfish pigs" because they never expected to find themselves in the role of a carer (the UK word for caregiver), who were "pissed off" (3) about having to care for their "piglets," and who felt guilty about their anger.

Not even self-help books like *The Selfish Pig's Guide to Caring*, however, begin to capture the complexity and *lived experience* of caregiving that we see in novels, films, and memoirs. Nor do self-help books provide the aesthetic pleasure of seeing caregiving and care-receiving in action. Reading about or viewing caregiving is, admittedly, often wrenching, yet even at their darkest, caregiving stories deepen our understanding of one of the most fundamental experiences of life.

How can dark caregiving stories give us aesthetic pleasure? Noting that emotion animates literature, Patrick Colm Hogan points out two paradoxes: "First, we grieve over fictional events, thus events we know to be unreal. Second, we enjoy experiencing that grief." The explanation of these paradoxes of fictional emotion and tragic enjoyment, in Hogan's view, is *simulation*, a key process of the human mind. Simulation has an "adaptive function because it allows us to evaluate scenarios 'off-line,' thus without actual risk." We respond to simulations as we respond to "comparable realities." Literature is a form of simulation, a recreated reality. Invoking the latest neurological research in affective science, Hogan speculates that the act of simulation activates the reward system in the brain that governs the pursuit of pleasure.

Our receptivity to emotion in literature is heightened by our empathy, our ability to place ourselves in the situations of literary characters, and by our susceptibility to "emotional contagion," "catching" or "being infected" by dark emotions, such as grief, anger, disgust, guilt, and shame. Few experiences in life awaken more empathy and emotional contagion than caregiving, precisely because of its intense and prolonged nature, and because of the dissolving boundaries that often occur between caregiver and care-receiver. Empathy and emotional contagion, as we shall see, are the poles around which caregiving stories revolve.

Authors of self-help books on caregiving *tell* us about the inevitable problems that occur and then offer solutions. By contrast, novelists, filmmakers, and memoirists *show* us these problems, bringing them to life, making them real. We see the conflicts between caregivers and care-receivers, how each may grow to depend on and resent the other. We see burn-out and compassion fatigue, loneliness, isolation, and exhaustion. We see how boundaries between caregiver and care-receiver may dissolve, resulting in identity loss. We see how the caregiver may feel at times murderous rage and suicidal feelings—and act on these feelings.

And yet more positively, we see characters placing their lives on hold for parents, spouses, siblings, and children, the sacrifices caregivers are willing to make. We see a deepening of purpose and commitment, a reordering of priorities and values. We see the survival value of humor, the caregiving challenges that can be overcome, the healing of old conflicts, the discovery of spiritual and existential truth, and the new intimacy that may be gained. We see the life lessons acquired through caregiving: the meaning of love, devotion, courage, and grace. We see why caregiving is the ultimate form of attachment—and why caregiving may be the most profound experience of life. And we see how caregiving may inspire enduring literary and cinematic masterpieces.

Caregivers accompany us throughout life, from womb to tomb, but I have not examined the caregiver-infant relationship, a subject that deserves separate study. Many of Naomi Morgenstern's observations about contemporary parenting in *Wild Child: Intensive Parenting and Posthumanist Ethics* (2018) apply to caregiving: "Parenting, in the twenty-first-century works under consideration here, often takes the form of a kind of mad or incalculable commitment to another that bears no relation to reciprocal or contractual models of intersubjective responsibility" (31). Caregiving, too, often seems to be an impossible, unimaginable commitment, one that may transform caregivers into care-receivers themselves. Morgenstern's statement that parenting is perhaps the "art of the broken promise" (31) may also apply to caregiving. One of her questions remains implicit in any study of caregiving. "Does the wildness of caregiving consist in practices of absolute protection or in forms of abandonment or abuse?" (31). And her insight about the ethical ordeal of parenting—"of bringing and being brought, sometimes kicking and screaming, into being and relation" (38)—is often true of caregiving *in the reverse*, where care-receivers are brought into nonbeing and nonrelation.

My 2010 book *Companionship in Grief: Love and Loss in the Memoirs of C. S. Lewis, John Bayley, Donald Hall, Joan Didion, and Calvin Trillin* is indirectly about caregiving. Apart from the chapter on Bayley, which I have revised and expanded here, I have not discussed the other writers. C. S. Lewis was an exemplary caregiver, as can be seen in *A Grief Observed* (1963). Donald Hall, the former US poet laureate, wrote several memoirs about caring for his wife, the poet Jane Kenyon, including *The Best Day the Worst Day* (2005). My 2012 book *Dying in Character: Memoirs on the End of Life* is also indirectly about caregiving, especially the chapter on Roland Barthes, where he discusses in *Mourning Diary* (2010) being his mother's caregiver. In *Writing Widowhood* (2015), I discuss Kay Redfield Jamison's 2009 spousal loss memoir *Nothing Was the Same*, in which she writes about caring for her terminally ill husband, the physician Richard Wyatt.

## The Plan of This Book

The portrayal of caregiving in fiction, film, and memoir is a daunting subject, too large to be described in a single book, particularly if one wishes, as I do, to study caregiving in depth. In real life, caregivers may believe that they do not have a choice to be a caregiver, but novelists, filmmakers, and memoirists do have a choice—unless they believe, as I did when I was writing *Dying to Teach*, that they were following their obsessions. How does caregiving fit into an artist's larger body of work? How has the experience of caregiving changed one's life? What can we learn from a novel, film, or memoir about caregiving that may not be apparent from a self-help book? When might the depiction of caregiving in art be misleading or dangerous? In a film like Michael Haneke's *Amour*, when may caregiving in reel life lead us astray in real life?

Throughout my study, I discuss the literary and cinematic techniques used by novelists, filmmakers, and memoirists to describe caregiving. Like self-help books, novels, films, and memoirs offer psychological insights into caregiving; but, in addition, they convey, through metaphorical language, irony, ambiguity, imagery, shifting point of view, and fantasy, the continuities and discontinuities between health and illness, insight and blindness, lucidity and dementia, living and dying. Unlike self-help books, whose primary purpose is to offer solutions to vexing problems, caregiving stories or films dramatize problems and may be wary of solutions, agreeing with F. Scott Fitzgerald's insight in *The Crack-Up*: "The test of a first-rate intelligence is the ability to hold two opposed ideas in the mind at the same time, and still retain the ability to function" (69). In each chapter, I offer close readings of the story or film under discussion, showing how caregiving fits into the work's larger thematic concerns. Whenever possible, I discuss how writers' or filmmakers' experiences with caregiving affect their lives and art. Sometimes caregiving remains the *central* experience of life, one to which a writer or filmmaker keeps returning, either to honor a memory or to exorcise a ghost.

Chapter 1 focuses on Tolstoy's iconic *The Death of Ivan Ilych*, arguably the greatest story about mortality. No novella has shown in more painful or painstaking detail the various stages through which a person passes from health through illness to the moments before death. Tolstoy's masterpiece contains a young butler's assistant, Gerasim, who instinctively knows how to comfort his dying master. Never didactic, *The Death of Ivan Ilych* is taught not only in countless literature classrooms but also in medical schools, where the "Gerasim Model of Caregiving" is discussed. Gerasim may represent an impossible ideal for most caregivers, but we can strive for the art of empathic listening he embodies as well as his truthful words on caregiving.

One cannot imagine caregivers more unlike Gerasim than those in Edith Wharton's celebrated novel *Ethan Frome*, the subject of Chapter 2. Wharton explores an aspect of caregiving rarely discussed in how-to books: a caregiver's fantasies of martyrdom. The story opens with Ethan Frome caring for his ailing wife, Zeena, who had been his dying mother's caregiver. Ethan and Zeena enter into a cheerless marriage, and when Zeena invites her attractive young cousin, Mattie Silver, to help out in the home, Mattie and Ethan predictably fall in love. It doesn't take long for Zeena to detect the blossoming relationship, and when she dismisses her relative, the distraught lovers choose death over life. The double suicide fails, however, leading to horrible injuries and a startling reversal of the caregiver-care-receiver roles. Wharton offers a penetrating psychological analysis of the nature of psychosomatic illness, including the "complications" that arise from Zeena's illness, and Ethan Frome's struggle with what today might be diagnosed as depersonalization/derealization disorder. In addition, we see the ambiguities of caregiving and the fantasies behind caregiving and care-receiving. No novel, film, or memoir surpasses *Ethan Frome* in showing how caregivers and care-receivers, codependent on each other, become prisoners for life. *Ethan Frome* has noteworthy autobiographical implications. Wharton remained ambivalent toward her fictional caregivers and care-receivers, but in devoting herself to the craft of fiction, she became a literary caregiver, transmuting her own conflicts into art.

Chapter 3 explores Ingmar Bergman's masterpiece *Persona*, which reveals another aspect of caregiving seldom discussed by clinicians or self-help authors: the loss of boundaries between the caregiver, Alma, and the care-receiver, Elisabet Vogler, the actress who suddenly stops speaking during a performance of *Electra*. Bergman dramatizes boundary loss and identity transformation not through words, spoken dialogue, but through images, the two spectral faces merging into each other's. The women switch roles in the film, each taking on the worst aspects of the other. Narcissistic conflicts render the caregiving experience into a nightmare, where each woman betrays and is betrayed by the other. *Persona* remains a cautionary tale about the ease with which compassionate caregiving can turn into humiliation and rage, with disastrous consequences for both the caregiver and care-receiver. Bergman's mistrust of caregiving in *Persona* reflects his anger toward his parents and his traumatic childhood, a topic that appears in many of his films.

Alice Munro's "The Bear Came Over the Mountain," the subject of Chapter 4, highlights a different type of transformation, one involving the memory loss that occurs in Alzheimer's disease. Fiona, placed into a nursing home, falls in love with another demented resident, and her husband, Grant, not the most faithful of men, is faced with a caregiving conundrum. Should he encourage or discourage his wife's new love? What is best for her welfare—and his own? The bittersweet tone, along with the endless probing of the ambiguities of marital fidelity, makes "The Bear Came Over the Mountain" unique among caregiving stories. Munro's story became the basis for the film *Away from Her*, directed by Sarah Polley, who also wrote the screenplay. *Away from Her* captures Fiona's grace, but many of the complexities of Munro's story disappear in the film, where the motivation behind Grant's matchmaking becomes less intriguing.

The caregiving survival strategies John Bayley offers in his three memoirs, *Elegy for Iris*, *Iris and Her Friends*, and *Widower's House*, discussed in Chapter 5, have little in common with those found in how-to books. An ironist, Bayley delights in presenting counterintuitive truths. Recalling the early years of their marriage, he writes nostalgically about moving with his wife, in the words of A. D. Hope, closer and closer *apart*. Now, however, as a result of Alzheimer's, he experiences a suffocating closeness to her. Bayley was his wife's exclusive caregiver for many years. He never lost his humor, though it became darker toward the end of her life, when the strain of caregiving became almost intolerable and his own health began to suffer. His wife's death left him bereft, but in his final caregiving memoir he describes falling in love again and remarrying—and continuing to honor Iris's memory—an example of the continuing bonds approach to bereavement.

Of all the caregiving stories I've read, the one with which I most identify is Anna Quindlen's harrowing *One True Thing*, the subject of Chapter 6. Ellen Gulden's mother, Kate, dying of ovarian cancer and in irremediable pain, pleads for death. Barbara, too, was in intense pain shortly before her death and asked me whether I could give her a fatal dose of morphine, a question that froze me in horror, reminding me, as I discuss in *Dying to Teach*, of the guilt I felt when my mentor committed suicide thirty-six years earlier. *One True Thing* is unsurpassed in showing the limits of pain medication and palliative care. A pathology report indicates that the cause of Kate's death is an overdose of morphine. Ellen, who had written an essay in high school advocating euthanasia, is arrested. A grand jury deliberates whether she should be charged with homicide—the only untrue thing about a novel that is accurate in every other detail about caring for a terminally ill person wracked with pain.

We don't often think of a twelve-year-old child being the primary caretaker for her grandmother, dying of colon cancer, but that was Mary Gordon's situation, as Chapter 7 reveals. Traumatized by the experience, particularly when she was required to change her grandmother's colostomy bag, Gordon imagined being her father's caregiver in her first novel. She was a reluctant caregiver when her mother developed dementia decades later. In Gordon's world, caregiving is often associated with martyrdom. It's hard to imagine a darker caregiving memoir than *Circling My Mother*, where Gordon acknowledges feeling repelled by her mother's body. Gordon takes on the role of an avenging angel in the memoir, indicting her relatives for their long mistreatment of her mother. The caregiving memoir is an example of what Sandra Gilbert calls, in her spousal loss memoir *Wrongful Death*, "writing/righting wrong," allowing the author to record and rectify a cruel injustice. Caregiving remains a persistent theme in Gordon's writings, appearing in disguised form in several of her later novels.

Michael Haneke's controversial film *Amour*, the subject of Chapter 8, is about another type of rage, an octogenarian's impulsive decision to end his wife's bedridden existence as a result of a series of strokes. No film portrays more graphically the violence of euthanasia—or murder—depending upon whether the viewer is sympathetic or unsympathetic to an event that reflects either the supreme act of devotion imaginable, amour, or its opposite. No film makes greater demands on an audience's ability to endure cinematic violence. And no film shows more painfully how the experience of caregiving awakens homicidal/suicidal feelings that occur in real life all too often. The caregiver and care-receiver both play a double role in the film, each torturing and tortured by the other. Some viewers, including experienced film and literary critics, found themselves literally sickened when watching *Amour*, which remains a forewarning of the caregiver's isolation and despair. *Amour* remains Haneke's most personal film, dramatizing the question, how does someone respond to a loved one's suffering?

The murder mystery does not seem to be a genre conducing to caregiving, but this is only one of the surprises of Walter Mosley's ingenious novel *The Last Days of Ptolemy Grey*, examined in Chapter 9. Another surprise is the novel's creation of a credible language of dementia as the eponymous hero, a nonagenarian African American living in contemporary Los Angeles, tries to express himself. And a third surprise is the endearing seventeen-year-old Robyn Small, who becomes Ptolemy Grey's faithful caregiver. Ptolemy enters into a Faustian pact to regain his memory and language, albeit temporarily, to fulfill the promise he made to his slain mentor more than eighty years earlier to improve the lives of his race. The two protagonists, lovingly devoted to each other, enact the personal, familial, and historical implications of caregiving, and, in the process, Mosley's story transcends the constraints of its genre to earn a place in enduring literature.

Should caregiving stories be only "progress" rather than "decline" narratives? Chapter 10 focuses on this question raised by the age theorist Margaret Morganroth Gullette. Her belief that decline narratives are dangerous and antithetical to life compelled her not to publish a caregiving memoir she had written about her father, who had developed amyotrophic lateral sclerosis (ALS), an incurable neurological disorder. Decades later, when her mother developed dementia, Gullette decided to exclude the depressing elements of the story from her memoir. She even refused to read the leading how-to book on dementia, *The 36-Hour Day*, for fear of being infected by its perceived negativity. If we followed Gullett's recommendation, we wouldn't read several powerful "decline" memoirs such as Alix Kates Shulman's *A Good Enough Daughter* or Sue Miller's *The Story of My Father*. Gullette raises vexing questions about literature's contagion effect. What is gained—and lost—by reading only progress narratives of caregiving? How much of the truth of caregiving are we willing to learn? Few questions are more timely than this one.

Our discussion of Atul Gawande's *Being Mortal*, in the final chapter, returns us to the beginning of this study: *The Death of Ivan Ilych*. How do we begin the tough conversations about mortality and caregiving? Gawande, a physician, had a preferred way of responding to the questions his dying patients asked him, but his medical training did not prepare him for assisting his dying father, also a physician, with the caregiving decisions surrounding end-of-life care. The burdens of today's caregivers, Gawande points out, have dramatically increased. Throughout *Being Mortal*, Gawande invokes *The Death of Ivan Ilych* to help him speak the truth to his father. Gawande's discussion of his father's illness can be described as either an extended clinical vignette or a memoir, but whatever our label, he uses fictional techniques to end his father's story. By concluding our own story with a discussion of *Being Mortal*, we come full circle, showing how Tolstoy's novella remains central to caregiving.

Is caregiving a beautiful story? It can be, I suggest in the conclusion, but not in the way that Nicholas Sparks portrays caregiving in his sugarcoated novel *The Notebook*, made into an even more sentimental film. Sparks's notion of beautiful caregiving is cruel optimism, blinding us to the reality of the experience.

The history of caregiving is vast and beyond the scope of the present book, but whenever possible I have tried to historicize my discussion of caregiving in the arts. Increased longevity, the decline of the extended family, the rise of nursing homes, the growth of end-of-life care, and the burgeoning right-to-die movement have all affected caregiving. Historical shifts have affected our understanding of physical and psychological illness (as well as psychosomatic illness) and reconfigurations of the patient-doctor relationship, all of which impact caregiving.

There are many studies and surveys of our changing attitudes toward death, including Philippe Ariès's landmark *The Hour of Our Death* (1981), and some of his comments apply to the fictional characters in my study. Ariès notes, for example, that when Ivan Ilych visits a physician in the 1880s, "going to a doctor has become a necessary and important step, which it was not fifty years before" (564). And when Tolstoy's protagonist turns to the wall near the end of his life, lying on his side with one hand on his cheek, he instinctively imitates the "classical attitude of the dying when they had had enough of the world." Adds Ariès, the "Jews of the Old Testament lay like this; in sixteenth century Spain, this attitude was the mark of the unconverted marranos" (573). Changing attitudes toward death usually reflect changes in caregiving. Tony Walter observed in 1999 that the usual question asked in the nineteenth century was whether the dying person was sustained by faith; that question changed in the twentieth century to whether the death was pain-free. The nineteenth-century minister, priest, or rabbi was consequently replaced in the twentieth century by the caregiver, whose many responsibilities included pain management. Most books about dying, death, and bereavement do not discuss caregiving, while most books about caregiving discuss these subjects, to which we return in nearly every chapter.

There are also cultural and gender differences in caregiving. Robert C. DiGiulio observes in his 1989 study *Beyond Widowhood* that, based on extensive interviews and autobiographical and literary accounts, the "caregiving of women by men was out of character. Men are not expected to care for the ill or weak in our society; they thus feel powerless to help when confronted with the need to do so" (53). Widowed men's grief seems more despairing than widowed women's grief, adds DiGiulio, which helps to explain the aging caregiver's decision to end his wife's life in *Amour*.

In an article provocatively titled "#MeToo Is All Too Real. But to Better Understand It, Turn to Fiction," Parul Sehgal argues that to understand this troubling phenomenon, which the media too often portray with "numbing sameness," one should read novels. "They are remarkably various, and they trouble debates that traffic in certainties. They come laden with confusion, doubt, subtlety—is it excessively earnest to call it *truth*?" The same may be said about fictional, filmic, and memoiristic portrayals of caregiving, which raise inconvenient truths that often cannot be found elsewhere.

# 1

# The Idealized Caregiver in Tolstoy's *The Death of Ivan Ilych*

Leo Tolstoy's 1886 masterpiece *The Death of Ivan Ilych* remains, after more than a century, the most profound literary examination of the stripping away of the denials of mortality. No story analyzes more incisively the thoughts of the dying individual from the first hint of illness to the moments before death; and no story dramatizes more poignantly the defenses erected against death by relatives, friends, and colleagues. Godlike in his omniscience, Tolstoy convinces us that he sees and understands everything about the nature of dying. All the characters in the novella are human, all too human—all, that is, except one, who occupies the role of caregiver.

Ivan Ilych (the second name is a patronym) Golovin is an everyman figure, Tolstoy's version of John Doe, a 45-year-old member of the Court of Justice who throughout the story is judged and found wanting. "Ivan Ilych's life had been most simple and most ordinary and therefore most terrible" (18). He has attempted to live without suffering, an impossibility, as Tolstoy shows. The story opens with a climax, the protagonist's death, and what follows is acute psychological and sociological analysis. Each of the mourners attending his funeral thinks, "Well, he's dead but I'm alive!" (7). The expression on the dead man's face seems to contain a "reproach and a reminder to the living." In the pages that follow, the cautionary tale dramatizes the truth of the words inscribed on his watch-chain that he begins to wear upon graduation from law school: "respice finem"—reflect on your end.

Tolstoy describes the world of difference between sickness and health, the recognition, in Susan Sontag's memorable words, that "illness is the nightside of life, a more onerous citizenship" (3). Tolstoy captures the dark complexity of motivation surrounding illness and death, particularly self-interested motivation. Ivan Ilych's wife, Praskovya Fedorovna, cannot separate her husband's suffering from her own, as can be seen by her use of first-person pronoun. "For the last three days he screamed incessantly. It was unendurable. I cannot understand how I bore it; you could hear him three rooms off. Oh, what I have suffered!" (14–15). Her main concern, Tolstoy adds, gazing into her mind, is to secure as large a government pension as possible. Ivan Ilych's daughter's dominant emotion is anger, suggesting that others are to blame for her father's death. His morose son has the tear-stained eyes that are found in boys who are "not pure-minded" (17). Ivan Ilych's colleagues attend his funeral out of propriety; each of them wonders how the death will affect his own government transfer or promotion. Peter Ivanovich knows his deceased colleague as well as anyone, but he is the first to leave, trying to shield himself from further thoughts of mortality. On his way out, he encounters the butler's young assistant, Gerasim, and says, more out of convention than the desire for conversation, "It's a sad affair, isn't it?," to which the youth responds, without hesitation, "It's God's will. We shall all come to it some day" (18).

These are the first heartfelt words in the story, expressed by the only character who is not driven by self-interest. Tolstoy associates Gerasim with perfect health, vitality, and compassion. He walks briskly into and out of the dead man's room, without fear or self-consciousness. He has the "even white teeth of a healthy peasant" (18), a detail bound to strike envy among orthodontically challenged readers. The peasant lad, "always cheerful and bright," is uneducated but serves as the moral compass of the story. Everything about Gerasim is natural and spontaneous, which explains why he is the only one who provides Ivan Ilych with care and comfort.

There is no uncertainty over the outcome of Ivan Ilych's existence, only whether he has led a good life. His illness begins with a slight fall from a stepladder while showing an upholsterer how he wanted the draperies hung. The fall results in a "simple bruise" that has the gravest consequences. "With the benefit of hindsight," Gary R. Jahn observes in his 1993 edition of the novella, "it may well seem significant that Ivan Ilich falls from a ladder just at the point when, in his career, he has finally reached the upper rings on the ladder of success" (47). Ivan Ilych tries to distract himself from the gnawing thoughts of mortality, but nothing helps. Playing cards, one of the pleasures of his life, no longer interests him, nor does dancing with a princess whose sister founded a society called "Bear My Burden" (41), an ironic comment on his failure to control his rising agitation. Immersing himself in work no longer provides gratification, nor can he find psychological relief from reading. The panic attacks worsen, and as he finds himself veering closer and closer to the abyss, during the third month of his illness, Gerasim enters his life.

What makes Gerasim different from the other characters in the story? To begin with, he is satisfied with his place in society, uninterested in moving up the social ladder. Unburdened by the pressure of social advancement, the pursuit of material success, or the opinion of others, he is entirely present in the here-and-now, mindful of his service to Ivan Ilych. Gerasim never worries about what his life will be like after his master's death: the story implies he will continue to serve future masters in the same selfless way. His faith in the existing social order is absolute, as is his faith in life itself. He experiences no conflicts in his life, neither resentment toward the ruling class, as one might have expected among peasants in the decades prior to the Russian Revolution, nor a feeling of despair over a future filled with endless drudgery.

## An Unacknowledged Caregiver

Gerasim is a pantry boy, not Ivan Ilych's caregiver, and he doesn't worry about the problems associated with caregiving, such as burn-out, compassion fatigue, and compromised health. Nor does the servant need to confront the wrenching decisions that face caregivers regarding end-of-life issues. But in other ways Gerasim is a caregiver. He spends more time ministering to the dying patient than anyone, and he is the only one who manages to make the patient feel better. He is also the only character who does not evoke his master's anger and resentment. Gerasim succeeds through active listening. A natural healer, he understands the value of silence.

Gerasim's caregiving responsibilities begin when he is needed for what is for Ivan Ilych the most appalling detail of his progressive illness, probably abdominal cancer: the removal of his body waste. Tolstoy holds nothing back about his protagonist's feeling of shame arising from the loss of autonomy. "For his excretions also special arrangements had to be made, and this was a torment to him every time—a torment from the uncleanliness, the unseemliness, and the smell, and from knowing that another person had to take part in it" (65). Ivan Ilych is at first embarrassed by his dependence on the servant for this "repulsive task"; the latter's appearance, in his clean Russian peasant costume, only heightens his master's shame.

But Gerasim knows instinctively what to do and how to do it. While removing the commode, he refrains from looking at his sick master out of consideration for his feelings, and he also restrains the "joy of life" that beams from his face. Gerasim is afraid he has done something wrong when Ivan Ilych weakly utters his name, but far from criticizing the youth, the judge expresses a rare empathic comment: "That must be very unpleasant for you. You must forgive me. I am helpless," to which the youth responds, eyes beaming and teeth glistening, "What's a little trouble? It's a case of illness with you, sir" (66).

Flash forward a century, and Ivan Ilych's chamber pot becomes a dominant symbol of the unspeakable rituals of caregiving. Most caregiving self-help books skip lightly over urinary incontinence, bowel or fecal incontinence, and other bodily functions, problems that are often humiliating to the care-receiver and caregiver. No caregiver, Philip Roth nevertheless calls attention in his 1991 memoir *Patrimony* to his dying father's explosive evacuation while showering, viewing it as the supreme indignation of illness and aging. By contrast, John Bayley takes a more comic view of cleaning up the bowel movements of his incontinent wife, Iris Murdoch, who suffers from advanced Alzheimer's disease. Tolstoy doesn't regard his protagonist's chamber pot with horror, disgust, or amusement; instead, the novelist views it as part of the end of life.

Gerasim's words mark a turning point in the story, and from this moment on he is present when Ivan Ilych needs him. The dying man feels better, physically and emotionally, when Gerasim uses his shoulders to hold up his master's legs, a small but redemptive act of compassion that he performs "easily, willingly, simply, and with a good nature that touched Ivan Ilych" (68). Sometimes Gerasim supports Ivan Ilych's legs the entire night, resulting in the servant's loss of sleep, but he has no difficulty explaining his willingness to help. Addressing his master familiarly, Gerasim adds, "If you weren't sick it would be another matter, but as it is, why should I grudge a little trouble?" (70).

## Telling the Truth

Another person's health, strength, and vitality would have been threatening to Ivan Ilych, but these qualities in Gerasim are soothing. Why? Gerasim is the only character in the story who never deceives the dying man. Until the second half of the twentieth century, it was common for physicians to conceal from their patients a terminal diagnosis, fearing that the truth would rob them of hope and the will to live. Tolstoy describes Ivan Ilych's physicians as self-important men who display the same pomposity toward him that he has displayed toward defendants in his court. The physicians are motivated less by compassion than by the refusal to acknowledge their own limitations. They also use language to obfuscate meaning, rendering their words unintelligible. As Harold K. Schefski suggests, Tolstoy took pleasure in showing how physicians' diagnoses and treatments of patients were often wrong—and often callous.

But Gerasim is different. He has the native intelligence and humility to understand the truth of Ivan Ilych's situation. Gerasim gives no advice, makes no recommendations, offers no promises, seeks no rewards, and expresses no complaints. He is a man of few words, having learned, Tolstoy tells us, from the townspeople how to speak with "gentlefolk," but there is nothing obsequious or self-serving about his language. He never interferes in Ivan Ilych's family, who are content to allow him to ease their caregiving responsibilities. The other characters express their pity and condolences largely to mask hidden agendas, but Gerasim's sympathy is bedrock, the foundation by which he lives. Gerasim is willing to serve for as long as his master needs him. He leaves when requested, but his influence lingers.

What makes Gerasim an effective caregiver? Susan L. Taylor suggests in a 1997 article on the "Gerasim Model of Caregiving" that Tolstoy's novella affirms the four characteristics that are central to the patient-caregiver relationship: the caregiver's acceptance of the patient's illness, honest communication between caregiver and patient, patient-directed comfort measures, and a "consistent, gentle, and simple" approach to caregiving (303). Additionally, Taylor points out that the servant illustrates the three principles that the feminist ethicist Nel Noddings views as central to caring: receptivity, relatedness, and responsiveness. Noddings based her ethics of care on empathy, not on what she believed was a "peculiarly rational, western, masculine" view of empathy, based on projection, but on what she felt was a "feminine" view, based on "reception" (Noddings 30). As Sara T. Fry points out, Noddings's model of caring is gender-related, though Noddings maintains that the model applies to both females and males (98).

Regardless of its origins, mechanisms, or definition, empathy allows one to understand the other, not completely or fully but nevertheless powerfully. Empathy also has a cognitive element, Robert C. Solomon suggests, a way of construing the world (68). In Taylor's view, Gerasim demonstrates an "acceptance of the patient and the illness," "honest communication," "patient-directed comfort measures," and a "consistent, gentle, and simple approach to caregiving" (303). Taylor might have also mentioned another key feminist work advocating an ethics of care, Carol Gilligan's *In a Different Voice: Psychological Theory and Women's Development* (1982), which offers a theory of moral development based on relational values. "[M]ale and female voices typically speak of the importance of different truths: the former of the role of separation as it defines and empowers the self, the latter of the ongoing process of attachment that creates and sustains the human community" (156).

## Secure Attachment

Both Gilligan and Noddings build upon attachment theory, which helps to illuminate Gerasim's successful caregiving. First proposed by the psychoanalyst John Bowlby, attachment theory was initially used to describe an infant's relationship to caregivers, but the psychological model has been extended to adults as well. Four attachment patterns have been identified in adults: secure; anxious-preoccupied, insecure-avoidant, and disorganized/disoriented.

Tellingly, Gerasim is the only character in the story who is securely attached to Ivan Ilych. Nothing threatens their bond. The two experience a role reversal that is often common among caregivers. The youthful Gerasim, who is only a few years older than Ivan Ilych's son, becomes a parent figure, sensitive to all of Ivan Ilych's needs. The dying patient, now dependent on others, thankfully accepts Gerasim's assistance and trusts him with his life. *The Death of Ivan Ilych* has generated a vast commentary, but few readers have acknowledged that the novella offers insight into gratitude, which benefits both the recipient and donor. Significantly, Gerasim brings out the best in his master, who never treats him as an inferior. Nor does Ivan Ilych project upon Gerasim the deep ambivalence he feels toward his wife and children. He never utters a sarcastic word toward Gerasim, never regards him as a disappointment, never experiences any dark thoughts about him, as he does with his family members.

The image of Ivan Ilych's legs resting securely on Gerasim's shoulders evokes a merging of the two bodies. Ivan Ilych feels better, physically, emotionally, and perhaps spiritually when Gerasim supports his legs, infused by the latter's strength and vitality. The nighttime ritual conjures up not only the act of caretaking but also the intimate attachment that occurs when an infant suckles at a mother's breast, an image that is consistent with Dennis Patrick Slattery's observation that Tolstoy's peasant servant is the "incarnation of Holy Mother Russia herself" (174). Tolstoy associates Gerasim with the Russian people, as Jahn suggests in his 1999 edited volume. "In Russian, Gerasim is identified as a '*bufetnyi muzhik*,' thereby linking him closely to the Russian peasant (*muzhik*), even though he is working in an urban, domestic situation" (178).

The other characters in the story, without exception, exhibit varying degrees of insecure attachment. They dread being in Ivan Ilych's presence, either because they cannot bring themselves to face illness and death, or because they cannot endure the anger and bitterness the dying man expresses toward them. Once Ivan Ilych becomes ill, his relatives, friends, and colleagues begin to detach themselves from his life, leading to his isolation, loneliness, and depression. Unlike the others, who seek to distance themselves from Ivan Ilych, Gerasim welcomes involvement.

As his illness worsens and he finds himself thrust deeper and deeper into a black sack, Ivan Ilych demands to be left alone. He requests even Gerasim to leave, and the youth obeys sorrowfully. It is significant, however, that Ivan Ilych asks himself the most urgent question in the story in the presence of Gerasim: "His mental sufferings were due to the fact that that night, as he looked at Gerasim's sleepy, good-natured face with its prominent cheek-bones, the question suddenly occurred to him: 'What if my whole life has been wrong?'" (91).

## An Idea and an Ideal

Gerasim is, admittedly, a flat, two-dimensional character, devoid of the inner conflict that is necessary for aesthetic success. Tolstoy is an ironist and often a satirist with respect to the other characters in the story, showing the contrast between what they say and how they think, but he writes about Gerasim without irony or sarcasm. Gerasim is an open book, a metaphor that discerning readers never use. But the expression is apt, for Gerasim, utterly guileless, harbors no ulterior motives or hidden agenda. He has taken the words respice finem to heart.

Gerasim is, in fact, less of a character than an idea—and ideal: unselfish goodness, truth-telling, and devotion to the other. It is an ideal that Tolstoy came increasingly to value near the end of his life, when he experienced an epiphany as momentous as Ivan Ilych's, a spiritual awakening in which he dedicated himself to the ethical teachings of Jesus and sought fulfillment by striving for inner perfection.

Tolstoy's idealization of Gerasim's caregiving reflects one aspect of the novelist's personality, his belief in a life of purity and self-denial. This vision appears in his 1882 book *What I Believe*, in which he sets forth his view of ethics and true Christianity. Tolstoy knew, as his most recent biographer, Rosamund Bartlett, points out, that his dream of a morality based on perfection and self-abnegation went against his pursuit and enjoyment of a hedonistic life. "In August 1910, just a few months before his death, he noted in his diary that he had never encountered anyone else who had the full complement of vices—sensuality, self-interest, spite, vanity and, above all, narcissism" (333). These inner contradictions between moral perfectionism and hedonism tortured Tolstoy his entire life. His greatness as a writer, John Bayley suggests in his 1997 book on the novelist, came precisely from personifying this struggle. "He loved 'society' and he hated it. He believed in pacifism and nonresistance, but could himself be the most arrogant and quarrelsome of men. He was in every way a profound conservative, and yet he was sure that the future must be transformed by a whole new philosophy of peace, progress and love" (*Leo Tolstoy* 8). From these contradictions arose a masterful story.

## Empathic Tappings

Embodying Tolstoy's recognition of the role of empathy in healing relationships, Gerasim demonstrates the power of empathic listening, as Carl Rogers outlines it in *A Way of Being*:

> Almost always, when a person realizes he has been deeply heard, his eyes moisten. I think in some real sense he is weeping for joy. It is as though he were saying, "Thank God, somebody heard me. Someone knows what it's like to be me." In such moments I have had the fantasy of a prisoner in a dungeon, tapping out day after day a Morse code message, "Does anybody hear me? Is anybody there?" And finally one day he hears some faint tappings which spell out "Yes." By that one simple response he is released from his loneliness; he has become a human being again. (1)

Gerasim has heard the tappings of his master, a prisoner in the dungeon. Ivan Ilych knows that he has been heard by one person, and that makes all the difference. Gerasim cannot prevent his master from dying, cannot spare him from the three-day ceaseless howling that Tolstoy describes, but the servant's empathic listening begins the process of Ivan Ilych's release from the dungeon of fear. These empathic tappings never become deafening to Gerasim; he never worries about the deafening roar of suffering, as George Eliot describes it in a memorable passage in her 1872 novel *Middlemarch*: "If we had a keen vision and feeling of all ordinary human life, it would be like hearing the grass grow and the squirrel's heart beat, and we should die of that roar which lies on the other side of silence. As it is, the quickest of us walk about well wadded with stupidity" (189).

Tolstoy was obsessed with death while he was writing the story, as scholars have indicated. "The years 1885 and 1886 brought death into Tolstoy's house and serious illness to Tolstoy," Jahn declares in his 1999 edited volume (21). Richard Pevear suggests in his introduction to *The Death of Ivan Ilych* how Tolstoy's suicidal crisis, which he depicted in his 1882 memoir *A Confession*, bears upon his stories and moral teachings. "The idea of suicide came to me as naturally as ideas for improving my life had come to me before. This idea was so tempting that I had to use tricks with myself so as not to carry it out at once" (x).

*The Death of Ivan Ilych* cannot be reduced to a how-to book about caregiving, but the story reveals how the living can provide support and solace for the dying, and how caregivers can ease the plight of care-receivers who are on the brink of extinction. Tolstoy's novella remains, as Robert Weir points out in his introduction to his 1980 book *Death in Literature*, the "most comprehensive literary treatment of death available" (385), one of the "first 'modern' deaths," as Sandra M. Gilbert observes in *Death's Door* (125). "Beyond any doubt," the Russian-born French biographer Henri Troyat remarks, "this double story of the decomposing body and awakening soul is one of the most powerful works in the literature of the world" (461). In Lionel Trilling's view, *The Death of Ivan Ilych* is, quite simply, the most painful work of fiction to read (525).

## Inspiring Writers, Clinicians, and Theorists

According to George R. Clay, the "deathbed monologue" in twentieth-century fiction, such as Thomas Mann's *Death in Venice* (1912), Marcel Proust's *Time Regained* (1927), and Samuel Beckett's *Malone Dies* (1951), to name only a few modern masterpieces, can be traced to *The Death of Ivan Ilych* (206). In his 1988 study *The Illness Narratives: Suffering, Healing, and the Human Condition*, the Harvard psychiatrist and anthropologist Arthur Kleinman focuses on chronic, not terminal, illness, but many of his observations apply to *The Death of Ivan Ilych*. "If there is a single dimension of illness that can teach us something valuable for our own lives, then it must be how to confront and respond to the fact that we will all die, each of us" (157). Kleinman quotes Kafka's felicitous statement in "A Country Doctor": "To write prescriptions is easy, but to come to an understanding with people is hard" (209). No story dramatizes this truth more poignantly than *The Death of Ivan Ilych*.

As I wrote in 1980 in *Advances in Thanatology*, Tolstoy's novella anticipated by more than eight decades many of Elisabeth Kübler-Ross's insights into thanatology, including the "stage theory of dying," although the theory has been widely called into question because of its oversimplification. Contemporary thanatologists have pointed out that there are no universal stages of death and that Kübler-Ross largely ignored emotions such as fear, guilt, hope, and despair. She also failed to appreciate the cultural differences in death. David Wendell Moller likens those who accept her ideal of a "good death" to "travel agents for the dying, offering therapeutic intervention to a singular destination: tranquil, peaceful death" (51).

In rereading, after nearly forty years, my early essay on Tolstoy's story, I'm struck by my omission of any reference to caregiving, a subject about which I had no knowledge or experience at the time. *The Death of Ivan Ilych* does not offer a neat taxonomy for approaching the end of life, as Kübler-Ross does in *On Death and Dying* (1969). Instead, Tolstoy narrates a story that allows readers to draw their own conclusions about the right ways to live and die. For this reason, *The Death of Ivan Ilych* is often taught in medical schools, where, as Gerard Brungardt observes, it educates young physicians about the reality of end-of-life care. Rita Charon, a professor of internal medicine at Columbia University and a literary scholar, has created a new medical approach called narrative medicine. Charon uses Tolstoy's story in her seminars. In her 2006 book *Narrative Medicine*, she points out the narrator's movement over the course of the story. "The early scornful, distanced, judging teller of Ivan's life slowly moves in toward Ivan, closer, more forgiving, until, by chapter 4, he or she has attained Ivan's interior and can speak *for* him as well as of him. By chapter 9, the speaker is Ivan's soul" (118). Showing us how to cross the border between self and other remains part of Tolstoy's extraordinary achievement. Charon doesn't discuss Gerasim, but he is the key figure in the narrator's movement from distanced observation to empathic closeness.

## Another Ending

One can imagine a different ending to Tolstoy's story had he expanded Gerasim's role as Ivan Ilych's caregiver. The youth might not have attempted a direct answer to Ivan Ilych's question: What if my life has not been right? Gerasim probably would have remained silent, but it's likely he would have sat next to the dying man, providing him with much-needed presence in the face of death. He might have held Ivan Ilych's hand, conjuring the image of human connection. Gerasim would have been sad but not scared, and his acceptance of the inevitability of death would have been comforting to the dying man. Ivan Ilych still would have died, but he might not have been as isolated, lonely, and depressed. Nor would he have been in the presence of relatives who provide false consolation. Ivan Ilych still might have concluded that he had failed the test of his life review, that he had, indeed, lived by the wrong values, but Gerasim could have reminded him that all was not yet lost and that there was still time to see the truth.

Indeed, this is what happens at the end of the story, where Tolstoy, as narrator, merges with the authorial peasant servant. Gerasim drops out of the story a few pages from the ending, but, significantly, he is replaced by Ivan Ilych's son, Vasily, who, from his father's point of view, is the only other character apart from Gerasim who understood and pitied him. Slattery plausibly suggests that Gerasim's generous actions "exhibit a love that needs to be passed on, and this Ivan Ilych is able to do through his son" (175). Ivan Ilych's nurse and caregiver, Gerasim has taught his master how to express kindness and love. As the weeping schoolboy seizes his father's hand, Ivan Ilych kisses it, feeling sorry for both him and Praskovya Fedorovna, who is also weeping. For the first time in the story, Ivan Ilych feels compassion for his family. Forgiving his family is inseparable from self-forgiveness. He tries to express the words "Forgive me" but can utter only "forego" (90), a more ambiguous and ironic word. Irving Howe rightly cautions against an "uplifting" interpretation of the end of the story, and Ivan Ilych's agony continues for two more hours. There is no doubt, however, that the worst of his torment has ended, and his habitual fear of death gives way to joy.

As the dying man approaches the end of his journey, he sees a light. Anna Karenina sees the same light in the seconds before she throws herself in front of a locomotive: "suddenly the darkness, that obscured everything for her, broke, and life showed itself to her for an instant with all its bright past joys.... And at the same moment she was horror-struck at what she was doing" (760). The light comes too late for Anna Karenina but not for Ivan Ilych. The story's light and dark imagery serves as boundary markers in Ivan Ilych's transformation, as David S. Danaher indicates. Embracing the light, a traditional symbol of knowledge and power, Ivan Ilych experiences a spiritual rebirth, and he escapes from Anna Karenina's tunnel vision. He hears someone exclaim, "It is finished," an echo of Jesus' last words, which Ivan Ilych silently repeats to himself. The story ends where it begins, with his death, but with a crucial difference. Ivan Ilych's death has a far different meaning to the readers at the end of the story than to the mourners at the funeral, who, not reflecting on his end or their own, have gained little insight into his inner life.

Ivan Ilych's conversion at the end is more spiritual than religious. There is no suggestion that he has achieved everlasting life or has passed into a higher existence. After his own conversion to a radical form of Christianity in the late 1870s prior to writing the novella, Tolstoy tried to model his life after the historical Jesus. The center of Tolstoy's Christian faith, as his disciple Edward A. Steiner remarked more than a century ago, was based on the Sermon on the Mount (230). Tolstoy uses Gerasim to embody the story's affirmation of brotherly love and Christian charity. Ivan Ilych's nurse, teacher, and therapist, Gerasim is an early fictional example of a caregiver who helps ease the terror of death.

# 2

# Caregivers as Prisoners for Life in Edith Wharton's *Ethan Frome*

Few love stories are more haunting or bitterly ironic than Edith Wharton's (1862–1937) dark masterpiece *Ethan Frome* (1911). The novella focuses on the eponymous character's grim marriage to the ailing Zenoba (Zeena) and his passionate feelings for her young cousin and caregiver, Mattie Silver. Zeena soon realizes her husband's awakening love for Mattie and orders her to leave in an effort to thwart their blooming relationship. The two lovers cannot bear the thought of separation, however, and they agree to a suicide pact with unintended consequences. The ending of the story explores the unpredictable outcome of caregiving, the vagaries of psychological illness, and the shifting roles of caregivers and care-receivers. E. B. Greenwood's observation about the central theme of *The Death of Ivan Ilych*—"our need to be loved even when we are unlovely and unlovable" (122)—is no less true of *Ethan Frome*.

*Ethan Frome* contains a fourth character, the unnamed frame narrator who figures prominently in the story both as participant and observer. The prologue opens with the narrator traveling to the aptly named "Starkfield," a small town in the Berkshire Mountains in Western Massachusetts based on Lenox, where Wharton lived for many years. The narrator sees the most phantasmagoric figure in the village, Ethan Frome, a "ruin of a man" with a limping gait who appears far older than his age, fifty-two. "He's looked that way ever since he had his smash-up; and that's twenty-four years ago come next February" (4), the narrator learns from the village oracle, Harmon Gow, who adds that Ethan has been the caregiver for his two parents and wife. Intrigued by the spectral figure who looks more dead than alive, the narrator struggles to piece together the story, realizing that the "deeper meaning" was in the "gaps" (6).

The narrator's questions become the reader's questions, particularly the reasons Ethan chose to remain in Starkfield despite the fact that "Most of the smart ones get away" (8). How has Ethan been able to survive an accident that was "More'n enough to kill most men?" Confronting the villagers' reluctance to speak openly about Ethan's misfortunes, the narrator confidently assumes that he will learn the "missing facts" of the story or "rather such a key to his character as should co-ordinate the facts I knew" (9). The narrator succeeds in learning the facts, but the psychological key to Ethan Frome's character remains elusive.

Visiting Starkfield on business, the narrator hires Ethan as a driver for a week. A blinding snowstorm brings the narrator to Ethan's home, when the frame narration gives way to the story proper, an extended flashback leading to the events culminating in the smash-up. The frame narrator is not present during the lengthy flashback and has access to character motivation and dialogue that go beyond the details given to him by the villagers. Some critics have complained about this narrative inconsistency, but most readers have no trouble believing in the narrator's limited omniscience. One cannot assume that novelist and narrator are one and the same in *Ethan Frome*—though by the end of the story the narrator's conclusions are consistent with the information he has acquired. Wharton remarked in the author's Introduction that of all the characters in the story, "only the narrator of the tale has scope enough to see it all, to resolve it back into simplicity, and to put it in its rightful place among his larger categories" (xviii).

## *The Fruit of the Tree*

Euthanasia is not exactly the opposite of caregiving, but it eliminates the need for caregiving. Before turning to *Ethan Frome*, we should mention Wharton's little-known 1907 novel *The Fruit of the Tree*. In giving a fatal overdose of morphine to her childhood friend Bessy Langhope, who suffered a paralyzing spinal cord injury after being thrown from her horse, Justine Brent acts from the purest of motives, the desire to end another person's searing pain. "Keeping people alive in such cases is one of the refinements of cruelty that it was left for Christianity to invent" (402), opines Bessy's physician, Stephen Wyant, though in his view science demands that people should be kept alive at any cost. As a nurse, Justine had experienced cases where the "useless agonies of death were mercifully shortened by the physician: why was not this a case for such treatment?" (419). There is no question that the novel supports Justine's decision. Even if Bessy's heart continued beating, the rector bemoans, "it would probably be death-in-life: complete paralysis of the lower body" (406), a statement echoed by Bessy's sanctimonious lawyer: "I wish to God she had been killed!" (417).

Justine never doubts the correctness of her decision, but her situation becomes more complicated when she marries Bessy's husband, John Amherst, and finds herself blackmailed by Wyant. Justine initially does not disclose the mercy killing to her husband, and when she does, he cannot free himself from the suspicion that what she did was wrong. Justine's fault, in the narrator's words, "lay in having dared to rise above conventional restrictions, her mistake in believing that her husband could rise with her" (525). Ironically, in light of the extraordinary medical advances after the publication of *The Fruit of the Tree* and our heightened attention to disability studies, Bessy's spinal cord injury today would not be grounds for physician-assisted suicide.

Justine pays a heavy price for her act of "manumission," a term denoting an owner's freeing of his or her slaves but which Wharton uses to describe freeing Bessy from a life of relentless suffering. The only way Justine can prove her selfless love to Amherst is through heroic self-sacrifice, leaving her marriage. Not until the end of the novel does Amherst accept wholeheartedly the wisdom of the mercy killing. Justine's final lesson is that life is "not a matter of abstract principles, but a succession of pitiful compromises with fate, of concessions to old traditions, old beliefs, old charities and frailties." There is a vast difference, as we shall see, between the theory and practice of caregiving, and literature helps to fill the gap. Justine humbly accepts the lesson that human relations is a "tangled and deep-rooted growth, a dark forest through which the idealist cannot cut his straight path without hearing at each stroke the cry of the severed branch: '*Why woundest thou me?*'" (624).

## His Parents' Caregiver

*Ethan Frome* is about a different type of ineluctable wounding, a trauma with intergenerational implications. We learn in the prologue a few tantalizing clues about Ethan's role as his parents' caregiver. "Fust his father got a kick, out haying, and went soft in the brain, and gave away money like Bible texts afore he died," Harmon Gow explains. "Then his mother got queer and dragged along for years as weak as a baby" (12). Ethan attributes his mother's worsening health to the coming of the railroad; the once-busy farm now seemed cut off from the rest of the village, and she could no longer watch the stagecoach pass the house, which in the past seemed to cheer her up. The farm's isolation had a destabilizing influence on her. "But after the trains begun running nobody ever come by here to speak of, and mother never could get it through her head what had happened, and it preyed on her right along till she died" (19). It was during this time, Harmon Gow informs the narrator, that Ethan's cousin Zeena Pierce came to the farm: "she's always been the greatest hand at doctoring in the county. Sickness and trouble: that's what Ethan's had his plate full up with, ever since the very first helping" (12).

Because Wharton uses summary rather than scenic narration here—telling rather than showing us these caregiving experiences—we must rely on Harmon Gow's characterization. Nothing later contradicts his statement about Ethan's parents, but unlike Ethan's developing love for Mattie, which is *shown*, most of the caregiving activities are merely *told*. Love remains in the foreground, caregiving in the background. We see the stark differences in Ethan and Mattie before and after their smash-up, as well as the changes in Zeena, but we never witness Zeena's doctoring skills. By contrast, we vividly see Zeena as a patient.

## "Sickly"

"Nobody knows Zeena's thoughts" (155), exclaims the widow Mrs. Ned Hale near the end of the tale, and perhaps for this reason, Zeena remains the most enigmatic—and fascinating—character in the story. She is certainly the least sympathetic of the three main characters, the one we are most likely to dismiss as embittered and spiteful. In analyzing her baffling ailments, we must confront our own attitudes toward psychological illness. Wharton never uses "hypochondriacal," "neurasthenic," or the more problematic "hysterical" to describe Zeena, but her disease involves the mysterious interplay of mind and body and the difficulties that arise, for caregiver and care-receiver alike, when sadness is too impenetrable for words.

Zeena had "always been what Starkfield called 'sickly'" (31), the narrator asserts early in the story. Ethan dutifully travels to the post office to receive the patent medicine drugs she orders, pocketing them "without a glance, as if too much used to them to wonder at their number and frequency" (5). The nature of Zeena's sickness is never identified. One of her symptoms is insomnia, which she invokes, with confusing logic, to explain why she neglected to leave the house key under the mat to allow Ethan and Mattie to enter the house one cold wintry evening. She hadn't forgotten to leave the key, she says. "No. I just felt so mean I couldn't sleep" (47). The word "mean" occurs several times in the story; here it means "unwell," but earlier the word implies "contemptible," as when Ethan thinks about his rival for Mattie's love, Denis Eady, as a "mean fellow" (28). Zeena's statement that she felt too mean to sleep may imply that she was too agitated by dark emotions to sleep. There's little question that her mood and state of health are related. When she is fortunate enough to sleep, it is marred by "asthmatic breathing." Still another symptom is "heartburn," which sometimes prevents her from eating. Another symptom is "shooting pains," which sometimes extend to her ankles. A further indignity is that she wears dentures. Staring at his sleeping wife, Ethan sees her false teeth in a tumbler by the bed.

Believing that she is "losing ground every day," Zeena travels to neighboring Bettsbridge to see a new physician, Dr. Buck, whose name may evoke the expense of treatment. He had successfully treated a patient who was wasting away with kidney problems but is now "up and around, and singing in the choir" (96). There's no evidence that Zeena suffers from renal disease, but after her visit to the physician, Ethan sees her reading a book called *Kidney Troubles and Their Cure*; his only thought is that he had to pay extra postage when the book arrived. Whenever Zeena returns from one of her "therapeutic excursions," she feels overwrought, or "nervous," which explains Ethan's need for the "neutralizing presence" of his hired worker, Jotham Powell, to have dinner with them.

One needs to read between the lines to glimpse the nature of Zeena's illness, but the lines are deliberately blurred. The narrator does not hesitate to describe Zeena's "fault-finding," which was usually of the "silent kind, but not the less penetrating for that" (53). In the same paragraph, however, the narrator is less clear when describing how long summer nights have given Zeena "more leisure to devote to her complex ailments." One literary critic, Louis Auchincloss, has complained about Wharton's language in *Ethan Frome*. "Her sentences never have to be read and reread, like [Henry] James's, for richer and deeper disclosures" (44), but this comment misses the story's delicate irony. The narrator's language reveals a subtle blend of both acceptance and skepticism of the reality of Zeena's illness. Her decision to seek medical help as a result of her sleeplessness "showed that, as usual, she was wholly absorbed in her health" (56). The sentence would have lost its hint of irony had the narrator stated that she was absorbed in her "illness."

## "Complications"

We feel closer to Ethan than to Zeena, if only because we know his thoughts and feelings, not hers. When Ethan opens the bedroom door and sees his wife sitting by the window, he tells her that supper is ready, to which she responds, "I don't feel as if I could touch a morsel." The statement, he thinks, almost as if he were a diagnostician, betokens the "consecrated formula" that usually precedes her willingness to have dinner. This time, though, she remains seated, and he can't think of anything more felicitous to say than, "I presume you're tired after the long ride." The words immediately infuriate her, as if she was expecting his failure of empathic understanding. "I'm a great deal sicker than you think" (95). He responds with a conciliatory, "I hope that's not so, Zeena," but she continues to look at him "with a mien of wan authority, as of one consciously singled out for a great fate. 'I've got complications,' she said" (95).

Complications, indeed! The profound differences between Zeena and Ethan may be seen in their divergent uses of the word, betraying their clashing points of view. She views "complications" as an example of the uniqueness of her illness and, therefore, the singularity of her identity. She endures problems that other people can only imagine. One can hear her pride and resilience in articulating the word, which sets her apart from everyone else. Zeena's life, we sense, would be diminished without these complications. By pursuing every opportunity for health, she is proactive, demonstrating admirable strength of character. Why can't Ethan offer her empathic understanding instead of blame?

Ethan, by contrast, has limited insight into his wife's complaints. He is rightly worried about the ability to pay for her medical treatments, particularly in light of his struggling saw-mill. He can't help wondering what makes Zeena different from others in the community. "Almost everybody in the neighbourhood had 'troubles,' frankly localized and specified; but only the chosen had 'complications.' To have them was in itself a distinction, though it was also, in most cases, a death-warrant. People struggled on for years with 'troubles,' but they almost always succumbed to 'complications'" (95). From Ethan's perspective, Zeena's continued existence belies these complications.

Left unspoken is whether Ethan's life would be improved if he no longer had to live with his wife's complications. This is a jarring thought to him. Earlier in the story he allows himself to think about the possibility of her death. Gazing at his sleeping wife—she always went to bed after dinner—he sees a dead cucumber-vine hanging from the porch "like the crape streamer tied to the door for a death." Suddenly a thought flashes through his mind: "If it was there for Zeena—" (45). He breaks off the thought, which is too unnerving to pursue, but other times he reflects on death after a long life, as when he walks through a cemetery and sees a gravestone of a man bearing his own name, who dwelled together with his wife "in peace" for fifty years. Ethan can't help musing, "with a sudden dart of irony" (70), whether the same epitaph would be written about him and Zeena. History repeats itself in *Ethan Frome*, as Barbara A. White has noticed. "It is no accident that Zeena originally came to the Fromes, as Ethan's cousin, to nurse his mother; then Mattie, Zeena's cousin, came to nurse Zeena" (231). What seems so "grim," White adds, "is not Ethan's or any one character's individual tragedy but the unbroken chain of want and despair" (252).

Because we lack access to Zeena's thoughts, we don't know whether she struggles between the same two extremities of feeling, compassion and anger, that we see in Ethan. Compassion motivates him to say, in response to her complications, "Is that what the new doctor told you?" But compassion turns to anger when she discloses that she needs surgery—though tellingly, she never reveals the kind of surgery recommended by her physician. Worried about the expense, Ethan questions the doctor's judgment and immediately regrets his choice of words. "He saw his blunder before she could take it up: she wanted sympathy, not consolation" (96).

Wharton's novel has not generated the clinical attention that *The Death of Ivan Ilych* has, but Barry J. Jacobs has noted that Ethan Frome's anger toward his wife is complicated by the fact that she has taken care of his mother in the past. Jacobs offers several suggestions to health care professionals who work with angry, resentful caregivers like Ethan Frome, but, with one exception, none of the characters in the story help Ethan acknowledge the legitimacy of his emotions or offer him advice how to express anger constructively.

The fierce argument over the cost of surgery bespeaks deeper conflicts that began before marriage, when Zeena came to Ethan's home to help him care for his dying mother. Zeena appeared to be a different person then. Without Zeena's help, the story implies, he might have succumbed to his mother's fate. Mrs. Frome's medical ailments remain vague. She didn't lose the power of speech, but she stopped talking, and when her son desperately asked her to say something, anything, she answered, maddeningly, that she was listening to the wind: "They're talking so out there that I can't hear you" (61)—a confirmation, perhaps, of Harmon Gow's earlier statement that she "got queer."

## The Fear of Madness—and a Possible Psychological Disorder

During his mother's final illness, when Zeena helped to care for her, Ethan appears to have come close to suffering a breakdown. "After the mortal silence of his long imprisonment Zeena's volubility was music in his ears. He felt that he might have 'gone like his mother' if the sound of a new voice had not come to steady him" (61). The missing word in the preceding sentence may imply his fear of mental illness—the possibility that he might have "gone [mad] like his mother." Silence proves "mortal" and contagious in the story, and a "sense of unreality" (131) often overcomes Ethan during moments of stress. One suspects that the fear of madness preys on him, as it had preyed on his mother.

Ethan Frome's frightening loss of reality raises the possibility that he suffers from what was called, until recently, Depersonalization Disorder, and is now renamed Depersonalization/Derealization Disorder, or DDD. As Elena Bezzubova reports in her 2014 blog in *Psychology Today*, for almost half a century the official guide of the American Psychiatric Association, the *Diagnostic and Statistical Manual of Mental Disorders*, the *DSM*, referred to Depersonalization Disorder, defined as a feeling of unreality. The disorder included derealization as an associated feature. In the new fifth edition, published in 2013, the *DSM-5* changed the name to include the experience of the unreality of the world. The change is consistent with the first diagnosis made in 1873 by a French otolaryngologist, who viewed depersonalization and derealization as interconnected and inseparable. The *DSM-5* offers no explanation of the origins of DDD. "Even though neuroscience, genetics, psychology and other disciplines contribute significantly to understanding of the development of depersonalization," Bezzubova points out, "the exact cause of depersonalization remains unclear in the majority of cases."

There are several moments in the story when Ethan, suffering from intense anxiety, experiences the symptoms of DDD. Seeing Zeena open the locked door, Ethan "felt as if he had never before known what his wife looked like" (47). The entire scene has a dreamlike quality to him, one of the symptoms of DDD. Having dinner alone with Mattie while Zeena is out of town visiting a doctor, Ethan has a "confused sense of being in another world" (77). Watching Mattie sitting in Zeena's rocking chair, he has a momentary shock: "It was almost as if the other face, the face of the superseded woman, had obliterated that of the intruder" (78). Later that evening, when Ethan imagines Zeena rocking in the same chair the next day, he silently muses, "'I've been in a dream, and this is the only evening we'll ever have together.' The return to reality was as painful as the return to consciousness after taking an anaesthetic" (83). The metaphor of anesthesia is significant, for the use of drugs can trigger episodes of depersonalization or derealization. After ordering Mattie to leave their home, Zeena takes on a "mysterious alien presence" to Ethan, an "evil energy secreted from the long years of silent brooding" (103). The "sense of unreality" overcomes him again when he imagines life without Mattie, and moments before the smash-up, he sees his wife's face, "with twisted monstrous lineaments, thrust between him and his goal" (147).

We can understand Ethan's frightening loss of reality without invoking DDD, but our appreciation of the story deepens when we recognize Wharton's insights into the ambiguities of psychological health and illness. There is no sharp line between "neurotic" and "normal," Freud observes in his 1909 *Analysis of a Phobia in a Five-Year-Old Boy*—the case of Little Hans: "our conception of 'disease' is a purely practical one" (*SE*, vol. 10, 145-6). Ethan is not psychotic, but his persistent and recurrent episodes of depersonalization and derealization heighten his distress and disconnection. His psychological "complications" are different from but no less real than Zeena's.

Zeena seemed to be *Ethan's* caregiver as well as his mother's during her final illness. He felt awed by her efficiency, and she instinctively knew what to do when his mother died. After the funeral, he felt an "unreasoning dread of being left alone on the farm." It's unclear whether Ethan is helped more by Zeena's understanding of his situation or by her efficiency as a caregiver; but for whatever reason, he feels restored by following her orders. This is the moment in the story when Ethan is most impressed with Zeena, yet his admiration is tinged with ambivalence. "Her efficiency shamed and dazzled him. She seemed to possess by instinct all the household wisdom that his long apprenticeship had not instilled in him" (62). Shame is a key element of Ethan's relationship with Zeena, Lev Raphael contends (286); he points out that shame, the darkest emotion, suffuses the entire story.

Wharton offers us few clues into Ethan's near-collapse following his mother's death. He doesn't appear to have been especially close to either of his parents, and he never reflects on his earlier life with them. There is no mention of missing his parents: he never regards himself as an orphan. Nor do their deaths produce an existential or spiritual crisis. Rather, the loss of his parents leads to a regression to a childlike state in which he needs to be cared for by a parental surrogate—in this case, Zeena. During this harrowing time, Ethan loses confidence in his ability to live independently. He never talks about his near-breakdown, yet it is not an experience one is likely to forget.

Ethan feels manipulated into marriage, as Zeena later acknowledges: "my folks all told me at the time you couldn't do no less than marry me after—" (98). Motivated more by fear of isolation and silence than by anticipated joy over Zeena's continuing presence, Ethan impulsively asked her to marry him—and then, in a noteworthy sentence, we learn that he regretted his hasty decision. "He had often thought since that it would not have happened if his mother had died in spring instead of winter . . ." (62; ellipsis in original). In marrying Zeena so quickly after his mother's death, indeed, as a result of his mother's death, Ethan demonstrates the truth of the adage, marry in haste, repent at leisure. Does he see his wife as a replacement of his dead mother? Tricia M. Farwell makes this plausible interpretation. In "submitting to her fate, Zeena becomes the woman Ethan's mother was prior to her death": silent and closed off (67).

## "The Very Genius of Health"

Zeena's caregiving skills, Ethan later believes, are related to the illness she develops within a year of marriage. This sickliness is notable, the narrator adds, "even in a community rich in pathological instances" (63). Mary Gordon suggests how the idea of illness animates Zeena's personality, heightening her will to live. "The character of Zeena is a brilliant portrayal of the kind of woman whose métier is illness and whose strength comes from the certainty invented by the invalid's unlimited free time and the innocence born of the truth that most wrongdoing requires a physical capacity the invalid lacks or chooses to stifle" (*Good Boys and Dead Girls* 31). Freud did not write about *Ethan Frome*, but its insights into illness and health may remind us of *The Psychopathology of Everyday Life*, published in 1901, a decade before Wharton's story. Freud's discussion of the "secondary gain from illness" (*SE*, vol. 6, 115) helps us to understand Zeena's psychosomatic illness, what she gains as well as loses from ill health. Is her illness an intensification of what the Starkfield townspeople experience or qualitatively different? The narrator's next statement is even more puzzling. "When she came to take care of his mother she had seemed to Ethan like the very genius of health, but he soon saw that her skill as a nurse had been acquired by the absorbed observation of her own symptoms" (63). The hint of sarcasm in "genius for health" is palpable, particularly in light of subsequent events, yet the story also implies that illness, either present or incipient, may be the driving force behind productive or creative endeavors, as we shall see, in Wharton's own creativity.

Unlike Ethan, who believes that his wife's caregiving skills arise from intuitive knowledge of her own illness, Zeena dates the beginning of her illness to her caregiving experience. Both characters may be correct about this chicken-or-egg question. Emily C. Abel does not comment on *Ethan Frome* in *Hearts of Wisdom*, but she points out that nineteenth-century women "often attributed their own ill health to the stresses of caregiving" (49). When Zeena tells Ethan that she would be "ashamed" to tell her doctor that her husband "grudged me the money to get back my health, when I lost it nursing your own mother,!" Ethan cannot conceal his incredulity. In the narrator's words, though one could not see their faces during this heated exchange, "their thoughts seemed to dart at each other like serpents shooting venom" (98).

## A Dangerous Profession

Despite Ethan's stunned disbelief over Zeena's statement, the story implies that caregiving *does* endanger the caregiver's health, for he, too, began to lose his bearing while helping to care for his dying mother. Zeena enters Ethan's life as a caregiver, but soon she becomes the care-receiver as her own health starts to fail. She grows silent, like Ethan's mother, and marriage only exacerbates her situation. Wharton deftly hints at the reasons for their unhappiness in a passage that does justice to both husband and wife's points of view. "Perhaps it was the inevitable effect of life on the farm, or perhaps, as she sometimes said, it was because Ethan 'never listened.' The charge was not wholly unfounded. When she spoke it was only to complain, and to complain of things not in his power to remedy; and to check a tendency to impatient retort he had first formed the habit of not answering her, and finally of thinking of other things while she talked" (63–4). Marriage is the battleground on which husband and wife wage passive or active war, each blaming the other for discord, each viewing the other's selfishness as the key problem of misunderstanding and mistrust. Problematic marriages produce problematic caregiving.

## Depression?

Given the cheerlessness of Starkfield, especially during grueling winters, when nature resembled a "mute melancholy landscape, an incarnation of its frozen woe" (13), one wonders whether Zeena's physical complaints portend symptoms of clinical depression. She seems to be largely a prisoner of her dreary home and inhospitable community, with no friends or interests apart from her visits to doctors and reading medical textbooks. There's one question the story studiously avoids raising: whether either Zeena or Ethan wish to have children. They have been married for seven years, and Zeena is seven years older than her husband, which makes her thirty-five when the flashback begins. Does the "barren farm" (54) on which they live reflect her own fears of childlessness? Is this the reason

Ethan refers to her "flat breast" (47) when she opens the kitchen door to let him and Mattie inside? The Fromes' marriage is sexless and lacks either passion or emotional warmth. We cannot infer from the silence whether one or both of the Fromes wanted children or how the presence of offspring would have affected Zeena's health and marriage, but we can wonder whether these questions contribute to her silence. Elaine Showalter suggests in her Introduction to *Ethan Frome* that Zeena's unused wedding gift—the red glass pickle dish hidden in the china closet—may hint at an unconsummated marriage (xxiii). Zeena reacts to the shattered pickle dish as if it were the death of a loved one, gathering the shards "as if she carried a dead body" (111).

Zeena's frustration deepens as a result of the failure of the medical cures she has sought. A recent visit to Springfield has resulted in a $20 electric battery she has never learned to use. (Twenty dollars around 1900 would be the equivalent of nearly $600 in 2018.) She empties a large bottle of medicine but concedes, "It ain't never done me a speck of good, but I guess I might as well use it up" (58). One can understand Zeena's despair as well as Ethan's. He tries his best to accommodate his wife's illness, but his best is not good enough, and he recognizes that she is a "hundred times bitterer and more discontent than when he had married her." This leads to one of his central epiphanies: "the one pleasure left her was to inflict pain on him" (114). Zeena inflicts pain on *both* Ethan and Mattie. Zeena is not so self-absorbed that she fails to notice her husband's budding friendship with Mattie. Zeena intuits why Ethan begins shaving every day, something he had not done before Mattie's arrival. Zeena's physical complaints worsen, a sign of her seething rage, yet, paradoxically, she springs to life after she resolves to engage a "hired girl" and commands Mattie to leave, a decision that awakens her husband's fury. Ethan may not feel pleasure in inflicting pain on Zeena, but he cannot help wishing for her death. No paragraph in the story is more emotionally charged than this one: "Ethan looked at her with loathing"; "he abhorred her"; a "flame of hate rose in him" (103). Ethan doesn't immediately act on these volatile emotions, but he is headed in the direction of disaster and defeat.

Zeena now feels in control, and following the visit to Dr. Buck, she "regaled" Ethan and Mattie with several vivid descriptions of "intestinal disturbances among her friends and relatives" (108), taking full advantage of her own illness. The next morning, during Mattie's last breakfast at the farm, Zeena had an "air of unusual alertness and activity." After drinking two cups of coffee and feeding the cat, she prunes the geraniums, exulting in her victory over her defeated rival. Zeena's mood brightens during the last dinner together. "She ate well, declaring that the mild weather made her feel better, and pressed a second helping of beans on Jotham Powell, whose wants she generally ignored" (128).

Zeena's return to health depends upon undercutting her husband's health. Joy has entered Ethan's life for the first time with Mattie's arrival. She joins the Fromes' household under a cloud of suspicion: her father's extravagance, including his impressive funeral, had brought financial ruin to his and Zeena's family. Mattie's mother died of shame after the public disclosure of her husband's wrongdoing. Mattie's own health had broken down after her mother's death, though she recovers—temporarily. In a statement fraught with ominous foreshadowing, Mattie thus feels "indentured" to the Fromes, for whom she works without pay. Ethan tells Mattie, shortly before they go sledding, that he wants to be her caregiver. "I want to do for you and care for you. I want to be there when you're sick and when you're lonesome" (138). Ethan's wish comes true with a vengeance.

## The Value of Sympathy

Determined to leave Starkfield with Mattie and divorce Zeena, Ethan decides to ask Andrew Hale for the money that is owed to him, but he first encounters Mrs. Hale, who "in her youth, had done more 'doctoring' than any other woman in Starkfield, and was still a recognised authority on symptoms and treatment" (65). It's curious that Zeena has apparently never gone to Mrs. Hale for medical advice, but the older woman understands Ethan's adversities. "I don't know anybody round here's had more sickness than Zeena," she says to Ethan. "I always tell Mr. Hale I don't know what she'd 'a' done if she hadn't 'a' had you to look after her; and I used to say the same thing 'bout your mother. You've had an awful mean time, Ethan Frome." Mrs. Hale's expression of heartfelt sympathy is uncommon in a community in which most people were "either indifferent to his troubles, or disposed to think it natural that a young fellow of his age should have carried without repining the burden of three crippled lives" (123).

Caregiving doesn't evoke much sympathy among the Starkfield people, and for that reason, Mrs. Hale's words take on greater significance to Ethan. Embodying Nel Noddings's three principles of ethical care, receptivity, relatedness, and responsiveness, she is the character who comes closest to being a genuine caregiver in the story. Mrs. Hale embodies the four characteristics of the Gerasim model of caregiver discussed by Susan L. Taylor: acceptance of the patient's illness; honest communication; patient-directed comfort; and a consistent, gentle approach to caregiving. Mrs. Hale's sympathy makes Ethan feel less isolated; she alone grasps the difficulty of his situation and praises his efforts to fulfill his responsibilities. She appreciates his caregiving and helps him feel, for a brief moment, that he is a good person. Mrs. Hale also expresses sympathy toward Zeena and never questions the reality of her illness. "Beaming maternally" while speaking with Ethan, she offers the motherly support that has been lacking in his life.

Like Gerasim in *The Death of Ivan Ilych*, Mrs. Hale is admittedly a minor character, speaking only a few lines, but she embodies a major insight: the need for maternal approval. Gloria C. Erlich doesn't discuss *Ethan Frome* in her 1992 psychobiographical study *The Sexual Education of Edith Wharton*, but her suggestion that the novelist was on a lifelong search for a loving mother surrogate to replace her cold, unnurturing biological mother may be seen in Mrs. Hale's warm sympathy. It's impossible to know whether Mrs. Hale would have remained sympathetic had she known about Ethan's plans to run away with Mattie. Nor can we say whether Zeena would have felt less unwell had she received from her husband unqualified sympathy, not consolation. Nevertheless, sympathy remains at the center of both caring and caregiving in the story. Ironically, Mrs. Hale's sympathy forces Ethan to have second thoughts about leaving his wife and deceiving the Hales, "two kindly people who had pitied him" (124).

## The Smash-Up

Sympathy reminds Ethan of his moral responsibilities, allowing him to overcome briefly the "madness" (124) that has descended on him, yet he cannot give up Mattie, who has aroused his desire. He feels protective of her, a young woman with few resources and with nowhere to go, but Wharton also shows his acute jealousy, which clouds his judgment regarding what is best for Mattie. In their first open discussion of death, Ethan implies that the thought of her surviving without him, presumably with another man, is unbearable: "I'd a'most have you dead than that!" (138). Described by one critic, Susan Goodman, as "lovely" but "possibly the most inarticulate heroine in American literature" (73), Mattie supports his death wish, stating that no one has been as good to her as Ethan. In what proves to be the most joyful moments of their lives, they experience exhilarating coasts to the bottom of School House Hill. Wharton uses sexual imagery to convey the two lovers plummeting down the hill, evoking the symbolic consummation of their union. By contrast, sex is portrayed more graphically in the 1993 film version of *Ethan Frome*, directed by John Madden, where the two lovers, Liam Nesson and Patricia Arquette, passionately make love in the farmhouse while Zeena, played by Joan Allen, is visiting her doctor.

Mattie proposes the double suicide by crashing into the big elm at the bottom of the hill, and though Ethan dismisses the idea as "crazy," he agrees to it. Reminiscent of a Wagnerian *Liebestod* or the ending of George Eliot's 1860 novel *The Mill on the Floss*, where brother and sister Tom and Maggie Tulliver drown embracing each other in a flood, the intended act has been foreshadowed earlier when the two are walking through the Frome gravestones and Ethan declares, "I guess we'll never let you go, Matt," adding silently, "We'll always go on living here together, and some day she'll lie there beside me" (45). As they plunge down the hill, Ethan suddenly sees his wife's face, but he doesn't allow this momentary vision of guilt to slow their vertiginous rush toward death. The smash-up results in devastating injuries for both, leaving Mattie with a paralyzing spinal injury (recalling Bessy Amherst's similar injury in *The Fruit of the Tree*) that transforms her into an invalid.

The most stunning detail of the ending, however, is not that the double suicide pact failed but that Ethan and Mattie, thwarted in love and death, are now living with Zeena, who has become their caregiver. The act that brought Ethan and Zeena together, caregiving, has locked them into an indissolvable union with the woman, Mattie, who offered the possibility of Ethan's escape from a deadly marriage. Astonishingly, Zeena was the one, not Ethan, who sent for Mattie as soon as the doctors concluded she was able to be moved.

## A Double Caregiver

How do we explain Zeena's willingness to care for a woman she had ordered out of her home, over Ethan's outraged protests? Why does Zeena wish to live in the same house as her husband and the woman who almost broke up their marriage? Perhaps most intriguing of all, how is Zeena able to regain her health to become a double caregiver? This question amazes Mrs. Ned Hale.

> It was a miracle, considering how sick she was—but she seemed to be raised right up just when the call came to her. Not as she's ever given up doctoring, and she's had sick spells right along; but she's had the strength given her to care for those two for over twenty years, and before the accident came she thought she couldn't even care for herself. (155)

There's a startling disconnect between Mrs. Hale's reference to Zeena's strength as a caregiver and what we see—not strength but the absence of either emotion or thought: "opaque eyes which revealed nothing and reflected nothing" (150). The image is less human than zombie-like. One can hardly conceive of a more dehumanized caregiver, especially when Zeena refuses to acknowledge, either verbally or nonverbally, Mattie's complaints. Samuel Fisher Dodson calls Zeena at the end the "good, healthy nurse and Mattie the sullen, crippled patient" (256), but one would never wish to have a nurse like Zeena. Some of the statements made about the characters at the end of the story are unduly harsh, as when Gary Scharnhorst labels Mattie as a "two-faced *femme* near-*fatale*, a scheming temptress who not only lures Ethan to a worse hell than he could have imagined but in the end is consigned to it, too" (271).

Mattie is left at the end broken in body and spirit, bemoaning that Zeena has left her in the cold by allowing the fire to go out; Zeena performs her caregiving responsibilities silently and begrudgingly, in abject martyrdom. The expression on Ethan's face, when he listens to the two women quarrel with each other, intimates that he is the one who suffers the most. His worst nightmare has come true: not only does he remain entrapped in a loveless marriage but Mattie has also turned into another Zeena, cold and critical. It's as if he has two wives, both reminding him of his failures. Mrs. Hale implies at the end that it would have been better for all three had Mattie not lived. The last words in the story suggest that there is little difference between the Fromes at the farm and those in the graveyard—"'cept that down there they're all quiet, and the women have got to hold their tongues" (157).

Wharton holds her own tongue at the end of the story, refusing to offer any clues to what her three characters are thinking. Zeena appears to be in control at the end, but what are the motives for her caregiving? Compassion—or schadenfreude, rejoicing in the suffering of others? Does Zeena learn about the reasons for the smash-up? Does she assume it was an accident—or a failed double suicide? In short, what has Ethan revealed and concealed about the act? Why does Ethan agree to live with Zeena when he could have cared for Mattie alone? Does guilt alone, along with perhaps masochism, explain his willingness to continue to live with Zeena in a brutal marriage? Does he believe that Zeena will be a better caregiver to Mattie than he could be without his wife's help? What are Mattie's thoughts about the failed suicide pact? Wharton cites in *The Writing of Fiction* (1925) Nietzsche's comment that it takes genius to "make an end," and then she suggests, in her own words, that the writer must "give the touch of inevitableness to the conclusion of any work of art" (38). *Ethan Frome* ends with the touch of inevitability. Wharton might have cited another Nietzschean idea, one that tragically did not come true for the philosopher himself, who spent the last decade of his life in a vegetative coma: "Many die too late, and some die too early. Yet strange soundeth the precept: 'Die at the right time!'" (75), a fate that eludes both Ethan and Mattie.

The bleakness of caregiving in *Ethan Frome* is exceeded only by the gloom of marriage. Wharton describes both as forms of self-inflicted torture—life sentences that will end only at death. No one would want to be a caregiver or care-receiver in the world of *Ethan Frome*. The satisfaction of caring for another person, or being cared for, is absent—unless one regards caregivers as jailors, permanently imprisoned with their care-receivers. Before the decision to end their lives, when he regards his situation as hopeless, Ethan views himself as a "prisoner for life" (117), but the same may be said for Zeena and Mattie. Sartre famously said in his 1944 existentialist play *No Exit* that hell is other people; in Wharton's novella, all three characters find themselves in hellish company, without the possibility of escape.

## The Figure behind the Veil

Wharton observed in her 1934 autobiography *A Backward Glance* that *Ethan Frome* gave her the greatest joy in writing, a statement that might appear counterintuitive in light of the story's stony ending. The early reviewers recognized Wharton's brilliant achievement, but some of the readers, R. W. B. Lewis informs us in his 1965 biography, felt that the final image was "too terrible to be borne." The reviewer in the *New York Times* grumbled that the story was, in Lewis's words, "an exercise in subtle torture" (310). Diana Trilling called *Ethan Frome* a "cruel book."

Lewis regards *Ethan Frome* as "one of the most autobiographical stories ever written" (xiv) not because of the descriptions of caregiving, with which Wharton had little personal experience, but because of her portrayal of a loveless, passionless marriage, one that resembled her own, and her depiction of mental illness—her husband's and her own. By all accounts, the novelist's marriage to Edward (Teddy) Robbins Wharton was torturous from the beginning. "The marriage was a sexual disaster from the first," Hermione Lee avers in her 2007 biography of Edith Wharton, "and her misery and frustration expressed themselves as illness (notably, asthma) and depression" (363). Lee calls attention to the difficulty of finding a happy marriage anywhere in Wharton's fiction.

Wharton's marriage lasted for twenty-eight years, from 1885, when she was twenty-three, to 1913, when she received a divorce. Teddy Wharton suffered from severe mental illness for much of his adult life; he would now probably be diagnosed as having manic-depressive (bipolar) disorder. There was a history of mental illness in his family: his father demonstrated similar symptoms, was institutionalized, and committed suicide. Some of Zeena's physical complaints were those experienced by Teddy Wharton, such as piercing pains in his thighs, legs, and toes. Edith Wharton suffered from what appears to be depression prior to and during the early years of her marriage, experiencing many of the symptoms she projected onto Zeena Frome: insomnia, weight loss, headaches, asthma, fatigue, and nervous irritability.

Wharton never spoke publicly about her mental illness, making no mention of it in her autobiography, but she did write about it, sometimes in coded form, in her letters. It was a "form of neurasthenia," she confided to Sara Norton in 1894. "My 'seasickness' defied all cures, diets, and everything that the medical arts could devise (they mostly made me worse)" (Lewis 74). One can imagine Zeena making the same observation. In her 1977 biography *A Feast of Words*, Cynthia Griffin Wolff cites a 1908 letter the novelist wrote to Sara Norton that highlights additional details of her experience with depression:

> Tell Lily, if it's any comfort, that for *twelve years* I seldom knew what it was to be, for more than an hour or two of the twenty-four, without an intense feeling of nausea, and such unutterable fatigue that when I got up I was always more tired than when I lay down. This form of neurasthenia consumed the best years of my youth, and left, in some sort, an irreparable shade on my life. Mais quoi! I worked through it, and came out on the other side, and so will she [emphasis in original]. (52)

One can hear pride in Wharton's voice, the same pride that one hears when Zeena proclaims the "complications" of her illness. Creative writers do not need to experience their fictional characters' illnesses, only to imagine them, but in Wharton's case, she seemed to have first-hand knowledge of Zeena's complications.

Unlike Zeena, Wharton had the benefit of the "Rest Cure," devised by the foremost American neurologist of the age, S. Weir Mitchell, himself a famous novelist. Wharton never wrote about her experiences with the rest cure, as did Charlotte Perkins Gilman in her renowned novella *The Yellow Wallpaper*, but, unlike Gilman, Wharton benefited from the treatment, which she underwent in 1898 as an outpatient at the Philadelphia Orthopedic Hospital. The treatment proved successful, allowing her to return to life—and to writing. Edmund Wilson suggests in *The Wound and the Bow* that Wharton first "seriously began to write fiction . . . during the period of a nervous breakdown, at the suggestion of Dr. S. Weir Mitchell" and that thereafter "she seems to have depended on her writing to get her through some difficult years, a situation that became more and more painful" (160). The British physician George Pickering (1904–80) does not include Wharton in his 1974 book *Creative Malady*, which argues that illness played a major role in the lives of several great figures, including Charles Darwin, Florence Nightingale, Mary Baker Eddy, Sigmund Freud, Marcel Proust, and Elizabeth Barrett Browning. Pickering's thesis that an "illness that is not debilitating or disabling, or threatening to life, may provide the ideal circumstances for creative work" (16) is strikingly true for the author of *Ethan Frome*. Pickering's theory of creative malady may be applied to many authors of mental illness stories, as I suggest in *Mad Muse: The Mental Illness Memoir in a Writer's Life and Work*.

## Psychosomatic Illness

Part of Wharton's achievement in *Ethan Frome* is her depiction of psychosomatic illness, a physical disease that is caused or exacerbated by mental factors. "On any average day," writes the neurologist Suzanne O'Sullivan in an article appearing in *Psychology Today* in 2017, "perhaps as many as a third of people who go to see their general practitioner have symptoms that are deemed medically unexplained." Psychosomatic disorders, she continues, are physical symptoms that mask emotional distress. In a sentence that captures a central insight in *Ethan Frome*, O'Sullivan observes that "when words are not available, our bodies sometimes speak for us—and we have to listen." Wharton listened to her own body and then crafted one of the enduring masterpieces of twentieth-century American fiction. Like a master pianist, Wharton knew how to play silence, and Zeena's silence in *Ethan Frome* seems to "conceal far-reaching intentions, mysterious conclusions drawn from suspicions and resentments impossible to guess" (64). Wharton also dramatizes the caregiving challenges that arise from psychosomatic illness: the skepticism surrounding its reality, the frustration over lack of effective therapy, the worry about the cost of treatment, the interchangeability of caregiver's and care-receiver's roles, and the sense of helplessness experienced by both the caregiver and care-receiver. Wharton's story shows that caregiving puts an often unendurable strain on marriages already at risk.

Interestingly, Wharton's success as a novelist appeared to worsen her husband's illness. "Whatever the other possible causes," Lewis remarks, it is "hard not to suspect that one underlying source of these afflictions was the extensive change in Edith's position in life," when she began to earn a great deal of money from her writings. "His collapses were in part, one surmises, ways of drawing attention to himself in the midst of his wife's widespread recognition and her achieved independence and well-being" (273). Wolff make a similar observation about the reciprocal nature of illness in the Whartons' marriage: "If Edith persisted in getting well and taking care of herself, Teddy retaliated by becoming sick. Thus with an almost mathematical perversity, as Edith gave up the need for protection, Teddy asserted it" (103). Edith Wharton intuited this pattern: Zeena's recovery at the end of the story may thus only deepen Ethan and Mattie's despair, which in turn contributed to Zeena's recovery.

Teddy Wharton did not share or appreciate his wife's literary interests, and one can only imagine whether he recognized the autobiographical roots of *Ethan Frome*. "Like Edith Wharton, Ethan Frome is married to an ailing spouse a number of years older than he, and has been married for about the same length of time as Edith had been tied to Teddy," remarks Lewis. "Ethan sometimes wonders about Zeena's sanity, and he daydreams about her death, possibly by violence" (309). There are other conspicuous parallels between Wharton's fiction and life at this time. Ethan's relationship with Mattie Silver was based on Wharton's tempestuous relationship with the journalist Morton Fullerton. The affair, which began in 1906 and lasted until around 1910, did not end well, but the sexual awakening exposed her to an aspect of life, embodied in Mattie, that the novelist put to good use in her later stories. Fiction sometimes serves, like most dreams, as wish fulfillment, but in this case, writing *Ethan Frome* was an act of exorcism. Wharton imposed a cruel fate upon her characters, but she ultimately imagined an escape from both a deadly marriage and debilitating illness, in the process becoming one of the great American novelists of the century. She would later write *The Age of Innocence*, for which she received the Pulitzer Prize for Fiction in 1921, the first woman to receive the award. She was also the first woman to receive an honorary degree from Yale (Knights 6).

Wharton could not imagine caregiving as anything other than a gruesome duty in *Ethan Frome*, yet paradoxically, she believed in public caregiving. She helped create two organizations that led to the compassionate treatment of women and children who had fled to refugee centers during the First World War. After the Germans invaded Belgium in 1914, she helped organize the American Hostels for Refugees, and a year later she created the Children of Flanders Rescue

Committee, overseeing several hundred Belgian children who were displaced by the war. Shari Benstock points out that the private charitable organizations Wharton cofounded were the second largest private charitable trusts in France during the First World War (303).

It was, however, in her stories that Wharton succeeded spectacularly as a literary caregiver, to her fictional offspring. No one, including her close friend Henry James, was more devoted to writing fiction. Wharton regarded the writing of *Ethan Frome* as a turning point in her career, when she "suddenly felt," as she records in *A Backward Glance*, "the artisan's full control of his implements" (209). Wharton bore witness in *Ethan Frome* to the enigmatic illness that robbed her of years of health, but she wrote through it, penning a story whose gaps of silence continue to intrigue us.

3

# Unmasking the Caregiver in Ingmar Bergman's *Persona*

"He who fights with monsters," Nietzsche observes dryly in *Beyond Good and Evil*, "should look to it that he himself does not become a monster. And when you gaze long into an abyss the abyss also gazes into you" (102). Sister Alma (Bibi Andersson), the nurse and caregiver in Ingmar Bergman's 1966 film *Persona*, would have benefited from Nietzsche's oracular wisdom. She gazes long and hard at the bewitching face of Elisabet Vogler (Liv Ullmann), the stage actress performing *Electra* who has suddenly embraced maddening silence. In *Ethan Frome*, caregiver and care-receiver exchange roles; but in *Persona*, the nurse and actress exchange *identities*, each becoming the other. Caregiving proves to be a dangerous profession in both *Ethan Frome* and *Persona*, in part because of the dark motivation behind caring for another. In an interview with John Simon, Bergman called Elisabet a "monster, because she has an emptiness in her" (32). Alma's wish to change identities with her patient comes true, resulting in a monstrous transformation she never could have imagined.

"Everything one says about *Persona* may be contradicted," Peter Cowie stated hyperbolically in his 1982 critical biography of Ingmar Bergman; "the opposite will also be true" (231). Even if this is exaggeration, how does one respond to the inscrutable psychological horrors depicted in the film? Through silence? That's how Elisabet reacts to reality. Is her silence an effort to avoid speaking untruths or a symptom of madness? A way to protect herself from violence or a strategy to attack another person? An effort to avoid evil or the expression of evil itself? Alma ponders these questions, as do viewers. Silence is terrifying in *Persona*, but the alternative is equally unsettling insofar as the dialogue in the film exposes lies and duplicity. How is sincerity possible in a world where speech is wounding, where surface truths betray hollowness, and where caregiving results in a nightmarish loss of identity followed by acts of cruelty?

*Persona* is, as Egil Törnqvist enthuses, Bergman's "most daring and enigmatic film" (137). It is also one of the twentieth century's greatest and most complex films. *Persona* has generated vast critical commentary. Writing in 2011, Peter Ohlin pointed out that the reference guide to Bergman's works is a massive tome of over 1,100 pages (ix). Nothing, however, has been written about Bergman's disturbing vision of caregiving in the film, particularly his insistence that artists must be their own caregivers regardless of the pain they inflict on others.

## Masking and Unmasking

Persona, the Latin word for mask, referred initially to the mask worn by actors in classical Greek and Roman drama. By extension, persona is the public mask each person presents to the world—"To prepare a face to meet the faces that you meet," as T. S. Eliot writes in his 1917 dramatic monologue "The Love Song of J. Alfred Prufrock." Prufrock's next line, "There will be time to murder and create" (4), also illuminates Bergman's film, which explores artistic murder and creation. In Jungian psychology, which Bergman had been studying at the time, persona refers to the social mask designed to conceal and protect inner identity. "Alma" in Latin means "soul." Bergman's film relentlessly dissects the different personae worn by care-receiver and caregiver, both of whom unmask the other and, in the process, reveal exposed, isolated, and helpless souls.

Identity is tenuous in Bergman's world; the boundary between self and other is porous and unstable. Self-exposure leads to heightened vulnerability and cruelty. Self-disclosure usually begets self-disclosure, but as Alma opens up about her life, Elisabet remains withdrawn. Like Joseph Conrad's 1899 novella *Heart of Darkness*, *Persona* focuses on twinship, doubling, and secret sharers. Beneath the mask for Conrad and Bergman lies, in the dying Kurtz's words, "The horror! The horror!" Alma's compassion as a caregiver proves no match for Elisabet's impulse toward humiliation.

Bergman wrote the screenplay for *Persona* during the early months of 1965 while recovering at the Sophiahemmet, an exclusive private hospital in Stockholm, from double pneumonia, an inner-ear infection, and penicillin poisoning. For long periods of time in the hospital, Bergman told an interviewer, he couldn't read or watch television. "Just sat up in bed glowering at a black spot on the wall—as soon as I turned my head everything came tumbling down—I'd lost all sense of balance" (*Bergman on Bergman* 196). Death surrounded him: he had a "strong sense of corpses floating up through the bedstead. Besides which I had a view of the morgue, people marching in and out with little coffins, in and out" (199). Bergman intended to write a film called *The Cannibals* but abandoned the project in favor of *Persona*, which contains hints of cannibalism and vampirism.

Death also surrounded Bergman decades earlier, in his childhood, when he was shut inside the mortuary at the Sophiahemmet Hospital by a sadistic caretaker who was responsible for the transport of corpses. Lured into the inner room where the corpses lay, the ten-year-old Bergman found himself "alone with the dead or those in suspended animation," as he wrote in his 1988 autobiography *The Magic Lantern*. "At any moment, one of them might rise up and grab hold of me" (202). The experience simultaneously horrified and fascinated him, particularly when he lifted the sheet that concealed a young girl's body. "I moved so that I could see her sex, which I wanted to touch but did not dare" (203). The mortuary experience suggested to him that the "dead cannot die but are made to disturb the living" (204).

Bergman used the two surreal Sophiahemmet Hospital events in the experimental six-and-one-half minute pre-credits sequence of *Persona*. He called the pre-credits footage a poem, not in words but in images. The footage, which reflects the origins of the film, involves a projector running: we see a spider, figures in a morgue, a hand pierced by a nail, and a slaughtered sheep (suggestive of God's lamb). A strange boy pulls a white sheet over his head, curls into a fetal position, looks at and stretches out his hand to us, reads a book (Mikhail Lermontov's 1839 novel *A Hero of Our Time*), and then stares at two gigantic faces that turn out to be Elisabet and Alma on a movie screen. The two faces come into and out of focus, merge, and then dissolve, suggestive of the merging and dissolving of the women's identities. Bergman combines the image of the two faces into two illuminated halves that seem to float together to become a single face. The faces have a defamiliarizing impact on viewers. The two actresses were themselves stunned when they viewed the merged faces in the editing room, as Bergman took delight in pointing out in *Images: My Life in Film*. "Bibi exclaims in surprise: 'But Liv, you look so strange!' And Liv says: 'No, it's you, Bibi, you look very strange!' Spontaneously they denied their own less-than-good facial half" (61). The image of the floating faces represents one of the iconic moments in cinema history.

## Crimes against the Child

The boy in the prologue, Jörgen Lindström, who also starred in Bergman's earlier film *The Silence*, is both a childhood image of Bergman himself, a film director who was always fixated on his traumatic childhood, and an image of Elisabet's unloved child, from whom she is estranged. The boy may also be an incarnation of Alma's aborted baby. There are many parallels between caregiving and parenting, and any discussion of Bergman's vision of the former requires us to consider his vision of the latter.

"Ingmar Bergman is the quintessential auteur-confessor," Hubert J. Cohen asserts. "No other director has so frequently used his own life as the central matter of his works" (ix). Bergman returns repeatedly in his interviews and autobiographical writings to his vexed childhood and the ways in which his conflicted relationship with his parents influenced his films. On one occasion, Bergman spoke positively about his parents, as when he stated in the introduction to *Four Screenplays* that in his family "there was an atmosphere of hearty wholesomeness which I, a sensitive young plant, scorned and rebelled against" (19). More often, though, Bergman wrote about his troubled childhood with Dickensian indignation, feeling abandoned and betrayed by his parents, bereft. Bergman confesses in *The Magic Lantern* that his greatest problem as a child "was simply that I was never given the opportunity to reveal my game, throw off the mask and allow myself to be enveloped in a love that was reciprocated" (4).

As a child, Bergman was exposed to frequent humiliations: the word appears as a leitmotif throughout *The Magic Lantern*. Defying his minister father, who was often severely depressed, meant swift, pitiless punishment, including being shut inside the kitchen cupboard. In one of his most psychologically astute statements, Bergman recalls that he attempted to gain his mother's attention through illness. "As I was a sickly child with endless ailments, this did indeed become a painful but successful route to her tenderness. On the other hand, as Mother was a trained nurse, shamming was swiftly seen through and punished in public" (3). Bergman's comments may remind us of Zeena Frome, who similarly used illness to gain her husband's attention. Another way Bergman gained attention was through crying, but this proved no more successful than illness. "My mother saw through my tears and punished me. I stopped crying. Occasionally I sense an insane wail deep down in the pit, the echo alone reaching me, striking without warning, a child weeping uninhibitedly, imprisoned for ever" (43–4). How can one reveal the truth of one's feelings if the result is severe punishment? Masked emotions remained a lifelong problem for Bergman. "If I were to raise the mask for one moment and say what I really feel, my friends would turn on me and throw me out of the window" (34).

## Bergman's Metafilm

The original title of *Persona* was *Cinematography*, which the film's producer rejected as unwieldy. The film projector on which *Persona* opens, and which later breaks down, calls into question the nature of filmmaking and thus the mystery of artistic creativity. The pre-credits sequence renders *Persona*, in Törnqvist's words, into a "metafilm, a film dealing with itself, its origin, its relationship to other Bergman films, its media conditions, its characteristics as an artistic product" (137). The projector's approaching and retreating arc-rods conjure up a "self-conscious mindscreen," as if the film imitates mindedness (Kawin 114). The somber boy in the prologue appears to be watching us as we watch him, one of the many examples of the film's self-referentiality that has intrigued scholars.

I saw *Persona* when it first appeared in 1966, and I was haunted by it, especially by Sven Nykvist's masterful cinematography. I continue to be haunted by the film more than half a century later. *Persona* has always been one of my favorite films, if only because the intermingling faces of Liv Ullmann and Bibi Andersson captivate me. The spectral faces appear on a large poster I was allowed to take from the movie theater in which I first saw the film as an undergraduate. (The *New York Times* reproduced the ghostly image of the two faces in its April 14, 2019, obituary of Bibi Andersson, who died at age eighty-three.) The framed poster hangs in my home office, a few feet from my computer. The cardboard poster has faded and darkened over time, heightening its phantasmal eeriness. While streaming *Persona* on my computer, I could see my reflection on the monitor, driving home the question: How would I have acted if I were Elisabet's caregiver? My experience as a caregiver could not have been more different from Alma's, yet I can imagine her situation, the desire to enter into another person's life regardless of the consequences.

Bergman acknowledges at the beginning of the published screenplay of *Persona* that he has not produced a film script "in the normal sense." Rather, the script is "more like the melody line of a piece of music," which the director hopes, with the help of his colleagues, he will be able "to orchestrate" (21). Bergman has spoken dismissingly about his film scripts, which are "nothing but a collection of motifs which I work over with my actors as the filming proceeds. The final decisions I make in the cutting room, where I cut away all obtrusive elements" (qtd. in Törnqvist 18). The extraordinary power of *Persona* lies neither in its screenplay nor spoken dialogue but in its phantom images of the patient's and caregiver's faces. In what follows, I'll note how the differences between the screenplay (translated by Keith Bradfield), the spoken dialogue, and the evocative facial expressions of Elisabet and Alma affect our understanding of the latter's role as caregiver.

## A Patient without an Illness

After the pre-credits footage, *Persona* opens with a female doctor (Margaretha Krook), presumably a psychiatrist, who summons Alma to discuss the new patient. Speaking with icy clinical detachment, the psychiatrist tells Alma that in the middle of a performance of *Electra*, Mrs. Vogler suddenly stopped speaking, remained silent for a moment, and then resumed playing her role, later explaining her silence by saying, "I got this terrible fit of laughter" (24). There is nothing mirthful about her laughter on the screen, however. After the performance, Elisabet went home and has remained silent for three months. "So far as we can see," the psychiatrist explains, "Mrs Vogler is perfectly healthy, both mentally and physically. There is no suggestion of any hysterical reaction, even" (24).

The psychiatrist's failure to suggest the possibility of depression undercuts the reliability of her clinical judgment. Why would a woman who has always been of a "happy and realistic disposition" suddenly become mute for three months? Why would she reject the possibility of communication with her husband, son, and fellow actors? There's no evidence that the psychiatrist has engaged the silent patient in verbal therapy. That task falls to Alma. During their first meeting, Alma describes herself as twenty-five years old and engaged. Following in her mother's footsteps, who was also a nurse, Alma received her nursing certificate two years earlier. Untested, Alma will soon be initiated into the Bergmanesque reality of caregiving. She undergoes a rite of passage that involves a transition from innocence to experience along with the adoption of a new and frightening identity. Bergman describes Alma in *Images: My Life in Film* as "learning to know herself" (56), but the dark knowledge she acquires fails her when she most needs it.

Seeing Elisabet for the first time, Alma notices that her eyes are alternatingly gentle and severe, a contradiction that is never resolved. Elisabet's silence reveals both vulnerability and guardedness. Is her silence a version of Melville's Bartleby the Scrivener, whose line, "I would prefer not to," has a maddening effect on others? Alma fears that she might not be able to "manage" her patient. The problem is not Alma's lack of nursing skills, which she is never required to use, but her caregiving skills. It is one of the many roles she has never been required to play, along with other roles that test her experience: those of therapist, intimate friend, spurned lover, and psychological double.

## The Impossibility of Forgiveness

Throughout *Persona* lurks a cryptic crime and the need for forgiveness. An "indescribable" female voice proclaims on the radio: "Forgive me, forgive me, darling, you have to forgive me. All I want is your forgiveness. Forgive me so that I can breathe again—and live again" (29). But forgiveness seems impossible both in the radio play and in Bergman's film. Upon hearing the words on the radio, Elisabet begins laughing, laughter that is described, curiously, as "warm and hearty." But once again, the laughter is mirthless, chilling, unsettling. The radio voice becomes more menacing: "What do you know of mercy, what do you know of a mother's suffering, the bleeding pain of a woman?" (29). Elisabet bursts out in "another, equally cheerful, laugh," but a disconnect exists between her anguished state of mind and her inappropriate laughter.

The disconnect arises in part from the screenplay, which contradicts our assumptions of Elisabet's inner reality. As Elisabet turns up the volume, the female radio voice, swelling to "supernatural proportions," exhorts God to "look in mercy upon me. Thou who art love." In the screenplay, the terrified Alma turns off the radio, while in the film Elisabet turns it off. Despite Alma's "tremendous admiration for artists" and her belief that art is "tremendously important in life—particularly for people who are in some kind of difficulty," she admits that she cannot understand what she has heard on the radio and has no desire to move into "deep waters" (29–31). She knows she will never be an artist, like Elisabet. Instead, Alma reaffirms her long-standing goals: to marry her fiancé, Karl-Henrik, to have two children, and to continue with her work—all of which make her feel "safe."

And yet hearing the radio voice has thrust Alma outside of her comfort zone. Despite her instinctive caution, she cannot help entering the treacherous waters she has managed to avoid in her life. Notwithstanding her ghastly laughter, Elisabet cannot find the forgiveness that comes from her life as a mother. And the unwary caregiver finds herself pulled into her patient's life.

With her patient's permission, Alma reads a letter from Elisabet's husband conveying his fear that he has harmed her. He refers to the two of them as "anxious children" who are governed by forces they can neither understand nor control. The letter contains a photo of their son. Elisabet looks at the photo and then tears it in two. Does this suggest that she cannot forgive her son—or be forgiven by him? Has she become mute to avoid speaking with him? At the same time that Alma leaves the hospital to visit a cinema showing a film starring Elisabet, the patient watches television documentary footage of rioters protesting the Vietnam War and a Buddhist monk immolating himself. Both art and life are terrifying in *Persona*: violence is inescapable even in the safety of the hospital.

## The Meanings of Silence

Perhaps nothing is more difficult to interpret than silence, apart from death, which is permanent silence. The psychiatrist makes no effort to understand the aggressive implications of Elisabet's prolonged silence. Silence can be a way to drive another person crazy, which is what happens to Alma. Silence can also be, paradoxically, a way to silence others, rendering them mute, speechless. Alma's speech will soon begin to break down when confronted by the onslaught of Elisabet's silence. Words ring hollow when they remain unanswered. Bergman describes Alma as becoming "schizophrenic" (*Bergman on Bergman* 203), experiencing the disintegration of her speech.

Following the images of unendurable horror, the psychiatrist informs Elisabet that she is being discharged from the hospital because "it's only doing you harm." One cannot disagree with the psychiatrist's decision if only because we have never seen any treatment take place. How can a hospital help Elisabet when, according to her doctor, she has no physical or psychological problems? It's true that one cannot have a dialogue with a silent person, though sitting with a therapist who respects a patient's silence is sometimes clinically helpful. Elisabet and Alma are invited to stay at the psychiatrist's isolated summer home by the sea. "The countryside is a great healer, I promise you." The promise is broken, as is the psychiatrist's next promise, when she reassures Elisabet that Alma will "do you a world of good." The doctor adds, ominously, "You'd better have something to torture yourself with, now everything else has been taken away" (38–9). This promise is fulfilled, with a vengeance.

Not all problems in life are psychiatric, including existential dilemmas: the inevitability of suffering, loss, and death. Nor can philosophical and spiritual problems be reduced to psychological disorders. Psychiatry is only one of several lenses through which we apprehend reality. It's odd, nevertheless, that the psychiatrist claims to understand her mute patient when there is no evidence she has attempted to fathom Elisabet's psychological crisis. A film does not need to convey psychiatric authenticity, but the main story of *Persona* opens and closes with a psychiatrist offering a judgment that makes no clinical sense. Indeed, the psychiatrist never seeks to inquire into the psychological origins of Elisabet's muteness. Bergman recognizes the psychiatrist's intellectual arrogance, yet much of the time her words bear his signature as an auteur. Opining that Elisabet's life is a lie, both on and off the stage, and that she feels a "burning need to be unmasked," the psychiatrist is Bergman's instrument to strip away the deadly illusions of both the patient and caregiver. The psychiatrist predicts that Elisabet will continue to act (and, we might add, act out) her new role until she loses interest in it. "When you've played it to the end, you can drop it as you drop your other parts" (42). The film critic John Simon refers to the psychiatrist's words as a "master stroke. She has now equated Elisabet's refusal to act, on stage or in life, with yet another piece of acting" (265). Yet contrary to the psychiatrist's statements, Elisabet needs an authentic therapist who can help her explore the meaning of silence. Instead, in a role reversal, Elisabet plays the role of therapist to Alma when the two of them inhabit the psychiatrist's summer house.

## "We're Quite Alike"

"A lot of people have said I'm a good listener" (50), Alma boasts to Elisabet, a statement fraught with irony: pride cometh before a fall. As the youngest child and only daughter in a family of seven brothers, Alma has never had anyone listen to her while she was growing up. "I think you're the first person who's ever listened to me," she tells Elisabet gratefully (50). Unable to believe that her life is interesting, Alma craves Elisabet's attention. Elisabet willingly adopts the role of a caring listener, attentive to the caregiver's every word. As the camera focuses lovingly on the two women's faces, their intimacy develops. Elisabet's perceived— or posed—empathy proves beguiling. She smiles knowingly, encourages Alma's self-disclosures, nods sympathetically during the right moments, holds her hand, rubs her neck, teaches her how to smoke, and validates all of her feelings. Later, Elisabet cradles the weeping Alma in her arms like a mother comforting a child. The two women wear similar hats, sit next to each other on the beach, and seem to have an intuitive, nonverbal understanding of each other. The mirror image of the two women recalls Otto Rank's statement about narcissistic self-love in his classic psychoanalytic study *The Double*, first published in German in 1914 and translated into English in 1971. "We always find a likeness which resembles the main character down to the smallest particulars, such as name, voice, and clothing—a likeness which, as though 'stolen from the mirror' . . ., primarily appears to the main character as a reflection. Always, too, this double works at cross-purposes with its prototype" (32).

Alma confesses that there's much about herself that she doesn't like and proceeds to confide secrets she has never shared with anyone, reminding us of Freud's statement in *Fragment of a Case of Hysteria*, the story of Dora (1905): "He that has eyes to see and ears to hear may convince himself that no mortal can keep a secret. If his lips are silent, he chatters with his finger-tips; betrayal oozes out of him at every pore" (*SE*, vol. 7, 77–8). Alma's secrets include a five-year affair with a married man followed by an agonizing breakup, a passionless relationship with her fiancé, and an erotic experience while sunbathing nude on a beach with a woman named Katarina and two young teenage boys. The "orgy" seemed to heighten Alma's sexual pleasure with her fiancé. An unwanted pregnancy ended with an abortion. Opening herself up to Elisabet has been painful yet cathartic. "We're quite alike," Alma says laughingly; "I think I could turn myself into you" (58–9). Alma then falls asleep, and it appears that Elisabet speaks to her and visits her room later that night, though Elisabet shakes her head when Alma questions her about this in the morning. Was it a dream or reality? The viewer cannot be sure.

## An Analytic Mirror

Elisabet plays the role of Alma's trusted therapist and confidant perfectly. Her silence recalls Freud's injunction in his 1912 essay "Recommendations to Physicians Practising Psycho-Analysis" that analysts should model themselves "on the surgeon, who puts aside all his feelings, even his human sympathy, and concentrates his mental forces on the single aim of performing the operation as skilfully as possible" (*SE*, vol. 12, 115). Changing metaphors from surgery to technology, Freud urges the analyst to "turn his own unconscious like a receptive organ towards the transmitting unconscious of the patient. He must adjust himself to the patient as a telephone receiver is adjusted to the transmitting microphone" (115–16). Freud concludes that the doctor "should be opaque to his patients and, like a mirror, should show them nothing but what is shown to him" (118). As is well documented, Freud never adopted the role of analytic neutrality in his own practice, and the surgical metaphor of analysis has long been discredited. But Freud's intent was to do everything possible to elicit a patient's self-disclosures in the hope that the revelations would lead to heightened self-awareness and therapeutic relief.

Elisabet's opaque analytic mirroring results in Alma's humiliation, rendering her into a sterile psychiatric case history, shorn of feelings. Elisabet betrays her hidden motives in an unsealed letter she asks Alma to post to the psychiatrist. The unsealed letter suggests either a Freudian slip or, more likely, a deliberate effort to manipulate Alma into reading the merciless words. Alma is predictably horrified to learn that Elisabet sees her only as a scientific experiment. "It's extremely amusing to study her," Elisabet callously writes (64). Viewers share Alma's conclusion: "Such treachery!" Elisabet's facial expression reveals outrage when Alma acknowledges reading the letter without permission, but is this simply another pose? Has *everything* about the actress's professed interest in Alma been an elaborate role lacking in sincerity? What are the limits of Elisabet's treachery? Alma cannot answer these questions, nor can we. Alma now feels hurt and rage, which are precisely the emotions that lie beneath the actress's persona.

Only a few sentences of Elisabet's letter to the psychiatrist appear in the film, but in the screenplay the letter is much longer. Beginning the note with "My dear," Elisabet comes across as the psychiatrist's friend rather than patient. The letter is warm, chatty, and cheerful. One cannot infer from the letter that Elisabet has been silent and withdrawn for the past three months or that she has doubts about her eventual recovery. We never learn the psychiatrist's response to the letter. Would she recognize Elisabet's betrayal of Alma—or conclude that the latter's response is an overreaction?

Peter Cowie was among the first critics to notice that "Both Alma and Elisabet are divided in two; each is the other's missing half" (233). Alma treats Elisabet as an idealized mirror of herself, an alter ego. The mirror, suddenly darkening, reflects Alma's worst fears about herself. Alma's idealization of Elisabet leads to virulent devaluation, a familiar pattern of narcissism. Their relationship betrays other symptoms of narcissistic personality disorder. Behind the self-confident masks of both women lies fragile self-esteem that is threatened by the slightest criticism. Each woman uses and is used by the other in an exploitative way. Alma is preoccupied with Elisabet's success, fame, and beauty and wishes to merge with the actress's power. Despite her professional success, Elisabet remains unfulfilled. Is her muteness a way to receive a different form of attention? Alma begins the film as a caregiver, but she soon finds herself ill used by Elisabet, who cannot feel genuine empathy. As the film progresses, their relationship deteriorates into sadomasochism. Alma soon finds herself lost in her patient's emptiness. Or as the Knight says in Bergman's *The Seventh Seal*, "The emptiness is a mirror turned toward my own face. I see myself in it, and I am filled with fear and disgust" (*Four Screenplays* 149).

## Empathy and Its Discontents

Empathy is, nearly always, a pro-social value, to be encouraged whenever possible. The ability to empathize indicates our humanity, as we have seen with Gerasim in *The Death of Ivan Ilych* and Mrs. Hale in *Ethan Frome*. To walk in another person's shoes, to feel another person's pain, is almost always positive. The empathic tappings of which Carl Rogers speaks, resulting in being deeply understood, are nowhere to be heard in *Persona*. The empathy that appears in Bergman's film is antithetical to Rogerian empathy. Though we often equate empathy with sympathy, they are not identical. Sympathy is compassion and concern for another. It's possible to use empathy to understand another person's thoughts and feelings for destructive or evil purposes; in this case, empathy is the opposite of sympathy.

*Persona* reflects a dangerous form of empathy, antipathy masquerading as empathy, and for this reason we need to understand the uses and misuses of empathy. Academic studies of empathy have proliferated in recent decades, as Rebeccah J. Nelems states in her chapter "What Is This Thing Called Empathy?" appearing in the 2018 volume *Exploring Empathy*, edited by Nelems and L. J. Theo. Nelems informs us that there are nearly three times as many academic articles referencing the word "empathy" in 2016 alone, 41,000, than those published cumulatively between 1900 and 1970, 14,900 (17). In the same volume, Steve Larocco identifies three types of empathy. "Transformative empathy attends to the alterity of the other; it is curious, exploratory, open and concerned, dealing with difference not as a marker of absolute separation but as a spur to vulnerable, potentially destabilizing engagement. Passive empathy shows little of this, and narcissistic empathy exhibits none" (11). Viewed in these terms, Bergman depicts narcissistic empathy throughout *Persona*, which evokes in both Elisabet and Alma resentment, fear, and aggression, largely because the emotional boundaries between the two women are so porous and permeable.

## Emotional Contagion

The blurred boundaries between the two women make both of them highly susceptible to emotional contagion, particularly "primitive emotional contagion," which Elaine Hatfield, John T. Cacioppo, and Richard L. Rapson define as the "tendency to automatically mimic and synchronize facial expressions, vocalizations, postures, and movements with those of another person and, consequently, to converge emotionally" (81). The ability to "infect" others with emotions, especially dark emotions, has gender implications, with women being more susceptible to emotional contagion than men. In their 1994 book *Emotional Contagion*, Hatfield, Cacioppo, and Rapson do not discuss Bergman's film, but their comments have intriguing relevance to *Persona*, particularly the finding that people are especially vulnerable to contagion in certain relationships. Those who have a psychological investment in others' welfare are often vulnerable to contagion; "thus, psychotherapists may be prone to catch their clients' emotions, teachers their students' moods, and caretakers their dependents' feelings" (166). The statement applies to Alma though not to Elisabet's psychiatrist, who remains coldly detached throughout the film.

Those who have power over others are generally resistant to contagion: Elisabet has this power over Alma, who soaks up the actress's emotions while the actress herself never becomes genuinely empathic. Hatfield, Cacioppo, and Rapson conclude *Emotional Contagion* by noting a puzzling incongruity they have come across in their research, an incongruity that is borne out in *Persona*: "People seem capable of mimicking others' facial, vocal, and postural expressions with stunning rapidity and, consequently, are able to 'feel themselves into' others' emotional lives to a surprising extent; however, they also seem oblivious to the importance of emotional contagion in social encounters, and unaware of how swiftly and completely they are able to track the expressions of others" (183).

Alma strikes back, allowing Elisabet to step on a shard of glass, leading to a painful injury. Alma's need for revenge is understandable, but it destroys her role as Elisabet's caregiver. Alma's revenge anticipates a statement Bergman makes in *The Magic Lantern*. "On the whole I have no illusions about my own talent for friendship. I am indeed faithful, but extremely suspicious. If I think I am being betrayed, I am very quick to betray. If I feel cut off, I cut off, a dubious and very Bergmanlike talent" (263). Alma, too, feels wounded and betrayed, and she is quick to reciprocate. Though she makes further efforts to engage Elisabet in conversation, the actress remains stonily silent. Significantly, Alma cannot stop viewing Elisabet as an actress rather than as a patient who needs help. "I always thought that great artists had this tremendous feeling of sympathy for other people. That . . . they created out of sympathy with people, from a need to help them. Silly me" (74). Alma is so enraged that she is ready to hurl a pot of boiling water at Elisabet, forcing her to express her first unambiguous words in the film:

"No, stop it!" (77). Roger Ebert begins his laudatory 1967 review of *Persona* by referring to these words, translated as "No, don't!" in the film: "Shakespeare used six words to pose the essential human choice: 'To be, or not to be?' Elizabeth, a character in Ingmar Bergman's 'Persona,' uses two to answer it: 'No, don't!' . . . . 'No, don't!' translates as: I do not want to feel pain, I do not want to be scarred, I do not want to die. She wants . . . to be. She admits . . . she exists."

Alma later regrets her harsh words and asks for forgiveness, but their relationship has been irrevocably changed—not that it has ever been authentic. Alma falls asleep, and once again the film becomes dreamlike. Does Alma actually have sex with the blind Mr. Vogler (Gunnar Björnstrand) while Elisabet is watching, or does Alma only dream of this? Having intercourse with Vogler may represent Alma's wish to humiliate the onlooking Elisabet; it may also represent Alma's homoerotic desire for her, as Gwendolyn Audrey Foster has suggested. "Heterosexual sex is almost always associated with abortion and pain in *Persona*, whereas homosexual sex is associated with fear of and fascination at the merging of identity" (137).

## The Devouring Mother

Alma still wishes to unite with Elisabet, not as her caregiver but as her secret double. Each woman continues to merge with the other in a destructive symbiotic relationship that evokes maternal hostility and ambivalence. "Merging," Nancy Chodorow remarks in *The Reproduction of Mothering*, "brings the threat of loss of self or of being devoured as well as the benefit of omnipotence" (69). The screenplay indicates that Alma claws at her bare skin, resulting in a narrow streak of blood that Elisabet proceeds to suck, evoking both cannibalism and vampirism. In her influential essay on *Persona* published in *Styles of Radical Will* in 1969, Susan Sontag incorrectly attributes the "bloodsucking" to Alma (142), an error uncorrected in the republication of the essay in the 2000 volume edited by Lloyd Michaels (80). Elisabet has now become, literally and figuratively, a devouring mother.

Humiliated by Elisabet, Alma responds in kind by reminding the actress that she is a terrible mother. And now we realize, perhaps for the first time, the significance of Elisabet's performance of Electra on stage. In Euripides's play, Electra and her brother Orestes plot to kill their mother, Queen Clytemnestra, for the murder of their father, King Agamemnon. *Persona* abounds in matricidal as well as infanticidal imagery. The transference-countertransference dynamics in the shifting care-receiver-caregiver relationship, which becomes a variation of the patient-analyst relationship, dramatize the murderous aggression directed against a mother who consistently rejected the child's need for love and approval.

The film projector that appears in the prologue unexpectedly stops, shattering verisimilitude. We see Elisabet holding the torn photo of her four-year-old son. She became pregnant, we learn, because someone had once said to her at a party that the only thing missing from her life was a child. As Chodorow notes, "Motherhood may be a (fantasied) attempt to make reparation to a mother's own mother for the injuries she did (also in fantasy) to her mother's children (her siblings). Alternatively, it may be a way to get back at her mother for (fantasied) injuries done by her mother to her" (90). It turns out that motherhood was merely another role in Elisabet's life as an actress, a role she never wanted to play. In a mocking irony that reveals Elisabet's desire to be Alma, the actress tried to have an abortion, but it was too late. Forced to have the baby, she wanted her son to die, and when that failed to happen, she grew to loathe him. Leaving the baby with a nurse, Elisabet returned to the stage to continue her life of deception.

The final moments of *Persona* offer an analysis of a tormented parent-child relationship. We overhear Elisabet in an inner monologue confessing to her inability to respond to her son's violent love for her. "I'm cold and indifferent, and he looks at me and loves me and is so soft I want to hit him, because he won't leave me alone" (97). The actress's son has the same relationship with his mother as Alma has to Elisabet: both love a woman who cannot reciprocate their love. Elisabet's maternal anguish appears genuine—bedrock truth in a film that exposes many of her other emotions as a lie.

Near the end of *Persona*, Elisabet returns to her psychiatrist who, "mildly triumphant," updates us on her patient's life. Whereas in the beginning of the film the psychiatrist has claimed to understand her patient, now she concedes that "It is difficult, of course, to analyse her innermost motives." Nevertheless, she points to her patient's "strongly developed infantility" (99). What does this diagnosis mean? That Elisabet is still childlike? The psychiatrist's next words, with which she is "very pleased," betrays her attitude toward Elisabet's—and Bergmann's—profession. "Personally I would say you have to be fairly infantile to cope with being an artist in an age like ours" (99).

## "Hurtling through the Abyss of Life"

A diagnosis of "infantility" becomes more meaningful when viewed in the context of a troubled parent-child relationship, which indeed casts light on Elisabet's difficulties. The most illuminating section of *The Magic Lantern* occurs near the end when Bergman describes his mother's inability to give him the love he urgently needed as a child. Imagining a dialogue in which the roles of mother and son dissolve, he asks her a question as if she were a friend. Why couldn't Karin Bergman love him? Quoting his mother's confession to him that she had never received love from her *own* mother, suggesting the intergenerational nature of their loveless childhoods, Bergman asks, rhetorically: "Were we given masks instead of faces? Were we given hysteria instead of feelings? Were we given shame and guilt instead of love and forgiveness?" (284). These are the questions a therapist might ask Elisabet. Living with a "never-ending infected sore that went right through my body," Bergman has a "huge arsenal of explanations" for "hurtling through the abyss of life" (284–5), calling for a mother who never responded to his pleas for love. In *Images: My Life in Film*, Bergman states that he was certain he was an "unwanted child, growing out of a cold womb, one whose birth resulted in a crisis, both physical and psychological." Reading his mother's private diary after her death confirmed his worst fears: "faced with this wretched, almost dying child, she had feelings that were decidedly ambivalent" (20).

The psychiatrist's self-satisfaction matches Alma's at the end of the film. "I really do like people a lot," Alma silently muses. "Mostly when they are sick and I can help them. I'm going to marry and have children. I think that is what is going to happen to me here in life" (100). These words appear in the screenplay but not in the film. The latter ends with the two women leaving the summer home, refusing to speak to each other. We see an image of Elisabet returning to her role as Electra. Does this imply her recovery? Alma departs on a bus, presumably to return home, having completed her caregiving responsibilities. She has survived her glimpse into Elisabet's abysmal world. Does this suggest that whatever has not killed Alma has made her stronger? *Persona* closes with the boy gazing at the blurred faces on the screen—and then the projector abruptly stops.

Alma never reflects on her failure as a caregiver, oblivious to the disastrous consequences of identity loss, transgression of boundaries, and breakdown of empathy. Elisabet also remains unchanged, as the last image of her performance as Electra hints: "A howling wide-open face, distorted by terror, with wild wide-open eyes and furrows of sweat running through her theatre make-up" (101). The ending of *Persona* highlights the problems confronted by caregivers, including the contagious nature of many illnesses. Perhaps no film or novel dramatizes more powerfully than *Persona* the virulent contagion of dark emotions: jealousy, rage, and abandonment. The well-documented contagion effect appears particularly overpowering to those who, like Alma, have a precarious identity.

## Art as Humiliation

It is impossible to exaggerate the impulse toward humiliation in Bergman's films. "Fear and its accomplice, guilt, have remained at the heart of Bergman's work since his youth," observes Cowie. "Humiliation is both the cause of and the response to such fear. Every remark in *Persona* aims to wound, every question to provoke, every answer to lacerate" (235). Elisabet's humiliation of Alma reflects Bergman's belief that insofar as life is filled with humiliation, the artist must faithfully convey this theme. Tellingly, he identifies this theme with his childhood. "Isn't it a fact that children are always feeling deeply humiliated in their relations with grown-ups and each other?" (*Bergman on Bergman* 80–1).

Elisabet is involved in multiple acts of humiliation. Unable to love her son, she inadvertently rejects him, as Bergman felt his own mother had rejected him. We learn little about Elisabet's childhood, but perhaps, like Bergman's mother, she had failed to receive love from her own mother. This remains speculation, but there's no doubt that Elisabet humiliates Alma, who craves her love. As an actress, Elisabet is part of the world of art, playing classical dramas; but in her personal life, Elisabet enacts the humiliation theme, particularly in her relationship with Alma.

Significantly, when an interviewer asked Bergman whether he was concerned that a young woman who saw his film *Port of Call* had a breakdown, or whether he cared that other women were scared of having a miscarriage after seeing *So Close to Life*, the director appeared callous in his response. "Well, what of it?" Surprised, the interviewer began to question whether he "ever felt any moral . . . ," but Bergman cut him off. "I don't feel the least bit shaken by bringing out someone's latent schizophrenia just because someone in one of my films crawls under her bed—on the contrary" (*Bergman on Bergman* 130). Had Bergman reacted less defensively, he might have quoted Kafka's statement that the only type of books we should read are those that wound and stab us. "A book must be the axe for the frozen sea inside us" (16). But Kafka was not defending cruelty when he made this statement.

## Bergman's Experience with Psychiatry

Bergman often acknowledged in his interviews and autobiographical writings that at different times in his career he struggled with anxiety and depression. After he was charged and arrested in 1976 for tax evasion in

Sweden, charges that were later dropped, he suffered a nervous breakdown and spent three weeks in a psychiatric clinic. He attributed his recovery to rest, enforced isolation, and medication. Writing was also an important part of his recovery—writing was his treatment of choice to master otherwise disabling anxieties.

Sometimes Bergman made conflicting statements about his experience with psychiatry. When asked by television-host Dick Cavett whether he would "object to being analyzed by a psychiatrist," Bergman replied that a psychiatrist pronounced him "extremely healthy" after his third visit. A few minutes later, however, Bibi Andersson, with whom he was living and working at the time, contradicted him. The psychiatrist "had said that you were so full of neuroses, that if he took them away, you probably would stop making pictures." According to Hubert Cohen, who quotes this incident, Bergman "responded first with his famous explosive laugh and the denial 'I can't remember that'" followed, "in a slightly more serious tone, with 'I think she is lying.'" Bibi Andersson regretted and then attempted to qualify her statement. "But I didn't say that the psychiatrist was right, I just said that that was what he said" (xi–xii). One can imagine Bergman feeling ambushed by Cavett's question and further dismayed by Bibi Andersson's statement, which today strikes us a betrayal of confidentiality.

Bergman never wrote about being in psychotherapy, nor do his films dramatize the talking cure, though sometimes we come across curious utterance like the following from *Wild Strawberries*: "My wife loves to embarrass me in front of strangers. I let her—it's psychotherapy" (242). Bergman read Arthur Janov's 1970 book *The Primal Scream*, the basis of an influential though short-lived therapy in which patients were encouraged to act out powerful emotions in an attempt to come to terms with childhood traumas—a therapy that would appeal to a filmmaker's desire for constructing dramatic scenes leading to cathartic release.

But Bergman's celluloid psychiatrists do not fare well professionally or personally. In his 1997 film *Face to Face*, Bergman describes Dr. Jenny Isaksson as representative of her profession. "Despite her wide knowledge she is, to a pretty great extent, mentally illiterate (a common ailment with psychiatrists; one could almost call it an occupational disease)" (vii). Jenny attempts suicide, and a colleague tells her that a "lunatic quack psychiatrist once wrote that mental illnesses are the worst scourges on earth and that the next worst is the curing of those illnesses. I'm inclined to agree with him" (22). Bergman did too.

## The Artist's Self-Care

Bergman regarded *Persona* as his "breakthrough," a "success that gave me the courage to keep on searching along unknown paths" (*Images: My Life in Film*, 28). A few pages later, he makes a more extreme pronouncement. "At some time or other, I said that *Persona* saved my life—that is no exaggeration. If I had not found the strength to make that film, I would probably have been all washed up" (64). He adds that he had gone as far as he could go in *Persona* and later in *Cries and Whispers*. "I touched wordless secrets that only the cinema can discover" (65).

*Persona* may have saved Bergman's life, but how has it affected viewers, especially caregivers? It's unlikely that it will appear in the bibliography of many how-to books on caregiving. Yet *Persona* remains a cautionary tale for those who treat others as mirror reflections of themselves and who are susceptible to emotional contagion.

Bergman retired from filmmaking in 2003 and died in 2007 at the age of eighty-nine. *Persona* evokes a romantic image of the artist, suffering through the creation—and performance—of art, but Bergman rejected that vision near the end of his career. "You know, many people think that if an artist suffers, he will be a better artist," he told an interviewer in the early 1980s.

> There are those who think that if a lobster is cut into pieces while still alive, it tastes much better, because the lobster suffers when it's cut into pieces. Some people think that about artists: if they suffer, they are much better artists. I don't think it's right that way, because every neurotic behavior is some sort of rigid behavior.

In his personal life, Bergman admitted, he was a "very neurotic man"; in his artistic life, he believed he was "completely un-neurotic" (Jones 59).

## An Ethics of Caring and Caregiving

While watching *Persona* on my computer—and myself on the monitor—I couldn't help reflect on how I have changed as a viewer, and as a person, in the fifty years since I first saw the film. In my twenties I loved *Persona*, perhaps because I believed then in the possibility of knowing a person so intimately that I could become that person without a loss of identity. In my mid-seventies, I still love *Persona*, but I no longer believe in the romantic ideal of merging or the exchange of identities. Similarly, in my youth, I was less aware of the dynamics of projection and identification than I am now: the extent to which we see others as versions of ourselves. I'm also more conscious now of the limits of love in saving or curing another person. "You can never protect a single human being from suffering," declares a character in Bergman's *Smiles of a Summer Night*. "That's what makes one so terribly tired" (77).

Both caring and caregiving require a delicate distance between self and other; a respect for boundaries; an awareness of one's limitations; and a recognition of emotional contagion, burn-out, and compassion fatigue. Some people have found their identities threatened while watching *Persona*, as Norman N. Holland admits at the end of his reader-response discussion of the film. "Bergman portrays a pathological regression, and he achieves one—in me. In *Persona*, I think, he succeeded not just in communicating, but creating a psychic state. For me, it is an uncomfortable one" (110). Holland's discussion of *Persona* appears in *Meeting Movies*, published in 2006, eleven years before his death at age ninety. Holland's book contains many insights that one might apply to caregivers and care-receivers alike. "We don't change very much, as we age," Holland writes, "we need to accept ourselves as we are" (177). Holland also points out Bergman's ambivalence toward caregiving in *Persona*. "Bergman gets to be both the good caregiver, the director mothering and loving his actresses, and the bad caregiver, humiliating the characters he has created" (110).

Regardless of whether one admires but does not enjoy the film, as Holland does, or both admires and enjoys it, as countless others do, including myself, *Persona* is unsurpassed in showing how easily love can dissolve into hate, and how both caregiving and care-receiving can lead to humiliation. To return to Nietzsche, some readers who gaze into Bergman's abyss in *Persona* find the abyss staring into them. There will probably always be a tension between one's persona and alma, mask and soul, respectively. Acknowledging the tension is a first step in caring for others and oneself.

# 4

# The Caregiver as Matchmaker in Alice Munro's "The Bear Came Over the Mountain" and Sarah Polley's *Away from Her*

Few short stories anatomize more deftly a caregiver's devotion to a care-receiver than Alice Munro's "The Bear Came Over the Mountain," and probably no story describes a caregiver as a matchmaker. This alone makes Munro's story unique. But what's even more astonishing is that the caregiver serves as a matchmaker to his own wife, encouraging her romance with another patient suffering from cognitive impairment. "The Bear Came Over the Mountain" is full of plot twists, revelations, paradoxes, and surprises, including an ironic ending that no one could have imagined. "The Bear Came Over the Mountain" was the inspiration behind Sarah Polley's acclaimed 2006 film *Away from Her*, which remains one of the best films on dementia despite flattening many of the ambiguities surrounding the caregiver's role as matchmaker.

Born in 1931, Alice Munro has won nearly every literary honor. "Alice Munro has a strong claim to being the best fiction writer now working in North America," Jonathan Franzen opined in the *New York Times* in 2004, five years before she received the Man Booker International Prize and nine years before she received the Nobel Prize for Literature, the first Canadian since Saul Bellow and thirteenth woman to receive the award. The author of one novel, *Lives of Girls and Women* (1971), and more than a dozen short story collections, Munro has been famously called "our Chekhov" by Cynthia Ozick. "The Bear Came Over the Mountain" is the final story in the 2001 volume *Hateship, Friendship, Courtship, Loveship, Marriage*. Forty-eight pages long, the story first appeared in *The New Yorker* in 1999 and, after the appearance of the film, was republished as a separate book, *Away from Her*, in 2007.

## A Reluctant Caregiver

Munro is not an overly autobiographical writer, and it's uncertain whether her limited experience as a caregiver influenced "The Bear Came Over the Mountain." As Daphne Merkin reported in the *New York Times Magazine* in 2004, in what appears to have been the "defining emotional circumstance" of Alice Munro's youth, her mother began to suffer from the debilitating symptoms of what was later diagnosed as Parkinson's disease. "It fell to Munro, as the oldest, to keep the household running from the age of 12 or 13 on, an experience that both toughened her and damaged her relationship with her mother, bringing the deep sense of regret in its wake that appears and reappears in her stories." Munro's caregiving experience differed from Anna Quindlen's and Mary Gordon's, as we shall see, but all three writers viewed the event as emotionally fraught. Frightened by her mother's illness and feeling guilt over having "emotionally abandoned" her during her long decline, Munro didn't go home to visit her mother during the final two years of her life. "Whereas these daunting experiences might have trampled the fighting spirit of a weaker girl," Merkin concludes, "in Munro's case they served to fuel a writerly sense of marginalization and a conviction that she was cut out for different things, even if not always by her own choice."

In her 2001 memoir *Lives of Mothers & Daughters*, Sheila Munro provides additional information about her mother's conflicted caregiving experience. "It is understandable to me that young Alice shut herself off emotionally from her mother's illness, with its particularly isolating and grotesque symptoms, because she feared that she would not be able to bear the waves of pity and grief that would engulf her." Sheila Munro adds that her mother continues to be "deeply affected by the isolation and suffering of her mother's life, and tormented by the way she closed herself off from her" (161). Complicating Alice Munro's guilt over her experience as a caregiver was her need to counteridentify with a mother whose personality was antithetical to her own. "My mother has talked about wanting to be the opposite kind of mother from her own mother, whom she saw as moralistic, demanding, smothering, and emotionally manipulative" (61). The heroine of "The Bear Came Over the Mountain" is not a mother, but when she falls ill and requires a caregiver, she could not be more different from Alice Munro's mother.

Set in rural Ontario, Canada, where many of Munro's stories take place, "The Bear Came Over the Mountain" never mentions the name of Fiona's illness, but there is little doubt that it is Alzheimer's. The story does not proceed in a linear direction; rather, flashbacks take us to the beginning of her relationship to

Grant, with whom she has been married for nearly half a century, and then to the present, when we see the first troubling symptoms of cognitive confusion and memory loss. Nearly everything is filtered through the point of view of Grant, a literature professor who, like the English-professor-father in Quindlen's novel *One True Thing*, is more adept at reading fictional characters than in reading himself. "The Bear Came Over the Mountain" dramatizes the subtle intensity of a character struggling to make sense of his wife's disease that changes and then erases her identity. Munro is largely sympathetic to Grant, though he is human, all too human. He reaches several epiphanies about the nature of his wife's illness and the significance of marital love, loyalty, and sacrifice.

## A Professor of Desire

Fiona has the "spark of life," and when she proposes spontaneously to Grant—"do you think it would be fun if we got married?" (276)—he readily accepts. He never regrets the decision, nor does she, despite her many possible reasons to do so. As the story progresses, we learn about his history of infidelity, another similarity to the father in *One True Thing*. Part of Grant's history is revealed in a dream in which he shows, to one of his colleagues whom he thought was a friend, a letter he received from the roommate of a former student with whom he had an affair. "The girl herself was someone he had parted from decently, and it seemed unlikely that she would want to make a fuss, let alone try to kill herself, which was what the letter was apparently, elaborately, trying to tell him" (284). As the dream continues, Grant sees a group of "cold-eyed young women all in black robes, all in mourning," staring at him, in bitter disapproval, in a large lecture room. Fiona is sitting in the front row, untroubled. "Oh, phooey," she tells him, reassuringly, "Girls that age are always going around talking about how they'll kill themselves" (285).

Does the dream suggest that Fiona knew about her husband's affair with an undergraduate? The dream seems to be based on reality: decades earlier he had a sexual relationship with a student, and someone had painted the word "Rat" on his office door. Fiona knew about the student's "bad crush" on her husband, though Fiona was not overly disturbed, or so he thought at the time. Grant has little difficulty rationalizing his conduct. The colleague in the dream was even more transgressive in his behavior, though now he takes a "dim view of such shenanigans" (284). Rarely passing judgment on her characters, Munro allows Grant to judge himself guilty of a serious offense, though characteristically he seeks to exonerate his behavior. "Nowhere was there any acknowledgment that the life of a philanderer (if that was what Grant had to call himself—he who had not had half as many conquests or complications as the man who had reproached him in his dream) involved acts of kindness and generosity and even sacrifice" (286). Munro presents us with a complex character, a man who is an adulterer yet capable of kindness, generosity, and sacrifice.

"The idea of a hidden identity," Munro's biographer, Catherine Sheldrick Ross, observed presciently in 1992, "appears in many early stories in the form of a watchful child observer, where watching is associated with shame, betrayal, and exposure." In Munro's later books, Ross adds, quoting an earlier literary critic, Judith Timson, the idea of a hidden identity appears as a fascination with the theme of adultery and the "double life it creates, especially for a married wife and mother who is expected to live her life for other people" (20–1). In "The Bear Came Over the Mountain," it is the adulterous husband who lives a double life.

## Losing Her Mind

Fiona has always left herself notes, often containing titles of books she wanted to read, but her new notes are different, such as taping on the kitchen drawers: Cutlery, Dish Towels, Knives. "Couldn't she have just opened the drawers and seen what was inside?" Fiona's later behavior is even more alarming, such as calling Grant from a telephone booth in town and asking him how to drive home. Another time she walks home by the fence line. "She said that she'd counted on fences always taking you somewhere" (277).

In the beginning, Fiona has little awareness of her dementia, apart from annoyance and perplexity over her darkening world. She suspects that something is wrong, but she doesn't want to alarm or burden her husband. "With a slow moving disease like Alzheimer's," Philip S. Gutis wrote in the *New York Times* in 2018 after he was diagnosed with early onset Alzheimer's two years earlier, "there's still time for doubt." Munro captures this doubt. Fiona's forgetfulness becomes more pronounced, and she asks Grant when they moved into their home. "Was it last year or the year before?" Twelve years ago, he tells her. "That's shocking," she responds. Characteristically, she prefers to treat memory loss as "somehow like routine courtesy, not quite concealing a private amusement. As if she'd stumbled on some adventure that she had not been expecting. Or was playing a game that she hoped he would catch on to" (278).

Part of Munro's achievement in "The Bear Came Over the Mountain" is that she avoids melodrama or sentimentality in limning her character's deterioration. Did Fiona convince herself, as she had tried to convince Grant, that she was only playing a game? That she appreciated the comedy of her new behavior? Munro wisely avoids answering these questions. A master of economy, Munro depicts in two pages Fiona's radical memory loss and her rueful recognition, after wandering off in a supermarket when Grant wasn't looking, that it was time to enter a nursing home, perhaps to spare him from the trouble of caring for her at home. She accepts the decision with courage and resignation, but her conclusion is so wrenching for Grant that he cannot think of it as a permanent change. "A kind of experimental treatment," he informs her. "A rest cure" (280). Unlike most stories about dementia, the caregiver remains in denial here, not the care-receiver.

Grant's decision to institutionalize Fiona represents the dramatic shift in caregiving since the middle of the twentieth century. "Families have always cared for their older relatives," observes Steven H. Zarit, "but in the past it was a rare and usually short-lived event" (3). Most people did not live to old age, Zarit adds, and death was usually sudden. But as a result of extraordinary medical breakthroughs and striking improvements in life expectancy—the average American reached the age of forty-seven in 1900, but that age jumped to seventy-seven in 2000—grown children who had moved away from home were unable to care for their dying parents, particularly if they developed chronic diseases such as dementia. "Much of the care for the elderly with disabilities is provided in community settings, usually by family and sometimes with support from formal helpers" (4).

Fiona views her new life in Meadowlake, the nursing home she enters when she is seventy, as "sort of like in a hotel" (276). Munro captures in a single understated sentence Fiona's essence on the first day of her new life. "She looked just like herself on this day—direct and vague as in fact she was, sweet and ironic" (277). Fiona's sweetness is palpable, her irony more subtle, as when she tries to explain, before entering Meadowlake, that Grant should not be troubled by her strange behavior. "'I don't think it's anything to worry about,' she said. 'I expect I'm just losing my mind'" (278).

Fiona may be losing her mind, and soon her gift for speech, but she never loses her quiet dignity. Nor her droll humor, which is apparent from the first page of the story. Sororities were a joke to her when she was in college, along with politics. Sometimes she played the "Internationale" to her parents' left-wing friends. She delights in playing games with her husband like "made-up voices," which "had mimicked uncannily the voices of women of his that she had never met or known about" (278), perhaps the students with whom he might have been having affairs. She mocks the nursing home's name, calling it "Shallowlake, Sillylake" (280)—and she calls the residents "inmates." Fiona retains the ability to see expected and unexpected meanings to reality, a gift that her husband lacks.

To convey Fiona's rapid deterioration in Meadowlake, Munro devises an institutional regulation which, as far as I know, is not customary at most nursing homes: neither relatives nor friends are permitted to visit a new resident during the first thirty days. "Most people needed that time to get settled in" (280). Munro includes this plot twist to prepare us for Fiona's fearful change. We cannot be certain whether Fiona's dramatic deterioration is due to the progression of the disease, institutionalization, or both. It was the hardest month of his life, Grant thinks, a detail that is bound to earn the reader's sympathy, until his next thought—longer than the month that Jacqui Adams, the student with whom he had a sexual relationship decades earlier, spent on holiday with her family, near the beginning of their affair. These details underscore the limits of Grant's marital faithfulness in the past, yet he remains devoted to Fiona. He telephones Meadowlake every day and soon becomes familiar to Kristy, the capable nurse who finds his constancy amusing and bemusing. Is Grant's loyalty to Fiona throughout the rest of the story atonement for his infidelity? If so, guilt alone cannot explain the depth of his commitment.

During Grant's month of separation, Kristy expresses to him the details of Fiona's difficult adjustment to Meadowlake. Kristy knows how to put a positive spin on these changes. Fiona had caught a cold, but this was "not unusual for newcomers." Fiona is now off antibiotics and appears less confused than when she was first admitted, two details Grant had not been told. Fiona was now "coming out of her shell," again implying something ominous of which he had been unaware. Munro conveys through Kristy the insidious nature of dementia. "Things change back and forth, all the time and there's nothing you can do about it" (292). She advises Grant to take one day at a time, to realize that patients have short memories: "That's not always so bad" (306). Kristy is generally reassuring, recommending patience, understanding, and acceptance. She sounds a chilling note, however, when she describes patients who are sent to the dreaded "second floor," reserved for the sickest patients, those who inhabit a death-in-life existence. "Some just sit," she warns Grant. "Some sit and cry. Some try to holler the house down. You don't really want to know" (300).

Yet Meadowlake is not a house of horrors. Life goes on there. Avoiding sensationalism, Munro suggests that the residents, even those who were not engaged in any activities, "were living a busy life in their heads," adding, parenthetically, "not to mention the life of their bodies, the portentous shifts in their bowels, the stabs and twinges everywhere along the line" (298). Munro offers an unflinching portrait of the reality of nursing homes, but she never turns away in revulsion. She knows that the life that occurs in institutions like Meadowlake "could not very well be described or alluded to in front of visitors" (298). She succeeds, nevertheless, in conveying this world. The visiting children may be "dying of disgust," but the adults react with sympathy and discretion. "Women wiped away the dribble from shivery old chins and men looked the other way" (298).

Munro reveals to us, before his first visit to Meadowlake, Grant's compromised loyalty in the past. She conveys in a sentence or two his insights, rationalizations, and blindness, as when she suggests that during his teaching career, he had never stopped making love to Fiona despite his female students' "disturbing demands" (286). After his year-long affair with Jacqui Adams ended, when her husband was transferred, Grant had dalliances with other students. These relationships led to Grant's "gigantic increase in well-being" (302). He blames the "feminists" for his troubles: "The feminists and perhaps the sad silly girl herself and his cowardly so-called friends had pushed him out just in time" (287). Without confessing his transgressive behavior to Fiona, he promised her a "new life."

Grant may not have been better than many other husbands, Munro implies, but he was no worse. Like Tolstoy in *The Death of Ivan Ilych*, Munro has almost godlike omniscience into her character's state of mind, and she always finds a delicate balance between sympathy and judgment. Like Wharton, Munro has keen insight into her characters' moral and psychological "complications." And like Bergman, Munro recognizes the darkness in human nature though she never finds it appalling, as he does. Grant is, in many ways, an everyman figure. He is about to be tested as a caregiver. Ivan Ilych must, in the words inscribed on his watch-chain, reflect on his end; Grant must do something nearly as arduous: reflect on the end of his marriage.

## Another Husband

Grant enters Meadowlake carrying a bouquet of narcissus flowers, the perfect choice for a self-absorbed man. In Greek mythology, Narcissus was a beautiful and vain young man, beloved by women and men alike. One day he meets Echo, who has been condemned to repeat the sounds of others. Echo cannot express her feelings for Narcissus, who cruelly rejects her. After incurring the wrath of the gods, Narcissus falls in love with his own reflection in a pool of water, pines away, and is transformed into a narcissus flower. Narcissistic conflicts bedevil Munros' characters, as they do Bergman's, but in a different way. Poetic justice awaits Grant, for when he sees Fiona, after a month's absence, she barely recognizes him. She is sitting at a card table, watching intently the play of a man sitting next to her. She smiles at Grant, whispers the word "bridge" to him, and then, recalling a college friend, Phoebe, with whom she used to play cards, fails to understand how Grant knew her friend's full name.

Anyone overhearing Fiona's conversation with Grant would conclude she knew he was her husband, but she has forgotten everything about him, reducing him to an echo. She now believes that she is married to the man sitting next to her, Aubrey. Taken aback, as anybody would be, Grant asks about Fiona's "new friend," who is close in age to himself. Fiona continues talking about Aubrey as if they had known each other for decades, having met him, she tells Grant, at the hardware store where her grandfather used to shop—an assertion that Grant later can neither confirm nor disconfirm. When Grant responds that he knows where her grandparents lived, because he and Fiona lived there themselves, she can only respond with the word "Really?" and then turns her attention back to Aubrey, as devoted to him as she had once been to Grant. Now it's Fiona's turn to experience, as a result of her new relationship, a heightened pleasure in life, if not a gigantic increase in well-being. Her new "marriage" has transformed an otherwise dreary nursing home into a romantic setting.

Dear reader, what would you do in Grant's situation? Remind Fiona that *you* are her husband? Scold her for not remembering you? Insist that Aubrey not be allowed to remain with your wife? Withdraw her from the nursing home? Forget her as she has forgotten you? Pity yourself for being abandoned? One can imagine all of these responses. Grant might have reacted to Fiona's developing interest in Aubrey the way Zeena does to Ethan's passion for Mattie, with anger, jealousy, and spite. Grant might have withdrawn his wife from Meadowlake or have her new paramour transferred to another nursing home. Who would blame the caregiver for being threatened by the new situation? But Grant refuses to indulge his darker self. Instead, he tells Fiona, when she returns to Aubrey, that he will be "fine," and then he seeks an explanation from Kristy, who informs him that these "attachments" are not uncommon. "Best buddy sort of thing. It's kind of a phase" (292).

Another writer might have ended "The Bear Came Over the Mountain" with the nurse's casual epiphany. Grant would be understandably heartbroken, losing his wife to a man who, like her, has no memory of his history or identity. Grant might be able to comfort himself with the hope that Fiona is better off in a new relationship with a memory-impaired man than in an old relationship with a forgotten husband. The ending would be appropriately Chekhovian, confirming Cynthia Ozick's statement. Grant, who has betrayed his wife with his many student dalliances, would find himself inadvertently betrayed by a wife who is no longer responsible for her actions. Like Narcissus, Grant might then spend the rest of his life pining away. Poetic justice would be complete.

But Munro continues the story by complicating the plot and imagining a situation that is not only plausible but one that also tests Grant's character. Aubrey has no memory, like Fiona, but unlike her, he is confined to a wheelchair. He and his wife had gone on a vacation, and he developed an illness that left him with a high fever and then wiped out his memory. Aubrey is only temporarily at Meadowlake, placed there so that his wife, Marian, can have a break from the crushing tedium of caregiving. Fiona assumes, from Grant's constant presence, that he must be a new resident, and, trying to be helpful, which is central to her character, she reassures him that he will make an easy transition. "It must all seem strange to you, but you'll be surprised how soon you get used to it" (291).

Believing that Fiona may be playing a sick joke on him, perhaps in retaliation for his former infidelities, Grant continues to visit her, observing her behavior with Aubrey. "Meadowlake was short on mirrors," Munro declares in a poignant sentence, "so he did not have to catch sight of himself stalking and prowling" (296)—or pining away, Narcissus's fate. Grant becomes obsessed with his wife and her new admirer. "Sometimes he seemed to himself like a mulish boy conducting a hopeless courtship, sometimes like one of those wretches who follow celebrated women through the streets, convinced that one day these women will turn around and recognize their love" (297).

Munro elaborates on the implications of Grant as a rejected lover. She heightens the courtship theme by having Grant read to Fiona an old novel that he finds in Meadowlake's library about "chaste love, and lost-and-regained fortunes" (309). Ruth Franklin notes, in her *New Republic* review of *Hateship, Friendship, Courtship, Loveship, Marriage*, that the old novels about chaste love "suddenly seem an ironic commentary on Fiona's relationship with Aubrey, which even in its chastity has all the infinite pain of any betrayal; and Grant, after nearly losing Fiona in the episode with the student, regained her only to lose her again to Aubrey." Nevertheless, although the theme of the old novel contrasts Grant's history of impure love, he is now becoming for the first time a chaste lover, and the reader wonders whether he will regain his lost marital treasure.

Fiona is devoted to her new husband, doting on him, catering to all of his wishes. She shuffles and deals his cards during the card games, helps him into and out of his wheelchair, and remains at his side as he tries to walk. "The nurses thought that it was a marvel, the way she had got him out of his wheelchair" (295). Fiona becomes, in short, both a loving wife to Aubrey and his devoted caregiver. Cared for by Grant, she will now care for Aubrey: the three lives are interconnected, albeit temporarily. Fiona's double role as care-receiver and caregiver is entirely in character but also out of character because of memory loss and cognitive decline. In Grant's presence, Aubrey reacts like a jealous husband. Aubrey's face takes on the appearance of "somber consternation" when he sees Fiona smile at Grant. It seems to Grant that Aubrey is warning Fiona about the sinister man who watches her. *"Take care. He's here. My love"* (296).

Fiona appears to be doing well in her "marriage" to Aubrey, but everything begins to break down when they realize he will soon be leaving the nursing home. Visiting Fiona frequently, Grant gives her a book on nineteenth-century watercolors made by a woman who had traveled to Iceland, but Fiona, whose mother came from Iceland, accepts it without any enthusiasm, despite the fact that he had regularly taught Icelandic mythology and poetry to his students. Fiona is focused entirely on the departing Aubrey, who is saying a final goodbye to her. "What is it?" she asks the disconsolate Aubrey, "What is it, dear heart?" (305)—flowery words that she had never expressed to Grant during their long marriage. Munro's tone conveys both sorrow and gentle humor as she describes the couple's tearful parting. Aubrey begins to weep, and Fiona pulls a handful of tissues and would have wiped his nose had he not been embarrassed by his display of emotion in Grant's presence. Fiona then asks Grant if he has "any influence around here," meaning, would he be able to allow the couple to remain together? Aubrey is inconsolable. "'Hush,' Fiona was saying. 'Oh, honey. Hush! We'll get to see each other. We'll have to. I'll go and see you. You'll come and see me'" (305).

Aubrey's departure leaves Fiona bereft—and distraught. Unwilling to eat, she begins to lose weight precipitously and pine away, like Narcissus, no longer interested in living. Grant fears that, unable to care for herself, Fiona will be sent to the frightful second floor. The only solution to Fiona's despair, Grant realizes, is to persuade Marian to allow Aubrey to return to Meadowlake, perhaps once a week, to cheer up Fiona.

## A Matchmaker

But Grant's chivalric quest to aid the lovesick Fiona—lovesick for another man—does not go well. The meeting with Marian begins disastrously. She reacts defensively when Grant explains that Fiona and Aubrey have struck up a close friendship. "He did not molest her in any way," Marian hisses, adding, "From what I heard it was the other way round" (310). Grant patiently explains the reason for his visit, but she sees no benefit to herself or to her husband for befriending a strange woman in a nursing home. It matters little to Marian whether or not Aubrey knows who she is, and the possibility that he may develop a passing fancy for a woman in a nursing home is not something Marian wishes to encourage. Grant does not view himself as a matchmaker, but that is the role he plays for the rest of the story, doing everything possible to bring two "lovers" together again. Caregiving has suddenly become matchmaking. Munro never states that her character is acting selflessly, chivalrously, heroically, but Grant has Fiona's best interests at heart, and he assumes that what is good for Fiona will also be good for Aubrey.

Marian does not share Grant's assumptions, however. Like Grant, she is a caregiver, but she cannot afford a nursing home for her husband even if that would be best for him. Her hardscrabble life has toughened her, and she never imagined that she would have to take care of her husband, who no longer contributes financially or emotionally to their day-to-day struggle for survival. Aubrey's illness "pretty well gets *him* off the hook," Marian complains to Grant. "I don't mean exactly that he got sick on purpose. It just happened. He's not mad at me anymore and I'm not mad at him. It's just life" (316).

## Class Differences

Munro emphasizes the stark economic differences between the two caregivers. These differences become a barrier to Grant, complicating his efforts to help Fiona. He can afford to send his spouse to a nursing home. Marian cannot. Grant doesn't need to worry about losing his home if his spouse is in a nursing home. Marian does. Grant has the freedom to visit his wife whenever he wishes, but except for her brief respite from her husband, Marian feels trapped. There are also differences in their education. Learning from Meadowlake that Grant is a university professor, Marian admits that she's "not much of an intellectual," to which he responds, commiseratingly, "I don't know how much I am, either." Marian speaks with a bluntness and anger that leave him speechless.

Driving home from the meeting, Grant realizes that he has failed to convince Marian to act in Fiona's, if not Aubrey's, best interests. The reason for his failure, Grant concludes, was Marian's belief that he and people of his class had deceived themselves about life. "Educated people, literary people, some rich people like Grant's socialist in-laws had lost touch with reality. Due to an unmerited good fortune or an innate silliness. In Grant's case, he suspected, they pretty well believed it was both." This must have been how Marian saw him. In Grant's revised view of Marian, class trumps gender as the major determinant of human difference. He had underestimated the profound economic differences between them. Grant presumably came from Marian's class—his mother worked as a doctor's receptionist, but by marrying Fiona, the daughter of a cardiologist with progressive views, Grant had moved up in society: "his father-in-law's money was welcome in spite of the political taint" (279). Yet Grant had forgotten these class differences. He would never succeed in changing Marian's mind as long as he remained committed to "generous schemes that he believed would make another person happy" (318).

Understanding a character like Marian is exhausting to Grant, but he cannot stop thinking about her. What would marriage to her be like? Characteristically, his first thought is sexual. "She'd have been appetizing enough, with her choice breasts. Probably a flirt" (318–19). Would she have been more of a flirt than he has been? He doesn't raise this question. He then wonders why Marian has married someone like Aubrey. "She must have believed that she would end up better off than she was now. And so it often happened with those practical people. In spite of their calculations, their survival instincts, they might not get as far as they had quite reasonably expected" (319).

Grant finds two messages on his answering machine, both from Marian, when he returns home. The first invites him to attends a singles dance later in the week. "I am on the supper committee, which means I can bring a free guest," the word "free" reverberating with economic, psychological, and moral implications. The second message clarifies the nature of the dance. "I realize you're not a single and I don't mean it that way. I'm not either, but it doesn't hurt to get out once in a while" (319). What is the nature of her invitation? Is she seducing him—despite his earlier rejection of what might be called a sexual theory of human motivation? While he is near the phone, Marian calls a *third* time, expressing her fear that she might have missed his return call. Grant doesn't want her to know that he is torn by the decision to call her back, "weighing the pros and cons" (322).

## Gender Differences

In Munro's only novel, *Lives of Girls and Women* (1971), the authorial first-person narrator, Del Jordan, comes across a magazine article written by a famous New

York psychiatrist, a disciple of Freud, who describes the differences between male and female modes of thought. The psychiatrist offers, as an example, a boy and a girl sitting on a park bench. "The boy thinks of the universe, its immensity and mystery; the girl thinks, 'I must wash my hair'" (198). Del is appalled by this maddening nonsense—it's clear to her that she does *not* think this way, even if the male characters in "The Bear Came Over the Mountain" do. Grant refers to a *woman's* natural sexual jealousy, but Fiona is not jealous, unlike Grant and Aubrey, who are.

In a 2001 interview with Cara Feinberg, Munro characterized herself as a feminist though she immediately qualified the word. "In the beginning I used to say, well, of course I'm a feminist. But if it means that I follow a kind of feminist theory, or know anything about it, then I'm not. I think I'm a feminist as far as thinking that the experience of women is important. That is really the basis of feminism." Núria Casado-Gual notes that there are two interconnected narratives in "The Bear Came Over the Mountain" through which "diverse (and even divergent) representations of romantic love and memory in later life can be analysed." Crafting a story that simultaneously lends itself to and resists romantic and feminist interpretations of Grant's behavior, Munro shows how a caregiver, betraying and betrayed, finds himself cheating to be faithful—a story where you "never quite knew how such things would turn out" (321).

## Blameless Self-Interest

Is Marian interested in Grant because he might be a future partner after their spouses have died? Is her invitation a manifestation of her survival instinct? Is she proposing a quid pro quo, one caregiver granting a favor to another caregiver in exchange for the mutual satisfaction of both care-receivers? Would Grant's acceptance of Marian's invitation lead to Fiona's happiness? Grant finds these questions dizzying, as do Munro's readers. What lies in store for Grant if he succeeds in delivering Aubrey to Fiona? "It would not work—unless he could get more satisfaction that he foresaw, finding the stone of blameless self-interest inside her robust pulp" (321).

We see, on the last page of the story, the stunning consequences of Aubrey's return to Meadowlake. Fiona is reading the book on Iceland that Grant had brought her earlier—a "beautiful book," she now enthuses, though she cannot remember why someone would carelessly leave such a valuable book lying around. She can't remember much, sadly, though she is now ready to leave the nursing home. Grant has a surprise for her, the return of Aubrey, but she has a bigger surprise for Grant: the failure to remember her "husband." Fiona looks blankly at the stranger, and Munro conveys dementia's grim progression. But the story's biggest surprise is yet to come. In a gesture of "bantering grace," Fiona puts her arms around her husband, *Grant*, exclaims that she is "happy" to see him, adding that he could have driven away without a care in the world and "forsook me. Forsooken me. Forsaken," to which he responds, in the final words of the story, "Not a chance."

Nearly everything in "The Bear Came Over the Mountain" is ironic, and the word "Forsooken" is no exception, as Marlene Goldman and Sarah Powell observe. Readers wonder, as a result of the shifts of verb tense, "if Fiona is referring to Grant's reaction to her recent infidelity, to her illness, or to *his* past infidelities." Goldman and Powell see another possible irony. "Like Fiona's remark, Grant's comment remains opaque; although he seems to be professing his love for her, it is also quite possible that he has just been unfaithful to her again and he is satisfied to have Fiona out of the way so that he can pursue his affair with Marian" (90). Coral Ann Howells also finds Grant's last words ironic. "Not a chance" is an "echo of his old duplicitous reassurances" that affirm the irresolvable ambiguity of the closing scene (77).

One cannot rule out these possibilities, but I suspect most readers believe that "The Bear Came Over the Mountain" has a happy ending—as happy as one can realistically imagine given the situation. Ruth Scurr's commentary on the ending of the story strikes me as convincing. "'The Bear Came Over the Mountain,' unusually, ends with an affirmation of love: 'Not a chance', Grant says in reply to the suggestion he might have forsaken Fiona. This simple assertion places his commitment to her beyond the laws of probability, the ravages of irrationality, contingency, or circumstance." The ending is fraught with paradoxes that deepen our aesthetic pleasure in the story. We see in Fiona's last words the persistence of both memory and selfhood and also, as Jonathan Franzen describes in his essay "My Father's Brain," the persistence of will, which may last longer than expected in an Alzheimer's patient. Acting on behalf of their spouses, Grant and Marian find the stone of blameless self-interest inside their own robust pulp. Both remain committed to caregiving whatever the consequences.

## *Away from Her*

Sarah Polley was twenty-one years old, flying back home from Iceland, when she read "The Bear Came Over the Mountain" for the first time. The story staggered her. "I believe I can say, without danger of overstatement," she writes in the preface to *Away from Her*, "that I have had a relationship with this story that has been as powerful and as transformative as any I have had with another human being" (viii). After reading "The Bear Came Over the Mountain," she thought that "with all of this fictional marriage's failures, this was perhaps not the greatest love story I'd ever read, but the *only* love story I'd read" (xii).

Polley was, remarkably, only in her mid-twenties when she wrote the screenplay, adapted from the short story, and directed the film. "I thought it was the most interesting portrait of a marriage, of memory and guilt, that I'd ever seen," she told Andrew O'Hehir in a 2007 interview in *Salon*. Polley acknowledged that she was drawn to the topic of dementia because of her many visits to her grandmother in a nursing home. "I knew that environment and I wanted to capture it." She immediately thought of Julie Christie as the film's visual and thematic center. Polley wanted to create an "elegant and simple film," one that had a "certain grace."

*Away from Her* succeeds in demonstrating grace. The film destigmatizes dementia, awakens sympathy for both caregivers and care-receivers, and calls attention to end-of-life care. Released in 2007 and widely honored, *Away from Her* was named one of the top ten Canadian films at the Toronto International Film Festival. The film earned Oscar nominations for Sarah Polley's adapted screenplay and for Julie Christie as Best Actress. Roger Ebert gave the film four stars, his highest rating, called it a "heartbreaking masterpiece," and said it was the fifth and best film about Alzheimer's that he had seen in the opening years of the new century. (The others were Bille August's *A Song for Martin*, Nick Cassavetes's *The Notebook*, Erik Van Looy's *The Memory of a Killer*, and Richard Eyre's *Iris*.) Ebert makes one interpretive error in his review, stating that Grant tries to persuade Marian to move Aubrey to another nursing home, when, in fact, he wants Marian to return her husband to Meadowlake. The Canadian actor Gordon Pinsent is convincing as Grant, as are Olympia Dukakis (whose mother had Alzheimer's) as Marian, Michael Murphy as Aubrey, and Kristen Thomson as Kristy. Calling the film "deeply impressive and intelligent," Peter Bradshaw observed in *The Guardian* that Gordon Pinsent's face "has the impassive, leonine quality associated with Alzheimer's sufferers, and he is in fact at one stage mistaken for a patient." Some viewers were disappointed with the film, especially if they were familiar with the short story. The psychoanalyst Alan Stone concluded in *Psychiatric Times* that "*Away from Her* is not really a bad film, it just does not come close to the mind-bending wisdom of Alice Munro's story," a judgment I share.

Anyone who can remember Julie Christie's resplendent beauty in the 1965 film *Dr. Zhivago*, directed by David Lean, is probably old enough to be worried about Alzheimer's disease while viewing *Away from Her*, yet the actress's radiance remains unravaged by age or dementia, a consolation that subverts the film's authenticity. Fiona is *not* hauntingly beautiful in Alice Munro's short story. Fiona has a "slightly crooked mouth" that she highlights with red lipstick. She also has a "lopsided" smile. In Polley's film, Fiona's mouth, with her picture-perfect white teeth, is iconic. Fiona is so unself-conscious about her appearance that when Grant asks her, "Why did they chop off your hair?," she replies, "Why—I never missed it" (299). By contrast, Fiona's hair in *Away from Her*, which is platinum-blonde, not white, as in the story, is long and sensuous. This is only one of the changes in the film adaptation of "The Bear Came Over the Mountain," but it is instructive. Julie Christie's face seldom betrays the empty, vacuous expression that is symptomatic of advanced Alzheimer's. She still looks like thin, fit, and foxy, in short, a supermodel, albeit one for the baby boomer generation.

## A Didactic Film

*Away from Her* has a strongly didactic quality that does not appear in Munro's story. Unlike Munro, who, as her biographer notes, has a "resistance to lessons in literature," preferring instead to view fiction as an "opener for life" (Ross 84), Polley's intention was to create a film that would educate and sensitize viewers to the plight of those who suffer from Alzheimer's, including the hardship of caregivers. Fiona reads a book called *The 36-Hour Day: A Family Guide to Caring for People Who Have Alzheimer's Disease, Other Dementias, and Memory Loss*, by Nancy L. Mace and Peter V. Rabins. The book, published by Johns Hopkins University Press in 1981, and now in its sixth edition, remains the definitive dementia guide, with more than three million copies in print. There's even an article on the publisher's website, "The Story of *The 36-Hour Day*." The book's popularity was doubtlessly helped by Sarah Polley's decision to publicize it in *Away from Her*.

A brief section of *The 36-Hour Day*, "You Are Not My Husband," foretells the plot of *Away from Her*. "Occasionally a person with a dementing illness will insist that her spouse is not her spouse or that her home is not her real home." Few can disagree with the authors' sensible advice. "Reassure the person, 'I am your husband,' but avoid arguing. Although this may seem heartbreaking, it is important for you to reassure yourself that it is not a rejection of you (the person *does* remember you). It is just an inexplicable confusion of the damaged brain" (158). Not everyone is a fan of *The 36-Hour Day*, as we shall see in our discussion of Margaret Morganroth Gullette, who refuses to read the book because of the fear of being infected by its dark message.

A doctor in Polley's film offers up-to-date information about the neurological changes in Alzheimer's patients' brains. "Plaques now crown neurons from outside the cell membranes," and "knotty tangles mangle microtubial transports from inside the cells." All told, we learn, "tens of millions of synapses dissolve away." Fiona reads another book on dementia where she learns that the caregiver "must preside over the degeneration of someone he or she loves very much, must do this for years and years, with the news always getting worse, not better." Additionally, the caregiver must "put up sometimes with deranged but at the same time very personal insults . . . and must somehow learn to smile through it all." Fiona then ruefully smiles and quips to Grant, "sounds like a regular marriage"—a joke that few people in her situation might be able to grasp. Kristy reads Alistair MacLeod's novel *No Great Mischief* to Aubrey, and Grant reads Michael Ondaatje's 1989 poem "The Cinnamon Peeler" to Fiona. Later in the film, Grant reads W. H. Auden's *Letters from Iceland* to Fiona, a poem which, as Robert McGill remarks, "implicitly licenses Grant to dance with Marian both literally and figuratively soon afterwards" (108).

## Other Changes in the Film

As Sally Chivers remarks in *The Silvering Screen*, "Polley's film transforms Grant's betrayal by placing many of Grant's words from the story into Fiona's voice. In this way, she expands the potential of the silvering screen to an unparalleled sense of female agency" (88). The biggest change in the film adaptation is that we learn little about Grant's history of marital infidelity, apart from four flashbacks, totaling less than a minute, suggesting his attraction to students in the distant past. Polley includes nearly all of the dialogue of Munro's story, but Grant's rich interior monologue is missing. Grant's noteworthy dream in "The Bear Came Over the Mountain" is also missing in the film, nor is there exploration of his fascinating inner thoughts. Fiona knows about Grant's affairs in *Away from Her*, and she delivers in the film several of his unspoken thoughts in the short story, including, "You still made love to me despite disturbing demands elsewhere." Both the fictional and filmic Fiona embody unconditional love, but the latter has a greater knowledge of her husband's infidelities. In *Away from Her* it is Fiona, not Grant, who compares their marriage favorably to others' marriages: "you did all right compared to your colleagues." Polley's Fiona is quick, perhaps too quick, to rationalize her husband's indiscretions, criticizing those people "[who] want to be in love every single day."

Polley simplifies Grant's character, reduces the complexity of his motivation, and makes him into a nearly perfect caregiver. Viewers of *Away from Her* don't need to struggle, as readers of "The Bear Came Over the Mountain" do, with Grant's ambiguous moral identity. For example, Grant reveals in the film that he had quit smoking thirty years ago, but Munro invests this detail with wry irony in the story. "He had decided to quit around the time he started up with Jacqui. But he couldn't remember whether he quit first, and thought a big reward was coming to him for quitting, or thought that the time had come to quit, now that he had such a powerful diversion" (314). These details do not appear in *Away from Her*. Lest there be any doubt about his character in the film, Grant strikes up a conversation with a bored teenager, listening to heavy metal music with her headphones, who finds the nursing home "fucking depressing." Grant tells her that he visits his wife "just to see her, make sure she's doing well," despite the fact that she appears to have fallen in love with another patient. "I suppose that must seem rather pathetic." On the contrary, she consoles him, smiling empathically: "I should be so lucky." Most viewers of *Away from Her* feel this way about Grant, though not necessarily most readers of "The Bear Came Over the Mountain." Agnès Berthin-Scaillet concludes her discussion of the differences between Munro's short story and Polley's film with a question about the translatability of one language system to another, particularly a story as elusive as "The Bear Came Over the Mountain": "is it possible to cinematize a text with the guessed-at ambiguities it withholds?"

Grant is more conventional in the film. "Fiona, I'm your husband," he shouts at her in exasperation, distressed that she has forgotten his identity. He is also annoyed that she is wearing someone else's "tacky" orange sweater, something that does not bother Grant in the short story. "We've been married 45 years," he reprimands her in *Away from Her*. "Look at me, Fiona, that is not your sweater. We had a good life together." Grant never scolds Fiona in Munro' story, never expresses dismay over forgetting him, never tries to disconnect her from Aubrey. Munro's husband knows something that Polley's husband does not know: any effort to separate Fiona from Aubrey would probably result in her heightened confusion and anguish. This is indeed what happens in the film. "What are you doing with Aubrey?" Grant asks, demandingly, to which she responds, "He doesn't confuse me. He doesn't confuse me at all."

Some of Polley's invented scenes in *Away from Her* are effective. In an early scene, Polley offers a sly commentary on contemporary filmmaking. Performing a diagnostic interview, a doctor asks Fiona what she would do if she was the first person to spot a fire in a movie theater. Unable to answer the question, Fiona responds, "We don't go to the movies much anymore, do we, Grant? All those multiplexes showing the same American garbage." In another invented scene, Fiona hangs on her bedroom wall two evocative pencil portraits Aubrey has drawn of her, a reminder of their special relationship. Polley creates a new character, Madeleine Montpellier (Wendy Crewson), the Meadowlake administrator who, embodying bureaucratic impersonality, contrasts Kristy's warmth.

Polley also shows the importance of architectural space in the care of dementia. As Annmarie Adams and Sally Chivers explain, Polley chose the Freeport Health Centre in Kitchener, Ontario, designed in 1989 by leading architects, as the site for the imaginary Meadowlake Retirement Facility. Adams, an architectural historian, and Chivers, a cultural studies scholar, show how the representation of architectural space in *Away from Her* reveals popular stereotypes about long-term residential care. "Polley's filmic images of homes and homelike spaces for dementia care transform Munro's story into a vivid commentary on current fears about late life as automatically associated with decline."

Polley's use of sunlight and snow is masterful. She told Andrew O'Hehir that "every frame of the film is suffused with a brilliant winter sunlight"; cold light illuminates "unexpected corners of the 40-year marriage between Fiona and Grant." Most striking of all is the image of falling snow, a metaphor of the inexorable obliteration of Fiona's memory. "Sometimes there's something delicious in oblivion," she observes while looking at flowers. We feel the movement toward death and oblivion when Fiona lies on the snow-covered ground while cross-country skiing; the falling snow may remind us of the ending of "The Dead," the final short story in James Joyce's masterful 1914 collection *Dubliners*. But some of the invented scenes in *Away from Her* are ineffective. While watching newsreel footage of the Iraq War, Fiona recalls an earlier conflagration: "How could they forget Vietnam?"—a cautionary tale that Polley wants us to remember but that seems implausible in the situation.

Grant's major reason for striking up a relationship with Marian in *Away from Her* is to induce her to allow Aubrey to return to Fiona, as in Munro's story, but the filmic Grant does not appear as overtly calculating as he does in the story. Part of the reason is that we don't have access to Grant's thoughts, and his face, for the most part, is stoic and impassive, making it difficult to know what he's thinking. Polley minimizes the class differences between Grant and Marian: the latter's attractive suburban house reveals that she is comfortably middle class, not struggling for economic survival.

## The Art of Deception

Sheila Munro writes about her mother's "long training in the art of deception" (111), a training that Grant puts into practice in both the short story and the film. He has attempted to deceive Fiona about his many affairs with students, and although Marian is aware of Grant's devotion to Fiona in *Away from Her*, he conceals from Marian the depth of this love. "I know what you're doing," Marian says to Grant. "It would be easier for me if you could just pretend a little." We then see them smiling in bed in a postcoital scene. Is he pretending? We can't be certain. This invented scene parallels an earlier one in which Fiona says to Grant, seductively, on the day of her admission to Meadowlake, "I'd like to make love—and then I'd like you to go."

Munro has no interest in describing Marian's fate at the end of "The Bear Came Over the Mountain," whereas Polley shows how Marian, as a result of her relationship with Grant, is able to overcome her bitterness and anger, reaching final acceptance of the situation, almost as if she has gone through the stages of Elisabeth Kübler-Ross's stage theory of dying, now adapted to caregiving. In the penultimate scene in *Away from Her*, we see that Marian has moved in with Grant at his home. It is hard for us to imagine that he will be anything other than a distracted, ambivalent lover to her. Grant drives the mute Aubrey to Meadowlake, where he will be a permanent resident, though no longer remembered by Fiona.

Munro ends "The Bear Came Over the Mountain" by showing how a glimmer of memory breaks through Fiona's dementia. When she looks at Aubrey's face, she says *harshly*, "names elude me" (323). Polley omits the adverb and adds several lines of dialogue that restore part of Fiona's memory of her husband: "I seem to remember you reading this to me. You were trying to make me feel better. You tried so hard. You're a lovely man, you know. I'm a very lucky woman. You've been gone a long time." The new dialogue suggests that Fiona has overcome much of her earlier memory loss and confusion.

"If we had followed Fiona for longer," the New Zealand neuropsychologist and novelist Jenni Ogden wrote in *Psychology Today*, "her personality would have changed and her sweetness might have been punctuated by delusions, paranoia, apathy, and emotional outbursts." Despite the audience-pleasing ending, Ogden found *Away from Her* moving and argued that while few Alzheimer's patients are as beautiful in their sixties and seventies as Julie Christie, there is reality in this aspect of the film: many patients in the early stages of the disease retain their social skills and care for their personal appearance. Ogden recounts a story when she was working in MIT's clinical research hospital and mistook the husband of a couple sitting in the waiting room for an Alzheimer's patient. "He looked old, somewhat unkempt and grumpy, whilst his wife was beautifully made up, elegantly dressed, and greeted me warmly with a firm handshake. She was in the early middle stages of AD, already with significant memory loss, and beginning to wander. He was a highly intelligent and healthy retiree!"

Notwithstanding the differences between "The Bear Came Over the Mountain" and *Away from Her*, both the short story and the film illustrate the paradox, as Norman N. Holland remarks in *A Sharper Focus*, that fidelity is infidelity: "not the kind Grant carried on with the students, [but] something altogether different, even 'noble,' as Grant and Marian first call it." Both story and film link this higher infidelity to love, devotion, and sacrifice. Both explore the ambiguities of adaptation and survival. Both show, as McGill points out, the complexities of artistic adaptation: Polley's struggle to be faithful to Munro's story while at the same time adapting it to her own cinematic vision of love and loss. Whether we read *Away from Her* as a love story threatened by illness or as a dementia narrative redeemed by sacrifice and devotion, the film demonstrates, like "The Bear Came Over the Mountain," the importance of bantering grace: that of the caregiver and care-receiver. We are likely to remember both the short story and the film if we find ourselves in Grant's situation—or, if our memory does not completely fade, in Fiona's.

## Fiction Anticipates Reality

In an article aptly called "Love in the Time of Dementia" published in the *New York Times* in 2007, Kate Zernike reported that Alice Munro's story presages that of former Justice Sandra Day O'Connor's husband, John J. O'Connor III, who, suffering from Alzheimer's disease, fell in love with another woman at his assisted living center. The former justice is "thrilled," according to Zernike, and "even visits with the new couple while they hold hands on the porch swing— because it is a relief to see her husband of 55 years so content." Zernike's article focuses on the mysteries of love that can flourish in old age in unexpected environments, but it also highlights the caregiver's responses to these confusing situations. Seeing only heartbreak and betrayal, some caregivers respond with feelings of indignation, anger, or betrayal; but other caregivers, like Sandra Day O'Connor, react with sympathy and generosity, appreciating the value of intimacy when it arises among those who have forgotten their past.

Sandra O'Connor retired from the Supreme Court in 2006 in part to care for her ailing husband, who died in 2009 after a long battle with Alzheimer's disease. The first woman to be appointed to the Supreme Court acknowledged in 2018 that she was retiring from active public life because of a recent diagnosis of early-stage dementia. "While the chapter of my life with dementia may be trying," she was quoted by the *New York Times* on October 23, 2018, "nothing has diminished my gratitude and deep appreciation for the countless blessings in my life" (Haag). Kate Zernike doesn't mention "The Bear Came Over the Mountain," but it, too, could be titled "Love in the Time of Dementia," an incomparable story of love combined with matchmaking and caregiving.

5

# Caregiving Strategies for Survival in John Bayley's *Elegy for Iris, Iris and Her Friends*, and *Widower's House*

John Bayley had written one novel and several books of literary criticism before his wife, Iris Murdoch, began developing Alzheimer's disease in the mid-1990s, but he was not a memoirist, nor did he seem interested in autobiographical writing. He shared his wife's suspicion of self-disclosure; she insisted that her novels were about "fictional" characters rather than "real" people. Murdoch's biographer Peter J. Conradi notes that she not only denied drawing her characters from real life but also found the practice immoral. Conradi quotes a 1982 diary entry in which she expresses her distaste for the personal element of fiction. "Autobiography: 'to try to tell the truth about oneself'—why bother? So you are indifferent to truth? No one struggles with truth versus falsehood all the time. But that effort would be pointless, one must just try to be good. Idea of autobiography is utterly unattractive to me as an art form—and also somehow morally sickening" (529). Bayley and Murdoch were fascinated by psychology, yet neither spent much time reading literature as disguised self-revelation. They kept their personal lives separate from their literary lives—they had no interest in being celebrities. For all of these reasons, then, it was unlikely that Bayley would write a memoir about caring for his wife. In fact, he wrote three: *Elegy for Iris* (1999), *Iris and Her Friends* (2000), and *Widower's House* (2001).

They were, to be sure, two of England's most distinguished writers. In his critical study *The Saint and the Artist*, the British Conradi calls Murdoch "our most intelligent novelist since George Eliot" (5), a comparison that would not have entirely pleased her, since she was no fan of the nineteenth-century novelist. The author of twenty-six novels, two books on philosophy and ethics, and a book on Sartre, Murdoch was made a Dame of the British Empire in 1987. Her novel *The Sea, the Sea* received Britain's most prestigious literary honor, the Man Booker Prize, in 1978. She was also one of the century's key moralists, as Martha Nussbaum suggests: "Murdoch, more than any other contemporary ethical thinker, has made us vividly aware of the many stratagems by which the ego wraps itself in a cozy self-serving fog that prevents egress to the reality of the other" (36). In the afterword to his biography, Conradi cites Harold Bloom's pronouncement upon her death in 1999 that there are "no first-rate writers left in Britain" (595).

John Bayley was no less gifted. The Wharton Professor of Literature at Oxford, he was an eminent literary critic and a regular reviewer for the *New York Review of Books*. Murdoch believed—with justification—that her husband was the "greatest literary critic in England since Coleridge" (qtd. in Conradi, *Iris Murdoch* 403). John Fletcher called their marriage "one of the most fruitful literary and critical partnerships of our time, and remarkable in any time" (qtd. in Conradi, *The Saint and the Artist* 18). It was also an unlikely marriage, partly because they were so different. "'I intend to make my mark,' the young Iris had once said, long before I met her. Her genius lives in her books" (*Widower's House* 132). Murdoch indeed made her mark, as did Bayley, and their genius lives in their many books.

Bayley's decision to write about Iris Murdoch's illness was not an easy one, for he had always valued privacy, avoiding the glare of publicity. Self-disclosures about illness are almost always more fraught than those about health, if only because the former often involve feelings of pain and shame. As Robert Weil points out, Bayley, an authority on Russian novelists, was "following Tolstoyan precedent in redefining society's fear of disease and mental illness, echoing the words of Ivan Ilych, who had 'searched for his accustomed fear of death and could not find it'" (251–2). A key difference between the two writers is that unlike Tolstoy, who uses the veil of fiction to tell the truth about the reality of dying, death, and caregiving, Bayley writes autobiographically, opening two lives to public scrutiny. "Bayley's dramatic decision not only to come forward with a public announcement of his wife's illness, but also to write joyously and spiritually about his experiences in caring for her reflects his estrangement from a late twentieth-century society where old age is feared and where death has been sanitized by our mainstream culture" (Weil 252). To write joyously about grief is a daunting challenge. "How boring bereaved people are. They have only one subject," Murdoch wrote in a 1953 diary entry after the death of a close friend (Conradi, *Iris Murdoch* 340). To write joyously and *interestingly* about grief is a double challenge.

## *Elegy for Iris*

Of the three memoirs, *Elegy for Iris*—titled in the UK *A Memoir of Iris Murdoch*—is by far the best known. It was a *New York Times* bestseller, receiving both popular and scholarly acclaim. It is also the most self-disclosing about their marriage and Bayley's caregiving. Eight years younger than Iris Murdoch and less worldly and sophisticated, the 28-year-old Bayley fell in love with her at first sight when they met in 1953. She was his first and only love, though she had several lovers at the time. He is strikingly open and candid about her extensive sexual experience—and his own inexperience. As Bayley began to know her better, he was at first astonished and then dismayed by the sheer number of her lovers.

Bayley returns repeatedly to the paradoxes of human relationships, always surprising and delighting us with his unconventional wisdom. In the beginning, he had no interest in her affairs with others. "By some emotional paradox, being in love made me, or at least at first, more incurious about this, not less. Iris existed for me as a wonderful solitary being" (9). We expect that as their marriage developed, Bayley and Murdoch would praise the intimacy of marriage, and while this was true for both of them, he unexpectedly affirms that one of the "truest pleasures of marriage is solitude" (40). As close as they were intellectually and emotionally, they still retained their separate identities and independence, their otherness. Perhaps the central paradox of their life together was their "apartness," as he reveals in an extraordinary passage describing the early years of marriage:

> Already we were beginning that strange and beneficent process in marriage by which a couple can, in the words of A. D. Hope, the Australian poet, "move closer and closer apart." The apartness is part of the closeness, perhaps a recognition of it; certainly a pledge of complete understanding. There is nothing threatening or supervisory about such an understanding, nothing of what couples really mean when they say (or are alleged to say) to confidants or counsellors that their partner doesn't understand them. This usually means that one partner understands the other all too well, or that both do, and doesn't rejoice in the experience. (44)

Bayley sees a paradox but not a contradiction when he speaks about the joys of solitude in marriage. "The one went perfectly with the other. To feel oneself held and cherished and accompanied, and yet to be alone. To be closely and physically entwined, and yet feel solitude's friendly presence, as warm and undesolating as contiguity itself" (123). There is an implicit parallel between a novelist's love for his or her characters, a delight in their independent existence as other people, and a husband's love for his wife. Husband and wife can be intimate with each other while at the same time respecting their spouse's freedom, independence, and otherness. Whereas one might see separation and closeness as binaries, Bayley sees them as complementary, each necessary for the other.

Alzheimer's disease shatters this apartness, for the loss of Iris's memory, freedom, and independence increases her dependence on her husband, who finds that he can no longer leave her alone even for a moment as her illness worsens. "Life is no longer bringing the pair of us 'closer and closer apart,' in the poet's tenderly ambiguous words. Every day we moved closer and closer together. We could not do otherwise. There is a certain comic irony—happily, not darkly comic—that after more than forty years of taking marriage for granted, marriage has decided it is tired of this, and is taking a hand in the game" (265–6).

This passage is significant for several reasons. First, Bayley reveals his acceptance of his wife's illness and his role as caregiver—an acceptance that is, until the end of *Elegy for Iris*—largely free of anger, bitterness, or resentment. (These dark emotions appear more frequently in his next memoir, *Iris and Her Friends*.) Second, he displays here and elsewhere an ethics of caring; it is hard to imagine a more loving or devoted caregiver, one who is exquisitely attentive to her needs. Iris remains a character of love, long after she has forgotten the nature of love, and although he doesn't comment on this, his love is constant for better and for worse, in good times and bad. Third, he demonstrates his ability to see the "comic irony" of their situation, indeed, the comic irony of life, filled as it is with existential absurdity. This vision of comic irony could not be more different from the crisis of faith C. S. Lewis records in *A Grief Observed* after his wife's death, when he refers to God as a "Cosmic Sadist," a "spiteful imbecile" (30). A freethinker, Bayley never experienced a crisis of faith either during or after his wife's protracted illness.

Throughout *Elegy for Iris* Bayley reminds us of Sisyphus pushing his rock up a mountain, only to watch it roll down again, at which point he turns around and resumes his unending task. Iris is certainly not an inanimate rock, not even when she loses the power of language and volition; rather, her presence serves as her husband's support system, as he is hers. "One must imagine Sisyphus happy," Camus states at the end of "The Myth of Sisyphus" (91), and so one must imagine Bayley happy at the end of the story. The happiness rests on the knowledge that love inevitably ends with loss; that we are all alone in an absurd universe, devoid of God or an afterlife; and that we must create our own meaning and care for those we love. Illness, suffering, and death remind us of the importance of living as fully and deeply as possible. They also remind us of our responsibilities to each other, our connectedness to those we love—even if this connection shatters much-needed apartness. Bayley recognizes throughout the memoir that he is needed more than ever to allay his wife's anxieties. Unlike Edgar in *King Lear*, who concludes that "ripeness is all," Bayley knows that "helplessness is all" (267), a recognition that only strengthens his determination to care for his wife as best he can.

## An Ironist

Like Alice Munro, Bayley is an ironist, but whereas she sees comic—not tragic—irony in a fictional character's illness, he writes about a real person's illness. Maintaining ironic distance from a suffering real character, particularly that of a beloved spouse, is more challenging. "The eeriness of Alzheimer's beginnings is also its reassurance" (214). He knows that he should be worried about the future, but he also knows that time has no meaning to the Alzheimer's patient. "The exasperation of being followed about the house now by Iris is as strong and genuine as is my absolute need for it" (238). Were she to leave him, he realizes, he would compulsively follow her. "As the condition gets worse, it also gets better. It seems to compensate each new improvement"—to which he concludes, laconically, "[I] should be more thankful for that" (239). Without confusing the roles of care-receiver and caregiver, he can feel himself unconsciously developing Iris's symptoms, an example of emotional contagion. "Does the care-giver involuntarily mimic the Alzheimer's condition? I'm sure I do" (241). Bayley never comments on a paradox that remains implicit throughout the trilogy: although the dying care-receiver can become an unbearable burden to the caregiving spouse, the former also grants the caregiver a priceless gift—the opportunity to demonstrate love, compassion, and devotion.

Reading Bayley's memoirs, one senses that they worked through whatever feelings of selfishness or possessiveness that may have been present in their early relationship. Moving closer and closer apart meant that neither sought to dominate or possess the other. Bayley credits Iris with the ability to love unselfishly, along with the ability to empathize with friends' tempestuous emotions without experiencing these emotions herself. Murdoch's essential goodness, even more than her extraordinary intellectual talent, formed the basis of their lifelong marital love. Generosity, compassion, calmness, and wisdom formed the unchanging bedrock of her personality. Not even Alzheimer's changes that. She never displays any of the darker emotions that occasionally manifest themselves in Bayley's character, such as anger and jealousy. He always offers the most generous interpretations of her behavior, as when he tells us that her many sexual lovers were the "recipients of Iris's kindness. They had desired her, and not been rejected" (72). He does not idealize Murdoch, but she has a distinctly saintly character, which is consistent with her philosophical and novelistic interest in Christian ethics. Religious without believing in formal religion, she embodies the Christ-like virtues of humility and tolerance. Her instincts are always kindly, and she is genuine in her relationships with others, without guile or selfishness. His early impression of her—"She was a superior being, and I knew that superior beings just did not have the kind of mind that I did" (11)—is borne out by everything she says, does, and writes. The only qualification the reader may add is that Bayley, too, is a superior being: theirs was a marriage made in heaven, in which neither of them believed.

Throughout *Elegy for Iris*, Bayley remains discreet in what he reveals about his life with Iris Murdoch. There are no sensationalistic self-disclosures, no lurid descriptions, no titillating erotic stories, no shocking revelations of their life together. Written in a spirit of loving kindness, the memoir embodies an aesthetic of generosity. *Elegy for Iris* celebrates a long and fulfilling marriage, one that brought happiness to husband and wife and allowed both to nurture their own and each other's creativity. Apart from Bayley's fear that Iris might resume a sexual relationship with the Bulgarian-born German writer Elias Canetti, the recipient of the Nobel Prize for Literature in 1981, with whom she had an affair before she met Bayley, there were few, if any, dark secrets in their marriage. Husband and wife appeared to be happy and content, the opposite of artists who torture themselves and others.

If the plot of this enduring marriage is insufficiently complex or tempestuous to compel the reader's interest, there is enough conflict in his heartbreaking portrait of her slow, irreversible journey into darkness. Murdoch remains a character of love and a loving character even as she loses her memory, identity, and personhood. The brilliance and originality of *Elegy for Iris* lie in its unflinching honesty about the cruel ravages of Alzheimer's disease, which in many ways is more devastating for the caregiver than for the care-receiver. The memoir offers an inspirational portrait of a caregiver who remains tirelessly attentive to his wife's physical and psychological needs while at the same time transmuting her life, past and present, into the stuff of art. Bayley doesn't analyze his motives for writing about her in *Elegy for Iris*, nor does he question how she would have responded to the book if she were still able to read. It is safe to say, however, that he writes not to get her out of his system, or, worse, to move on with his life or seek "closure," but to honor the woman who has spent a lifetime bringing insight, beauty, and pleasure to him and her readers.

## Still Iris

Attuned to the subtle changes wrought by illness, Bayley informs us in the beginning of *Elegy for Iris* that his wife remains "her old self in many ways." She can still autograph a book for an admirer, please others, and enjoy her lifelong habit of swimming. She still loves to be teased, and she can even tell the difference between one of her husband's mirthful jokes, humor for its own sake, and his increasingly strained jokes that strike her as forced, designed to allay her worry. Like most Alzheimer's sufferers, she knows dimly that something is wrong, but she doesn't know how to react to memory loss.

As *Elegy for Iris* progresses, so does her disease. A cloud of anxiety and dread darkens her once-luminous disposition, and she pretends that nothing is wrong. The denial is reinforced by the anxious caregiver. During the early stages of the illness, Bayley reads to her old favorites such as *Agamemnon* and other Greek plays in translation, but the reading only reminds her of the loss of identity, although, as he tells us, "reminder is hardly the word, for an Alzheimer's patient is not usually conscious in any definable way of what has happened." Yet Bayley concedes that some Alzheimer's sufferers are aware of what is happening to them.

> The torment of knowing that you cannot speak or think what you want must be intolerable, and I have met patients in whom such a torment is clearly visible. But when Iris talks to me, the result seems normal to her and to me surprisingly fluent, provided I do not listen to what is being said but apprehend it in a matrimonial way, as the voice of familiarity, and thus of recognition. (63)

The memoirist learns to read his wife's words differently, not for their content and context, which make no sense, but for their clue to her affective state. For a person like Murdoch who has spent her entire life reading and writing, losing this ability while remaining alive is perhaps the worst fate imaginable. Now Bayley must read for her, read to her, and indeed read her as if she were an indecipherable text. He must not only speak for her, because she cannot speak for herself, but also manage her, because she cannot manage herself. The loss of identity is reflected in the empty expression on her face. "The face of an

Alzheimer's patient has been clinically described as the 'lion face'" (53). Bayley himself speaks like a clinician here, one who attends to a patient's outer and inner reality.

Bayley's instinctive ability as a caregiver is strikingly evident in an interview he gave to Joanna Coles that was first published in the *Guardian* (Manchester) in 1996 and reprinted in the 2003 volume *From a Tiny Corner in the House of Fiction: Conversations with Iris Murdoch*, edited by Gillian Dooley. Murdoch is present during most of the interview, and he is exemplary in his empathy, reassuring her that her writer's block is only temporary. "'It has occurred before, darling,' says Bayley, leaning towards her reassuringly. 'You've had periods of lying fallow, as one might say, rather like a field. Because what is really rather extraordinary about you darling, if I might say, is that you don't mind being interrupted and you don't keep pompous writing hours. You simply write whenever you feel like it'" (246). We know that this is a white lie—an empathic lie—because Murdoch tells us in *Elegy for Iris* that she never suffered from writer's block earlier in her career (218).

Bayley's humor may be silly in his interview to Coles, but it never fails to evoke mirthful laughter, as when he responds to Iris's request to pour a cup of tea for her and the interviewer. "'Pour? Oh, I thought you meant paw!' And he starts scrabbling at the air as if he's a cat, and we all laugh" (247). When Iris reveals a few moments later that she's in a place from which she's "trying to get out," which obviously distresses Coles and Bayley, he tactfully breaks the silence by asking the interviewer if she has written a novel. Coles confesses gloomily that she hasn't, to which he says, encouragingly, "It's well worth trying" (249). The interview ends with Bayley confiding privately to Coles, "We've been to see doctors you know and they say the old brain's very crafty. It can come up against a block and for a bit things seem a bit strange, but then it finds its way around things again" (249–50). Anyone reading the interview would agree with Coles that their relationship "is not only touching, it's still fresh and young, making sense of what marriage is for" (247).

Unlike other irreversible diseases, Alzheimer's generally does not cause unbearable physical suffering. The psychological suffering, however—anxiety, confusion, dread, and panic attacks—may be unbearable to patient and caregiver alike. Bayley describes these panic moments, when they both seem paralyzed by fear. Hearing others' stories may not always be comforting. A woman married to an Alzheimer's patient "cheerfully" remarks to Bayley that it was "like being chained to a corpse," and even though Bayley politely agrees, not wishing to deny her experience, he feels repelled by the suggestion that Iris's affliction could resemble that of the woman's husband. He is repelled, not because the simile is inaccurate but because he does not wish to see himself or his wife in such a self-dramatizing way. He then makes a telling observation about the need to see one's own challenge as different from others'. "My own situation, I felt, was quite different from hers. It's not an uncommon reaction, as I've come to realise, among Alzheimer's partners. One needs very much to feel that the unique individuality of one's spouse has not been lost in the common symptoms of a clinical condition" (49).

As a writer Bayley prefers understatement to overstatement, comedy to tragedy, irony to sentimentality, self-effacement to self-dramatization. He never pretends to have unlimited knowledge or patience. We learn more about his life than about Iris's, but he sees her as the starring character of the story, the heroine, and himself in the supporting role. His writing has a metaphorical richness that never fails to impress us, as when he says that his mode of communication with Iris "seems like underwater sonar, each bouncing pulsations off the other, then listening for an echo" (51)—not, we may add, a narcissistic echo. "Nobody less narcissistic than Iris can well be imagined" (65). More interested in presenting paradoxes than in explaining them, he is a keen and reliable observer. He reports that Murdoch once told him that the question of identity puzzled her. "She thought she herself hardly possessed such a thing, whatever it was" (64). He then speculates that those with a strong identity may suffer more from Alzheimer's than those who, like his wife, were not egocentric. "Iris's own lack of a sense of identity seemed to float her more gently into its world of preoccupied emptiness" (65). Iris's lack of identity is poles apart from that which Bergman anatomizes in *Persona*. We see no exchange of identities in any of Bayley's memoirs, none of the dynamics of narcissistic merging or splitting, or idealization followed by virulent devaluation. Iris has no persona or mask: despite her lack of identity, she still has an essential self—until Alzheimer's inexorable onslaught.

Until the end of *Elegy for Iris*, Bayley speaks lightly about his own emotions when caring for his wife, dwelling on the unexpected consolations of Alzheimer's for the care-receiver and caregiver, such as her ability to sleep soundly. "This ability to sleep like a cat, at all hours of the day and night, must be one of the great blessings that sometimes go with Alzheimer's, converse of the anxiety state that comes on in wakefulness and finds worried questions such as 'When are we leaving?'" (73–4).

Those who write autobiographically must be able to see themselves as both participants and observers, always a challenge when one attempts to record one's blind spots. Bayley is particularly effective in sustaining this double vision, which he does through self-effacing humor. We learn, for example, that in the "old days" he would sometimes throw a tantrum if something was not done properly, blaming Iris, rightly or wrongly, for the problems. She would then become "calm, reassuring, almost maternal," and find a way to solve the problem. Few memoirists would record such a detail, and even fewer would then admit that they exploited this buried reflex as a way to manage an ill spouse.

Bayley never tells us what, if anything, Murdoch said to him about caring for her. Did she acknowledge at some point that she could no longer care for herself? Did she express sadness that their lives would never be the same? Was she angry at him for being healthy? Did she feel guilty that he was wearing himself out by caring for her night and day? Did she express gratitude over his devotion to her? Bayley never raises any of these questions. Nor does he tell us in *Elegy for Iris* whether he began to wonder how his life would be different after her death—whether, indeed, he wished to outlive her? Or did he feel, to the contrary, that his life would end with hers?

## Survival Strategies

One need not be a caregiver to appreciate Bayley's devotion to his wife, but that devotion may perhaps be best understood by another caregiver who understands the day-to-day reality of caring for an ill person. "I readily understand the complex devotion Bayley had for Murdoch, but even his most empathetic friends, and certainly distant readers of his book, may speculate, Didn't the relationship become a duty, a habit, a chore?" Aaron Alterra raises this question in his 1999 book *The Caregiver: A Life with Alzheimer's*. Alterra, a pen name for E. S. Goldman (1913–2013), was in his mid-eighties when his wife, with whom he had been married for sixty years, began developing Alzheimer's disease. Reading *Elegy for Iris* affected him deeply, and he saw many similarities between Bayley's emotional life and his own. Nevertheless, Alterra couldn't help wonder how a caregiver like Bayley maintained his sanity without taking a break. "How could he not prefer a night at the theater with old friends to sitting alone reading while she slept in another room? Literary people have excessive imaginations; did Bayley talk himself into a mood of pseudo-gallantry?" (162).

It's unlikely that the self-deprecating Bayley, who later wrote a blurb for Alterra's book, regarded himself as having an excessive imagination. Bayley shows us, without gallantry, how he cared for his wife on a daily basis. Bayley (like Alterra) is one of the few memoirists who remained his spouse's exclusive caregiver, until he was forced to place her in a nursing home, in Oxford, England, where she died with Bayley by her side. He offers a full account of his caregiving experience from the beginning until the end. *Elegy for Iris* is not a how-to book, not a clinical story like those in *The 36-Hour Day*, but it offers caregivers practical survival strategies for impossible situations. Most of these survival strategies are *not* found in self-help books. The main strategy he credits to a contemporary of Jane Austen, the Reverend Sydney Smith, who urged his depressed parishioners to "take short views of human nature—never further than dinner or tea" (53). At first Bayley expresses this platitude seriously, but soon he repeats it as an "incantation or joke, which can raise a laugh if it is accompanied by some horsing around, a live pantomime of 'short views' being taken. It is not now intended to be rationally received, but it gets a smile anyway" (53). It also gets a smile from Bayley's readers, who recognize that words have little impact on Alzheimer's patients, apart from, perhaps, the loving tone in which they are expressed. And it is Bayley's loving tone that most affects his readers.

Another survival strategy, one that Bayley practices on every page but on which he never comments, is the reverse: taking long views. That is, one recalls a long and rich life spent together. It is the consolation of memory. He engages in a secular version of counting his blessings, expressing gratitude for what was and, at least for him, what continues to be. It is the same gratitude and deep appreciation for the countless blessings in her life that Justice Sandra Day O'Connor was quoted by the *New York Times* in 2018. Taking long views of life filled with gratitude is what the memoirist does, writing about a past that continues to live in the writer's memory. These long views remind Bayley how fortunate he and Iris have been. Blessed with a long and accurate memory, Bayley can reflect upon a lifetime of love, happiness, art, and achievement. Nothing in the future can destroy what they had in the past.

Another survival strategy is to be as close to the care-receiver as possible. "If Iris could climb inside my skin now, or enter me as if I had a pouch like a kangaroo, she would do so. She has no awareness of what I am doing, only an awareness of what I am" (127). Some readers may be disturbed by these analogies, which appear dehumanizing, but they capture the dehumanizing features of Alzheimer's disease, which robs its victims of their humanness. Iris's new closeness is for him, though not for her, suffocating, worlds apart from what their marriage used to be like, when they were separate but never separated.

They are now, for the first time, truly together, suffocatingly close, a closeness not to be wished for, as he suggests in a passage filled with heartrending irony.

> We have become, as is often said of a happy married couple, inseparable—in a way, like Ovid's Baucis and Philemon, whom the gods gave the gift of growing old together as trees. It is a way of life that is unfamiliar. The closeness of apartness has necessarily become the closeness of closeness. And we know nothing of it; we have never had any practice. (126–7)

Still another survival strategy is humor, which never fails Bayley. "Humor seems to survive anything" (51), and no matter how despondent or despairing he becomes, he finds some redeeming comedy in the situation. His humor is often corny but never cruel, and he usually directs it against himself rather than against Iris. There are not many writers who can entertain us with their offbeat humor while at the same time enlighten us about its evolutionary significance.

*Elegy for Iris* is not an overly self-conscious memoir, concerned with the theoretical difficulties of representing ineffable reality. Bayley is more a storyteller than a theorist, and he succeeds in showing how the story of his life with Iris Murdoch has changed irrevocably. Sometimes he pauses to comment on the impossibility of fully realizing Iris's character. His wife's absent presence calls into question his ability to remember and document her past. He does not suggest a solution to the problem of capturing Iris's essence, but he doesn't allow the unrepresentability of reality to prevent him from doing his best to conjure the old Iris Murdoch back to life. She remains his inspiration in life, death, and in the shadowy death-in-life netherworld of Alzheimer's disease.

Unlike cancer patients, whose lives change forever on the day of their diagnosis, Alzheimer's patients do not realize in a flash that they are suffering from an irreversible, fatal disease. They may be troubled for months or years by failing memory, but as the symptoms worsen, and the fog of forgetfulness slowly descends upon them, they often do not realize the gravity of their situation. But the caregiver does. The first indication of Murdoch's illness came during a presentation she gave in Israel in 1994, when she could not summon the words to answer questions from the audience. Everyone could tell there was something seriously wrong—everyone except Murdoch herself. "It was hard to say how conscious she was of her own difficulty, but the effect soon became paralyzing, for the listener as well as for her" (212). The slow decline began to accelerate, and she had trouble completing her last book, *Jackson's Dilemma*, which contains several internal inconsistencies that are a reflection of her loss of authorial control, itself a symptom of her illness.

Bayley's first response was denial. "I was somehow sure that everything would carry on just as usual. In a sense, I was right. When the Alzheimer's patient loses touch with time, time seems to lose both its prospective and retrospective significance" (214). He began taking the shortest views possible, even shorter than those recommended by the Reverend Smith. Doctors' visits and medical tests confirmed that she was indeed suffering from Alzheimer's. Bayley rejected friends' advice for Iris to take new experimental drugs that work only temporarily and then produce greater confusion and disorientation. "The friendly fog suddenly disperses, revealing a precipice before the feet" (219).

## Emotional Contagion and Compassion Fatigue

The final chapter of *Elegy for Iris* contains Bayley's diary entries from January 1 to Christmas 1997. Life is now different from the past. The couple never felt a need for television, being too absorbed in their work, but now Iris watches children's "teletubbies" all day, staring at the screen as if in a trance. He does too. On March 30, he makes a "savage comment" about their bleak situation, to which Iris looks "relieved and intelligent," responding, "But I love you" (233). Always a paradoxicalist, he observes that as her condition darkens, it brightens—brightens in the sense that anxiety and dread no longer torment her. Despair sometimes overwhelms him, and he is tempted to shout at her, "It's worse for me. It's *much worse!*" (249). He ends a May diary entry with the anguished words, "When are they going to let *me* out?" (249). Iris's anxiety and dread have infected him; he too is a victim. "Alzheimer's obviously has me in its grip . . . . Does the care-giver involuntarily mimic the Alzheimer's condition? I'm sure I do" (240–1). At times he cannot prevent himself from going "berserk."

Bayley offers a faithful description of compassion fatigue, a common problem among caregivers and hospice workers. As Carol Wogrin suggests, "Those who have enormous capacity for feeling and expressing empathy are the ones who tend to be at the highest risk of compassion stress" (385)—largely because, as we saw in *Persona*, those who have a psychological investment in others' welfare are especially prone to emotional contagion. Frustration and rage overcome Bayley as he watches Iris spill the contents of a passenger's pocketbook while taking a bus back to Oxford after a brief vacation. As he roughly shoves her into a seat, he gives her a "surreptitious violent push on the arm" by which he was holding her (255). These revelations lend authenticity to the memoir, reminding us that Bayley is human, all too human. Every person has a limit, and he has reached his. We accept his rage because we know he has a right to feel that way; it is earned rage. We know that his anger does not invalidate his lifelong love for her. We also know, if we are honest with ourselves, that we cannot predict how we will act as caregivers. Above all, he remains devoted to her care. Their journey together, he realizes at the end, is nearly over. Twice Murdoch has told Peter Conradi that she is "sailing into the darkness." By the time *Elegy for Iris* ends, the journey is all but complete.

*Elegy for Iris* became a bestseller in the United Kingdom and the United States, and in 2001 it was made into a film, *Iris*, directed by Richard Eyre and starring Jim Broadbent, who received an Academy Award for Best Supporting Actor, and Judi Dench and Kate Winslet as the older and younger incarnations of Murdoch, respectively, also nominated for Best Actress and Best Supporting Actress. The film captures Bayley's eccentricity and humor, as well as his love for and devotion to his wife, though it fails to convey his intellectual brilliance and originality, his delight in wit, irony, and paradox. Suddenly Bayley was an international celebrity, more famous, perhaps, than Iris Murdoch during the height of her career.

## *Iris and Her Friends*

*Iris and Her Friends* is more somber and desperate than the preceding memoir: Alzheimer's has taken its grim toll on husband and wife. Iris is now in the final throes of the illness, and there are few moments when she resembles her old self. Bayley's statement about his wife in *Elegy for Iris*—"Memory may have wholly lost its mind function, but it retains some hidden principle of identification, even after the Alzheimer's has long taken hold" (48)—is less apparent in *Iris and Her Friends*. The humor is now more trenchant than in *Elegy for Iris*, the author's mood and voice bleaker. *Iris and Her Friends* is less about the patient than it is about the caregiver who has also been rendered into a patient. We learn little about Murdoch's life that we have not seen in the earlier memoir; now the focus is almost exclusively on the memoirist himself.

Bayley's artistic challenge in the second memoir is more daunting than in the first one. How does a writer convey the emptiness and boredom of an Alzheimer's sufferer without making the narrative empty and boring? Bayley solves this problem in *Elegy for Iris* by contrasting Murdoch's past and present lives. The memoir focuses more on the past than on the present. We see the blossoming and maturation of love, the development of a celebrated union, the marriage of a future world-famous novelist and distinguished literary critic. Bayley never lets us forget the ghastly reality of his present situation, but the flashbacks enliven the story, reminding us that both husband and wife have had a long and rich life together.

Few of the flashbacks in *Iris and Her Friends*, by contrast, have anything to do with Murdoch. She is hardly a character at all, now ravaged by an illness that has transformed her into an insensible object—or so she seems most of the time. Nor does the title refer to Iris's "friends," who are conspicuously absent from the memoir. Rather, the title refers to the consolations and comforts Alzheimer's bring to both care-receiver and caregiver. "There may be rewards and alleviations on the way, for all parties. As well as anxiety in the patient, there may be a kind of merciful indifference, even lightness of heart, a shrugging off of responsibility for the things most of us feel we have to do every day—washing, dressing, keeping up appearances" (5).

*Iris and Her Friends* continues where *Elegy for Iris* ends, and the two could have been published as one long memoir. Bayley uses the same survival strategies in caring for his wife, but these compensations are now more solitary and unshareable. Once again, he is a paradoxicalist, stating that "certainty of things getting worse is our most unexpected friend; yet undoubtedly he is one" (12). Because Murdoch cannot speak, write, or presumably think about the past, it is Bayley's past that we see, his life before Iris's appearance. He writes about his service in the British army during the Second World War, his early encounters with women, including one to whom he proposed marriage and who, to his relief, turned him down, and another woman whom he transmuted into a fictional character in his first novel.

If Bayley's major surprise while writing the first two memoirs was the importance of finding consolations that would offer a welcome, indeed, life-saving respite from the intolerable strain of caregiving, no less surprising, even shocking, is the onrush of memories of the distant past. Here he rightly invokes Proust, who "dramatised the joy he received from that sudden flooding back of the past" (15). But Bayley goes beyond Proust in exploring how the floodgates of his own memory are opened while his wife's memory recedes. He cannot help wondering about this mysterious and unanticipated phenomenon. "Is it the absence of any such goings-on now in Iris's mind which stimulates the production of them in my own?" (63). Unable to determine whether this reciprocal relationship reveals causation or merely correlation, he is troubled by the pleasure of writing. "I am pleased with myself not only for remembering but for having recorded it in the mind with such precision. Most memoirs and autobiography have a 'clever little me' feel about them somewhere" (129). He is also troubled by the possibility that he may be exploiting his wife's vulnerability, a concern he did not raise in *Elegy for Iris*.

## An Upstairs-Downstairs Account of Caregiving

As with *Elegy for Iris* but to a greater extent, *Iris and Her Friends* affirms Bayley's survival strategies as a caregiver. These survival strategies become more important after years of caring for an Alzheimer's patient. Retreating into one's memory and fantasy life becomes not only a pleasurable form of escape but also essential for the caregiver's physical and mental health, an example of self-compassion and self-care. Bayley offers a psychological guide to caregiving, showing rather than merely telling us that the "caregiver finds himself becoming two people: one closely identified with the sufferer and her symptoms, as I was with Iris's downstairs; the other in a state of almost enjoyable detachment, much aware of any treat he can save for himself" (153). In effect, Bayley's memoirs are an *Upstairs-Downstairs* account of caregiving, in which he attends to Iris's here-and-now needs while escaping into his past life with her and, before that, his life as a single person. Though he admits that he doesn't care for the word *caregiver*, "just because it has become so unavoidable" (273), he writes authoritatively about his experiences, and, according to the book jacket of *Iris and Her Friends*, he was an active supporter of Alzheimer's International.

Part of the value of reading Bayley's memoirs is that caregivers learn not to feel guilty for becoming angry at their care-receivers. He writes about his love for Iris but also his hate for her at times. "Hardly a day goes by without my flying into a brief frenzy, shouting at Iris, or saying in level tones something like this: 'I don't know *what* to do with you—you exhaust me so much.' Or sometimes saying, with a reassuring smile, 'Have you any idea how much I hate you?'" (76–7). One recalls the Roman poet Terence's observation 2,000 years ago: "I am human; I count nothing human foreign to me." Sometimes Bayley becomes so enraged at her that he can scarcely control his violence. "Once she put her hands over her head and whimpered, 'Don't hit me.' She knew better than I did what might happen" (77). On one level he is shocked by his behavior, but on another level he is not. He then asks a question that is not entirely theoretical: "Would a child, or a senile adult, prefer to be looked after by a parent or partner who loves her and knocks her about, rather than go into some sort of state care?" His answer is equivocal—"Depends on the degree of knocking about, I suppose" (77).

Midway through *Iris and Her Friends* Bayley postulates two complementary laws, existential in nature, which are survival strategies for everyone, not just caregivers and care-receivers. "There is certainly a law of the conservation of trouble, the troubles we must all undergo in this vale of tears. If some are taken away, by God or the government or scientific discovery, we can be sure not only that the ones which remain will seem more burdensome than before but that quite new and unexpected ones will appear" (128). Phrased differently, there will always be suffering, though the causes and symptoms may change, and the elimination of one problem may cause a greater one. The second law is less obvious but no less noteworthy, the law of the conservation of pleasure. "As troubles get worse, small satisfactions increase, both in intensity and in expectation" (128). He looks forward to putting Iris to bed, pouring himself a drink, and reading a page or two of a book. "I cling to this pleasure grimly, as if I were holding on to the side of a lifeboat" (129).

One of Bayley's regrets in *Iris and Her Friends* is that his wife will not be able to read the memoir. "I am playing to an audience of one—myself. Iris is indifferent to my performance, and presumably unaware of it. I have to be my own audience; and giving a benefit for an audience of one is part of the solitude of this unchosen profession of caregiver" (154). It's true that Bayley is playing to an audience of one as Iris's caregiver, but he is playing to a much wider audience as a writer about caregiving. And so even when he states that he must be his own audience, it is hard to imagine that he is unaware of the thousands of men and women who would read his story. Writing a memoir about a demented spouse is also a form of literary caregiving—and self-caring.

We learn less about Iris in the second memoir but more about Bayley's motives for writing. We discover, for example, that a major reason he wrote the memoirs is to prevent his wife from becoming an empty character devoid of consciousness. "Did I write about Iris last year to stop her from becoming such a She? It didn't feel like that, but the urge may have been there. And when the book came out, she loved to see it, and the picture on the cover" (243–4). Did Iris intuit what Sandra Gilbert calls in *Death's Door* "textual resurrection," when an author like Walt Whitman implies that "through a weird process of transubstantiation, his flesh and blood will metamorphose into paper and ink, offering his devoutest readers a chance at communion with 'the origin of all poems' incarnated on his pages?" (72). Bayley creates what I call in *Writing Widowhood* a "posterity self" (195–6), a record of caregiving and care-receiving that will survive long after wife and husband are no longer alive.

Writing brought Bayley and Murdoch satisfaction, even pleasure—not surprising given the fact that they were both prolific authors who had devoted their lives to the craft of writing. And writing was for both of them a way to express their feelings about each other. Bayley does not analyze the reasons for his wife's happiness when seeing a copy of *Elegy for Iris*, but he does describe the look on her face as she gazed at the book. "I saw a glimmer of pride, almost of a fond and motherly pride, in the smile she turned on me. I had actually written a book about her!" (244). He tells us in the same paragraph that his brother, Michael, who was fond of Iris, also approved of the book, believing that it "helped the Alzheimer's cause." Bayley concludes the chapter by revealing that his wife's and brother's support was all that mattered to him about the book. "That was all the approval I needed, and disapproval there—from Michael or from Iris herself (and I know she would have expressed it somehow had she felt it)—would have been the only kind that I feared" (243–4).

## Revealing and Concealing

Many biographers worry about the possibility of exploiting their subjects, a fear that must be heightened in memoirists who write about deceased or ill spouses. The fear is probably greater when the memoirist's spouse is still alive. The biographer Peter Conradi acknowledges that while the vast majority of the hundreds of letters Bayley received after writing *Elegy for Iris* were positive, a few were negative: some people felt Iris was cast "in this very public role of quixotic benefactress without her consent" (591). Bayley never mentions this concern in *Elegy for Iris*, but he does in *Iris and Her Friends*.

Does Bayley disclose too much in *Iris and Her Friends*? He indirectly raises this issue when he refers to an interview with an American physician-journalist who began raising in Iris's presence personal questions about how her illness has changed their relationships. "The journalist's queries were euphemistic ('Do you have to help her on the loo?'), but we both glanced appealingly at Iris from time to time, as if for reassurance" (202). Bayley's appeal to "nature," and to Murdoch's lifelong belief in artistic truthfulness, leaves little doubt that he intended to write as honestly and openly as possible about their present lives. Iris herself, he adds, "at least gave the impression of knowing exactly what we were talking about: Her face had an expression of courteous but faintly amused interest" (*Iris and Her Friends* 202). Her "consent" here, however, is problematic, as Bayley knows. As the interview continues, interviewer and interviewee appear to exchange roles.

"A question seemed to be imminent—'Do you still have, er, sexual relations?' I could not help feeling curious to see when it would come. Feeling like a prostitute with a nervous client, I gave the lady a look of invitation, but Iris was now getting frankly bored and her air of polite amusement had disappeared" (203).

The journalist never does raise the question, allowing Bayley to raise it himself in the memoir. "To be honest," he begins—a verbal tic in that he never questions his own honesty elsewhere in the narrative—"it wouldn't have been an entirely easy one to answer" (203). He then proceeds to answer the question as delicately as possible. Noting that sex can be more complicated than "Do you or don't you?" he admits that the "old indeterminacy in our own sexual relations seems to prolong itself naturally into the unending confusion of Iris's present days." Again, he appeals to "nature" to suggest his acceptance of the present situation. If this is a circuitous way of answering "no" to the question of sexual relations, he implies that sex can still be "felicitous." Iris's "long periods of anxiety are followed by brief happiness, inconclusive moments of peace and close embrace" (203).

Few novels, memoirs, or films describe the caregiver's (or care-receiver's) dilemma over sex, and for this reason Hugh Marriott's comments are welcome. "Good sex requires sensitivity on both sides and, if one partner has lost that, it probably won't be much fun for the other one" (147). Not content with this platitude, Marriott then complicates the situation. Suppose your "piglet" wants sex but you "can't bear to give it to them"—perhaps because they have lost control of their bladder or bowels. What should a caregiver do? There's nothing platitudinous about Marriott's answer. "What are you looking at me like that for? You think I've got an answer to all this? Nope. Sorry. I've got plenty of sympathy, but that's not a help." He then reminds us that "If you try to do something you really can't bear to do, you'll be the first person to suffer but not the only person. Sooner or later your piglet will, too" (147–8).

## A Rich Fantasy Life

Bayley is not yet finished with the question, however, for he then reflects on the importance of the caregiver's sexual fantasies. This was not something he was prepared to disclose to the journalist, mainly because a newspaper article could not record the nuances of such a discussion. A rich fantasy life is one of the great "friends" of Alzheimer's disease. "My fantasies accommodate persons both real and imaginary, the real ones mostly from the past" (204). Nor are characters in novels exempt from being either the fantasizer or fantasied object; he gives the example of Holden Caulfield in *The Catcher in the Rye* fantasizing over Eustacia Vye in Thomas Hardy's *The Return of the Native*. "I still have a recurrent tendresse," Bayley confesses, sounding like Humbert Humbert in Nabokov's *Lolita*, "for one or two of Barbara Pym's female characters" (204). He concludes his discussion of his fantasy life with a paradox: "I am not exactly lonely—how could I be when so close to Iris, every hour of the day and night? And yet that closeness without communication, however loving it may be, is also its own kind of loneliness" (205). The observation—loneliness amid constant companionship, closeness without communication—is less startling than the next: "If Iris were to have to go from me, into a hospital or home, all these solitary and friendly pleasures, fantasies, too, would vanish like a puff of smoke" (205). He would not merely be lonely, then; he would be bereft. This knowledge makes the present situation, however wrenching it may be for him, more desirable—or at least less undesirable—than the future, however much relief he may feel from no longer being a carer. "The solitariness of a close relationship—and how much closer could we get now?—is, for me, the fertile ground for fantasy, as it is for memories, the ones that go far, far back" (205).

The memoirist makes other piquant observations about the role of sexual fantasy for both caregivers and noncaregivers. "Fantasy and enactment are separate, and their cohabitation, to use a word slightly ridiculous in this context, is part of the charm of each" (206). He then relates an "absurd story" about a sleepy wife telling her husband, "Oh, do get on with it, George," to which her husband responds, "Sorry, dear, I can't think of anyone at the moment" (206). In his pragmatic words of wisdom and ironic wit, Bayley sounds like a cross between an erudite Ann Landers and Dr. Ruth, spicing his lively insights with apt literary examples.

Bayley does not mention Alice Munro in any of his memoirs, but it would be interesting to know how he felt about her depiction of matchmaking in "The Bear Came Over the Mountain." Bayley, like the fictional Grant, is a literature professor, and both husbands are devoted to their demented wives, but they have little else in common. "Could my Perfect Woman lead me into adultery?" he asks in *Iris and Her Friends*. "I rather think not" (215). The idea seems so comic to him that he begins to laugh.

Bayley does not hesitate to describe the caregiver's most difficult challenges, including caring for an incontinent spouse. "I don't know how it is with three-year-olds, but Iris's toilet habits, if you can call them that, have become unpredictable. Sometimes she will go to the right place, even though she makes a mess of it. More often, she will do it on the carpet outside, or in another room.

Then she lays the results, as if with care, on a neighbouring chair or bookshelf. I don't mind a bit of cleaning up, an operation which seems mildly to amuse her. I can make a joke of it, too, and we can laugh about it together" (185–6). Bayley's response may remind us of Gerasim's consoling words to Ivan Ilych. "What's a little trouble? It's a case of illness with you, sir" (66).

Bayley's good-natured acceptance of his wife's incontinence is striking. "For adults, feces seems to be a universal disgust substance," Paul Rozin, Jonathan Hardt, and Clark R. McCauley observe in an article published in *Handbook of Emotions* in 2000, "with the odor of decay as perhaps the most potent sensory attribute associated with disgust" (646). Exploring the meaning of disgust within both developmental and cultural contexts, Rozin and his colleagues concede that we know little about the history of the dark emotion. "It is absent in nonhuman primates, yet extremely frequent and probably universal in contemporary humans" (650). Children do not show an aversion to feces; consequently, the authors suggest that disgust seems to require enculturation. Because the "prototypical odor of disgust is the odor of decay, which is the odor of death," the authors speculate that disgust can best be understood as a defense against the universal fear of mortality (642). Bayley's amiable acceptance of Iris's incontinence reveals not only his ability to overcome the disgust that other caregivers might feel in the same situation but also his recognition of her mortality—and his own. Rozin and his associates cite a study showing that "disgust sensitivity is negatively related to the enjoyment of disgust humor" (648). If so, Bayley's ability to find the humor of his wife's situation reveals his tolerance of disgust. Other caregiving memoirists show a less enlightened attitude toward incontinence.

## Truth Without Betrayal

Bayley's description of cleaning Iris after a bowel movement could not be more different from Philip Roth's graphic account in his memoir *Patrimony* of his incontinent father, suffering from a massive brain tumor. Roth's horror contrasts Bayley's cheerful acceptance. It is the difference between a tragic and comic vision of life. "Love accepts the comic," Bayley writes with philosophical wisdom (207). For Roth, art rests on betrayal: he promised his humiliated father that he would not tell anyone about his incontinence but then disregarded the dying man's wishes. Offering a similar view of art as betrayal, Janet Malcolm has described journalism in her 1990 book *The Journalist and the Murderer* as the art of seduction and violation. For Bayley, however, art involves no such betrayal, since he believed Iris would not have objected to readers knowing about her life as an Alzheimer's sufferer. His statement about Henry James and Dostoevsky—"True art never exploits" (247)—applies to his own writing as well.

Bayley and Murdoch were both devoted to writing about the truth, and they admired writers who were themselves truthful. Bayley quotes with approval Auden's statement that "insofar as poetry, or any of the arts, can be said to have an ulterior purpose, it is by telling the truth, to disenchant and disintoxicate." He believes that Auden was not only the most inclusive and technically skilled poet of the twentieth century but also the "most truthful" (*Selected Essays* 82). So, too, does Bayley tell the truth about Iris's illness. By refusing to romanticize Alzheimer's disease, he shows us how illness can disenchant and disintoxicate life. He captures both the horror and beauty of life, and, in doing so, he remains true to experience.

Is Iris Murdoch a "vulnerable subject?" G. Thomas Couser raises this question in his 2004 book on ethics and life writing. Murdoch is "doubly vulnerable," Couser suggests. "Her impairment makes her subject to harm (abuse and exploitation) in her life; and it also renders her vulnerable to misrepresentation in her husband's writing because it deprives her of the capacity to take part in, examine, respond to, or resist that representation" (x) Additionally, Couser points out that since Murdoch "would likely never have wanted to be represented as incompetent, there is some question as to the ethicality of such representation." Yet Couser doesn't wish to "adjudicate" the question. His conclusion is that because Bayley offers a loving and respectful portrait of his wife's condition, the memoir does not violate her integrity. I agree.

## A Muse

Iris Murdoch remains Bayley's muse in health and in illness—an "elusive muse, a muse who has to be coaxed, cosseted, rescued from herself" (*Iris and Her Friends* 190). This helps to explain his reluctance to place her in a nursing home until near the end of her life. Bayley's worst moments in the memoir occur toward the end when he fears he has lost his muse. "I can do nothing without her. Without her, I shall have nothing to write, and nothing to do" (265). While the context of this fear is a literal loss—Iris jumps out of their moving car and then disappears for several minutes—he cannot help dreading the time when she will no longer be alive. And yet Iris can still express her love in language, even if her words no longer make sense.

> The other day in the car, she laid a hand on my knee and said with emphasis, '*Susten poujin drom love poujin? Poujin susten?*' I hastened to agree, and one word was clear. As soon as I could stop the car, we kissed each other. She knew what she meant even when there was no meaning, and there *was* that word. (233)

This is one of the many loving and lovely moments in the memoir when their heartfelt intimacy comes through. Bayley can speak for her when she can no longer speak for herself, at least not in recognizable language. *Iris and Her Friends* leaves us with love, loss, and a hint of recovery, not for the Alzheimer's care-receiver, for whom recovery is impossible, but for the caregiver, even when he fears that recovery is all but impossible.

No matter how fatigued, stressed, or despondent Bayley becomes in *Iris and Her Friends*, no matter how close he approaches his own breaking point—he refers in the last chapter to having a breakdown, though he gives us no specifics—we sense that he would live his life all over again even if he knew how it would end for him and his wife. He recites lines from *Macbeth*: "Canst thou not minister to a mind diseas'd,/ Pluck from the memory a rooted sorrow" (188). He might have also cited Malcolm's words in the same play: "Give sorrow words: the grief that does not speak /Whispers the o'er-fraught heart, and bids it break."

As Iris's long, dark journey comes to an end, we wonder whether Bayley's sorrow will be too much for him to bear. Earlier he has presented, with little commentary, examples of friends, teachers, and acquaintances who have been unable to survive beloved spouses' deaths. He tells us in *Elegy for Iris* that one of her favorite Oxford professors, Eduard Frankel, was "devoted to his wife, and he had told a close friend that when she died, he would follow. He did, taking an overdose the same night" (61). How will Bayley do in widowhood? He observes at the beginning of *Iris and Her Friends* that he does not regard suicide or euthanasia as one of Iris's friends (13), repeating this a few pages later when he thinks of Dr. Kevorkian, "death's angel," who is the opposite of a friend. "Sweet are the uses of adversity," he exclaims, the "commonest, sanest Shakespearean wisdom" (17). He might have recited a line from *The Aeneid* that biographer Peter Conradi quotes: "The day may dawn when this plight will be sweet to remember" (402). And yet Bayley admits that he "longed for death, like Anna Karenina abandoned, as she thought—no, as she knew—by a lover who had become a stranger to her. The person beside me seemed a stranger, too" (255).

Bayley's darkest moments in *Iris and Her Friends* occur when he contemplates homicide and suicide, foreshadowing the plot of Michael Haneke's film *Amour*. Sometimes Bayley says to Iris, "Don't worry, darling, we shall soon be dead" (13), a threat or promise that is always met with disturbing silence. He admits that he "had frequent thoughts of doing ourselves in together, if there were a nice, reliable way" (13). He mentions that in 1983 the writer Arthur Koestler and his wife did precisely that. "He was ailing and had cancer. She was young and in good health, but she wanted to go with him. Hard to understand, and yet there it is" (13). He then reveals that when Alzheimer's disease began to ravage Iris's mother, her companion began to mass on her behalf a large quantity of sleeping pills. "After her death, I found and appropriated them, thinking they might come in handy one day—if they worked" (14). His house is so cluttered that he can't find the pills—a wry end to what may be the most unsettling moment in the memoir. Bayley never returns to this subject again in *Iris and Her Friends*, and one senses that he never seriously considered ending Iris's life or his own. Her illness, paradoxically, shored up his strength.

## *Widower's House*

Life without Iris becomes the subject of the final volume of Bayley's trilogy, *Widower's House*. With its lengthy and curious subtitle—"*A Study in Bereavement, or How Margot and Mella Forced Me to Flee My Home*"—the memoir alternates between a farcical and melancholy tone, strikingly different from the earlier memoirs. *Widower's House* fills in some of the gaps of the story of Bayley's caregiving experiences and explores for the first time his motivation in writing about his wife. The memoir also reveals that Bayley has found a new companion—an old friend who, like him, has lost a beloved spouse—with whom he can begin a new life.

*Widower's House* opens with Bayley's assertion that Iris's death has irrevocably changed his life. His insistence that his old identity is irretrievably gone is misleading, however, for if style is the man, he is still the same person, at least in many fundamental ways. Notwithstanding his self-pity, he is still an ironist and paradoxicalist. He delights in surprising his readers with statements like "How much I had suffered lately from [friends'] kindness, and from goodness" (18). He is even more self-effacing than in the earlier memoirs, preferring to focus on his weaknesses—his cluelessness, haplessness, and unworldliness—rather than on his strengths: his devotion to Iris, active support of Alzheimer's International, and commitment to educating the public about bereavement.

For the first time in the trilogy, Bayley raises the question of whether he exaggerates Iris's strengths: an unnamed "shrink" asserts "blandly" that "bereaved persons have a tendency to idealise the dead loved one" (167). I don't know who this unnamed shrink is, but Colin Murray Parkes makes this statement in *Bereavement*. One aspect of the work of grieving is the "re-evaluation of the dead person, an activity sometimes termed 'idealization,' since it is the happy memories and valued aspects of the relationship that we treasure and wish to perpetuate" (71). The memoirist may not idealize Iris, but he presents her as a human saint, aiding him even when she is ill. Another interpreter might locate agency, the cause of this protection, in the caregiver rather than in the care-receiver, but Bayley endows Iris with the power to protect him even when illness has destroyed her volition. She stopped eating and drinking about a month before her death in 1999 at age seventy-nine, but she retained her enigmatic benevolence. Thus, he perceives her smiling at him whenever he does something that enables him to live without her.

## Communing with the Dead

Garrett Stewart points out that death is the only event in life that novelists can only imagine rather than know. Iris's death scene is Victorian in spirit, not so much in the belief that the deceased spouse has gone to a better world, but in its aura of radiance, innocence, and spirituality. There is a startlingly playful quality about the way in which Bayley opens and closes her eyes, almost as if she were a doll. He does not fantasize reunion with his deceased wife, but there is a sense of communication with the dead: their love seems to survive her passing. In contrast to the ravages brought on by Alzheimer's disease, Bayley portrays Iris's death as an example of *ars moriendi*—the art of dying well. We see, in short, a beautiful death, worlds apart from the long process of depersonalization and dehumanization that preceded it. Unlike Nietzsche, who believed that we have art in order not to perish from the truth, Bayley portrays art in the service of truth.

Geoffrey Gorer has observed that just as sex was the great unmentionable subject in the nineteenth century, so is death the great unmentionable subject in the twentieth—and now, we may add, the twenty-first century. Other researchers, such as Howard Spiro, have reached similar conclusions. "Once, when grandparents, parents, and sometimes children—too often children—died at home, everyone knew death first-hand. Death is as common as birth, but it went into hiding in our twentieth century" (xv). Bayley's description not only removes death from its fearful hiding place, exposing it to full view, but also destigmatizes Alzheimer's disease, showing us how he continues to love and honor Iris. She seems mysteriously aware of his devotion even at the moment of extinction.

Midway through *Widower's House* Bayley begins a discussion of why he wrote about Iris. Unlike John Milton, who believed that "thoughts wander through eternity," Bayley maintains that "eternity is not in the afterlife, but, rather, in our minds"—from which he concludes that "communing with the dead in this way must be one of the oldest of all human indulgences. And the most comforting?" (107). Despite the question mark, there is little doubt that Bayley found comfort in writing about his deceased beloved. Noting ironically that the "dead expect the attentions the living bestow on them, and almost unconsciously, the living assume this must be so" (107), he declares that in Thomas Hardy's late poetry, "the dead continue to converse with the living, quarrel with them, patronize them for still being above ground, become satirical at their expense. They can be downright nasty sometimes, too" (108). Bayley then reveals, in one of his most psychological insights, that writing about the dead "is a way not only of continuing to feel in touch with them but of expiating guilt" (108), a statement that clearly applies to Hardy, who was nasty to his first wife, Emma, throughout their long and grim marriage but wrote hundreds of love poems about her immediately following her death. "Hardy's poetry flourished alike on his lack of belief and on his devotion to the uses of poetic survival" (108–9).

## Writing as Rescue

So, too, has Bayley flourished in his devotion to the uses of artistic survival, his wife's artistic immortality and his own. Brooding over such issues "cheered one up"; now he could understand why Hardy wrote those love poems. "Not only was she still very much there for him but she carried him back . . . to the days and places where he had first met her, when their 'days were a joy.'" But, Bayley continues, there is a major difference between the two writers. "I could write about Iris again, as I used to before she died. But I was writing about her the other way round. Hardy kept Emma alive, at least for a while, by writing about her. I had felt that Iris was alive with me until this morning. Now I felt, quite suddenly, that she really had ceased to exist; and that is why I could write about her as if she were still alive" (*Widower's House* 109).

Bayley doesn't elaborate on why it was only when his wife ceased to exist that he could write about her for the third time. His diary entries in *Iris and Her Friends* indicate that he was writing about her throughout much or most of her protracted illness. As with Hardy, writing was a way for him to remain in touch with his deceased wife, but there seems to have been little, if any, guilt, existential or otherwise, toward her that required expiation—unless we assume that he felt a degree of guilt over his "occasional tantrums." One cannot imagine the dead Iris quarreling with Bayley, as Hardy imagined his dead wife doing with him. Bayley does not idealize Iris, as Hardy idealized Emma, but he acknowledges the obsessional intensity with which he wrote about Iris, implying that this was something he *needed* to do. Writing was for him nothing less than rescue work, an essential part of his life support system during and immediately following his wife's death. "I clung to writing as a form of belief. I didn't believe anything else, but I believed in Iris, and believing in her was a belief in her survival, both for me in my own way and for everyone who read her work. How could I not believe that?" (*Widower's House* 134).

## Obsessional Review

Bayley does not cite the extensive research that has been published on bereavement, but many of his observations support the major clinical findings. As I report in *Dying to Teach*, one characteristic of widows and widowers is obsessional review, which Ira Glick, Robert Weiss, and Colin Murray Parkes define in their book *The First Year of Bereavement* as "going over and over the same scenes," an integral part of the mourning process. "It was distressing to the widows that they were so absorbed by their review and could not simply recognize their loss and be done with it. But they seemed unable to stop" (126). Nor could Bayley. "For the bereft, memory grows into obsession: It grows and grows." It was not simply remembrance of things past. "It was remembering the time that still seemed present" (*Widower's House* 136). After her death, he read all of her books—a formidable task. Unable to speak to her, he communicated in the way he knew best: "writing to her—with her, as it seemed—was the only way of communicating I still had" (136).

And then something peculiar happened. Bayley could not remember that he had started the present book about Iris. His short-term memory was so impaired—

he doesn't use the word *traumatized* but that seems to be what happened—that he forgot he had lain in bed in the early mornings after Iris's death and written about her illness and their life together. When he does remember, he searched the drawers and folders of his house, looking through old papers on the floor, to no avail. Mystified not only by what he had written but also by where he had misplaced the post-Iris writings, he continued the search. He describes his state of mind immediately following her death as like being in a "trance, when I seemed to live with the dead, and not with the living" (104). Then one day he found the writings, in a cardboard box stuffed with letters on the kitchen table. "I was still amazed, as I read, by the way I had forgotten all about it, as if memory had lost all function and purpose now that Iris was dead, and could refer only to the time she had been ill, and we had been together" (105).

Iris's death shattered Bayley's health. The grief immediately following her death had kept alive some of his feelings, "frenzies of rage and despair" as well as "fits of love," but with the passing of grief came thoughts of death, to which he returns for the first time since the beginning of *Iris and Her Friends*. "I felt not only that I had not been living since grief, now so much missed, started to go away, but that I hadn't wanted to live. I preferred the other thing: just waiting to die" (*Widower's House* 198). The arrival of two unusual women who do their best to attend to his emotional, physical, and sexual needs, Margot and Mella—pseudonyms, we learn, in the author's disclaimer at the beginning of *Widower's House*—helps to create the comic and at times farcical tone of the story. Neither woman, though, can supply Bayley with what he needs after Iris's death: mature companionship. That he received from an old friend, Audhild ("Audi") Villers, whom Bayley married in 2000, a year after Iris's death.

John Bayley died in 2015 at the age of eight-nine, leaving behind three memoirs that represent, to date, the most detailed and eloquent account of caregiving. No other author has written more lovingly about caregiving over an extended period of time, and no other author has dramatized the survival strategies necessary for caregiving. Nor has a memoirist expressed deeper gratitude toward a spouse. In an essay first published in the *London Review of Books* in 1985 and reprinted in *The Power of Delight* in 2005, Bayley noted that both Tolstoy and D. H. Lawrence omitted much from their autobiographical writings, particularly indebtedness toward their spouses. "The last ingratitude is the need to leave the person who has helped you become what you are" (584). No one could say that about Bayley. Combining psychological realism, philosophical wisdom, and literary power, Bayley's *Elegy for Iris*, *Iris and Her Friends*, and *Widower's House* reveal a vision of caregiving that will continue to inspire countless readers.

6

# A Few True Things about Caregiving in Anna Quindlen's *One True Thing*

In her 2000 book *A Short Guide to a Happy Life*, Anna Quindlen divides her life into two periods, before and after her mother's death from ovarian cancer on January 18, 1972, at age forty. "Before" was her freshman year of college, when the nineteen-year-old student enjoyed life away from home, free to do whatever she wished. "After" was the beginning of her sophomore year, when she reluctantly left Barnard College to return home, cook for her family, and administer morphine to her dying mother. The dividing line, she adds ruefully, was "seeing the world in black and white, and in Technicolor. The lights came on, for the darkest possible reason" (34). Prudence Quindlen's death profoundly changed the future writer's life, and her experience as a caregiver is the central event in her gripping 1994 semi-autobiographical novel *One True Thing*.

It took Quindlen several years before she was ready to confront the haunting specter of maternal loss. She opens her first book, *Living Out Loud*, a collection of essays originally published in the *New York Times* and republished in 1988, with a statement about how her mother's death transformed the lives of everyone in her family in ways that took them years to understand. She acknowledges in the second paragraph of *Living Out Loud* that writing about her mother's death is an "odd way" to begin the story of writing a column of personal reflections. In a later chapter, she admits that when she was the "temporary female caretaker" of four younger siblings, she was "desperate" to return to college to continue her education (87). After the death, she felt about Mother's Day the way recently divorced people feel about Valentine's Day. She offers few details about Prudence Quindlen's life apart from being a stay-at-home mother with traditional values. Mother and daughter evidently had little in common, particularly in their literary taste: pronouncing one of her daughter's favorite novels, *Portnoy's Complaint*, a "dirty" book, Prudence Quindlen hurled it across the living room "with such force that it bounced off the wall opposite" (197). Would mother and daughter have become closer in time? "I suspect that we would have been friends, but I don't really know. I was simply a little too young at nineteen to understand the woman inside the mother" (237).

It was not until the aftermath of her mother's death that Quindlen realized she would have to create a new life for herself. Orphaned and adrift, she felt that only by becoming a professional writer would she be able to come back from the dead. Some of the sentences in *Living Out Loud* have special significance to those who, like Quindlen, experienced early maternal loss. "No girl becomes a woman until she has lost her mother" (101)—a statement that also appears in *One True Thing* (331). Other observations describe the fears of those who have lost relatives to cancer, such as the fear that the disease is contagious. "If that had been true, of course, my father and I would have been goners. But deep inside, I, too, believed cancer was contagious—that is, you caught it from your parents" (231–2). The statement also appears in *One True Thing*: "'they all think cancer's contagious,' my mother had said wearily one afternoon of her friends" (154).

## Early Writings on the Caregiver's Dilemma

In 1992, Quindlen won the Pulitzer Prize for her *New York Times* column "Public and Private," but she never devoted a column in the *Times* or in *Newsweek*, where she worked from 1999 to 2009, to her experience as a caregiver. She wrote two columns, however, on subjects often associated with caregiving: physician-assisted suicide and euthanasia. Both columns prefigure *One True Thing* and deserve further scrutiny.

Quindlen's early writings capture the fierce controversies and shifting public attitudes surrounding end-of-life care. As Elizabeth Atwood Gailey observes in *Write to Life* (2003), a study of the American media's coverage of euthanasia news stories published from the 1970s to the late 1990s, only 37 percent of American adults in 1947 and about half of those polled in 1977 supported euthanasia. These figures rose dramatically by the beginning of the twenty-first century, when 65 percent of American citizens supported physician-assisted suicide and close to 75 percent supported euthanasia. The increased public mandate for the right-to-die movement is striking, Gailey reports, but powerful institutions remained opposed to it, including the American Medical Association and nearly all religious institutions, including Evangelical Christian denominations, the Roman Catholic Church, and orthodox Jewish, Greek, and Islamic faiths (1–3).

"Seeking a Sense of Control" was first published in the *New York Times* on December 10, 1990, and then reprinted in *Thinking Out Loud* in 1994. Quindlen draws attention to two fiercely controversial cases that highlighted the ambiguities of the right-to-die movement. The first case involved Janet Adkins, a fifty-four-year-old former English teacher who suffered from Alzheimer's disease and committed suicide. She was assisted by Jack Kevorkian, a "euthanasia entrepreneur" who used his home-made "suicide machine" to help her "go quietly into that good night" (49), an allusion to Dylan Thomas's iconic poem "Do Not Go Gently into That Good Night." Quindlen was no supporter of Kevorkian, "Dr. Death," whom she describes in the column as an "assisted suicide zealot" (50). Quindlen reports that Kevorkian was charged with first-degree murder, though three days after the publication of her article the charge was dismissed. Nine years later, Kevorkian, who claimed to have assisted 130 people end their lives, was convicted of second-degree murder and served eight years in prison. He was released on parole in 2007 and died in 2011.

The second case Quindlen discusses in "Seeking a Sense of Control" involved Nancy Cruzan, whose family sued the state of Missouri to allow her feeding tube to be removed after being in a vegetative coma for seven years. While commenting on the two cases, Quindlen refers to a friend's situation that clearly resembled her own, though her readers did not know it at the time. The friend's mother, dying of ovarian cancer, had a superb oncologist. "He was kind and considerate and explained all procedures thoroughly. But she blurted out what was his great virtue: 'He told me how many of my mother's painkillers constituted a lethal dose'" (49). Without elaborating on her friend's dilemma over whether to give her mother a lethal dose of morphine, Quindlen praises the doctors who temper science with mercy. Noting that "hard cases sometimes illuminate hard issues," Quindlen ends the column with a question that has become only more urgent over time: "The question of how and when we die, in an age of respirators and antibiotics and feed tubes, has become one of the great 'who decides?' issues of modern time" (50).

Quindlen opens the next essay in *Thinking Out Loud*, "A Time to Die," first published on June 3, 1990, with a vignette that foreshadows the narrator's dilemma in *One True Thing*: a man who, hearing stories by his wife, Ann, a nurse, of patients hooked to respirators and feeding tubes, declares, "If that ever happens to me, I want you to shoot me" (51). Years later, finding himself in the situation he most dreads, tethered to a feeding tube in a nursing home as a result of a grave accident, he is told by his wife that she cannot fulfill his request. Quindlen then returns to the caregiver's dilemma when ministering to the "living dead." Someday we may be the caregiver or care-receiver, she tersely reminds us. "There must be some reasonable way to allow someone to speak for us when we cannot speak for ourselves, some reasonable way to make the distinction between real life and the mirage modern medicine can create" (53). Near the end of "A Time to Die," Quindlen speculates that most people would want Ann to honor her husband's request to end his life. The last sentence prepares us for *One True Thing*. "'If he could talk,' Ann said, 'he'd be really angry at me for not doing what he asked'" (53).

Quindlen wrote "Seeking a Sense of Control" and "A Time to Die" to highlight the issues that she explores in greater depth in *One True Thing*. She began her career as a journalist and then became a novelist, much like Dickens, whose novels she cites throughout *One True Thing*. Details from real life pervade Quindlen's novel. Jack Kevorkian's prosecution parallels what happens to Quindlen's protagonist, Ellen Gulden, who cannot mitigate the suffering of her mother. Kate is desperate to retain a degree of control over her life, having reached the time to die, and her daughter confronts the horror of the living dead. The title of *One True Thing* is understated, for there are many authentic aspects of this moving story. Despite a serious flaw at the end of the novel that weakens its medical credibility, few caregiving stories are more emotionally wrenching or intellectually riveting than *One True Thing*.

## Beginning the Story

The prologue opens with Ellen reflecting on her brief experience in jail. She recalls in vivid detail lying on a cot and thinking about her mother who has died of cancer. Closing her eyes, Ellen imagines her mother crying for help: "for a cup of tea, a glass of water, a sandwich, more morphine" (5). Gradually we learn that Ellen's family lives in Langhorne, a small college town, and that her father is the chairperson of the English Department of Langhorne College, "a fine but somewhat obscure small liberal arts college, a kind of poor relation of the Swarthmores and the Haverfords" (52). Ellen has just been charged with killing her mother, and she cannot understand why her father has not come to bail her out of jail. The prologue ends with Ellen declaring that she did not kill her mother—though she wished she had, a statement that becomes more ominous as we progress through the nearly 400-page novel.

The power of *One True Thing* lies in its ability to show how illness disrupts a caregiver's personal and professional life. Ellen is a twenty-four-year-old Harvard honors graduate when she learns from her father that her mother is stricken with ovarian cancer. "'Your mother procrastinated,' he said, as though she was somehow to blame. 'First she thought she had the flu. Then she imagined she was expecting. She didn't want to make a fuss. You know how she is'" (24). The accusation reveals more about George Gulden than it does about the 46-year-old Kate, particularly his need to blame someone for her illness, which he finds inconvenient. It is difficult to sympathize with a person who appears to love his wife for better but not for worse, who refuses to take responsibility for his actions, and who is condescending and self-absorbed. Ellen has always been distant from her nonintellectual mother, with whom she counteridentifies, and close to her academic father, who is witty, ironic, and courtly. George Gulden looks better from afar—especially to his adoring students, who are willing to engage in amorous activities with this professor of desire. Part of Ellen's dilemma is to understand her father's weaknesses and her mother's strengths, and to align herself with a woman whom she has underappreciated her entire life.

George Gulden assumes that his intellectually accomplished and ferociously ambitious daughter, an editorial assistant and rising reporter for a major New York magazine—Anna Quindlen's life following her mother's death—will put her career on hold to nurse her dying mother so that he can continue to teach and, as he rationalizes, pay the medical bills. There is the implicit assumption in *One True Thing* that caregiving is a woman's responsibility. And indeed as I reported in the introduction, 80 percent of caregivers are women. When Ellen resists and instead recommends that her father hire a nurse or apply for a sabbatical, he responds angrily, "you have no heart" (30). The father knows how to play upon his daughter's guilt, especially when he tells her that "another woman is what's wanted here" (33). The relationship between father and daughter is not precisely that of Miss Havisham to Estella in Dickens's *Great Expectations*, but there is some of the parental coldness, self-centeredness, and manipulation. Professor Gulden has an apt pupil in his daughter, who has internalized his values and judgments. When he tells her that she must display empathy toward her mother, she retorts, reminiscent of Estella's response to Miss Havisham, "Empathy is the one thing I never really learned.... You never taught me empathy" (142). Unlike Miss Havisham, George Gulden has never been jilted in love, and so there is no explanation for why he is so unempathic throughout the novel, so unable or unwilling to care for the woman who has unselfishly dedicated her life to her husband and children.

Few stories capture more convincingly caregivers' reluctance to suspend their personal and professional lives to aid a loved one. Ellen believes during the beginning of her five months of caregiving that she has been forced against her will to play a role for which she has no interest, talent, or training. "I felt as though I was sinking beneath the weight of a life I had always viewed with something even more dismissive than contempt, a life I had viewed as though it were a feature in *National Geographic*, the anachronistic traditions of a distant tribe" (84). It's not simply the domestic responsibilities she resents: doing laundry, cooking meals, cleaning house, shopping for food, making the beds, not to mention driving her mother to the hospital every three weeks for chemotherapy. Watching her mother suffer is the worst part of caregiving, an ordeal that is almost unbearable.

Kate remains the moral center of the story, the character who doesn't allow suffering to blind her to others' needs. She not only brings out the best in people but also knows how to make others feel comfortable in her presence. Thus, she tries to hide the disintegration of her body from her daughter, not because she is in denial but because she doesn't want to burden her family. Kate is also, unexpectedly, the literary center of the novel, endowed with insights that would make her husband proud—if the English professor could understand them. She forms with Ellen the "Gulden Girls Book Group" in which they read *Pride and Prejudice*, *Great Expectations*, and *Anna Karenina*. She recalls reading the Jane Austen novel years earlier and being annoyed that Jane Bennet, the "sweet and domestic and good" sister—like Kate herself—is always playing "second fiddle" to the "smart and outspoken" Elizabeth (54). Kate's insight into *Pride and Prejudice*, which never feels didactic or out of character, conveys her own marital situation and the life lessons she tries to teach her daughter.

Quindlen's admiration for Kate never wavers. Until the end of the story, Ellen is often an unreliable narrator, overvaluing her father and undervaluing her mother. Kate, by contrast, has authorial knowledge. Referring implicitly to her husband's many infidelities, which Ellen can never forgive, Kate tells her, "There is nothing you know about your father that I don't know, too," adding, "And understand better" (224). The novelist never sentimentalizes the mother-daughter relationship. In the beginning Kate is an uncomplaining patient, distressed that Ellen has taken a leave of absence from work to care for her. "You'll hate me" (45), Kate predicts grimly. Months later the premonition appears to be correct. Hearing her mother make a shuffling sound, Ellen cannot prevent herself from thinking, "you have ruined my life. You have ruined my life with your damn selflessness, your damn accommodations, your damn illusions, your damn husband, and now your damn death" (151). Quindlen allows both care-receiver and caregiver to voice their darkest feelings, not simply grief and sorrow but also fury. Ellen feels like dying with her, breaking down, giving up, and she finds herself increasingly sobbing, losing control. As the disease spreads, and Kate is confined to a wheelchair, she begins to rage against family and friends. No longer able to care for herself, Kate feels humiliated by her dependence on others. "You want me to be dead," she shouts at her daughter, "You want me to die so you and your father can get on with your lives" (110). The wounding accusation conveys the darkest fears and wishes of the care-receiver and caregiver, respectively. Ellen finds herself tearfully telling her boyfriend that "If I had any guts at all I would hold a pillow over her face" (111), a statement that comes back to haunt her.

## Irremediable Pain

Nowhere is *One True Thing* more authentic than in depicting the harrowing pain of metastatic cancer. "Few novels have depicted so vividly and with such unflinching detail exactly what dying of cancer looks, smells and sounds like," Lynn Sharon Schwartz wrote in her *New York Times* review. "The physical renderings of helplessness and decay, however grim, are the transcendent passages, the moments in which the writing finds its best and truest voice." Of all the caregiving novels or memoirs I've read, none surpasses *One True Thing* in the evocation of physical and psychological suffering. Pain management becomes the overriding and all-consuming issue, and the need for ever-increasing doses of morphine for "breakthrough" pain is heartrending. Quindlen captures the brutality of suffering and the way it enfeebles Kate despite her previous strength. "'I need a pill, Ellen,' she said, the trace of a whine in the ebb and flow of her inflection" (151). Kate experiences hallucinations as a result of the morphine and gradually loses the will to live. Many caregivers will identify with George's statement that he cannot conceive of life without his spouse, as when he says to Ellen, "I can't imagine the light going out," to which she responds coldly, "You're talking about her as if she was already dead" (145), a reply that fails to understand the depth of anticipatory grief.

Gazing silently at her mother's suffering, Ellen feels like a "Peeping Tom" (219), the exact expression Quindlen uses in *Living Out Loud* to describe writing articles about others' unspeakable pain while she herself was healthy. "I did a magazine piece not long ago about breast cancer and I sat one night in a conference room listening to eight women talk about the feeling of taking off their blouses and seeing the zipper of the scar, and I sat there, my two perfectly good breasts slowly swelling with milk for the baby at home, and felt like the worst sort of voyeur, a Peeping Tom of the emotions" (226). Quindlen confesses feeling "disgust" at herself, yet at the same time she is proud of her newspaper article. Quindlen's honesty in both *Living Out Loud* and *One True Thing* reveals that empathy is seldom pure.

## Teresa Guerrero

Ellen refuses at first to allow a visiting nurse to make home visits to monitor Kate's vital signs. "Having a stranger in the house is too upsetting," Ellen tells Teresa Guerrero, the novel's "shrink-nurse" (206). "I cannot afford to fall apart," to which Teresa responds, "Falling apart is curling up into a fetal position and staying in bed for a week . . . . What you were doing is having the emotional response an individual has to the loss of someone they love. We cry to give voice to our pain" (161). Quindlen knows how unbearable it is for caregivers to witness their loved ones dying, how even when caregivers believe they cannot go on, they are able to call upon resources they didn't know existed. Ellen is comforted by Teresa's experiences with other terminally ill patients, including a woman with pancreatic cancer who died in her husband's arms in bed. Quindlen uses Teresa to bring clinical insights to the many challenges of caregiving, including offering practical advice to Ellen about how to clean her mother's urinary catheter and the side effects of morphine. Teresa makes other prescient observations to Ellen, reminding her that illness brings out different qualities in different people. "Some people have a talent for it and some rise to the occasion. And some are diminished by their fear. They often deny, or withdraw" (209–10). Quindlen ends the discussion perfectly, with Teresa maintaining that suffering "transforms," Ellen responding with "Suffering sucks," and Teresa having the last word: "I agree. With both conclusions, actually" (210). Illness indeed becomes in the novel a test of character: Ellen rises to the challenge, while her father retreats into himself.

*One True Thing* is unsurpassed in its depiction of suffering surrounding the end of life for both care-receiver and caregiver. Quindlen describes Ellen's horror when helping her mother, now broken in body and spirit, into the bathroom. The heartrending descriptions of her mother's wasted body, and the shame each feels over the degradation of life, are unforgettable. Like the dying Catherine Barkley at the end of Hemingway's *A Farewell to Arms*, only to a greater degree, Kate finds life no longer bearable, and her last words to Ellen are a cry for help that her daughter cannot heed. "'Help me, Ellen,' she whispered. 'I don't want to live like this anymore.'" They stare at each other, each wanting something the other cannot give. "'Please,' she said. 'You must know what to do. Please. Help me. No more.'" Ellen tries to be helpful by telling her that she will feel better in the morning, but Kate cannot be distracted. "'No,' she said, and groaned again. 'It will not. It will not.' She sounded like a tired and irritable child." The repetition of the dialogue emphasizes the desperation of her pleas. "'Help me,' she whispered. 'You're so smart. You'll know what to do.' Then her eyes closed completely. 'Please,' she whispered once more" (229). Days later, Ellen sees her father feeding Kate, slowly lifting a spoon of rice pudding into her mouth, hears them talking softly, and then he walks into his daughter's bedroom and repeats twice Kate's agonized plea to end her suffering: "No one should have to live like that. No one." Rubbing his eyes, he says, "She wants me to sleep with her in there," adding, "I can't. I can't. Not tonight. I'm going upstairs" (245). Ellen then goes into her mother's room, witnesses her strained breathing, falls asleep, and when she wakes up in the morning, Kate is dead.

Two weeks after her mother's death, Ellen is informed that a pathologist found something suspect during her mother's autopsy, and thus begins another nightmare for her, almost excruciating as watching Kate die. The cause of death is not cancer but an overdose of morphine. Suddenly Ellen is the only suspect in what appears to be an act of euthanasia—the word means "easy death" in Greek. Events conspire against Ellen. The media publicize her prize-winning high school essay advocating euthanasia, and her statements sound incriminating, as when she exclaims to her mother's oncologist, Dr. Cohn, who ordered the autopsy and then dutifully conveys the results to the district attorney, "Who cares how she died? She should have been put out of her misery weeks ago. If she had been a dog they would have" (257).

Ellen fails to take seriously the charge against her, which only increases public support for her prosecution. The district attorney asks for help from a famous pathologist in Florida, and the school board considers disciplinary action against Ellen's high school English teacher, Mrs. Forburg, who befriends her. Meanwhile, community opposition to her is fueled by a Kevorkian-like "doctor death" who hooks patients up to IV drips elsewhere in the country. Ellen receives crank calls from both opponents and proponents of euthanasia, despite the fact that she keeps saying, "I didn't do it." Most of the residents of Langhorne assume that Ellen killed her mother, but they believe that she has done it out of kindness, not malice, as some people claim. Her boyfriend, with whom she has broken off relations, vindictively provides evidence against her, and her father, whom she suspects gave her mother the fatal overdose, refuses to support her. Ellen remains silent about her suspicions, vowing to protect him one final time. Her estrangement from him is now complete. She neither forgets nor forgives his accusation that she is heartless.

## Rejecting Sensationalistic Language

How does Ellen feel about euthanasia? She admits that her jejune high school essay now strikes her as glib and self-righteous. Quindlen intersperses the language written by the seventeen-year-old with the mocking criticisms of her lawyer, Bob Greenstein, who voices the novelist's disapproval over Ellen's sensationalistic prose. Ellen's tabloid style could not be more different from Quindlen's nuanced language in her *New York Times* op-ed columns. "True, but reductive," the reader wants to say about Ellen's essay, to use the refrain expressed by Mrs. Forburg, who functions as an authorial guide in the story. To contrast further the differences between novelist and narrator, Quindlen has Ellen acknowledge to her lawyer that she had invented some of the details of her high school essay, such as the incident in which she describes a fifteen-year-old dog being euthanized.

Ellen now recognizes a world of difference between the theory and practice of euthanasia. When her attorney asks her whether she discussed the essay with her parents, Ellen recalls vaguely that her mother thought euthanasia was a "horrible subject" and that her father was "livid" because the essay contained a grammatical mistake near the end: "A 'that' where a 'which' should be" (301). Ellen cannot bring herself to carry out her mother's request for death, but she admires her father for apparently doing so.

> Perhaps she had asked of him, that last night when I heard them talking, what she had asked of me and he had had the courage and the love to do what I had not. For that possibility alone I believed he deserved my protection. At least that is how I think I felt when the woman I am today analyzes the one I was then. (267)

Quindlen interjects much-needed humor during this moment in the form of the lawyer's mocking evaluation of Ellen's prose style. "Blah blah blah blah" is spot-on in its recognition of Ellen's oversimplifications. Greenstein puts into practice Hemingway's injunction that the most essential gift for a good writer is a "built-in, shockproof, shit detector. This is the writer's radar and all good writers have had it" (*Paris Review Interviews*, vol. 1, 61). George Gulden's response, criticizing his daughter for confusing a restrictive clause with a nonrestrictive one, only calls attention to his pedantry. And what is apparent only on a second reading of the novel is the masterful plot that contains a stunning surprise for the reader.

During the grand jury proceedings, the prosecutor, Ed Best, asks Ellen whether she believes that her mother's life in her final days was "worth living." Ellen objects to the wording and offers the same language that many caregivers would use to describe their loves ones' final weeks alive:

> I think my mother had lost her dignity, her place, all the things that made her life happy. She was wearing diapers. She was sleeping almost constantly. And for a woman like her, who'd always been so capable, so full of life, so lively—it was a terrible thing. It was terrible for her and it was terrible for me. (345)

The prosecutor then asks her, quoting her earlier words, if she believes "there are times when someone's quality of life is so compromised that death, whether natural or assisted, would be preferable," to which she answers in the affirmative. She responds in the same way when asked whether she believes that her mother's quality of life was "horribly impaired at the end of her life" (347). But she denies that she gave her mother a fatal overdose and then offers a moving statement about why she wrote an essay supporting euthanasia but could not act on her beliefs. "It's so much easier to know just how you feel about things, what you believe, when you're writing it on paper than when you really have to do anything about it or live with it" (348).

This comment underscores the differences between caregiving in theory, revealed in self-help books, and caregiving in reality, dramatized in complex novels like *One True Thing*. Quindlen shows us the endless challenges of caregiving, conveying the tangled emotions experienced by both the care-receiver and caregiver. She reveals as much of the *lived* reality of caregiving as is possible in a novel, the subjective truths, rarely spoken or written, surrounding grief: "Loss as muse. Loss as character. Loss as life," as she wrote in the 1994 article "Public & Private; Life After Death" published first in the *New York Times* and then in her 2004 book *Loud and Clear* (224). One of the ironies of *One True Thing* is that Professor Gulden has the experience of witnessing caregiving, but he misses the meaning of it. He remains, despite his graduate training in literary studies, the least authorially reliable character in the story, both narcissistic and solipsistic. Another irony is that Ellen, who speaks for Quindlen here, fails to convey how penning a novel about caregiving helps the writer understand feelings that rarely can be understood at the time of caregiving. And a third irony is that Ellen never speaks about the aesthetic pleasure of reading a masterfully crafted novel like *One True Thing*.

The grand jury decides not to indict Ellen for her mother's death, and the news makes the AP wire. In an epilogue that takes place eight years after Kate's death, we learn that Ellen has changed careers, rejecting the life of a writer for that of a psychiatrist. It is never entirely clear why she has gone into psychiatry. Perhaps she believes that it is more important to help people deal with psychological problems than to write articles and books about issues that fail to capture the complexity of the truth. "It was the idea of facing a future skimming the surface of life, winging my way in and out of other people's traumas, crises, confusions, and passages, engaging them enough to get the story but never enough to be indelibly touched by what I had seen or heard" (366). Perhaps she is drawn to psychiatry as a career to help others work through their grief and guilt over loss, as she herself has been helped. Only once does Ellen refer to being in therapy after her mother's death, but the reference is significant. "'As her daughter, would you have behaved differently?' my therapist asked once, with an unaccustomed gleam in her eye. And the answer is that, knowing then what I know now, I would have. I would have given her more opportunities to talk, to complain, to fantasize, to weep, to speak. But that is what I am in the business of doing now, and it sounds easier in retrospect" (373–4). Caregivers serve many roles, including that of listener, enabling care-receivers to narrate the stories of their lives, especially feelings about the end of their lives. Another possible reason Ellen has changed careers is because the life of a writer is too close to her father's profession.

## A Startling Ending

Ellen is estranged from her father at the end of the story, while her mother's absent presence is alive and real. Ellen remains bitter about the legal proceedings against her, but far worse than the bitterness is her inability to exorcise the memory of her mother's horrific death. In her final encounter with her father, a serendipitous meeting at a play in Manhattan, she sees him standing outside the theater. They begin their conversation in the old bantering way, and when she tells him that she has become a psychiatrist, working with depressed and suicidal adolescents, he responds glibly—and in character: "the stuff of fiction." Ellen is the true student of literature, recognizing its profound insights into life and its value as a therapeutic instrument. She tells her father that she has asked one of her patients, a young woman who tried to drink herself to death at a small liberal arts college, to read *Wuthering Heights*, which explores the impact of maternal loss on a husband, lover, and daughter. "You assign the Brontës to the mentally ill?," George asks Ellen, incredulously, to which she responds, "It will help her understand compulsion" (381).

Quindlen then discloses the most electrifying irony in the novel: each believes the other has been responsible for Kate's death. "I never, ever blamed you," George tells his daughter. "I would have done what you did in your position. Perhaps I should have." As Ellen stares in shock and disbelief, he adds, "It was the right thing to do. It took a good deal of courage. Real courage. Valor. I couldn't say that at the time because of the circumstances.... I wish I'd done it myself" (381).

"Two brilliant fools," Ellen thinks as she realizes suddenly the unthinkable. Kate had deliberately taken the overdose of morphine. Like her father, Ellen didn't believe that her mother "had it in her," implying that the suicide was an act of desperate courage and strength. Ellen decides to withhold the truth from her father. "I suppose in some strange way he honored me with his assumption and I was damned if I would tell him otherwise. Let him think of me as a heroine from some little story" (383). Wondering how she could have so misread her mother, Ellen questions how she could have misread herself. Her final revelation is the lesson her mother has taught her, that "it was possible to love and care for a man and still have at your core a strength so great that you never even needed to put it on display" (386). In death, as in life, Kate remains a muse, providing life lessons for her daughter.

Among these life lessons is the power of empathy, understanding another person's hidden life. Tellingly, the three people who teach Ellen the most about empathy are her mother, Teresa Guerrero, and Mrs. Forburg, confirming psychological research that women tend to be more empathic than men. All three reflect Quindlen's own empathy. Not all of Quindlen's readers have appreciated her empathy—a few have sharply criticized it. In an article published in *The New Republic* in 1999, Lee Siegel characterized Quindlen as one of the "monsters of empathy," a demonization that displays the resistance empathy engenders in some readers.

## The Double Effect

The grand jury investigation of Ellen is the only serious flaw in *One True Thing*, the one detail, ironically, that is not true. Few if any oncologists, either during the time the novel was written or now, would order an autopsy to determine if a terminally ill cancer patient, whose body was wasted from disease, died of an overdose of morphine. As Ira Byock states, "With severe pain, there is no maximum dose of pain medication; the right dose is the one that works" (206). Kate's oncologist would have prescribed as much morphine as necessary to diminish the pain. Some oncologists would have ordered, with the dying person's or family's permission, sufficient morphine to alleviate the pain even if the dose is fatal. This principle, called by the Roman Catholic Church the "double effect," implies, as bioethicist Margaret Pabst Battin states in *The Least Worst Death*, that "one may perform an action with a bad effect—for instance, the death of a person—provided one foresees but does not intend that bad effect; one must be doing the act to achieve a different goal (hence the name, 'double' effect)" (17).

Four conditions must be met to justify the double effect: "the action must not be intrinsically wrong"; "the agent must intend only the good effect, not the bad one"; "the bad effect must not be the means of achieving the good effect"; and "the good effect must be 'proportional' to the bad one, that is, outweigh it" (17). Battin cites the example commonly used in Catholic moral theology: "a surgeon may remove a cancerous uterus in order to save the life of the mother, though this will also bring about the death of a fetus developing there, provided the surgeon's intention is to save the mother: the surgeon foresees, but does not intend, that the procedure will kill the fetus" (17). An even more common example is a physician prescribing a massive dose of morphine to allay a terminally ill patient's unendurable pain, knowing that it will lead to death.

Kate's situation meets all four criteria of the double principle, and for this reason no autopsy would have been ordered. Nor would there have been a suspicion of foul play, regardless of a caregiver's stated position on euthanasia. Ellen's legal problem undoubtedly heightens the novel's plot interest, but it is not medically realistic. Given the novel's flawed assumption that a fatal overdose of morphine to a terminally ill patient is illegal, it is surprising that Ellen does not feel resentment toward her mother for potentially implicating the family in a crime. And it is unlikely that a lucid Kate would have taken a fatal overdose had she realized that her actions might lead to her daughter's or husband's arrest.

What *is* realistic is Ellen's psychological conflict over euthanasia. Since neither the doctors nor nurses informed her about the possibility of prescribing a massive dose of morphine that would end Kate's suffering and life, Ellen cannot avail herself of this option. Nor is the option discussed publicly. As Ian Dowbiggin explains in *A Merciful End*, a study of the euthanasia movement in the United States, there is often a sharp difference between what physicians do and say regarding end-of-life care. Dowbiggin's observation about the 1960s is no less true of the present. "Privately, doctors often withheld treatment from dying patients or eased them out of their misery. Publicly, however, they tended to dodge the issue and stand behind their profession's position that the doctor's goal was to try to keep patients alive, not hasten their departure from this world" (78).

Ambiguities inhere in the double effect. As Bonnie Steinbock observes in the introduction to her edited volume *Killing and Letting Go*, doctors may perform a hysterectomy on a pregnant woman if she has cancer of the uterus, but, by contrast, a "woman whose life is endangered by a pregnancy because of a heart condition, kidney disease, or tuberculosis may not abort, according to Catholic law" (13). Dan Brock points out that there is "controversy in the anesthesia literature about whether heavily sedated persons are actually free of suffering or simply unable to report or remember it. Although such patients are probably not conscious of their condition once sedated, their death is unlikely to be dignified or remembered as peaceful by their families" (133). The double effect has generated controversy over "how to distinguish direct and indirect intention, between effects that are intended and effects that are foreseen but not intended" (17).

Many authors of books on dying and death do not mention the double effect, even when they discuss euthanasia and physician-assisted suicide. Sherwin Nuland, for example, does not discuss the double effect in *How We Die*, his acclaimed 1993 study that Quindlen includes among the "10 Nonfiction Books That Help Us Understand the World" (*How Reading Changed My Life*, 73). Ira Byock does not mention the double effect in *Dying Well*, but it's clear from his discussion of a patient named Terry, who is in horrific pain despite taking "megadoses of morphine," that the decision to give her an infusion of the drug thiopental will produce a deep sleep from which she will probably not awake. Both she and her family agree to this, and she never regains consciousness. Byock concludes his discussion by noting that the "story of Terry and her family explores the fine line between sedation for the treatment of extreme terminal pain and euthanasia . . . . People unfamiliar with the purposes of palliative care may see little difference between sedation to control persistent physical distress and euthanasia. What may appear philosophically a fine line is, in practice, a chasm" (216).

There are also uncertainties over the effectiveness of pain medication. The oncologist Alan Astrow concedes that the "line between relief of suffering and end of life is often blurred" (45). Despite treating many patients whose uncontrolled tumors have produced "intractable pain," he nevertheless opposes physician-assisted suicide, maintaining that "in most cases . . . a withdrawal of active medical treatment combined with unstinting use of analgesics and sedatives to control symptoms allows the patient to die comfortably and peacefully" (45). Astrow doesn't indicate whether "most instances" is closer to 51 percent, 99 percent, or somewhere in the middle. One physician, Ira Byock, *guarantees* that his patients will not suffer physically. "Pain and other physical symptoms caused by advanced disease usually yield to relatively simple treatment" (215).

## *Lots of Candles, Plenty of Cake*

In her most recent memoir *Lots of Candles, Plenty of Cake* (2012), Quindlen offers new information about her role of caregiver and her mother's death, allowing us to see the similarities and differences between real life and fiction. She emphasizes how unprepared she was to be her mother's caregiver, and how unwilling her mother was to be a care-receiver. "When I showed up, with bad grace and humor, to take over her life, it must have seemed as though she was diminished, defeated, perhaps already dead" (176). Prudence Quindlen died in a hospital, not at home, and there's no hint of physician-assisted suicide or euthanasia. Quindlen saw her as a "sacrificial mother" (164), the same image that appears in *One True Thing*. Quindlen characterizes herself in the memoir as a "reluctant caregiver" (81), resentful of the role her father thrust upon her. "When my father demanded that I quit college to care for my mother when she was ill, I occasionally made bitter comments about the tradition of Irish Catholic households sacrificing their daughters for the greater good. But it wasn't just my father, and it wasn't just the Irish, and it wasn't just then" (134). For whatever reasons, Quindlen tells us little about Kate's ethnicity or religious beliefs; we learn only that she was a lapsed Catholic—"or perhaps not so lapsed, in her heart" (27). Like Kate, Prudence Quindlen's belief that she was again pregnant compelled her to visit her physician, only to find out she had metastatic cancer. During the last months of her life, she indeed looked pregnant, swollen with cancer. "A woman who had spent the best years of her life in maternity clothes, she sickened and died in them as well" (163).

English professors, unlike high school English teachers, do not fare well in Quindlen's world. She describes in *How Reading Changed My Life* an English professor who may have unwittingly inspired the portrait of Ellen's father. Recalling her love for John Galworthy's 1922 *The Forsyte Saga* despite her recognition of its aesthetic weaknesses, Quindlen confesses that she cannot read it without remembering the one-word reaction of the chairperson of the English department at her college who responded: "'Galsworthy!' he spit out with a mixture of condescension and disbelief, as though he had found a pit in a fruit that had promised to be seedless. And so a dream died" (35).

## Robert Quindlen

There's some evidence that Quindlen's fictional portrait of George Gulden is loosely modeled on her own father, Robert Quindlen, particularly his demand that she return home from college to care for her mother. Sounding like a less embittered Ellen Gulden, Quindlen remarks in *Loud and Clear* that she was raised as her father's "oldest son" and that their relationship was "man-to-man" (42–3). Her father's expectations—"A curse, a blessing, all in one"—were hard on her but took her places she would never have gone otherwise (44). Without elaborating on the terrible irony, she observes that her father's second wife died of the same disease that killed his first one. In her commencement address given at Villanova University in 2000, the novelist mentioned a postcard her father had sent her: "If you win the rat race, you're still a rat" (*A Short Guide to a Happy Life* 7), an aphorism that George Gulden might have expressed sardonically. In a 2014 article in *Good Housekeeping*, Quindlen refers to her father as a "single older man who would reflexively and unobjectionably propose to waitresses and nurses," another quality that we can imagine to be true of an aging George Gulden.

Robert Quindlen resembled his daughter in his wish to retain control over his life, as she reveals in the *Good Housekeeping* article, in which she describes a one-page document he wrote to her, "The Funeral," containing his wishes for his funeral service. "The funeral memo was detailed and specific: the name of the funeral home, the readings from the Old Testament and New Testaments, the priests who should be on the altar." When he suffered third-degree burns in the fall of 2013, at the age of eighty-three, he was taken to a burn unit, where his daughter asked tough questions about the realistic benefits of aggressive treatments. The physicians made her feel "like a good daughter, and not the opposite," for asking those questions, she stated at the American Academy of Family Physicians Assembly in Washington on October 23, 2013. "They made me feel like I had power and control in a situation where I could have felt powerless" (Mitchell). Quindlen kept her father's end-of-life document in her purse. Anna Quindlen's father died, presumably without aggressive treatment, in October 2013.

## Grist for the Writer's Mill

Anna Quindlen discloses in *Lots of Candles, Plenty of Cake* that she felt "powerless, trapped, enfeebled" in her role as her mother's caregiver. This had less to do with her mother, whom she loved, than her mother's life as a suburban housewife in a large family. "I was afraid of the briars of housewifery turning me into a Sleeping Beauty, taking away Doris Lessing and Simone de Beauvoir and leaving me with *Joy of Cooking*, Jacqueline Suzanne, and slipcovers" (164). As happens often, the dying care-receiver has much to teach the caregiver. "She sat in the kitchen in her wheelchair and taught me to cook, mostly things I still make for my family today, tomato sauce and meatballs, meatloaf with a latticework of bacon on top, chicken Parmigiano" (163).

Quindlen is keenly aware of the intergenerational nature of caregiving and care-receiving, how children of caregivers wonder how they will themselves become caregivers one day. She never romanticizes caregiving or implies that she knew what she was doing at the time. "When my daughter was nineteen she wrote to me that she could scarcely believe she was the age at which I had taken over the house and the children, the pain management and the hospital visits. But I didn't take them over so much as live through them" (164). The hardest part of caregiving for Quindlen was helping her mother deal with the spiritual and existential aspects of dying, a task she felt she was too young to perform.

Perhaps the most intriguing insight in *Lots of Candles, Plenty of Cake* is the dying Prudence Quindlen's recognition that her daughter would later write about her life and death. "Now you'll have something to write about," her mother told her, a comment the daughter found "appalling" because of the suggestion that she could be generous only if there was something in it for her, material for a future story (165). Did Prudence Quindlen's comment about the opportunistic nature of art, where everything is grist for the writer's mill, heighten her daughter's fear that she was voyeuristic, a Peeping Tom, turning the most private act imaginable into public art, for everyone to read? The dying mother may not have expressed this remark maliciously, but it's easy to see how she might have felt ambivalent about the situation. We can only begin to imagine Quindlen's formidable challenge in writing about her mother's death, the single most transformative event in her life, as she implies in her memoir: "motherhood, and loss. That's what I write about most often" (168).

Readers are left with many questions at the end of *One True Thing*, including the impact of Kate's suicide on her family's future life. This may seem a curious question, but suicide often has unintended consequences, as Andrew Solomon reveals in his magisterial study of depression, *The Noonday Demon* (2002). His mother, Carolyn Bowers Solomon, suffered from metastatic ovarian cancer for two years, and after several rounds of chemotherapy, she made the fateful decision to end her life, with her husband's and two sons' reluctant support, on June 19, 1991, at age fifty-eight. As I discuss in *Mad Muse*, Solomon describes the suicide in his largely autobiographical 1991 novel *A Stone Boat*. Mother and son are so closely intertwined that each feels sickened by the other: "my mother accused me of giving her cancer," an accusation that he suspects is true (33). The mother's suicide infects the son with the same desire for self-extinction. "I imagined it as though it were a form of vengeance" (141). Solomon is a proponent of "rational suicide," but in *The Noonday Demon* he discusses how, through the contagion effect, his mother's suicide heightened his own suicidality. "It is not savory, in political terms, to conflate suicide in the face of psychiatric illness with suicide in the face of physical illness, but I think there are surprising similarities" (280). Unlike Solomon, Quindlen never wrote about becoming clinically depressed after her mother's death, nor did she write about becoming suicidal, but it's likely that she identified with his ambivalence in disclosing the event, including a writer's fear of invading his family's privacy. Solomon believed the publication of *A Stone Boat* would free him from his demons, but the novel's appearance had the opposite effect, consuming him with self-reproach: "the more I tried not to think about my mother in this situation, the more the 'internalized love-object' of my mother obtruded" (*The Noonday Demon* 326).

In light of Solomon's statement, it is possible to interpret the grand jury proceedings against Ellen as a metaphor of her guilt for harboring the wish for her mother's death. Like Solomon, Ellen is filled with anger, regret, and self-reproach. This is often caregivers' plight: struggling with dark emotions they can neither understand nor at times control. Indeed, in many, if not most, caregiving novels and memoirs, the caregiver expresses homicidal thoughts toward the care-receiver and then, feeling guilty for these musings, internalizes them in the form of a suicidal wish. There is, admittedly, one serious objection to viewing the grand jury proceedings as a metaphor of Ellen's need for self-punishment: she never reaches this interpretation herself either during her long therapy or as a psychiatrist working with troubled adolescents. Nevertheless, many caregivers harbor aggressive feelings toward both care-receivers and themselves, and sometimes they place themselves on trial and judge themselves guilty of crimes committed or imagined.

## The Film

"I'll sell my story to television" (360), Ellen jokes near the end of the novel. Sarcasm became prophecy, and in 1998 the film version of *One True Thing* appeared, directed by Carl Franklin and starring Meryl Streep (nominated for an Academy Award for Best Actress) as Kate, William Hurt as George, and Renée Zellweger as Ellen. Although Siskel and Ebert awarded the film "two thumbs up!," the director made several changes that weaken the story's ironic ending. Throughout the film Ellen is talking to the district attorney, and we see her in one scene crush several morphine pills into powder, but she is never brought before a grand jury. The last scene in the film occurs a couple of months after the funeral, when George visits Kate's grave and sees Ellen planting daffodils. As in the novel, each believes the other has been responsible for Kate's death, but unlike the novel, Ellen does not withhold the full truth from her father. "Dad, I didn't do it. I didn't do it. I thought that—All this time, I thought that it was you." Ellen does not change careers in the film nor is there the suggestion of a long-lasting estrangement between father and daughter. "My one true thing," George intones in admiration of Kate's strength to end her life. "Of course she did it. Who else would've had the strength?" Both novel and film link Kate's suicide to the right-to-die movement without suggesting, as opponents of physician-assisted death have warned, the slippery slope leading to the duty to die.

## Later Writings

Quindlen's internalized love-object, to use Solomon's words, is apparent in her later novels, where she affirms the importance of caregiving and explores the dynamics of survivor guilt. The caregiver in *Blessings* (2002) is a young man, Skip, who comes across an abandoned infant and cares for her as if she is his own. He is an only child, "the last healthy thing his mother had managed before she faltered and faded into a life of vague physical complaints that ended with the big finale of breast cancer" (19). Called "Mr. Mom," Skip instinctively knows how to care for the baby, and at novel's end he unselfishly gives her up to the returning mother. In *Every Last One* (2010), Mary Beth Latham confronts a shocking act of violence, the murder of her husband and two of her children. Her only surviving child, Max, is now in therapy, and his therapist helps her realize the reality of survivor guilt and the need to talk about death, the one subject no one wishes to discuss.

It's not usual for a young Quindlen character to put her life on hold to care for an aging relative. This can be seen in *Miller's Valley* (2016), when Mimi, in a moment reminiscent of Quindlen's own life, wryly thinks of herself as a spinster, "cooking, cleaning, taking my father for hospital appointments and long drives with no destination. Somewhere nineteen-year-old girls were going to parties, but I wasn't one of them" (180). In *Still Life with Crumbs* (2013), Quindlen fictionalizes her younger sister's difficulty in coming to terms with early maternal loss. Polly Bates

> was ten when her mother died, although all of that dying stuff was only words, as far as she was concerned: no one took her to the hospital or the funeral home or the cemetery. It was all considered too upsetting for a child. Her brother argued otherwise, but conventional wisdom prevailed, which was how she wound up thinking that her mother had merely packed up and moved away, perhaps impressed by a TV news story at the time about a woman who had done just that, left her five sons behind with their father and turned up later in Portland, selling real estate. (161)

Polly has never been the same following her mother's death. Doctors variously described Polly as schizophrenic or bipolar, and her brother, Tom, who attempts to be her caregiver, can only speculate on whether she would have been healthy if their mother hadn't died. Before her own premature death, when she lies down on the snow and freezes to death, Polly has given away her scant possessions, "suicide notes," in Tom's bitter words. Rebecca Winter, the novel's aging heroine who is at a crossroads in life, photographs these objects, transmuting them into startlingly original art. A meditation on love and loss, *Still Life with Crumbs* shows, like *One True Thing*, how fiction often arises from loss, and how the novelist is a caregiver for the living and the dead.

Literature abounds in countless insights into caregiving, but not everyone can appreciate these truths. The Guldens are a literary family, but George Gulden can find neither comfort nor solace in reading when his wife becomes ill. "All fiction takes as its great central mystery death, mortality, but it seems to me now that all of it misses the point" (145). How can a literature professor fail to see the healing power of fiction, both for the writer and reader? Hasn't he read *The Death of Ivan Ilych*? Ellen loves literature but rejects it as a career. Of all the characters in *One True Thing*, Mrs. Forburg remains "ever anxious," in Ellen's words, "to discuss the link between literature and life but not judgmental about opinions that diverged from her own" (289). Quindlen acknowledges in *How Reading Changed My Life* that literature has saved her from isolation, loneliness, and despair. Quoting

Kafka's statement, "a book should serve as the ax for the frozen sea within us," she argues that women writers, in their efforts to understand the "emotional underpinnings of other people's problems," should be willing to break the ice (28). Quindlen ends *Imagined London* (2004) by proclaiming that she could not fathom living without the writers mentioned in her book. "In a world that seems increasingly senseless and graceless, they bring intelligence to bear on the human condition" (162).

## The Legacy of Maternal Loss

"Throughout history," Hope Edelman writes in *Motherless Daughters*, "early mother loss has acted as an impetus for a daughter's later success" (260). She gives several literary examples of eminent women who lost their mothers during childhood or adolescence, including Dorothy Wordsworth (at birth), Harriet Beecher Stowe (age five), Charlotte, Emily, and Anne Brontë (five, three, and one, respectively), Virginia Woolf (thirteen), George Eliot (sixteen), and Gertrude Stein (fourteen). Edelman might have also included Mary Shelley, the author of *Frankenstein*, who lost her mother, Mary Wollstonecraft, at birth. *Motherless Daughters* was published in the same year, 1994, as *One True Thing*. Edelman was seventeen when her mother died of breast cancer at age forty-two in 1981, and she recalls in the introduction how she read and reread Quindlen's newspaper column about being a motherless daughter. "It was the first time I'd come across another woman who admitted to feeling as I did—very much as I did" (xix).

For her research, Edelman interviewed 92 motherless women in person and surveyed 154 by mail. Many of her observations about motherless daughters who become caregivers apply to Quindlen. "The adolescent who must become the nurse for an ailing mother, a parent for younger siblings, or a caretaker for a grieving father may develop characteristics such as compassion and empathy that serve her well in the future" (53). But the caretaking role is a premature one for an adolescent girl, Edelman adds; "it hurtles her into the responsibilities of a later developmental stage before she can complete the one she was in. It also forces her into maturity at exactly the time she needs to regress and be taken care of" (53–4).

Edelman found that children who lose their parents at a young age generally respond in one of two ways: they either become fatalistic, expecting and succumbing to failure, or resilient, finding the motivation to succeed after loss.

According to Edelman, two conditions must be necessary for a motherless daughter to succeed: "the drive to accomplish goals early and evidence of an already existing artistic or intellectual talent" (260). Both factors may be seen in Ellen Gulden and her creator, Anna Quindlen. Maternal loss hovers over a daughter's later life, even, indeed, especially, when she becomes a mother herself. In the epilogue, Edelman makes a statement that is no less true of Quindlen as a parent, caregiver, and writer: "To be a motherless daughter is to be riddled with contradictions and uncertainties, but it is also to know the grit of survival, and to hold an insight and maturity others did not obtain so young, and to understand the power of renewal and birth" (279). *One True Thing* remains, of all caregiving novels, an example of art arising from loss, penned by a caregiver whose devotion to her mother continues in story after story.

# 7

# The Avenging Caregiver in Mary Gordon's *Circling My Mother*

Like Anna Quindlen, Mary Gordon was herself a caregiver, nursing her maternal grandmother during the year before her death in 1962, when Gordon was not yet a teenager. "When I think about it now," she told Alma Bennett in an interview published in the *South Carolina Review* in 1995, "and I would think about it when my daughter Anna was twelve . . . the kind of things I was asked to do at twelve was just unbelievable. I was changing colostomies, I was using suction machines when my grandmother was choking. Everybody just thought, 'Well, she's there.' It was really awful . . . awful" (9; ellipses in original). As if caring for her grandmother was not difficult enough, Gordon volunteered in a nursing home for a week, an experience that demonstrated the depth of her commitment to elderly people. "It really did depress me," she admitted in an interview when she was twenty-eight. "They wanted so much—I just felt their desire for connection and for love was so overwhelming that I felt swallowed up by it" (*Conversations with Mary Gordon* 4).

Gordon, born in 1949, and Quindlen, born in 1952, have much in common. Both have been strongly influenced by Irish Catholicism. Both suffered early parental loss. Both were forced, reluctantly, to become caregivers at an early age, an experience that each found wrenching and life-transforming. Both counteridentified, as did Alice Munro, with their nonliterary mothers. Both graduated from Barnard College and had similar careers (Gordon as a literature professor, Quindlen as a journalist) before becoming novelists. Both authored several books before they were ready to write about their caregiving experiences. The differences between the two women are also significant. Gordon has *twice* been a caregiver, first for her grandmother, who died of cancer, and then, decades later, for her mother, who died of Alzheimer's disease.

Why, asked Bennett in her 1995 interview, was Gordon forced to become a caregiver at such a young age? "My mother, I think, was so worried that they [Gordon's maternal grandmother's children] were going to throw us out of the house, and also my mother thought I could do anything. She thought I was endlessly competent. And it was that kind of peasant thing where adolescence was already the end of childhood." When asked how she felt about living in her grandmother's home, Gordon laughed: "I would just torch it if I could" (9–10).

Gordon did not set her grandmother's house on fire, but her literary reputation was ignited with the publication of her acclaimed debut novel *Final Payments* in 1978, which was named one of the outstanding books of the year by the *New York Times* and nominated for the National Book Critics Circle Award. The author of many bestselling novels and memoirs, as well as the recipient of a number of literary prizes, including an O. Henry Award, Gordon was named the official New York State Author in 2008, receiving the Edith Wharton Citation of Merit for Fiction. She is also the McIntosh Professor of English at Barnard College. A fearless writer, she has aroused sharp controversy for exposing the dark side of subjects like caregiving and martyrdom, topics to which she returns repeatedly in her novels and memoirs.

## A Traumatic Subject

In her 2000 book *Seeing Through Places: Reflections on Geography and Identity*, Gordon reveals the agonizing details of caring for her grandmother. She succeeds in awakening within the reader the sense of revulsion she experienced at the time. "She lay in her bed, silent, and stunned. Like a child, she had to be changed several times a day. The smell of the shit that came out of the hole in her stomach permeated the house, and I was never free of it" (170). Gordon's language suddenly becomes startlingly metaphorical, and she uses a word to describe her dying grandmother, "rot," that she uses elsewhere, in her two memoirs, to describe her own mother. "I felt as if I was watching a giant tree rot steadily from the blight that spread inside her, a blight whose manifestation I could see: the red, raw bump on her stomach that had to be kept scrupulously clean" (170).

Gordon doesn't accuse her mother of child abuse, but that's what she implies when she recalls being ordered as a twelve-year-old to care for her dying grandmother. "Her smell, and the constant gurgling in her throat overpowered me. They were the atmosphere in which I lived, I had to give in to them, take them into my own body, I was saturated in them, they were too powerful for me to escape or to avoid" (170-1). The only able-bodied person living in the house—her mother was struck by polio at the age of three and permanently handicapped—Gordon was forced to take over nearly all the caregiving responsibilities:

> Retching, I would dip rags into the blue tin basin by her bed. I undid the colostomy's complicated bandage with its twelve interlocking tails. I washed around her bump, then disinfected it. I rubbed Vaseline on her stomach and covered the area in gauze. I took a new bandage from the pile of clean ones and rebandaged her, weaving the tails securely so that there would be no leaks. It didn't occur to me to ask if I could be spared these jobs. (172)

Gordon's traumatic experience as her grandmother's caregiver reminds us of Charles Dickens, who was ordered at the same tender age of twelve to paste labels on blacking pots at Warren's Blacking Warehouse. Dickens later wrote about his piercing shame first in the unpublished "Autobiographical Fragment" and then in *David Copperfield*. "My whole nature was so penetrated with the grief and humiliation of such considerations," he confided near the end of his life to his friend and biographer John Forster, "that even now, famous and caressed and happy, I often forget in my dreams that I have a dear wife and children; even that I am a man; and wander desolately back to that time of my life" (Forster 26-7). Gordon doesn't compare her chilling experience to Dickens's, but she has never forgotten it. The two formative events that have driven her work are both rooted in biography, the early loss of her father and the image of her mother's "broken" body (*Conversations with Mary Gordon* 142).

Gordon explores the subject of caregiving in *Circling My Mother*, published in 2007. She opens the book with a question seldom raised by writers: "Why have you done this? With the implication: why have you done this to *me*?" (ix). The question is less about the book's genre, memoir or biography, than about the motives behind its creation. *Circling My Mother* is primarily about Anna Gagliano Gordon's life before she entered a nursing home, when she became increasingly demented and could no longer take care of herself, but it also offers insight into the caregiver's dilemma overlooking at a parent's body, a sight that Mary Gordon found unbearable. To understand *Circling My Mother*, it is helpful first to look at two of Gordon's earlier books, *Final Payments*, where she imagines being her *father's* caregiver, and her 1996 memoir *The Shadow Man*, where she discovers the shocking truth about her father's life.

## *Final Payments*

*Final Payments* begins at a graveside in Queens, New York, where her first-person narrator, Isabel Moore, mourns the death of her beloved father, Joseph, whom she has nursed and cared for from his first stroke, when she was nineteen, to his death eleven years later. "This strikes everyone in our decade as unusual, barbarous, cruel," Isabel bemoans. "To me, it was not only inevitable but natural" (4). Gordon describes Isabel's "balletic attraction" of caregiving routine: bringing her father breakfast, shaving him, bathing him, cutting his food for him, sliding a bedpan under him, smelling his urine and feces. "It is impossible to explain to anyone how long it takes to do the most ordinary things for an invalid," she laments (6), all the time elaborating on the numbing details of caregiving. Her father suffered three more strokes before his death, and though family and friends recommended that she get help to care for him, she stubbornly refused: "if he were with a stranger he would have been deprived even of the consolation of his rage" (7).

Religious duty compelled Isabel to be her father's exclusive caregiver. Preferring deprivation to loss, she shared her father's assumption that she would sacrifice her life for him. "Behold the handmaid of the Lord, said Mary to the angel; be it done unto me according to Thy word. As a reward for the loss of a normal life, she became the mother of God" (229–30). Isabel's father may not have been divine, but she found herself unable to refuse his demand to subordinate her life to his, despite the fact that she rejected his orthodox Catholic beliefs. The religious impulse behind the caregiver's self-sacrifice approaches self-immolation, a friend warns her. Isabel concedes that there were days when she hated her father, wanting him to die, yet she continued to care for him. Unable to weep at his funeral, she acknowledges that she still bears emotional scars—wounds that the novel unerringly explores.

Apart from religious and filial duty, Oedipal desire motivated Isabel to be her father's primary caregiver. When she was two, her mother was killed by a car in front of their house, and an intimate bond formed between father and daughter following the tragedy. Margaret Casey was hired as a housekeeper, but sensing that the outsider, described as sanctimonious and self-pitying, was falling in love with her father, Isabel had her fired after eleven years of service. With her hated rival out of the picture, and her mother long dead, Isabel devotes herself completely to her father. A professor for nearly thirty years, he was the "neighborhood intellectual" (11), Isabel informs us. "I love you more than I love God," she recalls her father saying to her, "I love you more than God loves you" (251). Isabel fears that this may be blasphemy, but she never questions the sincerity of his words. She knows that she received "puzzled neo-Freudian arched eyebrows" (63) whenever she describes her years of caring for her father, but she always speaks proudly about this experience.

*Final Payments* endorses Isabel's idealization of her father, for the other characters affirm the intensity of their love for each other. "But, my God, how he loved you," exclaims a friend. "You've had your great love, and you can't expect another. I don't think that people get two per lifetime" (78). The other men in Isabel's life pale in comparison to her father, whose stature in the novel remains undiminished.

Not that Isabel shares her father's ultraconservative political and social views. "For my father, the refusal of anyone in the twentieth century to become part of the Catholic Church was not pitiable; it was malicious and willful." His sympathies were with the "Royalists in the French Revolution, the South in the Civil War, the Russian czar, the Spanish Fascists" (4). Perhaps most damning of all, her father wrote speeches for Joe McCarthy during the communist witch hunts of the 1950s. An ardent feminist with strong liberal beliefs, Isabel cannot fathom why her father held these views, so different from her own, but her admiration of him is untarnished.

Yet if her father's immoderate love for Isabel constitutes her core self, her identity is threatened when Margaret Casey shows up, uninvited and unwelcome, at the funeral. Isabel hasn't seen her for seventeen years, but there is something about the former housekeeper that Isabel finds unsettling, even haunting. Isabel struggles throughout the novel to find a way to pay back the housekeeper for her long service, but we suspect that her indebtedness to the spectral Margaret can never be discharged. "I would take care of Margaret," Isabel thinks; "I would devote myself to the person I was least capable of loving. I would absorb myself in the suffering of someone I found unattractive. It would be a pure act, like the choice of a martyr's death which, we had been told in school, is the only inviolable guarantee of salvation" (240).

Isabel's motives for wanting to be Margaret's caregiver are never clear. Isabel wants to believe that if she can love a person who is entirely unlovable, like Margaret, she will achieve a pure act, but she also recognizes that such martyrdom will lead to the renunciation of happiness and the rejection of everything she holds valuable. But why is Isabel so willing to give her life to a woman who is so hateful, so incapable of loving or being loved? Why is the thought of martyrdom so appealing to Isabel—and why does she equate martyrdom with caregiving? A religious fanatic who is broken in body and spirit—she suffers from crippling arthritis later in life—Margaret is one of Gordon's most repellent characters. Why is Isabel drawn to her? Given her belief that Margaret is unattractive and stupid, why must Isabel reinvent herself "in her image, as her opposite" (27)? Why does Isabel describe the sound of Margaret "slopping around the house in her slippers" as the "sound of my nightmares" (28)? Why, if everything about Margaret is so offensive, does Isabel allow the housekeeper to wield so much power over her? "There's something very wrong with you," Margaret hisses. "There's something disgusting and unhealthy. People like you aren't fit for normal life" (232–3), a judgment with which Isabel strangely agrees. Calling Isabel a "stubborn, willful child" who had her father wrapped around her little finger (278), Margaret is as baleful as any witch invented by the Grimm Brothers. If Margaret functions as a dark mother figure, competing for Isabel's father's love, we can begin to understand her menacing power.

By novel's close, Isabel finds a way to reward the housekeeper's eleven years of service, giving her the equivalent of a pension, funded by the cash Isabel receives from selling her family home. In discharging her final payments, both financial and psychological, to Margaret, Isabel preserves her freedom and identity. *Final Payments* is the first but by no means last book in which Gordon explores the implications of martyrlike self-sacrifice implicit in caregiving. The question of Isabel's indebtedness to the sinister housekeeper remains—one that leads twenty-six years later to *The Shadow Man*, Mary Gordon's search for her lost father.

## *The Shadow Man*

The single most noteworthy detail anyone could learn about her, Gordon reveals in *The Shadow Man*, was her father's death in 1957, when she was seven. An omnivorous reader and autodidact, David Gordon suffered a heart attack at the New York Public Library from which he never recovered. "I placed what I called my memories of him at the center of what I called myself" (38). She was shaken to the core when, following the paper trail of her father's writings, she discovered that nearly everything he claimed to be true was false. Unlike Isabel, Gordon was too young to be her father's caregiver, but she could imagine the experience in her first novel. *The Shadow Man* allows us to see, retrospectively, Gordon's deep attachment to her father in *Final Payments*, the man for whom she could envision sacrificing her life, and, prospectively, her ambivalent feelings toward her other parent in *Circling My Mother*, for whom she became a reluctant caregiver years later.

Throughout *Final Payments* we see Isabel in the throes of paternal love, an adoration that the novelist shares, but in *The Shadow Man* this idealization is cruelly shattered when Gordon discovers that nearly everything her father had told her about himself was a lie. In searching for her father's origins, she assumed he was born in in Lorain, Ohio, in 1899, as he claimed, when in fact Israel Gordon was born in Vilna, Russia, in 1894, immigrating with his family to the United States. Unlike Isabel's father, an esteemed professor, David Gordon boasted that he attended Harvard, but he was a high school dropout. Nor did he study in Europe in the 1920s, as he asserted: he never had an American passport. Nor had he admitted an earlier marriage before meeting Anna Gagliano.

Mary Gordon became a writer because of her father, also a writer, but imagine her dismay when she discovered that his literary "work" was a "series of schemes to get rich men to bankroll him and his magazines" (xv). One of the magazines he edited, *The Children's Hour*, defended the Japanese during the Second World War; another, *Hot Dog*, began as a girlie publication and morphed into a pornographic magazine. Gordon used some of this biographical material in her 1985 novel *Men and Angels*, where she described a journalist who went to New York to start a "girlie magazine. Then he went far right. Supported Franco with a vengeance. Had a dramatic conversion to Catholicism at the feet one supposes of the Generalissimo" (166). The tone of these comments in *Men and Angels* is farcical, but there is nothing amusing about Gordon's revelations in *The Shadow Man*. She knew before her research that her father had converted from Judaism to Catholicism, in 1937, but she didn't know he was a virulent anti-Semite who believed that modern literature was "infected" by "Jewish" writers: Gide, Proust, and Bergson. Aware of the Nazi concentration camps, David Gordon believed the worst that could be said about Hitler was the closing of Catholic schools in Bavaria. Growing up, Mary Gordon was the target of anti-Semitic statements from her mother's Catholic family, who would jeer, "That's the *Jew* in you" (*The Shadow Man* 20), whenever she said something they disliked. There is not a hint in *Final Payments* or *Men and Angels* that Isabel's father was born Jewish, converted to Catholicism, and became aggressively anti-Semitic.

For years Gordon believed that her father was the greatest man she had known. That's how she began her unpublished biography of him, written when she was ten. She named her son after her father, but the only truth of his life that she could hold onto following her research was his overwhelming love for her, which she never disputes. "'I love you more than God,' he once told me" (xviii), the same statement Isabel's father proclaimed to her. Yet how could Gordon appreciate this unconditional love when her father maintained such despicable views? She can never decide whether his beliefs were mad or evil—"not a happy position for a loving daughter to be in" (xvii).

Paradoxes surround Gordon's relationship with her father. She has no memory of him that doesn't include the knowledge that he was a writer, yet he was a failed writer; even his prose style was inferior. How does one write successfully about a poor writer? Gordon believes that if her father had lived, she never would have rebelled against him. "You went against me," her mother once told her, "but you wouldn't have been able to go against your father" (53). Nor would she have discovered the truth about him. Now that he is dead, she feels compelled to expose his fraudulent identity. She became a writer because of her father, yet her mission is now to bear witness against his writings. She can imagine her father asking, "Why have you done this to me?" (187), a question that cannot easily be answered. In betraying him, she believes she is betraying herself. Throughout *The Shadow Man* she finds herself in an impossible position, "both the perpetrator and the victim of a crime" (162).

Gordon was willing to imagine being her father's sole caregiver in *Final Payments*, and she might have considered caring for him in real life had she been older, but she is blunt about not willing to be her mother's caregiver. A month before she was to leave for her third year of study at Barnard College, her mother fell and was confined to a wheelchair for six months. "Heartlessly, I kept to my original plan, leaving her to the care of her cousin's wife, a plain and dour German woman who despised me and adored my mother" (239). After Barnard, Gordon went to graduate school in Syracuse and for three years traveled home as little as possible.

Anna Gagliano Gordon spent the last eleven years of her life in a nursing home, dying in 2002 at the age of ninety-four. For the last five years of her life, she did not recognize her daughter. Mary Gordon was in her forties when she began the protracted search for her father's identity. The search involved literally unearthing her father's bones, exhuming the remains of his body, in an unnamed grave in the Gagliano family plot, and reburying him in a new plot reserved for Mary Gordon and her husband—a "crazy idea," her mother tells her. Gordon cannot stop asking herself why she was exposing her father's memory to the public if he was mad, evil, or pathetic. "This is the story of my reluctance, of my flinching from the loss I knew would follow the truth" (93). Gordon also began interrogating her mother's identity, which, while not counterfeit, cast its own ominous shadows.

Gordon had a problematic relationship with her mother, whom she unquestionably loved, though not in the same way as she revered her father. Polio rendered Anna Gagliano into a "cripple" (30), a word that appears throughout *The Shadow Man* and *Circling My Mother*. As a result of her "dwarf leg and foot," which was six inches shorter than her other leg, she had to wear "high shoes, cruel-looking boots" and leg braces (30). Is this one of the reasons Isabel loathes the sound of Margaret shuffling in her slippers in *Final Payments*? Gordon tells us that her parents were always fighting, usually about money, and were temperamentally unsuited for each other. Her mother never liked to read—and never read her daughter's books. Mary usually sided with her father, details that support the idea that Margaret is a portrait of the novelist's worst feelings about her mother. Anna Gordon's body evokes her daughter's most frightening emotions—and most vivid prose:

> She had the, I suppose, necessary lack of physical shame that helps cripples get by. She would do things that mortified me, like going down a steep flight of stairs on her behind. She even had an expression for it: "Assing down the stairs." She would crawl up hills on her hands and knees. I would want to beg her not to, so deep was my mortification when she did something like this, even if no one could see us. But I knew that she was right: there was no alternative. It made me literally want to die, because there was too much to feel. It was easier to die than to feel all of it. There was mortification at the spectacle, pity for her, shame at my own shame, pride in her, hatred for her, perhaps a vague sense of her sadism in insisting that all this be visible. It was too much for a child. It has never stopped being too much. (222–3)

## Writing as a Countershame Technique

There's little one can say about Gordon's fraught relationship with her mother that Gordon doesn't already know—except to add that the memoirist uses writing as a countershame technique to detoxify poisonous feelings that might otherwise destroy her. Shame is the most virulent emotion, and it is the dominant affective state in *The Shadow Man*, along with sadness and grief. Shame is often compared to guilt, but whereas the latter reveals that our behavior is wrong, the former reveals that our entire character is wrong—and horrible.

*The Shadow Man* presents us with the appalling truth of a deceitful father and a mother whose body awakened revulsion in her daughter. Gordon offers us a fearless portrait of a mother-daughter relationship that challenges us not to turn away in horror. If the mother had a vague sense of sadism in insisting that her efforts to walk and crawl be made visible, the daughter's decision to write about this involves stronger sadism—aggression in the service of truth-telling.

Gordon's use of writing as a countershame technique recalls Leon Wurmser's identification of three separate meanings of shame: (1) shame as the "*fear of disgrace*," the "*anxiety* about the danger that we might be looked at with contempt for having dishonored ourselves"; (2) shame as the "*affect of contempt*" directed against the self; and (3) shame as an "overall *character* trait preventing any such disgraceful exposure," as in discretion or tact (67–8). We see all three meanings of shame in *The Shadow Man*. Gordon expresses shame over her mother's body; shame at her own shame, self-contempt; and shame as filial indiscretion. Gordon may have felt that it was easier to die than to witness her mother descending stairs on her behind and crawling up hills on her hands and knees, but there was another option: transmuting her shameful feelings into memoiristic art.

Gordon's relationship to her mother was no less paradoxical than her relationship to her deceased father, albeit in a different way. She confesses in *The Shadow Man* that she wants her mother to die, yet she feels rage if anyone disrespects her. She associates her mother with a "secret devotion to rot" (the same word she had used in *Seeing Through Places* to describe her dying grandmother), which she associates with polio: "Buried beneath her grief and shame about her body, and beneath the stoicism that conceals her grief and shame, like a softening tuber underneath a field" (*The Shadow Man* 206–7).

After a section of *The Shadow Man* was published in the *New York Times*, Gordon explained, in a 1995 interview with Alma Bennett, why she wrote about her mother who was still alive. The main reason, she told Bennett, was to help other caregivers who were deeply conflicted toward their own care-receivers. Gordon admitted that she had received complaints from mental health professionals about the harshness of "rot," but she defended her use of the word, believing that truth-telling trumps political correctness. In her 2009 book *Reading Jesus*, Gordon characterizes the last seven words of Jesus as "[r]adical honesty, radical porosity," language "used to obviate the work of language: the naming of differences, of distinctions" (196); she aims for the same radical honesty in all her writings.

Lacking the agility to step into or out of a bathtub, Anna Gordon never took a shower or bath. After her husband's death, she stopped grooming herself and became an alcoholic. Gordon knows that she is her mother's advocate when the elderly woman is placed in a nursing home, yet she wants to punish her for not taking care of herself. At the same time, she wants to sit in her mother's lap and say, "Don't you understand that I'm your child, and a child shouldn't have to do this?" (*The Shadow Man* 228). She admires her mother for working her entire life as a legal secretary, financially supporting her many siblings and her own mother, even paying the mortgage on her mother's house for a quarter of a century. Unlike her deceased father, who lied about almost everything and was a failure in work, her mother was a positive role model. Yet it is the mother who incurs the daughter's wrath. "My desire, my need, to punish my mother is very great. I am conscious of no need to punish my father" (220). How does a daughter punish her mother in print without punishing herself?

Near the end of *The Shadow Man*, Gordon makes a telling distinction between caregiving and *writing* about caregiving. Now that her mother is in a nursing home, having forgotten nearly all of her memory—she can remember being a daughter but not being a wife or mother—Gordon believes that nothing she does or doesn't do for her mother matters any more. If she takes her mother to a play, the daughter muses, she will have to stop writing *The Shadow Man*. She decides not to visit her mother: she would rather write about her than strain her back pushing her uphill in a wheelchair. Gordon doesn't put it in these terms, but, ever the writer, she chooses art over life—though paradoxically it is her parents' lives that she transmutes into art.

In her harrowing search to understand her tangled feelings toward her parents and the darkness in their lives, Gordon wonders whether writing is an act of vengeance or love. She frequently raises either/or binaries like this, when the answer is usually both/and. Part of her challenge is to transform her parents and herself into human portraits that do justice to them and herself. In her comments "To the Reader" at the beginning of *The Shadow Man*, she cites the psychoanalyst Hans Loewald's statement that a successful analysis is one that transforms ghosts into ancestors. Gordon doesn't tell us how, where, and when she came across Loewald's article, published in the *International Journal of Psycho-Analysis* in 1960, but many of his statements about analysis also apply to novelists and memoirists such as herself who seek to understand and work through traumatic caregiving experiences. "Those who know ghosts tell us that they long to be released from their ghost-life and led to rest as ancestors. As ancestors they live forth in the present generation, while as ghosts they are compelled to haunt the present generation with their shadow-life" (Loewald, 29). Loewald's reference to "shadow-life" may have been one of the inspirations behind the title *The Shadow Man*.

## Writing/Righting Wrong

Gordon's narrative strategy in *The Shadow Man* foreshadows that in *Circling My Mother*. She regards herself as playing all the roles in a public trial—detective, police artist, witness, prosecutor, judge, and executor. She will accuse everyone responsible for destroying her once-beautiful image of her father. She will not allow her father to be the villain in his story or in her own. "I will accuse so loudly, so cogently, my accusation will be so final and so damning that none of them will dare to speak again" (184). Gordon's role of accuser recalls Emile Zola, who penned *J'accuse* to defend Alfred Dreyfus, the Jewish captain in the French army falsely accused of treason. But even more than Zola, Gordon's role of accuser recalls that of an avenging angel, who in the Bible set out to destroy the enemies of God.

As an accuser both of others and herself—she fears that she has failed not only her parents but also herself—Gordon engages in what the literary critic Sandra Gilbert calls "writing/righting wrong." Gilbert uses the expression in her 1995 memoir *Wrongful Death*, which chronicles her successful malpractice suit against the University of California at Davis Medical Center, where her husband, Elliot, chair of the English Department at UC-Davis, died of complications following routine prostate surgery in 1991. Gilbert then wrote the magisterial *Death's Door: Modern Dying and the Ways We Grieve*. In writing *Wrongful Death*, Gilbert observes, "I understood that I was writing (recording) as well as seeking to right (to rectify) wrong, and now, as I retell the tale, I realize that 'I am still at the same subject,' still engaged in the same fearful and fierce activity—writing and seeking to right a mortal wrong" (*Death's Door* 86–7). Writing/righting wrong similarly characterizes Mary Gordon's narrative strategy in her next memoir, where, engaged in a fearful and fierce activity, an act of circling the wagons, she defends her mother from those who sought to destroy her dignity.

## *Circling My Mother*

*Circling My Mother* is, in part, Mary Gordon's anguished confession that she could not endure visiting her mother in a nursing home without feeling overcome by revulsion. In the eleven years she saw her mother once a week, sometimes less, while supervising her care, Gordon felt her mother's presence was unbearable. "The sight of her blackening teeth, now only stumps; her hair, scraped down almost to her scalp; above all the smell of her made me panic, made me want to cover my face with my hands and cry out, 'I can't, I can't, I can't do this'" (215).

No memoirist, to my knowledge, has written more graphically about the horror of visiting a loved one in a nursing home—and no caregiving memoir has conjured up stormier emotions than *Circling My Mother*. Gordon doesn't name the contagion effect, but she appears to be swept away by a torrent of frightening emotions whenever she sees her demented mother. Every aspect of Anna Gordon's appearance drives her daughter mad—in both senses of the word, infuriated and unhinged. Work is impossible after visiting her mother: "the rest of the afternoon is a struggle not to give in to a hopelessness that makes the creation of something made of words seem ridiculous, grotesque, a joke" (9). Gordon had imagined being her father's caregiver for eleven years in *Final Payments*, but that was fiction, not reality. Not for a moment does she now imagine being her mother's exclusive caregiver, absorbing herself in the suffering of another, martyrlike, as Isabel Moore imagined caring for Margaret Casey. Gordon is not prepared to renounce her life and everything she holds dear: her work and her own family. She is prepared, though, to denounce those who humiliated her mother—and herself.

Gordon has little to say specifically about her mother's final years. She was "much more a problem to me than a joy" (x). Gordon is not interested in describing the changes in her mother's health during these years or the nature of end-of-life care. The little we learn reveals the caregiver's difficulty in accepting these changes. By the time of her ninetieth birthday, Anna Gordon no longer remembered her daughter. "My mother has erased me from the book of the living. She is denying the significance of my birth. I do not take this personally" (5). And yet she does appear to take this as a personal betrayal. Why else would she attach agency to her mother's forgetting? Perhaps it would be more accurate to say that although Gordon knows intellectually her mother is not responsible for the erasure, the daughter believes, emotionally, that she has been abandoned and betrayed. There is nothing affirmative about her mother's "slow disaster" (7), nothing that suggests the "emptiness" at the center of her mother's life was anything other than obdurate blankness. "And there is nothing I can do about it. Nothing" (14). Nothing, that is, except to write about it.

Yet if *Circling My Mother* revealed only dark emotions, it wouldn't be as poignant or heartbreaking as it is—largely because we see the daughter's love and devotion. The title implies not only an image of defense against external attack but also a full perspective of a nonagenarian's life. In an effort to be close to her mother, who retired when she was seventy-five, Gordon bought her a house in 1983 two blocks from her own house in the mid-Hudson Valley, where she lived at the time. This proved to be the best and worst time for Gordon. As Bennett notes in her 1996 book on the novelist (13), five days after Gordon's son, David, was born, her mother fell and was incapacitated. For the next seven years, Gordon shouldered the responsibilities of caring for her husband and two young children, along with being a professor and novelist, while she also looked after her mother, who became increasingly depressed and demented.

There are two curious omissions in *Circling My Mother*. Gordon never reveals that she was her maternal grandmother's caregiver, a detail that might have deepened the reader's understanding of Gordon's horror of "rot," a reminder that the nightmarish present was a repetition of the traumatic past. Nor does Gordon tell us, in the chapter "My Mother and My Father," that David Gordon was anti-Semitic, though she implies the depth of his anger toward his former religion. "She would buy, at his request, jars of Rokeach gefilte fish: a throwback to the faith he had rejected with such vociferous energy, such rage" (170–1).

Of all the chapters in the memoir, "My Mother: Words and Music" comes across as the most lyrical and high spirited, conjuring good times together. She captures her mother's personality in this chapter, particularly her verbal power to sting. "For her, I think the pleasure of words was directly related to the joy of insult, its corrosive power" (37). Throughout *Final Payments* and *The Shadow Man*, Gordon comes across as her father's offspring, but in this chapter, she is unmistakably her mother's daughter, deriving pleasure from barbed language. Even at the end of her life, when she had forgotten nearly everyone, Anna Gordon retained part of her personality. Gordon reports that when she told her mother that she could allow herself to die and be with God, her mother "looked at me with her old gimlet eye, focusing as she hadn't for quite a long time. 'Why would I pull a crazy stunt like that?' she said" (39).

Some of Gordon's other characterizations are also self-characterizations, as when she writes about her mother's use of irony "to protect herself from disappointment" (42). So, too, is Gordan an ironist, protecting herself from disappointment and using language as attack. But unlike her mother, who had no use for analysis—"I don't dwell on things. I don't harp on things, I don't dig things up like you" (37)—Gordon does analyze, dwell, dig up, ruminate—and use emotionally charged language to convey happiness and sorrow. "My Mother: Words and Music" captures the joy of their time together in the nursing home. "The music was wonderful," she recalls. "It enabled me to weep. I did not weep at all learning of her death. But I wept when I heard the music. When the music came, I missed her. I wanted her singing, beside me once again" (53).

What also makes Gordon weep is the way in which her mother's family treated—or, rather, mistreated—her. Of the ten chapters in the memoir, the most devastating is "My Mother and Her Sisters," the longest, at forty-seven pages, and the most scathing. It is in this chapter, a striking example of writing/righting wrong, that Gordon seeks to redress the cruelties inflicted upon her mother by three of her sisters. Admitting that if she were writing a novel about her aunts she would, by necessity, treat them more sympathetically, Gordon declares that no such mercy awaits them in her memoir. "It was their hatred, their disdain, that destroyed her. There is nowhere else to lay it but at their feet" (58).

## Anger

To grasp the depth of Mary Gordon's anger in "My Mother and Her Sisters," along with anger's close cousins, spite, vengeance, and rage, we may turn to her article alluringly titled "The Deadly Sins/Anger; The Fascination Begins in the Mouth," first appearing in *The New York Times Book Review* on June 13, 1993 and then republished in the same year in *Deadly Sins*, a volume consisting of eight commissioned works by different writers. No one in recent memory has written more poetically or passionately on anger than Gordon, the emotion that constitutes her artistic muse. "More than any of the other sins," she declaims in the first paragraph, "anger can be seen to be good, can perhaps even begin by being good. Jesus himself was angry, brandishing his whip and thrillingly overturning tables: coins, doves flying, the villainous sharpsters on their knees to save their spoils. It would seem to run in the family; by far the angriest character in the Old Testament is God" (*Deadly Sins* 27). Of all the sins, she continues, anger alone is exhilarating, intoxicating—and divine. Gordon's avenging angels are holy creatures who use fierce anger to protect and care for righteous people. "The angry one is radiant in strength, and, blazing like the angel with the flaming sword, banishes the transgressors from the garden they would only now defile" (29).

There is joy in anger, Gordon avers, the knowledge that one can both inflict and endure. "To live in anger is to forget that one was ever weak, to believe that what others call weakness is a sham, a feint that one exposes and removes like the sanitizing immolation of a plague-ridden house" (29). But there is a darker side, for unlike vengeful anger, deadly anger feeds on itself. "Once fed, the creature grows hypnotized by itself" (29). The desire to hurt others, Gordon suggests, may be explained by the need for blame. What is wrong must be someone's fault. "Yours. And I must punish you. Furthermore, I demand that you see the rightness of your punishment" (31). Deadly anger "emanates a styptic breath that withers hope and youth and beauty" (33).

Gordon then describes one of her own angry outbursts, when she became like a frightening animal. While preparing for a dinner party of ten people on a swelteringly hot August afternoon, with no one to help her, she heard her mother and two children honking the car horn, demanding that she take them swimming. "They leaned on the horn and shouted my name out the window, well within hearing of the neighbors, reminding me of my promise to take them to the pond" (34). Infuriated, she lost it, lost herself, and began jumping on the hood of the car, pounding the windshield. She could feel herself turning into a carrion crow, with a monstrous beak, entranced by the taste of blood, wanting to feed on the three battered corpses until her stomach swelled. Nothing surprising here—except that she denies she is using figurative language: she had become that terrifying bird. Her behavior later appalled her, particularly when her son said to her, "I was scared because I didn't know who you were" (36). The only way to stop this anger, Gordon writes at the end of the article, is through forgiveness. "To forgive is to give up the exhilaration of one's own unassailable rightness" (38).

## "My Mother and Her Sisters"

Mary Gordon doesn't turn into a carrion crow who feasts on the battered copses of her mother's family in "My Mother and Her Sisters," but the depth of her voracious anger is stunning. The chapter describes the five Gagliano sisters, now all dead, and mentions briefly the four brothers. All the sisters prided themselves, like Gordon's mother, on not dwelling on things. Anna, the oldest daughter and head of the family, paid the family mortgage and financed the education of two of her sisters in nursing school and two of her brothers in college. Her siblings apparently felt entitled to this support. When the family fell apart, after their Irish mother's death, three of her sisters turned against Anna; "it was my mother's largest source of aggrievement, drunken rage" (*Circling My Mother* 56).

Of the many crimes for which Gordon holds her aunts responsible, one is notable. Recalling nearly half a century earlier how she felt after her father's death, paralyzed by grief, she had received from her Aunt Christine, the youngest sister, nicknamed "Tiny," a postcard of Alfred E. Neuman from *Mad* magazine with the printed words "Keep smiling." Gordon felt wounded by the card, "with his idiotic gap-toothed grin." She believed that the postcard not only diminished her father's memory but also trivialized the role of mourning, which has no time limit to a bereft child. Gordon never forgot the incident. "I never forgive my aunt, I cannot forgive her still, for insisting that I weep in secret, as if it were a cause for shame" (71). Years later, newly married, Gordon and her husband were invited to her aunt's home for dinner. Tiny was cold to her the entire night. Gordon silently simmered.

"I would like to tell her I do not forgive her for forbidding me to weep the summer after my father's death, for hanging the face of Alfred E. Neuman beside my need." But she says nothing, and the evening ends with her feeling enraged. She receives neither comfort nor understanding from her husband, who "insists" that she stop weeping. "I do not sleep with him that night. I write the first real story of my life. About the summer after my father's death" (73).

This moment in *Circling My Mother* is noteworthy for several reasons. The need to avenge a perceived wrong is the driving force behind much of Gordon's writing, particularly her two memoirs, *The Shadow Man* and *Circling My Mother*. She will not allow shame to silence her permanently. Writing/righting wrong becomes her central goal in *Circling My Mother*. She may feel irritation and sometimes rage at her mother—she recalls being angry at her mother for sending her to typing school when she was twelve "so you can support yourself, because no man will ever want to marry you" (75)—but she will not allow others to abuse her mother. There is no statute of limitations on either grief or writing/righting wrong.

One more example of writing/righting wrong may suffice, the story of Aunt Rita, the source of "all the villainous cold-hearted women" in Gordon's fiction (84). Writing about Rita forces Gordon to decide the major reason she writes this chapter. Is it to heal wounds or to exact revenge? Unlike other binaries, this one appears to be either/or, not both/and. She acknowledges that writing can lead to healing and that it can be, indirectly, a moral force, but this is not her main reason for writing "My Mother and Her Sisters," if not the entirety of *Circling My Mother*. Rather, she must punish Rita for her barbarous behavior, even though her aunt is long dead. Later Gordon admits that "when it comes to my parents, I pride myself not on being fair but on being on their side" (118), an admission that calls into question her reliability as a narrator.

Having conceded that Rita was also betrayed by the Gagliano family who sent her away to a "school for crippled children" from the age of six to twelve, Gordon then documents her aunt's many heartless acts to her mother and herself. Rita was responsible for turning Gordon into an "indentured servant" on Saturdays, insisting that she spend the entire day cleaning the family house and scorning her academic success with the statement: "I don't see what good being a bookworm will do you." To a writer, there is perhaps nothing worse than venomous criticism; seeing a newspaper article on Gordon, Rita crumpled it and sneered, "I looked at this and I saw it was garbage, so I figured you wanted it thrown away" (98). Rita married a loathsome man, the devil incarnate, one who occasions the most mystifying moment in the memoir:

> It must be said: with his visits a darkness entered our family, and it was miserable for me; I was the child in the house, and there were things done to me, things I should not have seen, ways that I was looked at that I should have been kept from. But this is not the way I want to tell the story, because I escaped, and I have to thank them for making it so clear to me what must be escaped from. (92)

What shall we say about this murky passage? It's surprising that Gordon's editor did not recommend her either to elaborate on these sinister "things," with their undeniably portentous sexual connotations, or to delete the passage. If Gordon felt that this was not the story she wanted to tell, why didn't she revise it? She is not a writer who works through innuendo: she confronts the truth head-on, regardless of the consequences.

If one can imagine a darker version of Margaret Casey, it would be Rita. Gordon's task in *Circling My Mother* is to fulfill her lifelong promise: "one day I will expose the murderous true heart of my aunt: the Law Abiding, the Destroyer" (97). In exposing Aunt Rita's black heart, Gordon crafts an incendiary prose style that combines military metaphors, incantatory repetition, cruel caricature, and pitiless rage. The Christian forgiveness Gordon preaches in her essay on "Anger" is strikingly absent from the memoir. Her most damning statement occurs in the revelation that near the end of Rita's life, having lost her "hysterical fastidiousness," she refused to bathe and stopped using the toilet in her home. "When she needed to move her bowels, she defecated in empty Cool Whip containers, which she would empty in the kitchen sink at the end of day" (98). Gordon's image of Rita could hardly be more scathing. Paul Rozin and his associates (whose research I cited in the chapter on John Bayley) point out that in an extensive cross-cultural study of emotional responses in thirty-seven different cultures, "disgust shows the highest score on immorality of all seven emotions (including anger and shame)" (643). However unbearable the sight of Anna's body may be, Gordon never discusses her mother's incontinence; she reserves these details for her hated aunt. Placed in a nursing home, Rita developed a "sexual mania" for one of the male residents and stalked him in her wheelchair. The revenge is now complete. Gordon acknowledges that the story of the Gagliano sisters is not a good one, but one that she needed to tell for her mother's benefit.

## "Remember This"

Gordon's deepest shame centers around her mother's body, which is both the sight and site of assaultive violence. Gordon recalls a trip to Ireland she took with her mother in the early 1970s when, competing for the attention of the same man, her mother called her a "common whore." Overcome by rage, Gordon slapped her mother's face. "We were both terribly shocked. But she took control of the situation. 'Remember this,' she said, remember this for the rest of your life. That you struck your mother" (205). The incident reminded Gordon of an earlier childhood experience when, after one of her parents' frequent fights, her father, "fed up, wheeled away from her to walk out of the room" and accidentally knocked his wife to the floor. "'Remember this,' she said, 'remember this all your life. That you knocked your wife onto the floor. That you threw me on the floor, a cripple'" (205). Bursting into tears, Gordon states that never in her life, either before or since, has she felt such remorse. She can never forget that, in different ways, she and her father were both guilty of assaulting her mother's afflicted body.

It would be a mistake to imply that Gordon wrote *Circling My Mother* to rationalize her unwillingness to be Anna's caregiver or her perceived failures as a daughter. Yet one may wonder: Was her rage toward Anna's enemies a projection of her own unresolved ambivalence toward her mother, an example of what psychoanalysts call projective identification? "I let my mother down in many things," she admits, "but I was excellent at punishing people who let her down" (126). She rarely doubts that she has put this rage to good use in *Circling My Mother*. "I have kept her alive," she declares near the end of the chapter; "my love, my care, has been stronger than their darkness. My mother lives longer than any of her sisters" (99). Might Gordon's efforts to recreate her mother, giving her life through words, have been as successful if she had avoided some of the "flamboyant hate" (97), her wry expression to describe her family's history of seething hostility?

Of the five Gagliano sisters, Rita was the one with the "cutting tongue, the one of whom everyone was afraid" (56); but Gordon's tongue is no less lacerating or fearful in *Circling My Mother*. At what point does righteous anger turn into self-righteous rage that feeds on itself? At what point does revenge become not only unwise but also counterproductive? "Every act of revenge," the philosopher Robert Solomon suggests, results in a "new offense to be righted." "And when the act is perpetrated not against the same person who did the offense but against another who is part of the same family, tribe, or social group (the logic of 'vendetta'), the possibilities for escalation are endless" (113). Where is the line between truth-telling and brutality? Gordon raises this question herself but doesn't answer it.

Gordon admits in the closing pages of *Circling My Mother* that she wasn't with Anna when she died. "I didn't live with her because I could not. Because she was, to me, unbearable" (252). Yet she wrote about her, giving her new life and dignity. Yeats, a poet whom Gordon "worshipped as a god," wrote about the dilemma of choosing between the perfection of the life or of the work. Mary Gordon's choice is never in doubt.

## Annie Ernaux

Gordon's attitude toward being her mother's caregiver has much in common with that of the acclaimed French writer Annie Ernaux, the author of the 1997 memoir "*I Remain in Darkness*," the last sentence written by her mother, who died of dementia in 1986 at age seventy-nine. Like Gordon, Ernaux cared for her mother at home before placing her in a nursing home. "I am accumulating bags of guilt for the future. But letting her stay at my place would have meant the end of my life. It was either her or me" (37). Like Gordon, she was repelled by her mother's body but still felt deeply connected to her. "She had ceased to be the woman who had always ruled my life and yet, despite her misshapen features, because of her voice, her manners and her laugh, she remained my mother, more so than ever" (8). Like Gordon, Ernaux does not hesitate to disclose shameful details of caregiving, such as discovering a "human turd" in the drawer of her mother's bedside night table. "I slammed the drawer shut in utter confusion. Then it occurred to me that if I left it there, someone would find it, and that subconsciously, I probably wanted this to happen so that they could see how low my mother had fallen. I found a piece of paper and went to flush it down the toilet" (35).

Like Gordon, Ernaux felt rage toward her mother and was appalled by the intensity of her own cruelty. "My sadistic streak reminds me of the way I behaved toward other little girls in my childhood. Maybe because I am terrified by her" (22). Like Gordon, Ernaux fell heir to her mother's wrath. "I notice that I have inherited her brusque, violent temper, as well as a tendency to seize things and throw them with fury" (66). Like Gordon, Ernaux delights in painting and likens her mother to Courbet's *The Origin of the World*, which depicts the open thighs of a recumbent woman. Like Gordon, she was unexpectedly overcome by grief when her mother died. "This moment was something I had never imagined or foreseen" (84). And like Gordon, Ernaux shuddered at the thought of writing a memoir about her mother. "Literature is so powerless" (86), she concludes, nevertheless crafting a powerful memoir that remains, along with *Circling My Mother*, a jewel among caregiving literature.

## Bonnard

We don't ordinarily think about looking at a care-receiver's body as a major problem of caregiving, but this is part of the uniqueness of Gordon's story in *Circling My Mother*. She could not endure the sight of her mother's misshapen body before she entered a nursing home, but the problem was exacerbated when the elderly woman became demented and unkempt. "In the last years of her life, she was, in her wretchedness, my tormentor. Her body tortured me: the sight of it, its smell. Living, she was a torturer, and now, among the dead, she is entirely innocent" (215). Without indulging in the lies of beautification, Gordon seeks a way to transform the sight of her mother from that of a repulsive woman, with her leprous flesh, into a beguiling one. She decides to begin and end her book with the French painter Pierre Bonnard, who created *The Bathroom* in 1908, the same year in which her mother was born.

It's not surprising that Gordon found herself drawn to Pierre Bonnard (1867–1947), who was praised by *The New Republic* art critic Jed Perl, on the occasion of the painter's 2009 exhibition at the Metropolitan Museum of Art, for his visual taste, psychological insight, and poetic feeling, qualities apparent throughout Gordon's writings. Bonnard's canvases remind us, in Perl's words, that "beauty is unreliable, that blossoms will decay, that ripe fruit will rot, and that the bright afternoon sun will fade to darkest night. No other artist offers such complicated bliss." A similar complicated bliss appears in Gordan's writings.

Gordon sees several parallels between Bonnard's life and her own. Both lived with people who suffered from physical afflictions: Bonnard's wife, Marthe, had a skin disease and tubercular laryngitis. Bonnard lied to get away from his wife, who didn't want him seeing other people; Gordon lied as a teenager to her mother, who disliked her friends. Bonnard's painting *The Sewing Lesson* reminds Gordon of her mother and grandmother, a master seamstress. Marthe Bonnard was from the working class, as was Anna Gordon. Looking at a photograph of Marthe Bonnard, Gordon sees a striking resemblance to her mother's face: "the high cheekbones; the light, wide-apart, almost staring eyes" (250). She sees another photograph of Marthe Bonnard wearing a cloche hat and a close-fitting coat, both of which Anna Gordon also owned. Suddenly the writer experiences an epiphany. "In the photographs, Marthe becomes my mother. At last, I have accomplished what I have always wanted: I have given my mother a beautiful body" (250).

## The Antigone Complex

Gordon writes about caregiving mainly in *Final Payments*, *The Shadow Man*, and *Circling My Mother*, but we may note her preoccupation with martyrdom fantasies, which she often associates with caregiving in many of her fictional and nonfictional writings. In her 2005 novel *Pearl*, the eponymous twenty-year-old American heroine, ostensibly studying linguistics in Ireland, chains herself to a flagpole in front of the American embassy in Dublin in an effort to starve herself to death as an act of solidarity to those who supported the peace process in the war-ravaged country in 1998. Pearl hasn't eaten in six weeks, and, delirious, she is close to death.

Hazel Morrisey, the psychiatrist who supervises Pearl's forced feeding, is an expert on eating disorders and suicide and seeks a psychodynamic explanation for her patient's hunger strike. Dr. Morrisey believes that anorexia is caused by internalized rage: "the desperation of their hatred for their own flesh, which they would burn up, consume, with the avidity of the old saints. Feed them and wean them from an ideal of perfection, which was really the ideal of death" (198). Gordon's psychiatrist has a keen insight into the psychology of martyrdom; additionally, she is a student of literature, which deepens her authenticity. "I've observed that some young women seem to have a special impulse toward martyrdom," the psychiatrist explains to Pearl's mother, Maria. "I think of it as the Antigone complex," adding, "Although you mustn't go looking for it in the medical journals. It's only the way I name it for myself" (245). Recognizing her filial duty, Antigone, in Sophocles's ancient Greek play, became the caregiver for her father, Oedipus, after he blinded himself. Pearl is not a caregiver, but she believes it is her duty to sacrifice herself for Irish peace—and to atone for a harsh statement that she fears led to another person's death. Significantly, as a martyr, Pearl forces others into the role of caregiver, and she is fortunate that her psychiatrist, with a knowledge of transference and countertransference dynamics, offers her exemplary care.

Pearl bears the authorial signature of many of Gordon's female characters. Pearl was a quiet, bright, studious child who loved to read, much like Gordon herself. Like Isabel in *Final Payments*, Pearl, attracted to saints' lives, longs for a pure death, a martyr's death, which she believes is an inviolable guarantee of salvation. Pearl had a grandfather who was a Jewish convert to Catholicism; like Gordon's own father, Pearl's grandfather never talked about the German concentration camps. Pearl's father was a Cambodian physician who disappeared into his own country before she was born, leaving his daughter with a father-hunger that is evident throughout the novel, as is Gordon's throughout *The Shadow Man*. Pearl announces her intention at the end of the story to travel to Cambodia to look for "something connected" to her father.

Tellingly, Pearl has a highly conflicted relationship with her mother, Maria, from whom she is largely estranged. Learning that Pearl has pulled the feeding tube out of her nose and throat, Maria feels like screaming. "Rage crawls over her skin like mites; it begins on her arms, then over her skull, settles at the name of her neck, enters the soft spot there, liquifies, spreads, coats the skeleton" (210). By novel's close, the fraught mother-daughter relationship is partly healed, and we are left with the hope, in the narrator's words, that "we must live with mercy and forgiveness, which may be a series of mistakes, of overpayments, rather than the blame we seize, the blame we believe is shining, singular, the burning brand we use to mark with our own name" (337–8). The reference to *overpayments* recalls *Final Payments*, where Isabel considers and then rejects embracing martyrdom in the form of masochistic caregiving.

Gordon's fascination with martyrdom may also be seen in her 2000 study *Joan of Arc*. "She was a virgin, and she died for what she believed, but she does not fit the type of the virgin martyr. Ardent, impatient, boastful, resistant, implacable, she is, like all great saints, a personality of genius. Unlike most of the saints, she defined the Church on her terms, not its own" (172). Joan of Arc is, in short, the type of saint and martyr that captures Gordon's imagination, and who informs the essence of her most complicated characters.

## Art Out of Rage

Some of Gordon's family ghosts have been transformed into ancestors at the end of *Circling My Mother*. The others remain consigned to hell, where they will burn forever for their sins. *Circling My Mother* remains the darkest and most painful caregiving memoir to read, largely because of the depth of its anger. In her 1998 novel *Spending*, Gordon's heroine, Monica Szabo, is a world-famous painter who generates the same ferocious criticism from conservative Catholics that Gordon has herself received. Undeterred, Monica visits an art collection, located in the World Trade Center, and comes across a video screen on which appears what looks like a tepee in flames and a quotation, presumably from the artist, "I make art out of rage" (284), a comment that applies to *Circling My Mother*. Gordon could not have predicted that three years after the publication of her novel, the World Trade Center would itself be in flames, the target of terrorist rage.

And yet by the close of *Circling My Mother*, Gordon's rage has yielded to tenderness. Not that she has forgiven her mother's sisters. Rather, she has seen her mother in a new light, achieving through literary art a miraculous transformation of the ordinary that Bonnard effects in his paintings. Alluding to Bonnard's artistic injunction, she vows to keep her mother from vanishing. "I will try to understand distance, but to understand that I will also have to understand closeness" (254). In the end, she has found a way to balance distance and closeness, bringing her mother back to life.

8

# Murderous Caregiving in Michael Haneke's *Amour*

Two thousand years ago, Ovid imagined the perfect ending for an elderly married couple who lived a lifetime together. The Roman poet describes in the *Metamorphoses* two devoted lovers, Baucis and Philemon, who ask the gods never to be separated by death. "Since we have lived out harmonious years together, let the same hour take the two of us, so that I never have to see my wife's grave, nor she have to bury me" (Book VIII). The gods grant Baucis's wish, and he and Philemon are simultaneously transformed into trees, entwined in each other's branches. Ovid's rapturous ending, where old lovers die concurrently, never having to endure the sting of separation or the other's suffering, or having to be a caregiver or care-receiver, rarely happens in real life, and certainly not in the 2012 film *Amour*, directed by the Austrian director and writer Michael Haneke. *Amour* is probably the most devastating filmic portrayal of a spouse who can no longer fulfill his caregiving responsibilities. The emotionally charged film explores several interrelated problems, including the ravages of disease, the perils of caregiving for both the caregiver and care-receiver, the ambiguities of love amid the onslaught of death, and the intended and unintended consequences of euthanasia.

Haneke selected three iconic French actors for *Amour*, two of whom were octogenarians in real life, Jean-Louis Trintignant and Emmanuelle Riva, to play the roles of Georges and Anne Laurent, retired music teachers living in an elegant Paris apartment. Haneke said that he wrote the film for Trintignant, who catapulted into fame when he appeared with Brigitte Bardot in . . . *And God Created Woman* in 1956. Trintignant came out of retirement to make *Amour*, his first film in fifteen years. The no less legendary Emmanuelle Riva had starred in another "Amour" film more than half a century earlier, *Hiroshima Mon Amour* (1959). Trintignant and Riva are perfectly cast in their roles: their advanced age is palpable, and we can see them grow infirm as a result of illness and caregiving.

The two characters who began their careers portraying vernal youth will be immortalized in *Amour* for depicting the autumnal years of life. Eva, their self-preoccupied middle-aged daughter in the film, is played by Isabelle Huppert, who appeared in two of Haneke's earlier films, *The Piano Teacher* (2001) and *Time of the Wolf* (2003). Both Huppert and Trintignant appear in the 2017 Haneke film *Happy Ending*, a title that belies the film's unrelenting grimness.

## "The Most Unbearable Thing in Life"

In a conversation with Anne Thompson in *IndieWire*, Haneke related a story that Trintignant had expressed to several interviewers. Driving home from the hospital following an accident in which he was seriously injured, Trintignant wondered whether he should crash into a tree and end it all. "And my producer told him: 'Make the film first. You can commit suicide after that.' And now he says he doesn't want to commit suicide anymore." Film-lovers are grateful for Trintignant's decision, but if we are to take the anecdote seriously, one wonders why making *Amour* didn't provoke the opposite reaction, smashing into the tree. Nor is this a flippant observation, for as the director and actors revealed in the "Making of *Amour*," the film posed excruciating challenges. Watching someone you love suffering from illness is "perhaps the most unbearable thing in life," Haneke observed, "even worse than having a disease yourself."

Riva was eighty-five when she starred in the film, and sometimes her identification with the disintegrating Anne was so intense that she felt acutely depressed. "She was so shaken up," Trintignant remarked, "that for a few hours she couldn't speak," adding, "She gave it her all, working herself to death! It could have killed her." Riva admits that playing the role of Anne was so traumatic that she had to remind herself she was making a film, to break the dire spell that was overcoming her—an example of emotional contagion infecting the actress. If *Riva* had difficulty convincing herself she was not Anne, how are viewers supposed to remember the difference between life and illusion? Or as Francine Prose recounts, the actors in *Amour* deliver performances "so convincing and delicately nuanced that we forget they are actors, let alone French movie stars."

It's always valuable to hear novelists or film directors speak about their intentions in a work, even if their comments are not the final words about their creations. Haneke didn't intend to raise in *Amour* a "problem" that has a straightforward solution. "I don't want the film to be reduced to the issues of old age. Instead, I think it's a film about love, as it says in the title. And about dealing with the pain of a loved one" ("The Making of *Amour*"). Nevertheless, for those who have primary responsibility for the caring of a relative or friend, love and caregiving are often inseparable. The failure of one may betoken the failure of the other.

*Amour* is Haneke's most personal film, and it is based on the question, as he expressed in an interview with Peter Conrad, "How do I deal with the fact that someone I love is suffering?" The private source of the film arose from the agony of his 92-year-old aunt who had brought him up in the absence of his parents, actors with little talent for or interest in child-raising. Disabled by rheumatism, she overdosed on sleeping pills. Haneke found her in time and rushed her to the hospital, thwarting her suicide attempt. In Conrad's words, "She had previously begged him to help her die; he pointed out that since he was her heir, he might have ended in prison. A year after her first attempt, she swallowed more pills and put herself out of her misery." To add personal authenticity to the film, Haneke modeled Georges and Anne's Paris apartment on his parents' Vienna apartment. The apartment itself, as Dave Calhoun has suggested, is a "character itself," revealing the Laurents' age, background, and interests. In addition, the funeral Georges attends in the film, the only time when he is separated from Anne after her return from the hospital, was based on Haneke's father's funeral. In an interview with James Mottram, Haneke referred to what he imagines to be the perfect death, that of his wife's grandmother. "She was 95. She was sitting at a table, surrounded by friends. At one point she said, 'I feel tired' and laid her head on the table and died." *Amour* dramatizes the opposite of a perfect death.

Few films have generated more acclaim than *Amour*. The film won the Palme d'Or, the top prize, at the Cannes Film Festival in 2012; three years earlier, Haneke's *The White Ribbon* received the same coveted award, making him at the time only the seventh director to have received the award twice. *Amour* won the Best Foreign Language Film at the 85th Academy Awards and was nominated in four other categories: Best Picture, Best Actress in a Leading Role, Best Original Screenplay (by Haneke), and Best Director. In her *New York Times* review, Manohla Dargis referred to *Amour* as a "masterpiece about life, death and everything in between." David Thomson used the same word in *The New Republic*, calling *Amour* a "masterpiece," not just the best of the year, but "one of the best ever." What makes *Amour* "so strong and clear," Anthony Lane wrote in *The New Yorker*, "is that it allows Haneke to anatomize his own severity." In a review airing on *NPR*, Ella Taylor observed that *Amour* makes the "perfectly fine Julie Christie film *Away from Her* look like an ad for a swank retirement home, but it will stir your soul." Every Haneke film has provoked criticism, often ferocious denunciation, and *Amour* is no exception. Reviewing the film in *The New Yorker*, Richard Brody found the subject matter "powerful and true" but the treatment objectionable. "That's what makes Haneke's rigid contrivances—the pristinely repressed and filtered script and images, the directorial straight face held with iron bands to suppress laughter—all the more repellent."

## A Wrenching Film

Some reviewers lauded the film but admitted that it was nearly impossible to watch. "I almost didn't make it through *Amour*," Hannah Goldfield confessed in an article aptly named "Surviving *Amour*" appearing in *The New Yorker*. The problem was not that she was unprepared for the film: she knew what it was about. Nor was she put off by "depressing" films in the past. But Haneke's film saddened her in ways that she found intolerable. "It depressed me to the point that my chest felt tight, that fat tears streamed down my face as I struggled to keep my shoulders from heaving too noticeably. It depressed me to the point that I seriously contemplated escaping to the bathroom to have it out and collect myself, and considered leaving the theatre altogether." Goldfield felt shaken because the film hit too close to home, reminding her of the devastation she experienced when her elderly grandparents died.

*Amour* speaks personally to young viewers, like Goldfield, worried about their parents' and grandparents' deaths. What prevented her from bursting into convulsive sobs while watching the film, she notes ruefully, apart from respect for her fellow moviegoers, was that she was sitting next to her boyfriend and his parents, "whom I did not want to think I was a basket case." Yet the film has greater urgency for the elderly. Writing in *Psychology Today*, Kathryn Betts Adams commented that although the theater was full when she and her husband saw the film, she was surprised that she did not see more people her own age: midlife adults. "I speculated that people my age and younger do not wish to think about the possibility of our parents, spouses, or ourselves becoming disabled in old age and needing care." Adams, a gerontological social worker, found the film compelling, but like all the clinicians who have written about *Amour*, she felt the need to correct or at least call attention to many of the film's troubling assumptions about old age and caregiving. *Amour* is not the first film to elicit cautionary statements from mental health professionals, but no film in recent memory has dramatized more mightily art's ability to make viewers suffer—in this case, implicating viewers in the caregiver's anguish and helplessness that culminate in an act that has been interpreted as either euthanasia or homicide.

Haneke has compared filming to the making of a ski jump: "you have to build a good jump, but viewers have to take the leap, and how far they go depends on how good your ski jump is" (qtd in Walker, 91, n31). The director aims for maximum ambiguity, allowing viewers the freedom to reach their own interpretations about what they see. As he observes in the documentary *24 Realities Per Second*, "My whole work consists of preserving a certain ambiguity, allowing the spectator to find his own interpretation." Haneke fears that by answering the questions he poses in a film, he will destroy its art. "It's up to you to decide what it means." Haneke's artistic credo recalls Chekov's observation that the role of the artist is to ask questions, not answer them. But Chekhov did not have in mind the murderous actions in *Amour*.

## Critiquing or Exploiting Violence?

Haneke cannot be faulted for maintaining ambiguity, but the controversy surrounding his films is whether his portrayal of violence and cruelty is an act of critique or exploitation. The director's incendiary statements about art have not always won him supporters. "I've been accused of 'raping' the audience in my films, and I admit to that freely," he told John Wray in a *New York Times Magazine* interview in 2007: "all movies assault the viewer in one way or another. What's different about my films is this: I'm trying to rape the viewer into independence." Filmgoers have predictably reached opposite conclusions about this filmic independence. Some viewers have bemoaned the impossibility of locating Haneke's authorial position in relation to violence. "It's Haneke's usual strategy," complained Brody: "to make viewers complicit with morally dubious deeds while keeping his own hands resolutely clean." But other scholars, like Elsie Walker, the author of the 2017 book *Hearing Haneke*, stress his "moral compass, political progressiveness, and compassion for humanity" (5).

Haneke's reputation for shocking violence and cruelty long preceded *Amour*. His first three films, which he has called his "glaciation trilogy"—*The Seventh Continent* (1989), *Benny's Video* (1993), and *71 Fragments of a Chronicle of Chance* (1994)—stunned viewers. *The Seventh Continent* describes a family of three who commit suicide together after destroying all of their possessions. *Benny's Video*, despite its innocuous title, opens with a fourteen-year-old boy obsessively watching footage he has taken of a squealing pig being slaughtered by a butcher gun. Benny then uses the same gun to shoot a teenage girl he has lured to his family's apartment. We see her writhing in pain, but he never displays emotion or regret about the callous murder; afterward, he proceeds to do his homework, as if nothing has happened. No less horrifying are his parents' responses. The father, in an effort to conceal the crime and protect his son, disposes of the body by chopping it into small pieces and then flushing the body parts down the toilet, though Haneke mercifully spares the audience from watching the dismemberment. Asked by his father near the end of the film why he has killed the girl, Benny replies indifferently, "I wanted to see what it was like." Benny's motives for killing the stranger remain as unfathomable as the reasons for his unexpected betrayal of his parents at the end when he shows the police a tape he has made of them planning the cover-up. It is hard to know which is more morally outrageous, Benny's irrational but unpremeditated murder or his parents' methodical cover-up. A mass shooting takes place at the end of *71 Fragments of a Chronicle of Chance* along with a character committing suicide.

Haneke's later films are no less unsettling. *Funny Games* (1997) depicts two sadistic youths who invade a home and torture a family of three. As with the earlier films, the violence here is graphic and gratuitous. Haneke captures the mind's obsessive rumination over violence. After the distraught mother uses a rifle to kill one of the marauders, the other uses a television remote to replay and magically undo the violence, bringing his dead comrade back to life. The killers remain at large at the end of the film, eager to unleash evil on new victims. Unable to find any explanation for the killers' sadistic violence, viewers may be reminded of Iago's motiveless malignity. Stephen Holden concluded his *New York Times* review of *Funny Games* by comparing the film to the "patient delight of a cat luxuriantly toying with a mouse that it is in the process of slowly killing. Posing as a morally challenging work of art, the movie is really a sophisticated act of cinematic sadism. You go to it at your own risk." Part of the risk is identifying Haneke's moral and ethical vision. In his statements about the purpose of art, the director always insists on the struggle to portray the truth. "Film is 24 lies per second at the service of truth, or at the service of the attempt to find the truth," he remarked in the documentary, a pronouncement that recalls Picasso's more succinct declaration that art is a lie that tells the truth.

*The Piano Teacher*, based on the 1983 novel by the Austrian Nobel Laureate Elfriede Jelinek, presents a sadomasochistic woman who sits on the edge of a bath and, placing a mirror between her legs, uses a razor blade to cut her genitalia. Later, she puts a shard of glass in a rival's coat pocket. Near the end of the film, Haneke shows her being raped and plunging a knife into her breast. In

*Cache* (2005), we witness an unexpected suicide of a desperate man who takes out a knife and slits his throat, the blood spurting out on the wall behind him. *The White Ribbon* narrates the violent attacks on a German village during the months leading up to the First World War. In a 2014 interview published in *The Paris Review*, Luisa Zielinski characterized the polarizing Haneke as, "depending on whom you ask, the minister of fear, a master of horrors, Europe's greatest auteur, or simply a sadist."

The violence in *Amour* comes as a shock, but it is not entirely unexpected. There is external violence, as when Georges and Anne return to their apartment after attending a concert and discover that a burglar has attempted to break their door lock. Most of the violence in the film, however, is internal, as when we see Anne's body and mind breaking down. *Amour* dramatizes the violence of time and nature leading to inevitable decay and time. There is also the violence of Anne's ending, which has understandably sparked much debate. But hardly anything has been written about Georges's role as caregiver, or even his enigmatic fate at the end of the film.

## "You Want to Torture Me?"

*Amour* opens with firemen and police breaking into an apartment. They discover in the bedroom sealed with tape the corpse of an elderly woman lying in bed, her body strewn with desiccated flowers. Opening the windows, a fireman holds his nose to avoid being overcome by the stench of death. By revealing Anne's fate at the beginning, Haneke eliminates the element of surprise. As with the opening in *The Death of Ivan Ilych*, where we see the deceased protagonist, the remaining questions in *Amour* are how and why the death occurred. The film proceeds backward, chronicling the events leading to her demise. *Amour* then cuts to a concert hall, the Théâtre des Champs-Elysées, where an audience eagerly awaits a performance by Anne's protégé and former student, the real-life pianist Alexandre Tharaud, playing himself. The camera, which appears to be located on center stage, scans the audience, where we see (though we do not yet know it) Georges and Anne sitting patiently for the concert to begin, which opens with Schubert's melodic Impromptu, No. 1 in C minor, Op. 90. *Amour* feels, as Uma Anyar remarks, "as if one audience is watching another," suggesting not only the fact that we are always watching and being watched but also a "postmodern deconstruction of the illusion of film and its ability to reproduce reality."

After the concert, Georges and Anne congratulate the pianist, and they then take a trolley car home. The next morning, while they are having breakfast, Georges asks Anne a question, but she is suddenly motionless in her chair, speechless. "What's going on?" Georges asks, alarmed, but she doesn't answer. A couple of minutes later, as Georges prepares to telephone their physician, Anne regains consciousness, unaware she has had a mild stroke. Her inability to explain what has happened provokes her husband's exasperation, to which she responds, in an exclamation laced with irony, "You want to torture me?" Thus, begins Georges's life as a caregiver, in which he is both the tortured and the torturer.

While her mother is still in the hospital for what turns out to be failed surgery to relieve an obstruction in her carotid artery, Eva visits her father, but instead of asking how she is, or visiting Anne in the hospital, she prattles on about her life: her finances, her travels to other European cities to concertize, her children, and her conflicted marriage with Geoff. She informs her father about her husband's brief affair with a viola player in their ensemble. "What can I say? It caused a huge drama. She tried to kill herself. He got scared and came back to me, riddled with remorse." (Elsie Walker refers to *Eva's* suicide attempt [182], but this is factually incorrect.) Was Geoff's remorse due to his adultery, his guilt over the violist's suicide attempt, or both? The question is important because at the end of the film, when Eva returns to her parents' empty apartment, she is lost in her thoughts, almost certainly riddled with regret, guilt, and remorse.

Georges, whose back is to the camera, listens carefully to Eva, but one infers the emotional distance in the father-daughter relationship. When Eva finally asks, almost as an aside—"What can I do to help?"—her father responds brusquely, "nothing," suggesting that he alone will be Anne's caregiver. "We've always coped," he adds, but he has never before been in a situation like this.

## "Promise Me"

The word "nothing" reappears when Anne makes Georges promise not to send her back to the hospital. The elliptical dialogue conceals more than it reveals:

> "Promise me something."
> "What?"
> "Please, never take me back to the hospital."
> "What?"
> "Will you promise me?"

"Anne."
"Promise me. Don't speak. Don't explain. Please."
"What can I say?"
"Nothing. Say nothing, okay?"

Unable to read Georges's unspoken thoughts or his impassive facial expression, we don't know whether he agrees to Anne's promise. In a 2012 *New York Times* interview, Larry Rohter reminded Trintignant of a statement he had made early in his career that "the best actors in the world are those who feel the most and show the least." Recalling the comment, the actor observed that he finally found in Haneke, whom Trintignant believes is the world's greatest living auteur, a director whose philosophy of acting coincided with his own. "He said that he always tells actors not to exteriorize, to feel emotions deeply but never to show them, that it's up to him and the camera to capture those feelings." It's impossible to read George's continued silence, which does not necessarily imply consent to Anne's request; his silence may imply only that he doesn't know what to say—an understandable response to a new and frightening situation.

Georges could have responded to Anne's request by reassuring her that he will always be present to help her and that he will never abandon her. The dying often need these reassurances. Indeed, the fear of abandonment may have been the unconscious meaning behind Anne's request. Her command to say "nothing" is fraught with irony. One recalls Lear's response to his daughter Cordelia's use of the same word. "Nothing will come of nothing," he warns her in an ominous self-fulfilling prophecy. Shakespeare's play is one of the few works with a bleaker ending than *Amour*. We can't tell from this scene whether Georges's silence means that he agrees to the promise, though he refers to upholding the vow in a later scene with Eva.

## The Beginning of Caregiving

Georges performs some of his early caregiving duties with zest, such as cooking for Anne. "I haven't seen meals involving older people that affected me so keenly since Ozu's *Tokyo Story*," enthused Stanley Kauffman in *The New Republic*. "Georges knows what she likes, and she knows that he knows, saying nothing about it. The meals are both memories and markers."

Little has changed after Anne's arrival home. "You don't have to hold my hand all the time," she gently scolds Georges after he has helped her into bed. "And don't feel guilty. It would be absurd and oppressive. For me, too." They are cheerful and affectionate with each other, smiling, bantering, nodding attentively. She encourages Georges to "find yourself something to do," and he obliges by reading, an activity that has sustained them throughout their lives, as Catherine Wheatly suggests. "The spines of their paperbacks are cracked and worn; in their tired but cozy kitchenette, they pour each other tea and compare notes on the new biography of conductor Nikolaus Harnoncourt."

Georges then relates to Anne a story he has never disclosed before, about being overcome by emotion as a youth when he saw a film about a "schmaltzy romance" between a nobleman and a commoner's daughter. The emotion "bubbled up again" when he told a stranger about the film. "I stood there in tears in the courtyard telling him the whole damn story." Georges cannot now remember the film, but he recalls vividly the embarrassing experience of becoming emotionally distraught, the humiliation of crying. The experience, which is based on an actual event in Haneke's own youth, may help to explain Georges's emotional restraint throughout *Amour*: he never cries in the film or even tears up. His restraint, approaching frozen emotion, culminates in an explosive act of violence against his wife. Georges's frigid restraint recalls Ann Kaiser Stearns's metaphor of frozen emotion:

> Water, as it freezes and the molecules expand, has the power to burst steel pipes wide open. Likewise, frozen emotion assumes a power out of proportional to its original nature. In the middle of a very harsh winter it's wise to see to it that the water flows fairly regularly through your home plumbing system. Similarly, during the harsh seasons of grief, it is best to keep the channels open so that hurtful feelings are freely expressed. Frozen emotion, like a frozen pipe, has the potential for causing unexpected problems. (60–1)

Anne finds Georges's story "sweet," but she accuses him, in what may be the single most enigmatic line in the film, of being a "monster sometimes." She doesn't elaborate on the statement, but she immediately qualifies it, with a broad smile, "But very kind." Because we don't know anything about their lives or marriage before the film opens, we have no way of knowing whether Georges has been a scary or gentle monster in the past. In one of the most illuminating essays on *Amour*, Andrea Gogröf suggests the ways in which Georges *and* Anne are monsters, though they always remain human and relatable.

Returning home from Pierre's funeral, Georges finds Anne sprawled helplessly on the floor in her bedroom, possibly because of a failed attempt to throw herself out of a large opened window. "Forgive me," she says, without looking at Georges. From this moment on, they both seem increasingly worried.

Georges's reluctance to speak about Pierre's funeral may reflect their unspoken fear of Anne's own impending funeral. Strikingly, at no point in the film do Anne and Georges talk about end-of-life issues. Georges's reference to Pierre's distraught widow evokes Anne's despairing words, "There's no reason to go on living. I know it can only get worse. Why must I inflict pain on you and me?" Georges responds by denying that he feels tortured, but she accuses him of lying. "Put yourself in my shoes," he counters, but she cannot or will not attempt to empathize with his situation. "Imagination and reality have little in common," she opines, a statement that the film seeks to undercut by showing how much *Amour* has to do with reality. Anne's failure of empathy reveals the limits of her imagination. Illness has darkened her love, preventing her from not only being in Georges's shoes but also trying to be as protective of him as possible. The scene ends with Anne going to bed, withdrawing further into herself.

## "I Owe You a Lot"

Both Anne and Georges are beginning to retreat from the world, as the next moments dramatize. Alexandre knocks on the door, wishing to see his former teacher but reluctant to intrude. He had telephoned Georges, who admits that he has largely stopped answering the telephone, suggesting his growing isolation. Anne is genuinely happy to see Alexandre, and he expresses his gratitude to her: "I owe you a lot." In response to his polite inquiry about her health, she admits that the right side of her body is paralyzed, but she attributes this to aging rather than to a stroke and quickly changes the subject. She asks him to play a Beethoven Bagatelle, but we hear only a few notes. Later she orders Georges to stop playing Alexandre's CD: "Turn it off." Music, once Anne's entire life and career, no longer provides her with pleasure, consolation, or solace. She cannot find much comfort in the knowledge that she has contributed to the success of Alexandre's career. The recognition of a future without her presence is terrifying. Later, Anne looks through old photos of herself. "It's beautiful. Life. So long. Long life." Georges looks at her, anguished, and she responds, "Stop peering at me." Although the artifacts in the Laurents' apartment reveal the beauty and richness of a long life, *Amour* does not celebrate the fullness of existence, life's plenitude, but rather the embrace of death. Erik Erikson's notion of generativity, the seventh of his eight stages of psychosocial development, in which people derive joy from helping to make the world a better place, is denied to Anne.

Nor does Georges find much comfort from music: he plays a few chords on the piano and stops, as if grief-stricken. We next see him shampooing Anne's hair, fully engaged in the task, but in the following scene, she falls out of bed, provoking his first angry response in the film: "Can't you call me when you need something?" In the next sequence, Georges appears to be menaced by the familiar Haneke threat of external violence. The doorbell rings, but when Georges opens the door, no one's there; he walks through his flooded apartment and someone grabs him from behind, attempting to smother him—a premonition of what is soon to happen, though with Georges in the active role of smotherer. Screaming, he wakes up from a nightmare, and Anne comforts him, the last time she will do so, momentarily becoming *his* caregiver.

## The Next Stage

Mortified when she becomes incontinent, Anne is unable to look at Georges as he struggles to lift her out of bed into her wheelchair. A second stroke has incapacitated her. Her speech has become disconnected, making it difficult to understand her. The film dramatizes the changes in her appearance, speech, and state of mind. "Sometimes it's as if she's totally unaware of her state," Georges informs his son-in-law. "A moment later it's the opposite." Weeping, Eva cannot endure her mother's deterioration. "She's talking gibberish. We can't leave her lying there like that. She's unrecognizable. It's mad." Noting that witnessing pain may be difficult to watch, Manohla Dargis argues that *Amour* "willingly" holds the viewer throughout the film, but a better word might be "forces" because of the viewer's resistance to viewing searing pain.

We realize that outside help is necessary for both care-receiver and caregiver. "Don't you think you're taking on too much?" Eva asks her father, though she doesn't offer to help. Tensions mount in the father-daughter relationship. Haneke gives us details about caregiving that we seldom see in other films. The image of Anne's vacant eyes while Georges feeds her spoonfuls of puréed food is heartrending, recalling Meryl Streep's performance in *One True Thing*, but unlike the director of the Quindlen film, Richard Eyre, Haneke dwells obsessively on his actress's face. From this moment on, *Amour* is wrenching to watch, perhaps because the camera dwells searchingly on Anne's interminable suffering. Peter Conrad reports that Emmanuelle Riva "had to strip naked for a scene in which a bossy nurse bathes her; she didn't believe, until the moment came, that Haneke was really going to oblige her to undress." The aide doesn't seem domineering in this scene—she is simply performing her job efficiently and compassionately. Nor is there anything exploitative or voyeuristic as we watch her shower. We see Georges's other caregiving responsibilities, including learning how to change Anne's diaper when she becomes incontinent. The end of life, *Amour* dramatizes, is like the beginning of life, a state of helpless dependency.

If it is excruciating for us to witness these scenes of caregiving for a few minutes—*Amour* is 130 minutes long—what must it be like for Georges to fulfill his caregiving role for twenty-four hours a day, seven days a week, without respite? The Laurents' fashionable apartment, as reviewers have discerned, is now a prison and a mausoleum. David Sorfa's 2006 observation about Haneke's use of domestic space in his films—"the place of safety . . . is the very place of danger" (98)—is strikingly true in *Amour*.

Georges hires a second nurse but then fires her for treating Anne harshly, yet ironically, his own treatment of her a few minutes later is crueler. He pries open Anne's mouth while trying to give her water, but she refuses to cooperate. "I need your help," he pleads, but when she spits the water in his face, he slaps her. Appalled, he asks for her forgiveness. We identify with both caregiver and care-receiver. How would we respond if we were in these roles? *Amour* challenges us to raise this question, but unless we have occupied both roles, that of the caregiver and care-receiver, we don't know how we would react. Georges whispers something to Anne that we cannot hear. Her eyes reveal her wish to die, but he is not ready for her to leave. We then see several landscape paintings in the apartment, perhaps conjuring a contrast between idyllic art and discordant reality. Georges's walking begins to change imperceptibly; he seems to shuffle unsteadily, tired, dejected, and broken.

"What's going on with Mom?" Eva asks at the beginning of her surprise visit. She has left four phone messages that her father has not answered, again emphasizing his disengagement with the world. Georges declines to recount for Eva all of his caregiving duties, stating, "None of that bears showing," yet what's remarkable about *Amour* is that it *has* shown these acts in perhaps greater detail than any other film. In what proves to be their final encounter, Georges says to his daughter, chillingly, "Your concern is of no use to me. Don't take it personally." He then softens the criticism. "You two have your own life. Leave us with ours." We sympathize with both characters, but our main concern is with Georges, who is being pushed to the breaking point. Yet Eva, too, is under stress. If we can imagine the impact of his words on his daughter after the film ends, she will have a lifetime to ruminate over her father's bitterness. To his credit,

Haneke doesn't demonize their relationship. "The tea's not very hot," George softly murmurs to her, offering her a cup, "but it perks you up."

Small kindnesses like this abound in *Amour*, offsetting its grimness. Anne and Georges still have a few more smiles left for each other, after a lifetime of living together. In one of the film's most poignant moments, they sing the children's song "Sur le Pont d'Avignon." The Laurents' neighbors express their sympathy and goodwill. "We're very impressed by the way you're coping," the building manager tells him, eliciting George's sincere thanks. Near the end, Anne attempts to talk to Georges, and though we can't hear her words, we are struck by their closeness. Anne touches her husband's hand, and we see their wedding rings in close proximity, like the entangling branches of Baucis and Philemon metamorphosed into trees.

## Euthanasia or Homicide?

Nothing prepares us for the shock of Georges suffocating Anne to death, an act that is brutally violent and startlingly graphic. One moment he is dutifully attending her, the next moment, pouncing on top of her, pressing a pillow over her head. The suffocation is unbearably long, nearly twenty seconds, and we see her leg jerking under the blanket, not unlike the image of the writhing victim in *Benny's Video*. Early in *Amour*, Eva tells her father that as a young child, she remembered listening to her parents making love. "For me it was reassuring. It made me feel you loved each other and that we'd always be together." Her words foretell her parents' final moment together, evoking an image of love and death. Another proleptic moment occurs at the beginning of the film when, after discovering that a burglar has attempted to break into their apartment, Anne exclaims, "Imagine if we're in bed and someone bursts in . . . . It's horrible. I think I'd die of fright."

What's shocking about Georges's suffocation of Anne is the prolonged violence of the scene, not the idea of homicide or suicide. Indeed, in most of the caregiver stories, films, and memoirs we've discussed, homicidal or suicidal thoughts afflict the caregiver, care-receiver, or both. It would be unusual for a caregiver or care-receiver *not* to have these murderous thoughts, both as an end to suffering and anger over abandonment. The smash-up scene in *Ethan Frome*; Alma's threat to hurl a pot of boiling water at Elisabet in *Persona*; Bayley's ambiguous statement to his wife in *Iris and Her Friends*, "Don't worry, darling, we shall soon be dead"; and the daughters' wish for their mothers to die in *One*

*True Thing* and *Circling My Mother*, all testify to the threat or reality of caregivers' violence toward either care-receivers or themselves.

Not surprisingly, Georges's action has provoked widely—and wildly—divergent responses. One suspects that viewers' attitudes toward euthanasia and physician-assisted suicide strongly influence their feelings about this moment in the film. At one extreme is Richard Brody. "But what comes off onscreen is the filmmaking's smirking pleasure at depicting, with a chilling explicitness, a heinously affirmative killing—a peculiarly active variety of euthanasia." Alluding to Dylan Thomas's celebrated poem, Calum Marsh stated in *Slant* that there's "no going gentle into that good night; it's all useless rage."

At the other extreme is Elsie Walker, who makes the astonishing claim that the "scholarly tendency to dwell on the euthanasia scene reflects a sensationalist approach that goes hand in hand with comparing the film to horror" (200). Walker characterizes the act as one of "amazing kindness" and views Anne's quivering body as "more like a forceful embrace than a fight" (192). Catherine Wheatley is sympathetic to Georges's decision but without foreclosing the legitimacy of scholarly discussion. "[U]ntil the film's very end he is her fierce protector, as his final act of devotion makes devastatingly clear." Andrea Gogröf also regards the euthanasia sympathetically. "Georges's final act of killing his wife, ending the agony, transcends the barrier that keeps life, love, and death apart. It is monstrous, but is also a form of *Liebestod* that his mysterious vanishing from the film supports." In a long analysis of the film, Roy Grundmann believes the suffocation is both "merciful" and "clearly selfish"; as an "act of cruelty," it "ranks among the bluntest in Haneke's canon." Some reviewers, such as the film critic Jeffrey Overstreet, maintain that Haneke is critical of Georges's decision to end Anne's life. "I find *no evidence in the movie* that Michael Haneke is *honouring or recommending Georges*' rash and violent act" (emphasis in original). Bob Moss believes that Haneke is characteristically evasive, forcing viewers to reach their own conclusions and, in the process, sparking public debate on euthanasia.

## Clinical Discussions

The clinical discussions of *Amour* add a real-life dimension to euthanasia and caregiving. Writing in the prestigious English medical journal *The Lancet*, Hilary Rose and Steven Rose conclude that a "silent message of *Amour* is that the medical profession's traditional belief that its arguments for palliative care automatically trump the desires and needs of those confronting death is under cultural discussion." Hilary Rose, a sociology professor and a founding member of the British Society for Social Responsibility, and Steven Rose, a British neurologist, are both septuagenarians, and they end their coauthored article by saying that watching *Amour* was salutary; "after long discussion we each wrote the letters Anne, in her need and desire for death, might well have written" (1219). The British psychiatrist Joyce Almeida observes that *Amour* "offers an incredibly powerful portrait of the real stress that carers may experience, if they continue to want to provide the majority of the personal care required." Noting the film's depiction of familial and intergenerational tensions, Almeida raises the question, "who gets to choose what is best for an individual when mental capacity to make a particular decision about care is lost?" The film is a valuable learning opportunity, she concludes, for anyone interested or involved in caring for the elderly population.

Writing in *The Gerontologist*, Rick J. Scheidt, Jim Vanden Bosch, and Helen Q. Kivnick laud the film's "unblinking view" of aging but point out that although Haneke's vision of the *threat* of old age is correct, his vision fails in the assumption that we must cope with this problem alone. "In later scenes of the film, Anne is often crying out in pain. Why Georges does not seek out hospice care to help Anne with pain management at this point, is the huge unanswered question in this film." The authors criticize Georges for his unawareness of in-home hospice care, which would allow him to continue to honor his pledge to Anne while at the same time providing her with expert pain management.

In her critique of *Amour* in *The Guardian*, Margaret Morganroth Gullette objects to Haneke's vision of caregiving:

> [W]e have a film detailing Georges' protracted caregiving so respectfully and Anne's decline so cruelly that it becomes hard to disagree with Georges' masochistic choices, or even notice that he has broken down. It presents a nonconsensual termination of life as a solution for the carer: it justifies euthanasia. That such a film has been so widely acclaimed while remaining so ill-examined is a dangerous thing. ("*Amour*")

Gullette also points out that most caregivers do not end their own lives after a loved one's death. "The fact is that however stressful caregiving may be, this is the outcome in just 0.001% of cases, in the US anyway."

Philip A. Ringstrom's psychoanalytic interpretation of *Amour* illuminates the role of illusion in love. "Georges cannot allow Anne—the object of his romantic illusion—to die. And the reason for this is that with the exception of perhaps psychosis, our illusions require at least a whiff of the reality upon which we hinge them" (158–9). In Ringstrom's view, Georges cannot let go of the illusory or idealized Anne. Concluding his article with Lacan's paradoxical (and cynical) statement that "Love is giving something you do not have to someone you do not know," Ringstrom suggests that *Amour* questions "where our illusions and the reality we assume that they adhere to, converge, or remain assiduously apart" (161).

Kathryn Betts Adams questions the film's assumption about aging and caretaking. Arguing that Anne would have benefited from more social stimulation and supportive counseling, Adams suggests that she probably would have felt better had Georges not been her main caregiver. He, too, would have benefited from respite. Commenting on the stigma associated with end-of-life issues, Adams reaches a noteworthy conclusion. Though some elderly people may die in their sleep, others decline "gradually, in less appealing ways, losing this capability and that, requiring help to dress and bathe and eat, and yes, even to use the toilet. There is no shame in this; it should not be a secret."

## Disappearing

Like *Persona*, *Amour* focuses relentlessly on the caregiver and care-receiver's faces, which are both transformed as the film progresses. During the opening concert, Anne's face is radiant and serene, the image of ageless beauty, but then we see her during her first stroke, frozen and mute. The camera captures her inexorable decline. We see Georges transformed from a self-possessed senior to a man tormented by his wife's suffering. The two faces do not mysteriously dissolve into each other, suggestive of a blurring of boundaries or transfer of identity, as we see in *Persona*, but they undergo a more haunting and harrowing metamorphosis. In the still photo that appears in a half-dozen online reviews of *Amour*, Georges gazes horrorstruck at Anne, his eyes bulging out, while he touches her hair. We cannot see her face, but we can guess at her feelings. Throughout the second half of the film, Anne's eyes betray the wish to die: Georges's eyes, until the end, reveal the desire to keep his wife alive at any cost. Unlike his earlier films, in which he often shatters verisimilitude to address the viewer, Haneke does nothing in *Amour* to break the spell of reality.

Georges's expressionless face prevents us from knowing his thoughts at the end, but he appears to engage in a purification ceremony, ritualistically cutting flowers that will be strewn on Anne's body and carefully choosing an appropriate funeral outfit for her. He acts slowly and deliberately, as if he has meticulously planned what must be done, though the act of suffocation appears impulsive. The purification scene has a stark solemnity that contrasts the emotional excess of Pierre's funeral service. Georges seals up the bedroom door with tape and then writes a letter, which may be a suicide note to his daughter, sees a pigeon (for the second time), throws a blanket over it, returns to the letter, stating that he has "let it go again"—even though it appears for a moment that he has smothered it. Suddenly he imagines Anne alive, washing dishes. "Put your shoes on if you want," she murmurs, perhaps recalling his metaphorical use of the word earlier in the film: "Put yourself in my shoes." He silently complies with her request, and the two of them glide out of the apartment together.

There's no evidence that Georges or Anne believe in God, an afterlife, or in reunion after death. As in Ingmar Bergman's films, one of Haneke's major themes, Richard Porton avers, is the "struggle of modern, middle-class Europeans to live in a world where time-honored religious values have eroded." Georges's momentary fantasy at the end, imagining walking out of the darkened apartment with Anne, has more to do with an exit from life than an entry into another world. Their departure together is made possible through what appears to be an implicit homicide/suicide pact, one that culminates offscreen.

Most commentators assume that Georges commits suicide, or prepares to commit suicide, at the end of the film, perhaps by turning on the gas jets and asphyxiating himself. Georges's final scene, Ringstrom suggests, like other scenes in the film, "goes on at silent length so as to draw us into a sense of the real time he awaits before he passes out." Georges seals the apartment doors, according to Ringstrom, to ensure that "there can be no fresh air to mitigate the gathering poisonous gas" (160). The firemen and police who break into the apartment, however, do not behave as if there is a gas leak, and there is no evidence of suicide by asphyxiation, or by any other method. The question remains: *Why does Haneke conjure up an ambiguous suicide?*

*Amour* offers us many internal reasons to believe that Georges commits suicide. He has invested his entire life in Anne, and there is never a moment when he imagines existence without her. He appears to have nothing left to live for, neither family, friends, reading, nor music. Georges's thinking becomes increasingly constricted, symptomatic of clinical depression. Additionally, it's likely that he feels guilt over the euthanasia, no matter how strongly Anne wished to end her life. Georges has led a deeply meaningful life, but his life no longer has meaning without Anne. Paradoxically, caring for her has kept him alive, despite the sacrifice of his physical and mental health, and he has nothing or no one to live for after her death.

There are also biographical reasons to believe that *Amour* ends with an implied suicide: Haneke's lifelong preoccupation with the subject. Self-inflicted death figures prominently in four of his television films: *Three Paths to the Lake* (1976), the two-part film *Lemmings* (1979), *Variation or "Utopias Exist, Yes I Know"* (1983), and *Fraulein* (1986). Suicide also appears in *The Seventh Continent* and *71 Fragments of a Chronology of Chance*, both of which involve murder/suicide. Writing before the appearance of *Amour*, Oliver C. Speck presciently observes that "suicide in Haneke almost always happens in front of a witness who seems to be strangely unaffected by the horrible spectacle and not traumatized in any way" (173), an insight that may help to explain the hint of an offscreen suicide. Haneke may have feared that ending the film with an explicit homicide/suicide would lead *Amour* in the direction of melodrama. But Haneke depicts suicide onscreen in *Happy Day*, the film he made after *Amour*. After smothering his ailing wife and now wheelchair bound, suffering from dementia, Georges Laurent, again played by Trintignant—Haneke uses the same names in film after film—rolls down a slipway into the sea.

Haneke scholars have not probed the biographical implications of *Amour*, perhaps because they have accepted his injunction against personal readings of his films. David Thomson reports without elaboration that the death of Haneke's mother "freed" him to make *Amour* (he was seventy when the film appeared). Citing Flaubert, Isabelle Huppert compares Haneke to the "very great directors" who are "present by their absence" ("The Making of *Amour*"). The documentarian Yves Montmayeur relayed Haneke's belief that the attempt to understand a director's biography works against an understanding of the film. "If I give you some information about my life, my background, immediately after it will interfere with interpretation of the movie" (Titze). Nevertheless, one should not minimize the impact of suicide in Haneke's life, particularly that of the elderly aunt who raised him when he was growing up. Haneke is notoriously antipsychology, as well as antibiography, throughout his films, including *Amour*, rejecting efforts to explain the inscrutable motives of his characters. But as Erik H. Erikson points out in *Young Man Luther*, "there is always an implicit psychology behind the explicit antipsychology" (36).

## The Caregiver's Suicide

*Amour* has sparked intense controversy over euthanasia, but little has been written about the caregiver's suicide apart from whether Georges takes his own life at the end of the film. What will be the impact of his suicide on his daughter and grandchildren? This is, of course, a speculative question, but it is worth asking in light of suicide's powerful contagion effect. Dark emotions are as contagious as germs.

The best known literary example of the contagion effect is Goethe's 1774 novel *The Sorrows of Young Werther*, which ends with the hero, rejected in love, shooting himself. Werther's suicide led to the copycat suicides of dozens of young men, some of them holding copies of the novel and wearing clothes similar to the hero: a blue waistcoat and a yellow vest. Another example of the copycat phenomenon in literature is Sylvia Plath, when, deeply depressed in 1963 over being abandoned by her husband Ted Hughes, she asphyxiated herself by placing her head in an oven. Imitating her rival, Assia Weevil, the woman with whom Hughes lived after he left Plath, asphyxiated herself and her young child in 1969. I discuss these and other examples in my 1999 book *Surviving Literary Suicide*. The suicide rate often jumps when a celebrity commits suicide. Suicides increased in the United States by 12 percent in the month after Marilyn Monroe's self-inflicted death (Phillips 306).

While I was working on this chapter, the Centers for Disease Control in Atlanta released statistics indicating that the suicide rate has jumped 25 percent in the United States since 1999. The dramatic increase occurred in nearly every ethnic and age group. At the same time these startling statistics appeared, two of the country's most prominent figures, the designer Kate Spade and the television chef and entertainer Anthony Bourdain, ended their own lives. As Clay Routledge observed in the *New York Times* about the disturbing rise in the suicide rate, to avoid succumbing to existential anxiety, we must maintain a meaningful life. "We are a species that strives not just for survival, but also for significance. We want lives that matter. It is when people are not able to maintain meaning that they are most psychologically vulnerable."

There are no reports of the suicide rate spiking as a result of *Amour*, but this is what happened with the Netflix series *13 Reasons Why*, about a teenage girl's suicide. As Benedict Carey reported in the *New York Times* on April 29, 2019, a study in the *Journal of Child and Adolescent Psychiatry* found that after the series premiered on March 31, 2017, the suicide rate among boys aged ten to seventeen jumped nearly 30 percent and remained higher for the year. "The study estimated that 195 more suicides occurred in 2017 in this age group than would be expected given current trends." Counterintuitively, there was no significant increase in the suicide rate among girls in the same age group, the demographic likely to identify most closely with the show's protagonist. The reason for the disparity, one researcher conjectured, is that although females are three times more likely to attempt suicide, males are four times more likely to complete it. Any increase in suicidal behavior among girls thus may have been in the number of suicide attempts, information not included in the journal article. Although youth suicide is perhaps the most tragic loss, the age group with the highest suicide rate is the elderly—Georges's generation. Distraught, Georges never considers the impact of his suicide on his daughter or grandchildren, who may be touched by the dark legacy—or illegacy—of suicide.

## "The Courage of Caring"

It may be hard to imagine a caregiver killing his desperately ill wife and then killing himself as a courageous act, but that is what Gladys González-Ramos describes in her chapter "The Courage of Caring," published in *Always on Call: When Illness Turns Families into Caregivers* in 2000. An associate professor at the New York University School of Social Work, she took care of her mother, who was diagnosed with Parkinson's disease in 1988, as well as her father. González-Ramos reveals with unwavering empathy how her father, "in a careful, deliberate way," shot her mother and then, positioning himself by the window of their eleventh-floor apartment, sat on the ledge and shot himself in the mouth. "He chose the particular window well, for if he used any other his body would have landed on someone's car or the parking lot driveway. My father was a man of details, a man who always helped others and never wanted to be a burden" (66). Her parents had agreed to the homicide-suicide, each unable to live without the other.

Anticipating that her readers might be appalled by the violence of her mother's ending, González-Ramos tells us that the "medical examiner at the morgue, who I went to see personally two months after their death, used words like 'caring' and 'compassion' to describe the manner in which he killed her, words that don't usually belong to such a violent act" (66). González-Ramos doesn't reveal the advice she would have offered her father, but she never questions her parents' decision. Had González-Ramos seen *Amour*, she probably would have felt the same way about Georges's act.

Georges's disappearance reveals the caregiver's uncertain future. By vanishing without a trace—the firemen and police do not discover another body next to Anne's, which is what we might expect if he committed suicide—Georges becomes a spectral figure, inhabiting the death-in-life existence of those caregivers who are bereft without their love. Using an expression borrowed from Nietzsche, Speck characterizes Haneke as a "physician of culture" (133). Nowhere is this better seen than in *Amour*. The film's diagnosis of cultural, medical, and existential dilemmas will probably always remain fiercely polarizing. Contrasting *The Death of Ivan Ilych* to *Amour*, Francine Prose states that while she has read the former many times and expects to continue to read it, she cannot imagine wanting to see the latter a second time.

And yet it's the film's power to *dis*comfort us, to offer *un*settling truths, that makes the cautionary tale memorable. *Amour* affirms Nietzsche's belief that we have art in order not to die of the truth. Another Nietzschean aphorism comes to mind: "What is done out of love always takes place beyond good and evil" (*The Philosophy of Nietzsche* 467). *Amour* remains, as Roger Ebert concluded in his glowing review, a "lesson for us that only the cinema can teach: the cinema, with its heedless ability to leap across time and transcend lives and dramatize what it means to be a member of humankind's eternal audience." Death is the opposite of life, but dying is part of living, and no film describes more powerfully than *Amour* the plight of the living trying to care for the dying.

# 9

# The Divine Gift of Caregiving in Walter Mosley's *The Last Days of Ptolemy Grey*

I had never heard of Walter Mosley until I googled the word "caregiver" and was directed to his 2010 novel *The Last Days of Ptolemy Grey*. Before reading the novel, I discovered that Mosley is one of the most prolific and honored contemporary American writers. He is the author of the "Easy Rollins" murder mystery series, which contains fourteen novels, as well as two other murder mystery series. Additionally, he has written science fiction novels, plays, and nonfiction. Several of his novels have been made into films, most notably, *Devil in a Blue Dress* (1995), starring Denzel Washington. Mosley came to prominence during the 1992 presidential election when Bill Clinton named him one of his favorite writers. Mosley has garnered several prestigious literary prizes, including an O. Henry Award in 1996, the Pen Center Lifetime Achievement Award in 2004, and the NAACP Image Award in Fiction in 2007 and 2009.

I was not surprised that I had never heard of Mosley. Art is long and life is short, I rationalized to myself. But I was surprised that an author known mainly for crime fiction would be interested in caregiving. Only vaguely familiar with the hard-boiled murder suspense story, I couldn't understand how this category of fiction could be conducive to caregiving. *The Last Days of Ptolemy Grey* is dazzling in its insights, power, and humanity. The novel abounds in mysteries, not the least of which is the miracle of storytelling.

How does a novelist evoke the loss and temporary recovery of a 91-year-old's memory and his improbable love for a woman young enough to be his great granddaughter who becomes his caregiver, inspiration for life, and heir? There are two mysteries that Mosley must solve in under 300 pages: the enigma of his mentor Coy McCann, "Coydog," who stole a pile of gold coins during Ptolemy Grey's youth in the Jim Crow South and was then lynched and set on fire; and, in present time, the identity of the man who murdered Ptolemy's beloved great-nephew Reggie in a drive-by shooting. Will Ptolemy be able to fulfill his promise to Coydog to use the stolen treasure, a product of a "righteous crime," to improve the lives of his own people? Will Ptolemy's unlikely caregiver, seventeen-year-old Robyn Small, be the spark that reignites his life? Will Ptolemy be able to live up to his storied name? Mosley uses these questions to drive the plot, all the time seeking to illuminate the nature of personal, familial, and historical caregiving.

## What's in a Name?

Mosley endows his protagonist with a legendary name. The polymath Ptolemy (Claudius Ptolemaeus) was a mathematician, astronomer, geographer, musician, and poet who lived 1,900 years ago in Alexandria in the Roman province of Egypt. When asked the meaning of his name, Mosley's Ptolemy responds, "It was Cleopatra's father's name" (270), a reference to another bearer of the name, Ptolemy XII, the last ruler of the Ptolemaic kingdom of Egypt. Mosley's protagonist does not appear regal, yet he is keenly aware of the plight of his people as a result of the thousand-year scourge of slavery, the "Great Degradation." If characters' names betoken their destinies, he lives up to the image of Claudius Ptolemy, who later became known as "Ptolemy the Wise." Mosley gives his hero more affectionate down-to-earth names—Pity Grey, Petey, Li'l Pea, and Pity Papa, the last of which evokes his compassion.

As the novel opens, Ptolemy's life is severely compromised. His memory, language, and cognition are rapidly failing, and he cannot make sense of his world. Nor can we. Mosley reproduces Ptolemy's confusion and murk in the reader. Because of Ptolemy's advanced age, he has a large family, but many of his relatives are no longer alive, and he cannot distinguish between the living and the dead. On a first reading, Ptolemy's genealogy is impossible to understand. Time has stopped for him, partly because of his growing dementia, and partly because of a vision of time in which past and future are indistinguishable, recalling William Faulkner's gnomic observation, "The past is never dead. It's not even past" (92).

The key figure in Ptolemy's past was Coydog McCann, who taught him how to read. Mosley conveys Coydog's centrality to Ptolemy in a subtle way: nearly all of Ptolemy's coherent sentences come from his old friend and mentor, suggesting how deeply his memory of Coydog is wired in his brain. Coydog teaches Ptolemy not only how to read but also how to value what's important. "Money ain't the root of all evil," Coydog warns Ptolemy, "but it get a hold on some people like vines on a tree or the smell'a fungus on damp sheets. They's some people need money before love or laughter. All you can do is feel sorry for someone like that" (112). Stealing nearly 5,000 pre-civil war gold coins from a tyrannical white man who later enacts unspeakable revenge, Coydog commands Ptolemy to "take that treasure and make a difference for poor black folks treated like they do us" (140). Coydog plays many roles in the novel: friend, father figure, benefactor, teacher, thief, martyr, and visionary redeemer. His crime leads to a horrific punishment, one that Ptolemy can never forget despite memory loss. Ptolemy dutifully buries the gold coins in his ground floor apartment, where they have remained for nearly half a century, but his descent into dementia following the death of his second wife, Sensia, calls into question whether he can recall where he buried the treasure.

## "Locked on the Other Side of a Closed Door"

Mosley shows early in the novel that Ptolemy's memories still exist but are unavailable, "locked on the other side of a closed door that he'd lost the key for" (12). Part of Mosley's achievement in *The Last Days of Ptolemy Grey* is that he has invented the language of dementia that readers must learn if they are to understand the story. The novelist's rhetoric of dementia becomes more impressive when we realize that few novelists or memoirists have attempted to do this—even when they write about their own dementia.

For example, Thomas DeBaggio (1942–2011), an American author and herb grower, was diagnosed with early onset Alzheimer's in 2003, at age fifty-seven. His 2003 book *Losing My Mind: An Intimate Look at Life with Alzheimer's* records his courageous efforts to convey his growing loss of memory and cognitive skills. "I am writing in a panic, racing against an insidious disease that gobbles memory and ends up destroying life" (25). Statements like "This is the worst thing to happen to a writer" (48) affect the reader deeply. Nevertheless, although DeBaggio tells us that the disease "produces a literary trash of butchered words, once recognizable but now arranged in combinations neither I nor the spell-checker has ever seen" (125), the book is written in lucid prose. The disastrous impact of Alzheimer's remains at a safe distance from the reader. DeBaggio is aware of this paradox, for near the end of *Losing My Mind* he acknowledges that through the process of writing, which includes careful revision, he is able to achieve the linguistic control he has lost through speaking. Nor does DeBaggio's verbal control falter in his final book *When It Gets Dark: An Enlightened Reflection on Life with Alzheimer's*, published in 2004. By contrast, Mosley uses writing to illustrate how Ptolemy attempts spontaneously to make sense of dementia's linguistic tangles. Mosley *shows* us how the disease gobbles memory and speech; we see and appreciate the butchered words.

Language eludes Ptolemy, and he can only fall back upon the indefinite pronoun "thing," symptomatic of the breakdown of speech. The radio must be on continuously lest he lose his favorite stations. "But sometimes I turn the wrong thing an' then the wrong channel, station, uh, the wrong man is on talkin' to me, an' he, an' he don't know the right music" (14). An ATM machine confuses him because it sounds like "amen." Mosley captures the "floating detritus" in the old man's mind. To understand Ptolemy's situation, one must grasp the internal logic of his confusion. The reader must also understand his rhetorical figures of speech, including metonymy, a word that is used to represent something related to it, and synecdoche, using a part of something to represent the whole. "I got to do sumpin' before that damn pall is th'owed ovah me," Ptolemy tells Robyn (87). Unable to remember the word for "bank," where he will cash the checks in his wallet, he says he wants to go to the "place for in my pocket" (19). When he asks who shot Reggie, he is told, "Drive-by," from which he infers, not unreasonably, that "Drive-bee" is the name of the killer. Another metaphor of dementia is imprisonment. "It's like they's a jailhouse in my mind," he laments to Robyn, "an' I'm in the prison an' they's all these people I know outside yellin' to me but I cain't make out what they sayin'" (99). Some of Ptolemy's mistakes are darkly comic, as during the following exchange when a social worker knocks on his door:

> "Who is it?"
> "Mr. Grey?" a man's voice said.
> "You Mr. Grey too?" Ptolemy asked.
> "No," the man said patiently, "you're Mr. Grey." (53)

Ptolemy has been losing his memory for years, but the situation has become grave with the death of Reggie, the person who has looked after him for more than five years. No one has yet told Ptolemy about the death. When Reggie's first cousin, Hilliard Bernard Brown, "Hilly," shows up at Ptolemy's apartment, not to care for him but to steal his city retirement checks, he is horrified by the sight and unbearable stench.

## An Unusual Caregiver

Mosley establishes Robyn's identity as a caregiver when she knocks on Ptolemy's door and asks, "are you all right?"—a question that Hilly has not asked. Ptolemy first meets Robyn at Reggie's wake, where she leads him to the pine casket and, holding his hand, allows him to grieve silently. An orphan, Robyn lives with Hilly and Reggie's mother Niecie, but she is wary of Hilly. When Ptolemy reveals that Hilly has stolen the money from two of his three retirement checks, each worth $211.41, she responds, "Reggie gonna go to heaven an' Hilly gonna go to hell" (42). She speaks with a "grim certainty" that surprises Ptolemy, whose religious beliefs, like Mosley's, are less censorious.

Ptolemy's apartment horrifies Robyn no less than Hilly. She asks him how he goes to the bathroom without a working toilet, but when he offers only a partial explanation, she replies, "An' what about numbah two?" (64) without feeling shame or disgust. She isn't required to empty his bedpan, as Gerasim does with Ivan Ilych, but she begins the herculean task of cleaning up the apartment, which involves unstopping the toilet and cleaning the black mold growing on the commode. She also fumigates the roach-infested apartment. The one-bedroom apartment is so cluttered that Robyn can barely move through it. His closets are piled high with boxes that contain his grandfather's handwritten birth notice along with his deceased wife's old clothes and shoes. She had been a hoarder, and Ptolemy recalls Reggie's exasperated question to him, "Why you keep all this old junk, Uncle?" along with his reply: "It's my whole family, boy" (50). Respectful of his past, Robyn promises not to throw anything out without permission. She fills five thirty-nine-gallon lawn bags with trash from a single room. She knows what to save and throw out. When Ptolemy shows her a crumbling photo of his mother and himself, taken when he was a boy, she promises to make a photocopy of it to preserve the "fragile memory"—fragile both on paper and in his mind.

Robyn is more than a plumber, maid, and declutterer, however. She is also Ptolemy's protector from a drug addict, Melinda Hogarth, who has knocked him down and stolen his coffee-can bank in the past, and who continues to terrorize him whenever he leaves his apartment. "Don't you worry, Mr. Grey," Robyn reassures him, "I got me a six-inch knife in my purse and I know to use it." Robyn indeed knows how to brandish the knife that her mother had given to her. Robyn leaves no doubt in the reader's mind that she is capable of carrying out the threat. "You know I stick a mothahfuckah in a minute they try and mess with either one' a us" (67). Ptolemy is amazed how Robyn can change from a sweet girl into a demon, when necessary, to protect him. Later, Robyn vows to stab Hogarth, who is twice the size of the frail Ptolemy: "if I evah see you talkin' to my uncle again, if he evah tell me you even said a word to him, I'ma come out heah wit' my girls an' we gonna cut yo' titties right off" (93–94). Robyn is street tough, and when a young black man in a red jumpsuit menacingly approaches her and Ptolemy, she doesn't hesitate to hiss, "Niggah, get away from me" (99). No caregiver has ever spoken like this in a novel, but no caregiver has learned the art of survival in a dangerous world fraught with thieving relatives, drug-crazed assaulters, and drive-by shooters. Tough, wary, and smart, Robyn is never at a loss for words. When asked by a social worker why she refers to Ptolemy as "uncle" if they are not related, she has a ready answer: "I call my boyfriend 'honey' . . . but that doesn't mean I'ma put him in my tea'" (104).

Nel Noddings points out that caring is a relational ethic, "both self-serving and other-serving" (99). Mosley's characters demonstrate this truth. Ptolemy and Robyn need each other, but they also befriend and care for each other. Mutual need draws them together, and trust cements their relationship. Ptolemy loves Robyn for her goodness, but he also recognizes that he needs her to fulfill his promise to Coydog. Robyn is drawn toward Ptolemy because she feels safe in his presence, but she also wants to clean up the "mess" in his life. She flees when Ptolemy offers her all of the money in his suitcase, almost $94,000, fearful that she will remain with him for the wrong reasons. When she returns, she advises him to bank the money—and then tells a bank teller, suspicious that she might be trying to rob the feebleminded old man, that she doesn't want her own debit card. It is easy to victimize the elderly, especially when they are demented. Robyn's integrity is never in doubt.

## The Caregiver's Plight

While demonstrating the burdens and responsibilities of long-term caregiving, Mosley offers insights into one of its most vexing problems: the anger that arises over relinquishing control to a caregiver when one cannot be self-reliant. Caregivers and care-receivers have different challenges. Caregivers must act on behalf of those who can no longer act for themselves; care-receivers must entrust their independence and self-reliance to others. The more independent a person has been in health, the more difficult it is to relinquish independence in illness. We see only hints of the care-receiver's anger in earlier dementia stories—"The Bear Came Over the Mountain," *Elegy for Iris*, *Circling My Mother*, and *Amour*—but Ptolemy finds himself becoming increasingly demanding when Robyn takes over the everyday responsibilities of cooking and housekeeping. He even tells her what clothes she should wear. A brief paragraph captures the problematic caregiver-care-recipient relationship. "Instead of getting angry, the child almost always acquiesced to his demands. In his heart he knew that she was the one who made the important decisions, and she knew that he wanted in the worst way to be in charge" (108).

Ptolemy and Robyn are keenly aware of the age difference between them. If Ptolemy were fifty years younger, he tells her repeatedly, and she twenty years older, he would want to marry her. She agrees, but she hasn't reflected on the implications of their relationship, as he has. She offers to marry him in a few weeks, when she turns eighteen, but he declines. "I need a daughter, not a wife," he declares simply. "I need you to love me like I love you" (178). Despite Ptolemy's dependence on Robyn, he doesn't want her to sacrifice her life for his. "You cain't give up your life for me, child" (194).

Mosley handles delicately the sexuality between Ptolemy and Robyn. Spending two nights together after Robyn has fumigated his apartment, she coyly asks him, "Are you lookin' at my legs, Uncle," and after he confesses reluctantly, "I guess so," she asks him, "Are you a dirty old man?" They lie in separate beds, but she teasingly exposes her legs, which prompts him to respond, "You know I'm a old man but I still remember how much a girl can hurt you. I'm past ninety but that doesn't mean you could play wit' me like that" (97). Tellingly, Ptolemy recalls desire as something that can hurt a man. Yet he also wants to protect Robyn: one page later he explains that because he loves her, he *doesn't* want to think about her legs. We learn later that Robyn was sexually abused as a child by one of her mother's boyfriends—and that Hilly is constantly trying to "fuck" her.

Mosley acknowledges the sexual tension between Ptolemy and Robyn, but he doesn't let it interfere with their relationship. Ptolemy breaks down and weeps when she tells him that he cannot live in a house full of garbage and bugs, and after she hugs him, he rests his hands beseechingly on her chest. He immediately pulls his hands back and apologizes. "Don't worry, Mr. Grey," she comforts him, "I know you don't mean no harm" (66). Robyn sleeps in the living room in Ptolemy's apartment, and when he remarks that he had seen her making love with her boyfriend the previous night, she becomes embarrassed, not wanting him to know about this aspect of her life. Ptolemy offers a reassuring reply. "How can I adopt you as my daughter if you don't tell me all about you and your life?" (176). Ptolemy is always aware of Robyn's sexuality, and in one of the novel's most suggestive sentences, Mosley implies that advanced age has its benefits. "He could no longer feel sex, but he remembered . . . maybe knowing it better in hindsight than he ever did when he was able" (221).

## Shirley Double-u ara eye en gee

The other important female character in *The Last Days of Ptolemy Grey* is Shirley Wring. Mosley's gift of characterization allows him to paint memorable characters in a few brushstrokes, and he sometimes associates a character with a defining name. While accompanying Hilly to a bank to cash the retirement checks, Ptolemy is approached by a woman who asks for his help: she is $5 short of paying her telephone bill. "My name's Shirley," she begins, Ptolemy responds with his own name, and then, asked to explain its meaning, recites its significance. Shirley follows with her last name, which she spells phonetically: Double-u ara eye en gee. This is how Ptolemy remembers her throughout the story. We don't yet know the significance of her last name, but she offers to give Ptolemy her emerald ring as collateral for the $5. "You can hold on to it until I get my social security [check] an' then I can buy it back for six dollars" (28). Accepting the ring, Ptolemy experienced a "deep satisfaction in the pleasure of her trust in him" (28). Placing the ring in his pocket, he gives her a $10 bill and then returns the ring to her—*his* act of trust in her.

Shirley's ring turns out to have a history almost as fabled as Coydog's gold coins. Her great-grandmother had stolen the ring from her ex-master's house in 1865 when Lincoln freed the slaves. "She told her son that even though the ring was worth a whole lifetime for a poor black family that she should keep it as a treasure that stood for our freedom" (135). Receiving the ring, Shirley's grandfather changes his last name to Wring, which reflects a legacy based on a rare treasure, freedom. Shirley gives the ring to Ptolemy because he has befriended her, but he returns it to her because he doesn't need collateral. Befriending remains at the center of *The Last Days of Ptolemy Grey*, and compassion is a precious value that cannot be measured by gold coins or emerald rings. Giving treasures is better than receiving them, Mosley suggests. Shirley later asks Robyn to give Ptolemy the ring, a reminder that "he has been like a real man to me when I was down past my last dollar" (135). Ptolemy once again returns the gift to Shirley, and she is wearing the ring in our last image of her in the story. A septuagenarian, Shirley is Ptolemy's friend, not caregiver, but she knows how to respond when the nonagenarian becomes too confused to understand her during their frequent conversations. "She didn't frown or get bored, but her smile became soft and her dim eyesight focused on something other than what he was saying"—a signal that it was time for her to leave, "before the sun goes down and the thugs come out" (122).

Another novelist might have established an immediate sympathetic kinship between Robyn and Shirley, both devoted unselfishly to Ptolemy, but Mosley emphasizes Robyn's immediate suspicion of the other woman, a combination of mistrust and jealousy. When Shirley tells Robyn that Ptolemy helped her pay her telephone bill, Robyn rudely demands that she pay him back now. Nor does Robyn's attitude soften when she comes home and sees Shirley kissing Ptolemy's hand while the two of them are sitting on the living room couch that serves as Robyn's bed. Shirley beats a hasty retreat, and Robyn looks at him with a "stony stare" when he claims that the kiss "didn't mean nuthin" (232).

## Satan's Medicine?

Robyn is Ptolemy's caregiver, but even with her help, he is still tormented by his unfulfilled promise to Coydog to improve the lives of his people. To make good on the promise, Ptolemy must be able to remember the past and think clearly in the present—something that dementia cruelly prevents him from doing. "I wanna remember," he poignantly declares (115). Robyn takes him to a memory specialist, Dr. Bryant Ruben, who asks Ptolemy to repeat a list of words: apple, tomato, pinecone, orange, sparrow, and stone. "Orange, stone, and, and, somein'," Ptolemy sputters (125), defeated by the test. As I was typing the list, I realized, ruefully, that I could not remember it either.

With the help of a powerful experimental drug, Ptolemy's memory returns. Mosley exploits the ironies and ambiguities of Ptolemy's Faustian bargain. Both "life-preserving, life-taking medication" (256), the drug will work only for a few weeks or months, after which Ptolemy will die. Taking such a drug poses philosophical, psychological, and religious questions, but Ptolemy never hesitates, though he regards his decision to take the drug as a pact with the devil. Is the experimental drug "Satan's medicine" or simply risky medication with serious side effects? Mosley offers readers enough information to support either interpretation. The drug produces stunning memory recall and cognitive clarity, but Ptolemy feels as if his blood is on fire. As Jennifer Larson observes in *Understanding Walter Mosley*, the "hellfire" Ptolemy experiences from the medication "suggests damnation and parallels Ptolemy's slow death with Coydog's lynching" (81). Emily K. Abel reminds us in *Hearts of Wisdom* that religious beliefs "suffused the caregiving practices of enslaved women in the antebellum South. Caregivers viewed their healing knowledge and skills as divine gifts and assumed that their medicine had spiritual powers" (4). Ptolemy's Faustian compact conveys the ambiguous nature of this spiritual power.

Memory is a way to keep the dead alive, Ptolemy says to Robyn. "Ain't nobody full dead until no one remembah they name. Don't forget that, girl—as long as you remembah me, I'ma be alive in you" (248). Coydog had told Ptolemy that the "older you get the more you live in the past" (166), but now the dead assume a greater reality to him. Remembering the past, with or without the aid of an experimental drug, can be wrenching, for one remembers one's mistakes and failures. Much of the past is a burden for Ptolemy and his people, and while he takes pleasure in shocking his relatives with his new mental clarity, he is forced to relive the past, including the lynching and burning of his mentor and the aching memories of his childhood love, Maude Petit, who died in a fire when he was five. Ptolemy now remembers where he has hidden the treasure that will allow him to make good on his promise to Coydog, and he formulates a plan to avenge Reggie's death. Robyn's roles of caregiver and adopted daughter merge in the second half of the novel, and once Ptolemy regains his memory, he makes sure that she will be the instrument through which he enacts his promise to Coydog. His memory and cognition restored, Ptolemy feels in charge of his life. "Now he carried the past with him rather than being carried on the back of the brute that was his history" (167).

## Fatherhood: "His Words Were Not Wasted"

Fatherhood is a vexed subject for Ptolemy. Consequently, his decision to be a "father" or benefactor to Reggie's two children, as well as to his adopted daughter, Robyn, is noteworthy. Ptolemy recalls his father saying, "I love you, boy," and then thinking about "men who love their sons" (40), but he rarely speaks about his father. Significantly, Ptolemy has long been estranged from the two children of his first marriage, Rayford and Rayetta, who "despised him after their mother had taken them away" (151). Curiously, Ptolemy has made no effort to get in touch with his children. Two years after his marriage to Sensia, an eleven-year-old child, Pecora, knocked on their door after running away from a foster home. "I can't take you," Ptolemy coldly says to her, though he doesn't doubt that he had fathered the love child. Sensia insists that they take the child in—and we learn little else about her apart from a holiday account Ptolemy created for her "even though she never liked him very much" (24). Ptolemy's transformation from a negligent father to his legitimate and illegitimate children to the benefactor of Reggie's children remains one of the novel's greatest surprises.

Mosley's dedication of *The Last Days of Ptolemy Grey* to his own father, Leroy Mosley—"For the man who gave everything"—reinforces the crucial role fatherhood. In a 1993 interview, Mosley referred to his father's recent death, at age seventy-six, as the "worst thing that happened to me," adding, "My father gave me the feeling, when I was a kid, that nothing bad would ever happen to me. I knew that if the police came to get me that he would protect me. I knew that if somebody was trying to kill me, he would be out there with a gun, because that's just the way it is" (*Conversations with Walter Mosley* 9). Mosley characterizes his father as a "storyteller," a person who loved telling stories and listening to his only son's stories (141). One suspects that Leroy Mosley was the inspiration behind Coydog, Ptolemy's idealized father figure, whose earthy wisdom, gift for storytelling, vitality, and unconditional love of Ptolemy are never in doubt.

Mosley offers additional insights into his father's character in the 2003 political memoir *What Next*. Much of what Mosley says about his father can also be said about Coydog. "He told me what it meant to be a man and to be a Black man" (10). Leroy Mosley, a school custodian, was a "Black Socrates, asking why and then spoiling ready-made replies" (12). Ptolemy describes Coydog in similar terms, an "old man who taught me everything I know—almost" (190). Ptolemy's vow to make good on his lifelong promise to Coydog parallels, if not originates, from Mosley's devotion to his father. "He lived a long-suffering life so that I could tell his stories. I hope he knew that his words were not wasted" (*Conversations with Walter Mosley* 65). There are other parallels between Coydog and Leroy Mosley. Coydog's despair over the Jim Crow South coincides with Leroy Mosley's anguish during the Watts Riots in Los Angeles in 1965. Unlike Coydog, whose rebellion resulted in lynching, Leroy Mosley chose not to participate in the riots, a decision that mystified his thirteen-year-old son. Complicating young Walter's ambivalence was the fact that his mother, Ella Mosley, a school administrator, was both white and Jewish. "In Germany and most of Europe, at least before 1945, she was a race apart" (*What Next* 71–2). As Owen E. Brady points out, Mosley claims a "double minority heritage rather than a biracial one" (*Conversations with Walter Mosley* xii).

## The Personal Motive Behind the Novel

In a 2010 interview with Terry Gross on NPR's "Fresh Air," Mosley stated that he wrote *The Last Days of Ptolemy Grey* after watching his mother struggle with Alzheimer's disease. She struggled with dementia for years: "sometimes she'd turn the television off with the remote control and then try to use the telephone to turn it back on again with the buttons on the phone because she'd gotten confused." Mosley told Terry Gross that after his mother began suffering from Alzheimer's, her employer, the Los Angeles Board of Education, did not want to let her go because she had helped so many people. Though he lived in New York, he hired a car to drive her to and from work. "It cost more than her paycheck, but she would cash her paycheck and she had this thick, thick, thick wad of hundred dollar bills, and she would go wandering around the streets to stores with this thick wad of hundred dollar bills. I was so worried about her."

*The Last Days of Ptolemy Grey* is not a roman à clef, but it is intriguing to see that some of the fictional characters' conflicts reflect the novelist's. After Robyn's baby brother died, her parents became alcoholics. Her father disappeared, and her mother lost control of her life. "I am an alcoholic," Mosley abruptly discloses in *Twelve Steps Toward Political Revelation* (2011):

> For years in my late teens and early twenties I'd drink very close to a quart of whisky (or its equivalent) almost every night. I'd imbibe until I was a stumbling, mumbling drunkard—a danger to myself and to others. Twice, I almost died from *accidents* I had while inebriated. And then one night, at the bottom of a deep ravine and lucky to be alive, I realized that I had to stop drinking. (xiii–xiv)

## Fulfilling a Promise

Mosley meticulously crafts a plot that allows Ptolemy to establish a trust for Reggie's children. Ptolemy appoints Robyn to enforce the trust's conditions, which require that the two children be taken away from their irresponsible mother, Nina, who has known all along that her boyfriend, Alfred Gully, has murdered Reggie. Gully embodies rapacious violence, and though he wears a thick gold chain that holds a pendant with *Georgie* written on it, the name of his brother slain by a rival gang, his notion of honor is to profit from the killing of others. Recognizing Gully's baleful influence on Reggie's children, Ptolemy insists that they live with their grandmother, Niecie. Ptolemy even instructs Robyn how to pay her taxes every three months, a detail most novelists would not think to include.

To achieve his ambitious plan, Ptolemy must adopt Robyn and create a will in which he leaves all of his money to her. In the process, Ptolemy gives Robyn an informal education about money, law, and psychiatry—and cultural diversity. First, he takes her to an old friend, Mr. Mossa, an aging Palestinian antiquarian who will buy the gold coins at a fair price. "Your father is a great man with a long history" (201), Mossa tells Robyn. Next, Ptolemy takes her to a lawyer, Moishe Abromovitz, whose deceased father had provided legal services for Ptolemy years earlier. And then, when Ptolemy realizes he has made a mistake by telling Niecie he has made Robyn his sole heir, a decision his family will surely contest, he visits a psychiatrist, Nora Chin, who declares him to be of sound judgment. Mosley's belief in multiculturalism, creating a trio of sympathetic characters—a Muslim collector, Jewish attorney, and a Chinese American "doctor of the mind"—is not lost on the reader. Nor does Ptolemy's faith in his own people blind him to the reality of evil. The sullen Hilly is beyond redemption; Nina is unfit to be a mother; the drug-addled Melinda Hogarth is forever lost to addiction; and Reggie's murderer is vicious.

Ptolemy succeeds in avenging Reggie's death by enticing him to his apartment through the promise of gold coins, extracting a confession from him that he has murdered Reggie, and then, when Gully prepares to kill him, too, Ptolemy shoots him, an act that is as much self-defense as the fulfillment of retributive justice. Gully's death rids the world of a depraved murderer. There has never been any doubt over Ptolemy's fate, only whether he will fulfill his promise to Coydog. Ptolemy has lost his memory at the end, and when Robyn reminds him of his name, he responds, "That's a king's name" (276). Ptolemy's last thought evokes the memory of his beloved mentor. "A coyote that talked like a man whispered in his ear, and then licked his face, and then . . ." (277). The ending returns us to the beginning, with the letter Ptolemy writes to Robyn while waiting for the apocalyptic encounter with Reggie's murderer. The letter affirms Robyn's role as a caregiver. "I want you to know that everybody in my family is counting on you" (1).

## Existential Questions

The murder mystery genre is for Mosley an opportunity to write about burning social and political questions. As he explained to D. J. R. Bruckner in an interview published in 1990 in the *New York Times*, "Mysteries, stories about crime, about detectives, are the ones that really ask the existentialist questions." These questions include, "How do I act in an imperfect world when I want to be perfect?" No less crucial, Mosley continues, are the moral questions, which involve, in *The Last Days of Ptolemy Grey*, caregiving questions: taking responsibility for those who can no longer take care of themselves. Had Mosley chosen a different genre of literature, one that had nothing to do with avenging a murder, one can still imagine Ptolemy's gratitude at the end of the story for the caregiver who brought him comfort and dignity.

Like Ptolemy, Mosley has a strong desire to help his own people. In *Black Genius*, he characterizes this desire to help as developing "in those dark years when all we had was our fair share of little to nothing. In that world everything passed between us—our clothes, our old books, our food." Unlike help from whites, Mosley continues, which was usually based on charity, not equality, "If you wanted help, and self-respect, you looked to black folk" (41). Or as Ptolemy says about Robyn, "she have received charity, an' so she unnerstand how to give it out" (263).

## Hope for the Future

Mosley's hope for the future lies in characters like Robyn and in Reggie's two children. There's also hope that the power of goodness may eventually sensitize people to racism. Early in the story Ptolemy recalls an incident that occurred eighty-four years earlier when, standing in front of a Mississippi church, he is warned by a white minister that neither he nor his people can enter it. The boy doesn't challenge the statement, but his heartfelt explanation why he is staring at it—"You have to look when somethin's pretty"—leads to the minister's epiphany. He turns his back, looks at the church in a new way, and then, turning around again, a changed man, extends his hand to Ptolemy and thanks him. "You've shown me my own life in a new light" (34). No less than the minister, Walter Mosley's readers may realize from the story that there is much more to be seen. The novelist gives us a black American hero who has become, like his murdered mentor, a caregiver of his people. Mosley has also created a memorable caregiver in Robyn. Her decision to begin community college in the fall, to become either a nurse or teacher, affirms Mosley's belief in the power of education. Robyn has been for Ptolemy a "gift from God," a "child savior" (153). Together, they have changed the course of history.

# 10

# Caregiving as a Progress Narrative in Margaret Morganroth Gullette's Writings

Are caregiving stories "decline" or "progress" narratives? Margaret Morganroth Gullette, the leading advocate and namer of a new theoretical approach called "age studies," raises this provocative question in her writings. To understand Gullette's rejection of decline narratives, one must know something about the trajectory of her career as a theorist—along with the implications of turning away from what she perceives to be the dark reality of caregiving.

## Age Studies

The psychiatrist Robert N. Butler, the first director of the National Institute on Aging, coined the expression "ageism" in 1969 to describe prejudice against elderly people. Butler received the Pulitzer Prize for General Nonfiction in 1976 for his book *Why Survive: Being Older in America*. Since then, research has shown how stereotypes of aging affect the elderly. Becca R. Levy, a professor of Epidemiology at the Yale School of Public Health, probed the causal links between negative age stereotypes and impaired memory and cognitive functioning. In a coauthored 2016 article, Levy demonstrated how negative stereotypes predict Alzheimer's disease biomarkers. In a 2019 article in the *New York Times*, Paula Span cites Levy's recent research on ageism and cognition. "With negative stereotypes, older people have a higher risk of dementia," Levy told Span. "They have greater accumulations of plaques and tangles in the brain, the biomarkers of Alzheimer's disease, and a reduced size of the hippocampus," the region of the brain associated with memory.

Just as negative age stereotypes can harm the elderly, Levy has shown that positive age stereotypes can help the same population. The titles of Levy's coauthored articles convey the health benefits of positive age stereotypes:

"Subliminal Strengthening: Improving Older Individuals' Physical Function Over Time with an Implicit-Age-Stereotype Intervention" (2014); "Lower Prevalence of Psychiatric Conditions When Negative Age Stereotypes Are Resisted" (2014); and "Association Between Positive Age Stereotypes and Recovery from Disability in Older Persons" (2012). Span cites a recent study conducted by Karl Pillemer for the World Health Organization indicating that "Ageist attitudes don't seem as baked in as we think. They may be relatively malleable."

## *Safe at Last in the Middle Years*

Born in Brooklyn, New York, in 1941, Gullette did her undergraduate work at Radcliffe and earned a PhD in English at Harvard. She has taught as a visiting scholar at several universities, and in 1996 she became a Resident Scholar at the Women's Studies Research Center at Brandeis University, her major academic affiliation. Her first book, *Safe at Last in the Middle Years*, published in 1988, is primarily a work of literary analysis, exploring the "midlife progress novel" in Saul Bellow, Margaret Drabble, Anne Tylor, and John Updike. These four novelists portray adolescence as a "dangerous age" which, if safely negotiated, leads to a more serene period.

As the non-ironic title implies, *Safe at Last in the Middle Years* offers a reassuring portrait of midlife, reassuring, that is, as long as one does not adopt a decline narrative, by which Gullette means an ideology of aging that inevitably leads to physical and mental deterioration. "The midlife decline narrative clearly shows the dreadfulness of being-against-oneself or, in some cases, *turning against oneself as one ages*" (166). Gullette has more to say, in her later writings, about decline narratives than about progress narratives; decline narratives become, paradoxically, her muse. What awakens her anger and indignation, she contends, is not aging but an ideology of aging that is linked to decline.

*Safe at Last in the Middle Years* reveals a positive view of aging, one that "promises more benign self-judgments, better interpretations of the world, braver resolutions, more confident desiring—pieces of what we might want to call an education 'into gladness,'" an expression that a footnote explains comes from Elizabeth Barrett Browning (146). There's no mention in *Safe at Last in the Middle Years* about caregiving, but Gullette quotes a statement by Margaret Mead that takes on increased significance in Gullette's later books, when she writes about caring for her mother: "Watching a parent grow is one of the most reassuring experiences anyone can have, a privilege that comes only to those whose parents live beyond their children's early adulthood" (70).

Are writers of decline narratives gloomier than writers of progress narratives? Gullette thinks so. "There are plenty of writers who find ways of telling decline stories again and again: they never learn to describe reality in any other way; this way never comes to seem false to them; it never accomplishes catharsis" (52). Studies have shown, in support of Gullette's assertion, that although pessimism is closer to reality, optimistic people are more resilient than pessimistic people, as Martin Seligman, the leader of the positive psychology movement, observes in his 1991 book *Learned Optimism*: "Life inflicts the same setbacks and tragedies on the optimist as on the pessimist, but the optimist weathers them better" (207). Resilience, Seligman adds, allows the optimist to achieve more at work, at school, and on the playing field. Nevertheless, some of our greatest writers have created decline narratives in their novels, plays, and poems: Franz Kafka, Joseph Conrad, William Faulkner, Eugene O'Neill, Samuel Beckett, Sylvia Plath, and Philip Roth. Some authors achieve catharsis through their art, while others do not. Just as a writer's catharsis does not guarantee great art, the lack of catharsis does not imply inferior art.

## *Declining to Decline*

Academics seldom concede that a single idea may transform their lives, but this confession appears in Gullette's next book, one with a catchy title and a militant social agenda: *Declining to Decline* (1997). "Age theory saved me," Gullette proclaims, a double redemption in that a sudden insight gave birth to a new theoretical approach. "The idea I slowly came to understand—that age had to be socially constructed—pulled me in good time away from the bodily solipsism and bone-deep resignation that I've described as a midlife threat" (10). Like most new converts, Gullette writes with evangelical fervor about the social construction of age, an epiphany and turning point in her life. Her frisson, she admits, using effusive prose, is the joy of creating a new field of study that transcends academic disciplines. It is as if Gullette has discovered a magical anti-ideological aging potion that will defy the ravages of time.

Conceived, then, as an act of resistance, *Declining to Decline* offers early hints of Gullette's relationship with her parents, who are among the book's dedicatees. Her father, Martin Morganroth (1905–74), suffered from ALS and wasted away, losing first his speech, then his muscular power, and finally his ability to eat. "He wanted to die at home and we helped him do that. This is not the place to tell about them—his stoicism and bravery, her patience and resilience" (125). Gillett has never revealed in her subsequent books the details of caring for her father, except to tell us, glumly, that since his death, "decline" has not been a figure of speech that she uses lightly (125). Gullette and her mother were both caregivers, but we never learn how his dying and death affected them, what they learned from the ordeal, or how the experience of caregiving affected Gullette's husband, David, whom she married in 1964, or their son, Sean.

Some deaths might be viewed as progress narratives, at least for relatives who are able to move on with their lives, but other deaths, such as from ALS that involve inexorable deterioration, are inevitably decline narratives, no matter how they are told—unless they are told sentimentally, as Mitch Albom does in *Tuesdays with Morrie* (1997), his memoir about Morrie Schwartz, who died of ALS in 1995, a month short of his seventy-ninth birthday. How did Martin Morganroth's dying and death affect the theorist's faith that she was safe at last in the middle years? She never addresses any of these questions.

Gullette maintains in *Declining to Decline* that the "basic idea we need to absorb is that whatever happens in the body, human beings are aged by culture first of all" (3). One can cede the social construction of age, but does it have priority over the biological factors of aging? Can any ideology, including one based on the idea of an afterlife, which Gullette's doesn't endorse, make dying and death more palatable? It remains to be seen whether death will become acceptable even in an enlightened age that can somehow overcome ageist and other destructive ideologies. Perhaps the only good outcome of her father's dreadful dying and death, Gullette suggests, was that she and her mother bonded in a new and healthier way. Earlier in *Declining to Decline* she implies that they had a fraught relationship while she was growing up. She gives only one example of how her mother incurred her "wrath" in late childhood: by encouraging her daughter to use her time in doing schoolwork rather than reading novels (28), an act that hardly seems scarring.

In the chapter "Ordinary Pain," Gullette discloses that in middle life she began suffering from osteoarthritis that led to chronic pain and thoughts of suicide. "I've always believed in suicide as an option for the sane suffering from incurable degenerative diseases" (49). Is this a veiled reference to her father's situation? She rules out self-inflicted death because of its impact on loved ones. "I looked with hollow eyes at my dear husband; my son, whose wedding I might never attend; my mother, who would survive me" (49). She returns to the subject in later books when she describes her dismay over two well-known feminist academics who took their own lives, Carolyn Heilbrun and Sandra L. Bem.

Chapter 7 in *Declining to Decline*—"My Mother at Midlife"—offers us insights into their relationship. Betty Eisner Morganroth was thirty-seven, married with two children, when she returned to the workforce, teaching first-grade in Brooklyn. She was an excellent role model for a daughter who later became an acclaimed feminist scholar. Gullette received a tuition scholarship at Radcliffe, but her mother supplemented the award with money from her hard-earned savings, a decision of which Martin disapproved: he wanted his daughter to live at home and attend Brooklyn College, as her mother had done. Yet despite gratitude toward her mother, Gullette found herself ignoring her for a decade. "The loss of those years in my case is puzzling," she now laments. "It can't possibly be blamed on—dire word—*matrophobia*, the catchall term that muddles together factors I want to disaggregate" (127). Notwithstanding Gullett's denial of "matrophobia," a word Adrienne Rich uses in *Of Woman Born* to describe a daughter's fear of becoming her mother (235), the mother-daughter relationship appeared strained.

Gullette's refusal to describe in detail the years of estrangement with her mother is exasperating. Why did it take her, she asks, from age seventeen to thirty-three to repair the relationship? She raises the question but then retreats into theoretical explanations for why mothers and daughters drift apart. Gullette would be the first to grant that the personal is the political, yet she uses storytelling mainly to illustrate a political or theoretical insight. Stories, however, regardless of whether they are autobiographical or fictional, require conflicts; writers need not resolve the conflicts, but they must, as Chekhov noted, dramatize, them. Gullette alludes to tensions in the mother-daughter relationship but then refuses to elaborate on them, perhaps fearful of turning a progress narrative into a decline narrative.

In a later chapter of *Declining to Decline*, "Doing Age Theory," Gullette deconstructs decline narratives. She reproaches the noted literary critic Frank Lentricchia for conveying an anecdote about his elderly grandfather who muttered, in Italian, which Gullette then translates, that "Being old is a bitch." For Gullette, the statement demonstrates that humor is often "dying ideology" (205). An age studies killjoy, she ignores the possibility that black comedy or gallows humor, both of which make light of grave subjects generally considered taboo, can help us laugh instead of cry. One can tell ageist jokes to acknowledge our fears, as when Mary Pipher declares in *Another Country: Navigating the Emotional Terrain of Our Elders* that we joke most about the subjects we fear:

"You know you're getting old when someone asks if you're getting enough and you think about sleep" (41). Gullette would likely frown, not smile. One page later, she adds that gerontophobia is a cultural malady that must be resisted at all cost. Joking about age is not funny, Gullette insists. Being old is not a bitch; what *is* a bitch is the expectation that aging will lead to decline. But if so, how does a memoirist write about old age? About caregiving a dying parent? About confronting mortality?

## A Filial Memoir: *A Very Easy Death*

To answer these questions about referentiality, the appropriateness or inappropriateness of writing about a dying or aging body, Gullette turns to Nancy K. Miller's discussion of Simone de Beauvoir's 1964 *A Very Easy Death* (*Une mort très douce*), what Gullette calls a "filial" (as opposed to a parental) memoir about the dying and death of the iconic French writer's mother. Gullette is troubled by Miller's endorsement of the memoirist's attempt to reproduce "unnerving" (Miller's word) sights of the dying body. Disagreeing with Miller's contention that the memoirist should be relentless in the commitment to truth, no matter how disturbing, Gullette argues that it is a "trick of representation" to believe that one can know another person—or another person's suffering. She then refers to the memoir she wrote about a year after her father's death, *Determinations*, describing her family's experience of the event. Writing *Determinations* was a positive experience, she informs us, but, unexpectedly, she decided *not* to publish the memoir because to do so would have revealed her efforts to "own" her parents. "Writing it had brought me to understand that I did not have good access to my father's experience. That was a hard, hurtful discovery, but it eventually gave me space to conceive of something enormously different from our culture's filial accounts" (*Declining to Decline* 210).

One can appreciate the pain surrounding Gullette's decision not to publish the memoir, given the time, energy, and, yes, determination that must have gone into the project. She believes that she acted in the only responsible and ethical manner, the opposite way that Beauvoir acted. "Undeniably powerful, *Une mort très douce* nevertheless colonizes the body of the (older, female, once-rejected) m/other for Beauvoir's own therapeutic and writerly purposes" (210). In a footnote, Gullette quotes Kathleen Woodward's statement that Beauvoir's decision to write about her mother's last six weeks of life was an "unconscious act of reparation in the [Melanie] Kleinian sense" from a daughter who had always resisted identification with her mother (257, n.18).

Simone de Beauvoir's title, *A Very Easy Death*, is not entirely ironic, but the last line of the memoir makes no effort to conceal her mother's death, *all* deaths, as a narcissistic injury. "All men must die: but for every man his death is an accident and, even if he knows it and consents to it, an unjustifiable violation" (106). Unlike Gullette, I don't believe that de Beauvoir "colonizes" her mother's body. The opposite is true. She writes lovingly about her mother's refusal to use a bedpan, an attitude that bespeaks acceptance of mortality. "And Maman, who had lived a life bristling with proud sensitivities, felt no shame. In this prim and spiritualistic woman it was also a form of courage to take on our animality with so much decision" (54).

Gullette could have avoided any reference to her unpublished memoir, and we would have been none the wiser, but the mere mention of the book raises questions. Did her father know that she was going to write about him? How did her mother feel about the project? Did she urge her daughter to publish or suppress the memoir? If the latter, could Gullette have omitted material that was objectionable to her mother? Can one write a filial memoir about caregiving without owning or exploiting one's parents? Does Gullette believe that filial, end-of-life, or caregiving memoirs should not be written—or, if written, remain unpublished?

To support her argument, Gullette enlists the cautionary tale of Philip Roth, who acknowledges in *Patrimony* that he was haunted by a dream in which his deceased father accused his son of dressing him "for eternity in the wrong clothes" (*Declining to Decline*, 210; Roth 237). Gullette neglects to point out, however, that despite whatever guilt Roth may have felt writing *Patrimony*, he published the poignant memoir, which won the National Book Critics Circle Award for Biography in 1992. Moreover, not all filial end-of-life memoirs involve the betrayal of a parent's explicit wish for privacy, as we see in Roth's story. The memoirist had promised Herman Roth, who died in 1989 at the age of eighty-eight, that he would not disclose to anyone the incident occurring near the end of his father's life when, constipated for four days as a result of declining health, he explosively evacuated his bowels as he stepped out of the shower in his son's home in Connecticut, an act that filled the dying man with shame. "Don't tell the children," the father pleads, to which his son agrees. "'Nobody, I said.' 'Don't worry about it. It could have happened to anyone'" (173).

As I suggest in *Dying in Character*, Roth may be criticized for including information in *Patrimony* that he had explicitly promised not to use, but that is different from Gullette's argument that memoirists should not disclose the details associated with dying, death, or caregiving. Other memoirists may not believe they are betraying or victimizing loved ones by writing about their dying or aging. Gullette fears that the disclosure of these details will inevitably lead to decline narratives, thus infecting the reader's life. "It's not the motives but the age effects that concern me: these texts can erase the idea of old age as 'normal,' obscure the subjectivity of the old, and mar the readers' anticipations of our own aging, old age, and dying" (*Declining to Decline* 211).

It's true that dark writing can infect readers—the contagion phenomenon is well documented. Nevertheless, Gullette's call for self-censorship implies that readers will not be able to cope with the unvarnished truth of aging and caregiving. Yet this is precisely what writers attempt to do: to reveal the truth of their experience. As usual, Nietzsche says it best in *Thus Spake Zarathustra*: "Of all that is written, I love only what a person hath written with his blood. Write with blood, and thou wilt find that blood is spirit" (39). Some caregivers want to read and write memoirs that are reports from the front lines, blood writing, as Susan Allen Toth observes about her husband's worsening Parkinson's disease. "I wanted details," she exclaims, along with truth. "No one gave an unblinkered, running account as caregiving gradually grew from a mild nuisance to a constant worry to an all-consuming way of life" (15). One need not succumb to a decline narrative to realize the darker side of life. Gullette worries that children will objectify their parents in filial memoirs, but viewing one's aging or dying parents with love and understanding, along with the detachment necessary for truth-telling, is part of the challenge of writing about caregiving. How can a writer demonstrate convincing recovery or resilience without first showing the dreadfulness of being against oneself or turning against oneself?

## *Aged by Culture*

One has the sense in Gullette's next book, *Aged by Culture*, published in 2004, that she has paradoxically escaped from the worries of aging by becoming an age critic. "Exhilarated by the novelty of 'midlife progress novels' in the 1980s, and by my own ability to 'grow,' I was convinced that the proliferation of positive representations signaled a new paradigm." The euphoria proved to be short-lived, if only because of the harsh reality that "forces that make the life course bearable for some can unmake it for many more" (28). Undaunted, Gullette continues the campaign against ageism, including ageist jokes ("Has decline invaded your jokes, your vocabulary, your secret autobiography?" [33]), and master narratives promulgating inevitable decline. She is proud to be a "spoilsport" (36) because of "decline's flawed and injurious ideology" (13). She doesn't apologize for preferring recovering plots to those that end in death. The "cure stories walk us through the condition of grief and loss with more imaginative completeness," she opines, adding, parenthetically, "Meliorism deals with pessimism more persuasively than pessimism can ever deal with meliorism" (71). Perhaps, but one recalls Thomas Hardy's steely line in his 1895-6 poem "In Tenebris, II": "If way to the Better there be, it exacts a full look at the Worst" (557).

The only book in which she has almost nothing to say about her parents, *Aged by Culture* remains Gullette's least personal and most theoretical work. Yet she continues to reflect on her understanding of her parents from an increasingly postmodern perspective, rejecting other perspectives that emphasize a more stable self. She remains convinced that she needs to rethink her father's story: whereas she once believed that he was "stoically telling himself a decline story about his trajectory," she came to see that in his later versions "he had many selves, not all of which were ruled by decline" (146). Because she has refused to publish the story of her father's life, as told in *Determinations*, we can only take her at her word for this new insight.

## *Agewise*

Gullette's 2011 book *Agewise* remains her most extended meditation on caregiving, largely because her mother, who has lost most of her memory, constitutes the imaginative center. Gullette's challenge is to write about this chapter in her mother's life without rendering it into a decline narrative. She devotes most of *Agewise* to other subjects: the scenarios of premature death inflicted on the old, the mysterious suicide of the Columbia University literary critic Carolyn Heilbrun, the devastating impact of Hurricane Katrina on the elderly, the dangers of hormone therapy for menopause, the problem of cosmetic surgery, the belief that sex for women is likely to improve with age, the possibility that Emma Woodhouse's father suffered from dementia in Jane Austen's novel *Emma*, and the value of progress stories. Only in the penultimate chapter of the book, "Overcoming the Terror of Forgetfulness," does she write about her mother, and even then, she breaks away to discuss other subjects, revealing her ambivalence about turning *Agewise* into a filial memoir.

Gullette does her best to reassure readers that the incidence of dementia in old age is overblown. Conceding that most Americans over the age of fifty-five fear Alzheimer's more than any other disease, including cancer, she points out that "Only one in five people over the age of sixty-five have mild or moderate impairment of memory. The overwhelming majority have none." Only 37 percent of the people over the age of ninety have some form of mental impairment, she tells us, and then adds, for mathematically challenged readers, that the remaining 63 percent are not mentally impaired (178). Yet as the hint of sarcasm in my preceding sentence reveals, Gullette might have been more rhetorically successful had she acknowledged that dementia is a serious problem but not as widespread as the worried well may fear. The most current information on the number of people affected by dementia is mixed, as Paula Span pointed out in a 2018 article in the *New York Times*. The dementia rate is declining, probably because of rising education levels and better treatment for conditions like hypertension, both of which appear to help prevent dementia. Yet the number of Americans affected will continue to rise as the population grows.

Gullette's writings often read like angry jeremiads, and her stridence as an age critic compels her to take extreme positions. She avers in *Agewise*, for example, that the word "dementia" and its synonyms constitute "hate speech" (195). Asked by Julia M. Klein in a 2011 interview in *AARP Bulletin* whether identifying a disease is a useful step toward treatment, Gullette responded acerbically: "'Treatment' is a weasel word. So far there is no proven treatment for Alzheimer's. Today's pills, which my mother took at enormous expense, may turn out to be placebos."

## The Power of Placebos

One can understand Gullette's frustration, but she ignores the powerful, well-documented effect of placebos: anything that offers a glimmer of realistic hope is worth considering in the absence of proven treatments for dementia. "The history of medical treatment, until recently," Arthur K. Shapiro and Elaine Shapiro concluded in their 1997 book *The Powerful Placebo*, "has been essentially the history of the placebo effect. Despite the use of ineffective methods, physicians have been respected and honored because they have been the therapeutic agents for the placebo effect" (228). In his groundbreaking 2010 book *The Emperor's New Drugs: Exploding the Antidepressant Myth*, Irving Kirsch analyzed scores of published and unpublished clinical trials and concluded that antidepressants are active placebos. In a 2018 article in the *New York Times Magazine*, Gary Greenberg summarizes the evolving scientific hypothesis that the placebo effect is a "biological response to the act of caring." In a 2018 article published in *BMJ*, a weekly peer-reviewed medical journal, Ted J. Kaptchuk, a professor of medicine at Harvard Medical College, and Franklin G. Miller, a professor of medical ethics at Weill Cornell Medical College, discuss how placebos can be ethically and effectively used in clinical practice. "Patients were told that it was not known whether open label placebo worked for their condition and testing this question was the purpose of the trial, with information provided transparently and neutrality." The clinical outcomes surprised the researchers. "Intriguingly, the results of several, albeit small, randomised trials of open label placebo suggest that patients can experience symptom relief from taking pills that they know lack any medication."

Gullette tells us little in *Agewise* about her mother's feelings about dementia. We learn nothing, for example, about when she first suspected she was losing her memory. Was she in her seventies, eighties, or nineties when her life began to change? How did her daughter begin to react to these changes? How did both react to being a care-receiver and caregiver?

## REALITY

Chapter 9 of *Agewise* opens with an unfortunate incident that occurred in 2009 when Gullette was guiding her mother on her walker through the dining room of her residential community to a table with an empty seat. As her mother began to sit down next to a mid-septuagenarian named "Jack," another resident, "Edith," uttered in a sneering voice, "Jack won't like *that!*" (183), a comment that occasions Gullette's indignant discussion of sexism, ableism, and ageism. "Residents tend to shun those who are not their cognitive peers," Gullette observes, distressed by her mother's isolation in an otherwise communal setting (186). In an effort to encourage the others to include the cognitively impaired Betty in their conversation, Gullette proudly pointed out that in a recent game of Scrabble her mother had spelled out "REALITY," an ironic word given that much of her personality and awareness of her environment still remained intact despite radical memory loss.

Motivated out of love and loyalty for her mother as well as her belief in progress narratives, Gullet elicits our admiration for a woman who is still a font of wisdom. When Gullette's daughter-in-law remarks alarmingly that her nearly three-year-old daughter started saying "I want to cut you," Gullette appealed to her mother for advice. "Give her a scissors and let her cut paper. Say, 'We cut paper, we cut hair.'" The recommendation ingeniously solved the behavioral problem. "Vivi, handed rubber-tipped scissors, construction paper, and rubber cement, took to collage like a born artist" (187). Gullette captures other aspects of her mother's character that remain intact. Though she has forgotten most of her past, Betty Morganroth has relational memory, judgment, and emotional intelligence. Where others may see the glass three-quarters empty, Gullette emphasizes the remaining one-quarter, affirming her mother's indomitability. We have no way of knowing whether Gullette idealizes her mother because we have only the writer's point of view. Gullette dutifully reports near the end of *Declining to Decline* that after reading the chapter about her, her mother said, "characteristically," that her daughter gave her "too much credit" (251).

Gullette gives the reader enough credit by admitting her mother's anguish over memory loss.

> "What I don't remember is an abyss." She says, "I am an absentee" much more calmly than I believe I could. In the fall of 2007, she told me, "I seem to have lost my volition." It was true. She had analyzed what was happening to her as well as a neurologist could have. "I have no frame of reference," she states, factually, about a particular person she remembers once knowing well. (188)

Yet even then Gullette accentuates the positive, relating that her mother makes conversation out of her forgetfulness, in the same way that decline narratives catalyze her daughter's creativity. Gullette's identification with her mother is so intense that at times we wonder about her credibility as a narrator. Whenever her mother's nurse at the residential home would use the word "dementia" to describe her declining health, Gullette would "smilingly repeat" her mother's recent Scrabble score. "One day, almost in a fury, the nurse said to me, 'Your mother is *failing*!' To her, my mother's strengths were irrelevant" (188). Had we seen Betty Morganroth with our own eyes, would we have agreed with the nurse or the daughter?

In one of her most noteworthy admissions, Gullette is candid about her refusal to disclose the nightmarish aspect of being her mother's caregiver. Revealing that she lost sleep trying to adjust to her mother's worsening problems, she rules out including this part of the caregiving story: "to focus on her losses and my pity would be a waste of the time, emotional energy, and intellectual ingenuity I need to figure out her remaining lifelong abilities and help her relish them" (189). Readers, however, might not agree that this effort is a waste of time. We would be interested in knowing, for example, how Gullette overcame the shock and horror she experienced over her mother's deterioration, how she solved her mother's caregiving needs, and how the experience of caregiving strengthened both mother and daughter. Recall Gullette's statement in *Declining to Decline* about her family's assistance in helping her father to die at home. "This is not the place to tell about them—his stoicism and bravery, her patience and resilience" (125). The omission of a crucial part of the story, first as her father's and then as her mother's caregiver, makes it impossible for us to see the former's stoicism and bravery, the latter's patience and resilience, and her own determination and devotion to both parents.

Writers must always choose what to include and exclude from their stories, but Gullette's omission prevents us from seeing a vital aspect of reality—the word her mother had created in Scrabble. No brain scan can indicate a dementia patient's subjective reality, the nature of life with radically diminished memory, as Gullette realizes. "At best, tech imaging describes a static snapshot when we need an explanation for a dynamic video" (189). By refusing to imagine her mother's situation, Gullette deprives us of a key aspect of her mother's reality.

We have hints of this portentous reality, but Gullette usually conveys these details through summary rather than scenic narration: telling rather than showing. "She had a period of angry grieving over her forced removal from Florida, resettlement in frigid New England, new dependency on me, and feebleness. And in those years, I couldn't rev her up easily" (190). Gullette concedes that these details exist, all emphasizing a decline narrative, but she doesn't wish to portray them. When her mother fell for the first time, at the age of ninety, injuring two vertebrae, Gullette flew to Florida and for the first time in her life became afraid of her beloved mother:

> My trip down had been an agony of apprehension. When the door of her apartment closed on the two of us that first night, she at times shrieking, wailing, "I want to die," with only Tylenol in the medicine chest, I was suddenly responsible for curing the pain immediately, getting her healed, managing her care, her finances, her life—everything. It's hard to talk about that time now; it was so hard to endure. I force myself to write some of it mainly because it enables me to explain as much as I know about the fear, and to talk about how I overcame it. Even though every story is different, that might be useful. Even the anticipation of having to provide care provokes anxiety. (196)

This passage is, for me, the most memorable writing in any of Gullette's books, the moment when, traveling far out of her comfort zone, she demonstrates the worst time of caregiving. She acknowledges, in a footnote, that the last sentence of this passage is consistent with the research findings of an article she had read in a professional journal: "Anticipatory Caregiving Anxiety Among Older Women and Men," by Sarah B. Laditka and Maria Pappas-Rogich, published in the *Journal of Women and Aging* in 2001. The authors conclude that caregiving is often a stressful experience: "women and men who have served as caregivers have higher levels of anticipatory caregiving anxiety than those who have never served as caregivers. Among caregivers, individuals who are currently providing care had the highest level of anticipatory anxiety" (14).

The two-and-a-half-page section of *Agewise*—"My Mother and I Get Up; or, What I Learned"—would not be nearly as convincing were it not for the equally long section "My Mother and I Fall Down" that precedes it, a decline narrative in which Gullette reveals essential details about the crisis that affected both mother and daughter. "Living in the eternal kingdom of anhedonia, I became stupid from anxiety and insomnia" (197). Not so stupid, however, that she cannot recall Virginia Woolf's statement that she would not have a life of her own if her father, the eminent literary critic Leslie Stephen, lived to be ninety. Woolf reveals in *Moments of Being* how her father's health became her mother's fetish; "she died of overwork easily at forty-nine: he found it very difficult to die of cancer at seventy-two" (114). Gullette recounts the small steps she took to help her mother, such as encouraging her to make breakfast and exercise as much as possible. Hiring aides and then returning home, she telephoned her mother every day, listening to her complaints about the aides, food, and loss of independence. Once her mother stabilizes, Gullette is able to return to her own life. "I got my writing life back once she healed after the second fall and moved here. I stopped feeling her mental state might be contagious" (201). Gullette discovers that she can help her mother without experiencing her mother's sorrow. Another discovery is that instead of berating her mother, which inevitably evokes anger, she can try to distract her by changing the subject. A third discovery is that that she can invent a new conversational style with her mother with fewer complaints about politics, culture, and family struggles.

## A Good Enough Daughter

Gullette singles out some of the caregiving memoirs that she has found valuable, including Alix Kates Shulman's *To Love What Is*, a 2008 memoir about caring for her husband following an accident that left him severely brain-impaired. Curiously, Gullet does not mention Shulman's 1999 memoir *A Good Enough*

*Daughter*, a story about her reconnection with her elderly parents after her efforts to break free from them during adolescence and early adulthood. What makes the omission of the filial memoir even odder is that Shulman warmly acknowledges Gullette's help at the beginning of the story. *A Good Enough Daughter*, it turns out, is the type of memoir that Gullette does not wish to write, a decline narrative, which makes it all the more intriguing to discuss.

Shulman, the author of the bestselling 1972 novel *Memoirs of an Ex-Prom Queen*, does not distinguish between decline narratives and progress narratives. She has instead a different binary to characterize her own writing. "I once read that in all literature there are only two plots," she declares in the preface: "someone takes a journey or someone returns home. My other books have all recounted journeys. In this one I'm going home" (xiv). Shulman makes no effort to conceal the fact that her parents' lives in their eighties were dramatically declining, partly because of the 1989 death of her 57-year-old brother, Robert, from lung cancer. Evidence of her parents' decline—her mother, Dorothy Davis Kates, is in the early stages of Alzheimer's disease, and her father, Samuel Simon Kates, is no longer able to care for his wife at home—is striking every time Shulman travels to visit them in Cleveland, where she grew up.

Shulman tries to remain positive when she tells her story, obeying what she has been taught. "*Accentuate the positive, obliterate the negative* was our family's response to death" (51). Unlike Gullette, Shulman does not hold back in describing her many filial failures, including not being with her mother years earlier when Dorothy battled sarcoma in her early fifties. Shulman doesn't mention Gullette by name in the memoir, but she may have been thinking of her when she refers to her New York friends who have been holding meetings about establishing a feminist retirement home in Manhattan, though "words like *dementia*, *Alzheimer's*, and *nursing home* were quickly quashed as irrelevant to our project." These words "spooked" everyone in the group, Shulman adds, including herself. She agrees with the group's consensus that aging should be viewed as "ripening rather than decline" (65), but she doesn't hesitate to describe the darker side of caregiving.

The power of *A Good Enough Daughter* arises from Shulman's fear that she was not a good daughter in the past when she struggled to break away from her parents. She quotes a letter she wrote when she was pregnant with her first child in which she realizes painfully that she always loved her mother too much. "You should see that the colder I am to you, the more evident that my loving you is too much, more than I can handle" (68). Insights like this combine aspects of both decline and progress narratives. Shulman is prepared to transgress her parents' desire for privacy to convey these revelations. "That I must violate my family's privacy and betray their secrets seemed a small price to pay for rescuing them from oblivion" (69). This betrayal is never as unsettling as the one Roth describes in *Patrimony*, but it is necessary, Shulman implies, for telling the truth.

Shulman succeeds in filling much of the hole in our knowledge of motherhood both before and after her mother Dorothy's diagnosis of dementia. Shulman writes about her mother's sexual affairs, her father's impotence, and other details of their long marriage, which remained strong to the end of her parents' lives. Both died in 1996, not long after they entered a nursing home. She records some of the horrors of her mother's end-of-life existence, such as when her mother's physician had to clean her out because she was unable to move her bowels for several days. Shulman holds little back about her mother's end-of-life care. "Her once elegant room looked and smelled like a hospital, with a bedside potty, a plastic-covered path to the bathroom, a shelfful of pills, absorbent pads on the sheets" (26). She accepts the fact that her mother's version of the past is often strikingly different from her own. Dorothy Kates retains much of her "old quirky self—no less affectionate or fun to be with than before, with most of her traits and memories intact—I had to concede that the same was probably true of most of the other residents. That whatever their disorders they remained to the end for better or worse themselves" (241).

We can only speculate why Gullette included in her discussion Shulman's 2008 memoir *To Love What Is* but excluded the more relevant 1999 memoir *A Good Enough Daughter*. The latter is a filial memoir of which Gullette disapproves. *A Good Enough Daughter* blurs the boundaries between decline and progress narratives, revealing family secrets that Gullette would strenuously conceal. Portraying Alzheimer's as a cruel, debilitating disease, *A Good Enough Daughter* acknowledges the memoirist's many filial failures. Yet citing *A Good Enough Daughter* would have allowed Gullette to provide another example of an elderly woman who retained much of her identity despite dementia. Gullette would have found in Shulman an ally in affirming that caregiving, while exhausting and sometimes overwhelming, can strengthen parent-child relationships.

## *The Story of My Father*

We may mention briefly one more filial memoir—a decline narrative—that Gullette probably read but chose not to discuss, Sue Miller's 2003 *The Story of My Father*, which reveals how caregiving for a parent with Alzheimer's disease changes a daughter's perception of herself. James Nichols was a fourth-generation minister and a retired professor from Princeton Theological Seminary, having taught earlier for many years at the University of Chicago. Miller, the author of several popular novels, including *The Good Mother* (1986) and *While I Was Gone* (1998), both made into feature films, started caring for her father in 1988 when he began losing his memory, about six years after his wife's death. Miller felt burdened by the new responsibilities thrust upon her, temperamentally unsuited to be a caregiver.

In the beginning, the disease intensified aspects of Nichols's core identity, including his tendency toward self-effacement, but as his condition worsened, he became increasingly delusional, disruptive, and explosive. At one point, the once-gentle man slammed himself against his daughter when she tried to return him to his room in a continuing care retirement community in suburban Boston. She admits to us ruefully, though not to the staff, that he had crossed a line—"that he could *not know me*, that he could be as violent with me as he sometimes was with them" (239). One of the most disturbing moments occurs when he demands to speak to the "other Sue," the loving daughter Sue, not the evil *caregiving* Sue, a "cheerful, dismissal Sue. A Sue who, from his perspective, was grossly insensitive to the shocking and astonishing and sometimes painful things that went on daily in his universe." Perhaps worst of all, the father's new image of his daughter altered her own self-image: both of them, she concludes, were "*reduced* by Alzheimer's disease" (231).

Faced with the choice of having her father undergo exploratory surgery on his abdomen for what was likely cancer, a procedure that would likely lead to further mental deterioration and slow death, since he was not conscious enough to eat, Miller rejected further medical treatment for him and signed a Do Not Resuscitate order. She doesn't hide her relief over her father's death, which mercifully ended his though not her own suffering. Along with relief came a flood of dark emotions. For years she suffered from "seizures of grief, unexpected and uncontrollable bouts of sorrow and rage, triggered by the memory of my father's helplessness in his illness and my own in response" (263).

*The Story of My Life* is a decline narrative in Gullette's terms, but Miller would probably reject the classification and instead describe the memoir as an attempt to help someone else in her situation. "Someone who found herself taking care of a beloved parent as he disappeared before her eyes, leaving behind a needier and needier husk, a kind of animated shell requiring her attention and care—care she would offer in memory of the person who once lived inside it" (264). Miller admits that three times during the decade after her father's death in 1991 she tried writing the story—and three times she stopped, emotionally unprepared for the ordeal. During this time she wrote novels, including *The Distinguished Guest* (1995), a fictional treatment of her family dynamics while she was growing up, but she never had to "own" these feelings, as she would need to do in a memoir. Writing *The Story of My Life* forced her to confront her most terrifying demon: her childhood fear of abandonment. It was not that Alzheimer's had taken her father away from her; rather, the disease had taken him away from her *again*. She had always felt, unconsciously, that he was an absent presence in her life. This insight enabled her to complete the memoir and to feel, in the final word of the story, "consoled."

Reading *The Distinguished Guest* in light of *The Story of My Life*, one sees how Alzheimer's disease can haunt a family. Midway through the novel, Lily Maynard, who has suddenly become a famous writer at age seventy-two, reflects on her life in her early forties when her father, Henry, "had taken several years to die, from something no one would have known to call Alzheimer's disease" (162). His grandchildren shrink from the demented man as if he is a disgusting creature; one refers to him, in horror, as a *"cretin."* Henry's wife, Violet, is so terrified of finding herself in the same position that she makes her daughter promise to end her life if she begins to suffer from the same illness. Sounding like Kate Gulden in *One True Thing*, Violet asks, "I want you to help me" (164).

Lily agrees reluctantly, but fortunately, Violet dies peacefully in her sleep at age eight-one, mentally alert to the end. Lily develops Parkinson's disease, however, and, beginning to lose the power of speech and movement, finds herself in her father's situation. "She had come to understand that she was to live a life in which the words would simply be stopped" (166). Unwilling to live with the disease or be dependent upon a caregiver, Lily commits a disguised suicide. Writing about herself in her last published story, she pays tribute to the gift of memory, one achieved through writing. "And the transformation into memory of a parent is a gift we give gladly only to the dead, receive gratefully only from them" (256).

## *The 36-Hour Day*

Gullette ends "Overcoming the Terror of Forgetfulness" by raising the "burning question of loving caregivers": How does one escape grief? She references Tom Kitwood (1937–98), a British pioneer in the field of dementia care whose 1997 book *Dementia Reconsidered* argues for a person-centered approach based on empathy. Unlike Gullette, Kitwood makes no effort to minimize what he calls the "rising tide of dementia," which he asserts "may prove to be the most significant epidemiological feature of the late twentieth century" (1). After citing Kitwood's belief that caregiving crises center around failures of love, Gullette then tells us that she fought against the temptation to read *The 36-Hour Day*, by Nancy L. Mace and Peter V. Rabins, because of her suspicion of decline narratives. "It sits dusty on the bookshelf beside my bed," Gullette confesses in *Agewise* (202). There's nothing remarkable about a literary critic who dismisses an influential book, but it is unusual to renounce an unread book.

Of all the self-help books on dementia, *The 36-Hour Day: A Family Guide to Caring for People with Alzheimer Disease, Other Dementias, and Memory Loss in Later Life*, is undoubtedly the most famous. It is the book, we recall, that Fiona reads in the Meadowlake Retirement Facility in Sarah Polley's film *Away from Her*. First published in 1981 and now in its sixth edition, *The 36-Hour Day* is Johns Hopkins University Press's best-selling book. Considered the bible for families caring for Alzheimer's disease and other dementias, *The 36-Hour Day* has been unanimously praised in newspapers, magazines, and medical journals. The book had been recommended to Gullette by Shulman and other friends.

Part of Gullette's mistrust of *The 36-Hour Day*, I suspect, has less to do with the possibility that it is a decline narrative than academics' ambivalence toward the genre of self-help books. As Sandra K. Dolby notes in *Self-Help Books: Why Americans Keep Reading Them*, these books enable authors (and readers) "to bear witness to their own transformation or conversion" (48). Dolby concedes that although the genre tends to be formulaic and dogmatic, self-help books provide readers with the resources to manage crises that might otherwise be overwhelming. Gullette would be sympathetic to Dolby's belief that self-help books offer people the courage and knowledge to improve their lives. The abundance of self-help books demonstrates that Americans are "not dour and down in the mouth but instead hopeful and determined to improve themselves and meet life head on" (159).

There's much in *The 36-Hour Day* that Gullette would find appealing, including Paul R. McHugh's remark in the Foreword that caregiving affirms the "dignity of life embodied in every human being, young or old, sick or well" (xvii). Gullette would agree with the authors' statement that "[e]ven when the disease itself cannot be stopped, *much can be done to improve the quality of life of the impaired person and of the family*" (10). She would agree with their observation that a "frequent characteristic of dementia is that personality and social skills appear nearly intact while memory and the ability to learn are being lost" (122). She would agree with their belief that those who retire early because of a dementing illness are entitled to the same retirement and disability benefits as those with any other disabling disease. She would agree with their insight that a dementing illness "does not suddenly end a person's capacity to experience love or joy, nor does it end her ability to laugh" (213). And she would agree with their rueful recognition that self-help books may by necessity present a skewed picture of life. "Because this book is designed to help you with problems when they do occur, most of what we discuss are unhappy feelings and problems. We know that this is a one-sided view that reflects only part of what life is like for you" (187).

The main reason caregivers appreciate reading *The 36-Hour Day*, Emily K. Abel reports in her 2017 book *Living in Death's Shadow: Family Experiences of Terminal Care and Irreplaceable Loss*, is for its advice on stress reduction. Caregivers learn the warning signs of stress—"anger, irritability, loneliness, and exhaustion"—and how to forestall major crises. Perhaps most importantly of all, caregivers learn how to "cultivate positive attitudes." Abel then quotes from an AARP website. "Instead of dwelling on what you can't do . . . pat yourself on the back for how much you are doing and focus on the rewards of caring for someone you love" (77)—advice that Gullette would surely find valuable.

*The 36-Hour Day* has little to say about suicide beyond the obvious. "Statements about suicide should always be taken seriously. Notify your physician" (151). The authors don't raise the question whether a dementia patient's decision to commit suicide can be a rational choice—and, if so, how the patient's loved ones should react to this decision. Gullette, as we shall see, has strong feelings about these questions.

## *Ending Ageism, or How Not to Shoot Old People*

We learn in Gullette's most recent book, *Ending Ageism, or How Not to Shoot Old People* (2017), that Betty Morganroth died at age ninety-six in 2010, one year before her daughter's seventieth birthday. Gullette informs us that as her mother approached her mid-nineties, "her engaging midlife geriatrician had decided she did have Alzheimer's" (129), a diagnosis her daughter rejected. "My own verdict was still vascular events, since I had been present for a transient ischemic attack. 'It's not Alzheimer's,' I told my mother, marveling at her Scrabble prowess. We continued to call it 'moderate memory loss.'" Whatever the diagnosis, Gullette prides herself on not writing a filial memoir. "I've kept her closest secrets and I maintain her dignity posthumously" (130).

Some of these secrets involve, presumably, elements of a decline narrative. Gullette includes only the affirmative details of a progress narrative. Betty Morganroth expressed insights about her cognitive processes worthy of a neurologist. "'I have no frame of reference,' she stated factually, about people she recalled having known well" (130). Other times she spoke like a paradoxicalist. "My memory is my worst enemy and my best friend" (130). Angry and exhausted by the worsening situation, Gullette admits to reading the work of "brilliant gerontologists who engage with the memory-impaired"—presumably not the authors of *The 36-Hour Day*. Following the advice of these unnamed experts, she decided to focus on her mother's and her own strengths. She also started taking notes for what turns out to be the present scholarly book. "'Who knows, Mum,' I said happily, 'maybe this can go into another book'" (130). The idea of posthumous recognition delighted her mother. "Nothing cheered her like stories of our successes—true for so many parents" (131).

It is not hard to believe that despite profound cognitive impairment, macular degeneration that left her blind, and physical weakness, Betty Morganroth retained much of her identity to the end of her life. "If you say my mother and I were lucky, I won't argue much. We had five close years together off and on our best and our worse, before she died" (131). Gullette includes some of her mother's insights, expressed in 2009 and recorded by her daughter on note cards, which demonstrate that she was, like her daughter, an "instinctive anti-ageist" (186), as when she tells a friend, "Ageism degrades our social world. It will bring you a more bitter old age. Thank you for reading this" (188). Like mother, like daughter, we conclude. In an article titled "When My Mother Wanted to Die" published in *Tikkun* in 2018, Gullette reveals how she helped her mother overcome the wish for death. She offers details about her mother's peaceful ending that do not appear in *Ending Ageism*. "She died in her own bed, in my presence, with the help of a devoted physician's hospice team and adequate morphine. During those five years, she never took more than an aspirin. She never again had to say 'I want to die.'"

## Preemptive Suicide

Betty Morganroth's death was a best-case scenario, enabled by a caregiver who did everything possible to ensure that her mother escaped from a victimizing anti-ageist ideology. Other dementia patients choose different responses with their caregivers' permission. Gullette briefly mentions in *Ending Ageism* the distinguished Cornell women's studies professor Sandra L. Bem, a pioneer in the field of gender studies, who, five years after receiving an early onset Alzheimer's diagnosis, chose to end her life, with her family's sad consent. Gullette implies in three judgmental sentences that the suicide would not have occurred without the active assistance of her husband, Daryl, with whom Bem remained on good terms despite their marital separation fifteen years earlier. "Despite some remonstrance from other family members, her former husband seems to have suggested the day. On that day, he had to help Bem twice when she confused which glass was wine and which was the lethal beverage. He rested beside her as she breathed her last" (118).

Yet if one reads the account of Bem's suicide from which Gullette draws her information, Robin Marantz Henig's article "The Last Day of Her Life" appearing in the *New York Times Magazine* in 2015, one sees a different story. Bem was determined to end her life because she could not imagine existence without rationality and agency. Nothing her anguished relatives and friends could say or do changed her mind. The nonjudgmental Henig interviewed several people familiar with the suicide and offers a nuanced portrait of a woman who, living with moderate dementia for several years, found herself deteriorating rapidly. "She felt terror at the prospect of becoming a hollowed-out person with no memory, mind or sense of identity, as well as fury that she was powerless to do anything but endure it." Bem told her University of Rochester neurologist, Charles Duffy, whose own mother had had Alzheimer's, that she wanted to live only as long as she could continue to be herself. Duffy tried to convince her that she had much to contribute to knowledge by writing about the disease. His empathy touched her, but she remained resolute.

Henig implies in her riveting article that no one in the family pressured Bem into suicide, which was entirely her own decision. The family had one request, with which Bem entirely agreed. She would not choose a method that would be particularly disturbing or violent, such as shooting herself or throwing herself into one of Ithaca's seductively beautiful gorges, "gorging out," an event that has taken the lives of many Cornell students and faculty members over the years. "What I want," Bem wrote in her journal, "is to die on my own time table and in my own nonviolent way." An academic researcher to the end, Bem began reading books on the best way to die. According to Henig, Bem had read Derek Humphry's *Final Exit* when it was published in the 1990s, but now she read a book written by two Australian physicians in 2006, Philip Nitschke and Fiona Stewart, *The Peaceful Pill Handbook*, which recommended a liquid form of Nembutal, a brand name for the barbiturate pentobarbital.

Bem's resolution to end her life never wavered, but she enjoyed her role as a new grandmother when her daughter, Emily, gave birth to a daughter in December 2012. Nevertheless, throughout 2013 Bem wrote, using bold font, "**You know I plan** to kill myself," to which her daughter would respond, "Stop saying that!" According to Henig, Bem's main caregiver, Daryl, "proved steadfast" during this difficult time, especially as friends retreated from her. Steadfast but not insistent or directive, as Gullette implies. In Henig's view, Daryl had spent his entire life avoiding conflict, and now he was simply acceding to his wife's wishes.

Henig captures the feelings of all those involved with Bem, including Emily, who was not prepared to lose her mother. Emily believed that her mother's joylessness was a result of deep depression and that a change of medication might brighten her mood. Henig doesn't offer an opinion here; instead, she presents multiple perspectives and allows readers to reach their own conclusions. She conveys the arguments for and against rational suicide, including the difficulty of thinking clearly about this subject as a dementia patient. She quotes a statement by Rodney Syme, an Australian right-to-die advocate: "If you want to have personal control over what's happening, it means that you need to show considerable courage and considerable maturity." Syme concedes, in Henig's words, "that a person in a position like Sandy's might have to give up some period of time in which she might still be able to take some small pleasures in her life, just to be certain of ending it while she still could." Henig also points out that physician-assisted suicide for patients like Bem is a near-impossibility. Even in the few states that allow for physician-assisted death, two physicians must certify that the patient has fewer than six months to live; most Alzheimer's patients do not have that diagnosis.

"The time has come to end my life. I love you, Daryl," Bem wrote on May 20, 2014, one month shy of her seventieth birthday. Having tried every experimental treatment available, she felt she had run out of time. Contrary to the impression Gullette offers her readers, Bem executed every detail of the process by herself. She signed a statement indicating that she alone made the decision to end her life, took anti-nausea medication, poured herself a glass of wine to mask the bitter taste of the pentobarbital, which had been sent to her in a 100-millimeter bottle, and drank both glasses. Within a few minutes she was unconscious. Henig ends the article with Bem's husband and friend witnessing the death. "They were quiet, watching the sheet go up and down with each breath. Over the next hour, the sheet's rise and fall began to slow. Then it stopped." Gullette implies in her final sentence about Daryl—"He rested beside her as she breathed her last"—that he somehow did not take the event seriously, but Henig conveys the opposite impression. Having lovingly helped his wife to end her life, Daryl remains speechless, dazed by the event. To affirm his steadfastness, Henig quotes lines from a poem, by Fred Chappell, that Daryl recited at his wife's memorial service: "How powerful a presence is her absence."

Henig sought to capture as much of the truth of the event as possible, representing as many different points of view as possible. She did not have an anti-ageist agenda, nor was she trying to change readers' minds about dementia. Rather, she succeeds in conveying Bem's determination and dignity at the end, along with the complex feelings of her loved ones. One's praise for the article, on the other hand, is tempered by the possibility that by offering the concrete details of Bem's ending and dramatizing the event, Henig may be inadvertently contributing to suicide's dark contagion effect. End-of-life issues surrounding dementia remain inherently problematic and controversial.

The fictional Alice Howland considers suicide in Lisa Genova's 2007 novel *Still Alice*, hearing an inner voice, that of her "former self," urging her to end her life while she still has the opportunity. The fifty-year-old Harvard psychology professor, diagnosed with early onset Alzheimer's, does not yield to the beguiling inner voice, but the temptation is there, felt by the reader. Researching the novel, Genova, who earned a PhD in neuroscience from Harvard in 1998, discovered to her astonishment that everyone she knew who was diagnosed with Alzheimer's under the age of sixty-five had considered suicide. "That's extraordinary," Genova states in the "Discussion" section at the end of the novel. "The average fifty-year-old doesn't think about killing himself, but every fifty-year-old with Alzheimer's does. This is where this disease forces you to go."

## Final Thoughts

Every interpretation reveals something about the interpreter, Nietzsche taught us; sometimes an interpretation reveals more about the interpreter than the object of interpretation. Gullette's view of Bem's suicide is conspicuously different from Henig's. One can sympathize with Gullette's anti-ageist ideology without disapproving of Bem's decision, supported reluctantly by her caregivers, to end her life. How would we feel, to invoke a different belief system, if a person strongly opposed to suicide on religious grounds condemned Bem's final act? Would we believe, as I do, that a religious bias should not prevent a person from empathizing with the care-receiver and caregivers in this story? How would we feel if a person with strongly conservative values interpreted Bem's suicide as an indictment of feminism? Would we not reject that interpretation? Even if one subscribes to most of Gullette's anti-ageist assumptions, as I do, Alzheimer's remains a cruel and frightening disease. One can see Bem as dying in character, true to her beliefs.

I admire Margaret Morganroth Gullette for returning to issues about which few people dare to speak or write. She has the courage of her convictions, and she will not be silenced. No one has advocated more passionately for progress narratives. Age theory indeed saved Gullette, as she remarked in *Declining to Decline*. Nietzsche must have been thinking of her when he observed in *Twilight of the Gods*: "If we have our own *why* of life, we shall get along with almost any *how*" (468). Though some readers may be disappointed that Gullette offers a highly edited vision of caregiving, one consistent with her belief in progress narratives, others will find the portrait of her mother inspirational, a necessary corrective to bleaker portrayals appearing elsewhere, one that may provide hope and fortitude to caregivers and care-receivers.

# 11

# Caregivers Struggling to Make the Right Decisions in Atul Gawande's *Being Mortal*

Atul Gawande opens his 2014 book *Being Mortal: Medicine and What Matters in the End* with a reference to *The Death of Ivan Ilych*, conjuring his twin passions for medicine and literature. He recalls taking in medical school a weekly seminar called Patient-Doctor, "part of the school's effort to make us more rounded and humane physicians." Gawande believed at the time that Tolstoy's story betokens a "failure of character and culture." He and his fellow students were confident that, unlike Ivan Ilych's physicians, they would treat dying patients compassionately. Yet once he became a doctor and encountered patients confronting their mortality, it did not take him long to realize how "unready" he was to help them (1–3). The problem was not a lack of sympathy, training, or expertise but rather a failure to understand how the "seemingly unstoppable momentum of medical treatment" (165) often prevents doctors from having essential end-of-life discussions with their patients.

One of Gawande's great strengths as a physician-writer is his use of metaphorical language and historical analogies. "Death is the enemy," he states bluntly.

> But the enemy has superior forces. Eventually, it wins. And in a war that you cannot win, you don't want a general who fights to the point of total annihilation. You don't want Custer. You want Robert E. Lee, someone who knows how to fight for territory that can be won and how to surrender it when it can't, someone who understands that the damage is greatest if all you do is battle to the bitter end. (187)

The son of two Indian physicians who immigrated to the United States and settled in Athens, Ohio, Gawande received an undergraduate degree from Stanford in 1987; an interdisciplinary Master's in Philosophy, Politics and Economics (PPE) degree from Oxford in 1989 as a Rhodes Scholar; a medical degree from Harvard in 1995; and a Master of Public Health degree from Harvard in 1999. He is a professor at Harvard Medical School and the Harvard School of Public Health. A recipient of a MacArthur "Genius" grant in 2006 for his work on surgical interventions and medical ethics, Gawande is the author of three earlier books: *Complications: A Surgeon's Note on an Imperfect Science* (2002), a National Book Award finalist; *Better: A Surgeon's Notes on Performance* (2007); and *The Checklist Manifesto: How to Get Things Right* (2009). Arising from two articles published in *The New Yorker*, for which he is a staff writer, *Being Mortal* is his best known book, becoming a #1 *New York Times* bestseller and winning the British Medical Association Council Chair's Choice. Despite his impressive credentials and achievements, Gawande remains modest and unassuming.

## Gerasim Incarnated

If Tolstoy's Gerasim were a contemporary physician and could write as well as give comfort, he would resemble Gawande. Gerasim represents to him the ideal caregiver. "He provides care without calculation or deception, and he doesn't impose any goals beyond what Ivan Ilyich desires" (100). Gerasim embodies the importance of a large perspective on life, looking at the big picture and realizing that the dying need "someone closer to a companion than a clinician" (144).

Gawande's comprehensive perspective on medicine and life allows him to see the need for fundamental government reforms in healthcare and end-of-life care. His political activism brought him to the attention of Bill Clinton and Barack Obama, both of whom were influenced by his ideas for healthcare reform. He is a tireless advocate for universal health insurance and enlightened end-of-life facilities that are worlds apart from most traditional nursing homes where, in the name of "safety," few activities exist that make end of life interesting and worthwhile.

Gawande is also an advocate for hospice and palliative care. Many people view hospice as a turning away from medical treatment, a surrender to hopelessness and death, yet studies indicate that terminally ill patients on hospice care not only receive better pain management but also, contrary to belief, live longer than those not on hospice. As Emily K. Abel points out in *The Inevitable Hour*, a 2013 history of caring for dying patients in the United States, three explanations account for the popularity of the hospice movement in the second half of the twentieth century: hospices encourage family as opposed to institutional care; hospices minister to dying patients' emotional and spiritual needs; and hospices place a premium on physician honesty (169–70). Gawande endorses hospice for the same reasons. He is not opposed to physician-assisted suicide, but he notes that in the Netherlands in 2012, the fact that one in thirty-five people sought assisted suicide is a measure not of the success but of the failure of the Dutch system. The Dutch, he adds, have been slower than others in developing palliative care programs (245).

## Pit Crews

In his 2012 TED talk "How Do We Heal Medicine?", heard by nearly two million people, Gawande affirms teamwork—specialists working together collaboratively. In an age when all doctors, even primary care physicians, are trained as specialists, what's needed in medicine, Gawande asserts, is mainly pit crews, by which he means a system embracing "humility, discipline, teamwork," the opposite of the values on which he was trained: "independence, self-sufficiency, autonomy." He ends the TED talk by stating that the greatest challenge in healthcare, education, and climate change is the recognition that, despite our highly individualistic culture, ingenuity requires group success: collaboration. Gawande looks for practical solutions to intractable problems, such as designing nineteen-item, two-minute checklists that allow surgical teams to avoid potential complications—"making sure an antibiotic is given in the right time frame because that cuts the infection rate by half." The death rate in hospitals that implemented these checklists fell by 47 percent.

Gawande's medical stories show the complex interaction of personal, political, economic, and cultural factors in contemporary life. Caregivers can succeed only if they have an effective pit crew in place who work together to confront the ordinary and extraordinary problems that arise when caring for the ill. His stories focus not on daring physicians discovering miraculous cures to illness but on the protracted decision-making necessary when the dying patient's world narrows. Although Gregory Jusdanis has criticized *Being Mortal* for an "overreliance on anecdote," privileging narrative over analysis, most reviewers have found a seamless integration of story and instruction: "Gawande has plenty of engaging and nuanced stories to leave the readers with a good sense of what he means," as Sheri Fink wrote in her *New York Times* review.

Gawande calls attention to truths that are not always apparent, such as what is "natural" today was not natural a few decades ago. Until a couple of hundred years ago, for example, the average life span was around thirty years.

"The natural course was to die before old age" (32). Gawande then quotes the philosopher Montaigne about late sixteenth-century life: "To die of age is a rare, singular, and extraordinary death, and so much less natural than others: it is the last and extremest kind of dying" (32). Gawande points out other surprises, such as the fact that inheritance has little influence on longevity: "only 3 percent of how long you'll live, compared with the average, is explained by your parents' longevity; by contrast, up to 90 percent of how tall you are is explained by your parents' height" (33). Keenly aware of the medieval concept of *ars moriendi*, the art of dying, Gawande is also aware of the art of living: the two arts are often inseparable.

## Types of Physician-Patient Relationships

*Being Mortal* highlights three types of medical relationships that Gawande learned as a student when he read a 1992 article by the medical ethicists Ezekiel J. Emanuel and Linda L. Emanuel. He knew he didn't want to embody the "paternalistic" relationship, where authoritarian physicians believe they know what is best for their patients—*Father Knows Best*. "If there were a red pill and a blue pill, we would tell you, 'Take the red pill. It will be good for you.' We might tell you about the blue pill; but then again, we might not." The second paradigm was more appealing: the "informative" relationship. "We tell you the facts and figures. The rest is up to you." If there are only two choices, the decision is a no-brainer. Gawande became Dr. Information. But this type of relationship is unsatisfactory because patients want both information and guidance. A third choice exists, Gawande discovered, what the Emanuels call the "interpretive" relationship, where the doctor asks the patient, after presenting the inevitable trade-offs of different types of treatment, including no treatment at all, "'What is most important to you? What are your worries?' Then, when they know your answers, they tell you about the red pill and the blue pill and which one would most help you achieve your priorities" (200–1). The interpretive physician, like the relational or intersubjective psychotherapist, engages in a dialogical relationship with patients, more of an I-Thou encounter, in Martin Buber's terms, than an I-It. The interpretive relationship involves shared decision-making, with the physician serving as the patient's counselor and contractor.

Rereading the Emanuels' article years later, Gawande recognized something he had not earlier seen, the authors' recommendation for a physician to "deliberate" with patients on their larger goals. Curiously, Gawande omits telling us that the

Emanuels prefer the deliberative model as the best of the four. "In the deliberative model," the authors write, "the physician acts as a teacher or friend, engaging the patient in dialogue on what course of action would be best. Not only does the physician indicate what the patient could do, but, knowing the patient and wishing what is best, the physician indicates what the patient should do, what decision regarding medical therapy would be admirable" (2222). The Emanuels are quick to point out that the physician attempts to "*persuade* the patient of the worthiness of certain values, not to *impose* these values paternalistically" (2225). Gawande appears to be uneasy about the deliberative physician's use of moral persuasion, and perhaps for this reason, his favored mode remains the interpretive model.

Gawande's preference in *Being Mortal* for the interpretive model represents a significant shift in his thinking. He acknowledges in *Complications*, published more than a decade earlier, his struggle to make the right decision regarding his infant's medical treatment. When his youngest child, Hunter, momentarily stopped breathing, she was rushed to the hospital, where the doctors confronted a difficult question. Should she be intubated and placed on a ventilator? The procedure had its risks—as did doing nothing. Paralyzed by indecision, Gawande realized, both as a physician and as the infant's father, that he was the ideal person to make the decision, but he couldn't live with the possibility that he might make the wrong one. "I needed Hunter's physicians to bear the responsibility: they could live with the consequences, good or bad" (222). They made the correct choice—and Hunter recovered. Read together, *Complications* and *Being Mortal* demonstrate the challenge for physicians and patients alike of balancing autonomy and guidance.

Money remains a driving force in medicine for physicians and healthcare administrators. Physicians are less likely to pursue medical specialties that are not well compensated. Gawande observes ruefully that despite the aging of America, there is a startling decline in the number of geriatricians. "Mainstream doctors are turned off by geriatrics," reports one of his interviewees, Felix Silverstone, a geriatrician himself. "The Old Crock is deaf. The Old Crock has poor vision. The Old Crock's memory might be somewhat impaired. With the Old Crock, you have to slow down, because he asks you to repeat what you are saying or asking. And the Old Crock doesn't just have a chief complaint—the Old Crock has fifteen chief complaints" (36–7). Fewer physicians are willing to go into geriatrics despite, paradoxically, an increased need for them.

Gawande is a gifted storyteller, and throughout *Being Mortal* he emphasizes the role of storytelling in end-of-life care. "Whatever the limits and travails we face, we want to retain the autonomy—the freedom—to be the authors of our lives" (140). Life is meaningful because it is a story. "A story has a sense of a whole, and its arc is determined by the significant moments, the ones where something happens" (238). *The Death of Ivan Ilych* remains a cautionary tale for Gawande, reminding him of the limits of contemporary medicine and deepening his humanity and humility. As a junior surgical resident, he told the story in *Complications* of "Joseph Lazaroff," a man whose incurable cancer had spread throughout his body but who nevertheless insisted that his physicians do "everything" to keep him alive. "He was pursing little more than a fantasy at the risk of a prolonged and terrible death—which was precisely what he got" (5). Lazaroff's eight-and-a-half-hour surgery was a technical success, but he never recovered from the procedure. Gawande berates himself for never having discussed with the patient the reality of his disease and the likelihood that palliative care was a better option than surgery. "We did little better than Ivan Ilyich's primitive nineteenth-century doctors—worse, actually, given the new forms of physical torture we'd inflicted on our patient. It is enough to make you wonder, who are the primitive ones" (6).

## Honesty in Medicine

*Being Mortal* abounds in case study material, but the discussions are never dry or clinical. The first half of the book focuses on different models of senior living, including the inadequacy of most nursing homes, the second half on hospice and palliative care. Gawande never hesitates to show how, despite his best efforts to be an interpretive physician, he often reverts back to an informative one. *Being Mortal* illustrates the daunting challenge of honesty confronted by physicians, dying patients, and caregivers. The physician's own mortality, the fear of having distressing discussions of dying and death, often prevents patients from choosing the right medical decisions. Compounding the problem of honesty is that doctors routinely overestimate patients' survival time—by 530 percent! Moreover, patients prefer doctors who are optimistic. "In an era in which the relationship between patient and doctor is increasingly miscast in retail terms—"the customer is always right"—doctors are especially hesitant to trample on a patient's expectations" (168).

*Being Mortal* is not mainly about caregiving, but it has profound implications for caregivers. Gawande offers a number of caregiving vignettes, each only a few pages long, insightful and often moving, though not fully developed stories. The clinical vignettes are always in the service of Gawande's central thesis: terminal illness requires urgent conversations on ways to reduce suffering and maintain mental awareness as long as possible. Sometimes the bravest and best medical decision is to do nothing, to allow nature to run its course without technological intervention. The caregivers in these stories struggle to do their best in end-of-life care. Most of the caregivers are either a spouse or an adult-child, reflecting the fact that 80 percent of caregivers in the United States are family members. Because 70 percent of those over the age of sixty-five will require long-term care for an average of three years, the number of caregivers and care-receivers is huge. As Gawande shows, caregivers find themselves in the same quandary as physicians: the desire to prolong life often results in the loss of meaningful life.

Gawande's caregiving stories, unlike many of those we have seen, bespeak the importance of caregiver and care-receiver living together in a lively setting, one that is generally not possible in most traditional nursing homes. The integration of character and setting is as crucial at the end of life as it is in earlier stages of the life cycle. Traditional nursing homes are stultifying, Gawande admits. Bruce C. Vladeck's observation in his 1980 book *Unloving Care: The Nursing Home Tragedy* remains largely true: "the typical nursing home is a pretty awful place" (29). Studies indicate, Gawande reminds us, that most people wish to die in their homes, not in institutions. Many homes, however, are isolating. The success or failure of caregiving depends, to a large extent, on the caregiver's ability to provide compassionate care in a comfortable, familiar setting. Few care-receivers wish to spend their remaining days in a setting that is safe but empty of meaning; and while it may be easier for caregivers to deposit a loved one in a nursing home, they often feel ravaged by guilt, as we saw with Mary Gordon and Annie Ernaux.

End-of-life-decisions affect not only patients but also their caregivers. Gawande quotes a 2008 study published by the national Coping with Cancer Project indicating that terminally ill patients who received extreme medical treatment near the end of their lives or admitted, near death, to intensive care had a much worse quality of life in their last week than those who received no such medical interventions. Equally significant, six months after patients' deaths, "their caregivers were three times as likely to suffer major depression" (155).

## Felix Silverstone: "He Found Great Purpose in Caring for Her"

Gawande devotes twelve pages to a discussion of Felix Silverstone's care for his wife, Bella, with whom he has been married for sixty years. In looking for a brief statement to use as a caption, I considered several possibilities, beginning with "Eventually, the crisis they dreaded arrived" (57). This portentous quote certainly would have been an appropriate caption, as would the bleak sentence in Philip Roth's 2006 novel *Everyman* from which Gawande quotes: "Old age is not a battle. Old age is a massacre" (55; the words appear slightly differently in *Everyman*, 156). I could have chosen a more factual sentence that neatly sums up Gawande's discussion of Silverstone: "Felix's knowledge as a geriatrician forced him to recognize his decline, but it didn't make it easier to accept" (49). Or I could have selected a more self-mocking caption, as when Silverstone, after reminding his wife to chew her food carefully, soon finds himself choking and turning red: "Didn't follow my own advice" (51). Yet the quote I finally chose as a caption—"He found great purpose in caring for her," including the rest of the sentence, "and she, likewise, found great meaning in being there for him" (56)—is an insight that we have not often seen in our earlier discussions of caregiving.

Gawande never softens the ravages of aging, never chooses, as Margaret Morganroth Gullette does, to record only progress narratives, but he captures the dignity and courage of caregivers striving to do their best with the knowledge that, ultimately, their best is not good enough to prevent heartbreak. Silverstone was forced to retire from medicine at age eighty-two, not because of his own poor health but because of his wife's: Bella had become nearly blind, and he was her exclusive caregiver. Yet he soon found purpose in being his wife's caregiver; without him, she would surely have languished in a nursing home. Their marriage was hardly perfect: they often fought, but they were always forgiving of each other and themselves. Now eighty-seven, Silverstone retains many of his lifelong skills, including the ability to drive. Gawande injects humor into the story through his description of going for a ride with the octogenarian. "I was, I admit, braced for disaster. The risk of a fatal car crash with a driver who's eighty-five or older is more than three times higher than it is with a teenage driver. The very old are the highest risk-drivers on the road" (53). Gawande survived the trip: Silverstone is still a good driver.

Gawande's story of the two elderly Silverstones darkens as he chronicles Bella's worsening health: total blindness, memory problems, deafness, and a shattered fibula in both legs as a result of a fall. "What Felix feared most had happened" (57), writes Gawande, and we may be reminded of Job: "What I feared had come upon me; what I dreaded had happened to me." But unlike Job, Silverstone never curses his fate, never questions why God has tortured him, never rues the day he was born. Gawande visits Silverstone three months after his wife's death, and he condenses into a sentence the widower's sorrow over Bella's death and gratitude of their life together. "He had one great solace, however: that she hadn't suffered, that she'd got to spend her last few weeks in peace at home in the warmth of their long love, instead of up on a nursing floor, a lost and disoriented patient" (59).

## Lou Sanders: "The Burdens for Today's Caregivers Have Actually Increased"

Gawande's story of Lou Sanders and his daughter Shelley illustrates a different dilemma of caregiving. How can a caregiver fulfill an impossible promise to avoid placing an aged parent in a nursing home? Sanders was in his seventies when his wife, Ruth, developed metastatic lung cancer. She kept smoking, Gawande adds, a fact "which Lou [and Gawande himself, ever the physician] couldn't understand" (80). Sanders cared for his wife until her death, in 1994, at age seventy-three. His daughter worried about her father's health following her mother's death, but Lou's resilience surprised her. For the next decade he did well, making new friends and keeping busy, but a heart attack in 2003, when he was eighty-five, followed by the onset of Parkinson's disease, transformed the former caregiver into a care-receiver. Shelley became her father's caregiver. She and her husband, Tom, invited Lou to live with them, converting the living room of their modest colonial in a Boston suburb into a bedroom, but problems inevitably developed. Cohabitation required adjustment, Gawande remarks, adding, "Everyone soon discovered the reasons that generations prefer living apart. Parent and child traded roles, and Lou didn't like not being the master of his home" (83).

Gawande is no Tolstoy, but he has keen insight into his characters' inner lives. He rarely makes judgments. He understands earlier times and cultures, such as his grandparents' life in India, when it was taken for granted that infirm parents would remain in their homes, cared for by one or more of their children. Gawande doesn't idealize these cultures. "I learned of bitter battles in village families between elders and adult children over land and money" (19). He also understands contemporary times and cultures, where, because most children grow up, leave home, never to return, infirm parents are left on their own, without vital family support. This is an inevitable result of individualism. Gawande presents enough information to explain the dramatic changes in society, including what social scientists call intimacy at a distance. "Whereas in early-twentieth-century America 60 percent of those over age sixty-five resided with a child, by the 1960s the proportion had dropped to 25 percent. By 1975 it was below 15 percent" (21).

Novelists, filmmakers, and memoirists often comment on a caregiver's agonized decision to place a loved one in a nursing home, but Gawande captures Shelley's despair over the impossibility of caring for her father at home. The devil lies in the details of home caregiving, and Gawande conveys these details. Shelley did everything possible to accommodate her father's failing health, including installing bathroom grab bars, a sitting-height toilet, and a shower chair, but these efforts were not good enough. She hired a home health aide to shower him in the daytime, but he wanted baths at night, which required her help. This was in addition to Shelley's other duties as a wife, mother of two teenage children, and full-time worker. "She felt her sanity slipping." When a nurse tells her that, because of Lou's increased caregiving needs, he needs to be placed in a nursing home, Shelley looks at her father and knows what he is thinking. "Couldn't she just stop working and be there for him? The question felt like a dagger in her chest" (86).

If this were a novel, film, or memoir, we might see the desperate caregiver stab herself, the care-receiver, or both, or at least consider this possibility in a fantasy or dream. Just as Felix Silverstone's feeling of dismemberment over his wife's death recalls Georges's decision in *Amour* to suffocate his dying wife and then, presumably, end his own life, the stab in the heart Shelley experiences when her father asks her to sacrifice her life for his reminds us of Ellen Gulden's bitter resentment in *One True Thing* over being her mother's caregiver. Most caregivers, however, do not commit suicide or homicide, though they may, like Ellen, place their lives on hold for months or years. Gawande empathizes with all the characters in the story: Lou, Shelley, and Tom, who was admittedly not helpful at the time. Shelley finds herself betraying her solemn promise to keep her father at home. But Gawande's story doesn't end there.

Before telling us what happened when Shelley reached her breaking point, Gawande narrates in the next eighteen pages the fraught history of assisted living facilities. One story leads to another story in Gawande's world; he always wears his scholarship lightly. He introduces Karen Brown Wilson, one of the originators of assisted living residences, and then he discusses how her revolutionary idea changed from a bold alternative to nursing homes into diluted versions of fewer services. A colleague once told Wilson, "We want autonomy for ourselves and safety for those we love" (106), a paradox and problem that assisted living residences have failed to resolve. Shelley placed her father in an assisted living home, and over time he grew to hate it, partly because, as we learn when Gawande resumes the story, the staff members showed little curiosity in the quality of his life. "Their attitude seemed to result from incomprehension rather than cruelty, but, as Tolstoy would have said, what's the difference in the end?" (105).

## A Five-Star Hotel in *The Bonesetter's Daughter*

Gawande might have cited Amy Tan's novel *The Bonesetter's Daughter* as another example of early enthusiasm for assisted living residences. Ruth Young is hesitant to place her ailing mother, LuLing, suffering from Alzheimer's, in a nursing home, but Ruth's friend, Art, waxes poetic over a new San Francisco assisted living residence he has discovered. "They're the latest concept, the wave of the baby-boomer future, like senior Club Meds—meals, maid service, laundry, transportation, organized outings, exercise, even dancing. And it's supervised, twenty-four hours. It's upscale, not depressing at all" (312). Mira Mar Manor has amenities "typical of a five-star hotel" (312), Ruth tells her skeptical mother. Visiting the facility, Ruth and Art confirm that the residents are contented and safe. Mira Mar even has a "Love Nursery" where each resident has an orchid plant; many of the residents have named their orchids after deceased husbands. "It's really a carefree life, which is how it should be when you're this age, don't you agree?" (319), the cheerful director assures them.

Tellingly, Ruth must lie to convince her mother to enter Mira Mar, informing her that the California Department of Public Safety has found a radon leak in her home. Hearing the lie, the director exclaims admiringly: "The subterfuges people have used to get their parents here—wow, pretty ingenious. It could fill a book" (318). LuLing loves living in Mira Mar, though she finds the food too salty, a detail that is supposed to make the residence sound more credible. *The Bonesetter's Daughter* was published in 2001, around the time new assisted living residences appeared with great fanfare, but, as Gawande notes, the dream did not correspond to reality.

## The Reality of Nursing Homes

Gawande's realism allows him to see that human nature is imperfect, yet his idealism compels him to find solutions, however imperfect, for existing problems. His stories convey caregivers' dilemmas of trying to do their best for loved ones without sacrificing their own lives. Recall Annie Ernaux's statement about placing her mother in a nursing home: "letting her stay at my place would have meant the end of my life. It was either her or me" (37). Shelley and her father reached a compromise: he would spend three days a week in her home and the remaining four in his assisted living residence. The compromise worked until he began falling often, each time resulting in an ambulance ride to a hospital emergency room. Shelley then decided to place her father in a nursing home. Gawande is not critical of her decision to privilege safety over quality of life, but in a simple sentence he summarizes the similar decisions made by countless other caregivers: "So this is the way it unfolds" (108)—a sentence containing Tolstoyan omniscience. Gawande then devotes the next thirty-three pages to the reasons most people in nursing homes find themselves dying of boredom, loneliness, and helplessness. People need a reason to live, he reminds us. Lou Sanders lacked a reason after his daughter made her fateful decision, as Gawande reveals in a memorable sentence: he was "on his way to joining the infantilized and catatonic denizens belted into the wheelchairs of a North Andover nursing home" (141).

The story appears to be over—until a cousin told Shelley about a new, innovative nursing home, the Leonard Florence Center for Living in nearby Chelsea, part of a growing number of facilities committed to the reinvention of elder care. Here Lou was permitted to leave his wheelchair and move around without a walker, have his own room—most nursing homes have shared rooms—and live in a residence designed to be cozy and homey, not institutional. Gawande doesn't minimize Lou's growing health problems—"his teeth were like toppled stone. He had aches in every joint"—or his low moments, when he wants to die, but he enjoys his remaining time. During his last interview with Sanders, who was ninety-four, Gawande observes: "We'd been talking about the story of his life for almost two hours when it struck me that, for the first time I can remember, I did not fear reaching his phase of life" (146). Readers may feel the same way. Readers may also be interested in a 2018 article by Carol Weisse, Bernadette Sapienza, and Sophia Foster that outlines the ways in which community-run comfort care homes enable medical students to receive excellent training as caregivers for the dying.

## Atmaram Gawande: "Let Me Die Instead"

The most compelling section of *Being Mortal*, 40 pages long in a 282-page book, involves Gawande's decision to tell the story of his father's terminal illness and the family's struggle to make the right treatment choices. One can imagine the writer's challenge in exposing his family's private anguish to public scrutiny, as he hints in his acknowledgments. "In choosing to include the story of my father's decline and death, I know I dredged up moments they'd rather not relive or necessarily have told the way I did" (279).

The urologist Atmaram Gawande was in his early seventies, living an active personal and professional life—he had never missed a day of work due to illness in thirty years—when an MRI indicated in 2006 a tumor growing inside his spinal cord. Using personification, the writer declares, in horror, the "beast was outgrowing its cage." A neurosurgeon at Atul Gawande's own Boston hospital concluded that the tumor needed to be removed immediately, lest the patient become quadriplegic in weeks. Growing exasperated by Atmaram Gawande's worried questions, the unnamed neurosurgeon "had the air of the renowned professor he was—authoritative, self-certain, and busy with things to do" (197). In short, he resembled Ivan Ilych's physicians. The other neurosurgeon, Edward Benzel, from the Cleveland Clinic, was less "blithe" about the risks of surgery. Painting a more ambiguous picture, filled with doubt and uncertainty, Benzel thought it unlikely that there was an imminent risk of paralysis and recommended waiting until the patient's symptoms worsened. Recalling Fitzgerald's midwestern narrator in *The Great Gatsby*, Nick Carraway, the author of *Being Mortal* describes Benzel as not twitching or fidgeting when he spoke with his prospective patient. "He had that midwesterner's habit of waiting a beat after people have spoken before speaking himself, in order to see if they are really done" (198).

The family chose Benzel, a good decision, as it turned out, and surgery was postponed for four years, during which time Atmaram Gawande retired from medicine and became active as a Rotary district governor. Early surgery would not have eliminated entirely the relatively slow-growing tumor, an astrocytoma, which was incurable but treatable, and probably would have resulted in the loss of quality of life. The family had made the right choice with Benzel, but as Gawande dryly points out, the choices didn't stop. "Life is choices, and they are relentless. No sooner have you made one choice than another is upon you" (215). The next choices became harder. What were Atmaram Gawande's priorities, further treatment, with the possibility of added time but also further pain, or palliative care and relative freedom from suffering and discomfort? The radiologists urged immediate treatment, as did his son. "It seemed almost all upside, I said" (215). Pressured, Atmaram Gawande agreed to treatment. "But how foolish these predictions would turn out to be" (216), his son confesses. Prolonged radiation left Atmaram Gawande in agonizing pain and did nothing to shrink the cancer.

Atmaram Gawande, his pediatrician wife, Sushila, and his surgeon son, all physicians, with combined 120 years of medical experience, could not understand what was happening: why the radiologists' predictions were untrue, why the patient was in so much pain, why nothing went as planned. Gawande writes with admirable clarity about the family's confusion, showing the difficulty of seeing the whole picture surrounding the end of life. Atmaram Gawande's Cleveland Clinic oncologist was in information mode, not interpretive mode, and she infuriated Atul when she promised that his father, who until his illness had played tennis three times a week, would soon be back on the tennis court if he went on chemotherapy. The promise was not only irrational but also cruel. "I was spitting mad that she would dangle that in front of my father" (218). The oncologist made the false promises that, until recently, Gawande had offered to his own patients, promises based on fantasy, not reality. When pressed, the oncologist admitted that chemotherapy was not likely to give the patient much more time than no treatment at all. Gawande summarizes his father's dilemma in a stark sentence. "He was torn between living the best he could with what he had versus sacrificing the life he had left for a murky chance of time later" (220).

## Pulling Back the Veil of Caregiving

Atmaram Gawande rejected further treatment, unable to endure the torment he experienced from radiation therapy, but what's noteworthy is his wife's difficulty of accepting his decision. Phrased differently, the caretaker understood intellectually but not emotionally her dying husband's decision. She remained in denial, which appears to be the caregiver's default setting. Atmaram Gawande's medical condition worsened, resulting in several falls, and his wife's terror was so intense that she desperately pleaded to her son, "Maybe they can give him chemo" (222), contrary to her husband's explicit wishes. When her son brought up the possibility of a nursing home, she was aghast. "Absolutely not, she said." To which her son remarks to us, "We'd come to the same fork in the road I have seen scores of patients come to" (223).

Gawande is a loving, dutiful son, attentive to his family's needs, but he is also a writer, expressing heartbreaking truths, and he walks a tightrope in elucidating his cautionary tale. He is always more critical of his own actions than those of others. One must read between the lines to glimpse family tensions. Atmaram Gawande was willing to contemplate hospice, his wife less so. "'I don't think it's necessary,' she said" (225). But it was. When the hospice nurse practitioner stopped by and asked the patient whether he was ready for regular visits by a home health aide or wished to think further about the question, he replied, without hesitation, "Start now." His wife was speechless. "Her face was blank." Her blank face is the caregiver's horror story that can never be fully told. Atmaram Gawande had been thinking about hospice discussions, but his wife remained stunned. "This was not going where she'd been prepared for it to go" (227).

The hospice nurse advised Sushila Gawande, firmly though not unkindly, not to call 911, the police, or an ambulance company when her husband "passes away"; instead, she should call hospice, which would make the necessary arrangements. But when she couldn't rouse her husband, Sushila instinctively dialed an ambulance company. Caregiving decisions are grueling for physicians and nonphysicians alike. As wrenching as it must have been for Gawande to shine a light on his family's suffering, he did so for a reason, as he states at the beginning of his book. "I have the writer's and scientist's faith . . . that by pulling back the veil and peering in close, a person can make sense of what is most confusing or strange or disturbing" (9).

Gawande introduces a moment of rare humor in the otherwise heartrending vignette. When his father falls at home and his 75-year-old wife, suffering from arthritic knees, cannot lift him up, the two spend the night together on the floor. By the next morning, when their son arrives, father and mother are feeling less frightened. "It's been years since I've been down on the floor," his mother declared. "It was almost romantic," his father rejoined (222), giggling.

Furious when he is taken by ambulance to the hospital, Atmaram Gawande begins shouting at the medical staff, demanding to be taken home. His greatest struggle near the end of his life, his son tells us, remained the pain from his tumor. Gawande intimates the family's disagreement over how to help the dying man. Should he be given enough morphine to eliminate the pain, even if it meant remaining unconscious? Gawande and his sister, Meeta, thought so. Their mother disagreed. "'Maybe if he had a little pain, he'd wake up,' she said, her eyes welling. 'He still has so much he can do.'" Gawande is reluctant to criticize his mother, who was "not wrong" in her statement; in the next couple of days, the dying patient is able momentarily to ignore his pain to appreciate small pleasures, such as eating. But Gawande honors the pledge he made to his father to give him morphine every two hours, as planned. "My mother anxiously accepted it" (255)—a sentence that understates what was probably a troubling family disagreement over caregiving.

## The End of the Story

"Endings matter," Gawande reminds us, and he ends his father's story, which appropriately occurs at the end of the book, before a brief epilogue, by recording a family conversation that occurred during dinner a day before his father's death:

> "What are you thinking?" I asked.
> "I'm thinking how to not prolong the process of dying. This—this food prolongs the process."
> My mom didn't like hearing this.
> "We're happy taking care of you, Ram," she said. "We love you."
> He shook his head.
> "It's hard, isn't it?" my sister said.
> "Yes. It's hard."
> "If you could sleep through it, is that what you'd prefer?" I asked.
> "Yes."
> "You don't want to be awake, aware of us, with us like this?" my mother asked.
> He didn't say anything for a moment. We waited.
> "I don't want to experience this," he said. (256–7)

In writing this death scene, as memorable as one is likely to find in a memoir or clinical case study, Gawande relies upon his aesthetic instincts in crafting dialogue and distilling characterization into its essence. Even if he tape-recorded the conversation, which is not likely, it's improbable that all four characters—father, mother, daughter, son—would speak in perfect sentences. People do not speak this way in real life, certainly not in a deathbed scene, using an economy of words, without verbal tics, repetition, or inconsequential utterances. No one interrupts another in this final evocative conversation: each has a role to play in the solemn drama, and each waits patiently for his or her turn to speak. Gawande eliminates any ambiguity in what the four characters say or hear, so that there can be no misunderstanding or second guessing after the conversation. Each speaks in character: the dying father reaching the end of the line, accepting of death, wisely letting go; the distraught mother pleading with him to remain alive, not abandoning her; the empathic daughter, giving him an opportunity to express his feelings; and the physician-son, asking the right question to clarify the situation, making his father's death into a teachable moment. The caregiver's situation is especially poignant: she alone cannot accept what is happening before her eyes, cannot defer to her husband's wishes, yet her fear, disbelief, and perhaps anger are muted. End-of-life discussions are a process, Gawande maintains, not an epiphany, and that's what we see here. Atmaram Gawande died in character, knowing when his time had run out.

To make these observations is not to call into question the accuracy of the dying event but to appreciate how Gawande relies upon novelistic techniques to narrate the story—including creating suspense before the father verbalizes his final sentence in the book. Gawande's description of his father's dying breath does not contain the transcendent, religious transfiguration at the end of *The Death of Ivan Ilych*, but it conveys peaceful death, implying that the family's caregiving decisions were the right ones. Gawande doesn't prettify death, but he takes the sting out of it, affirming his belief that talking about the ending of life is better than not talking about it. Gawande's story of his father's death confirms Rita Charon's observation that the "telling of pain and suffering" enables patients to "give voice to what they endure and to frame the illness so as to escape domination by it" (65).

Attentive to the endings of his patients' lives, Gawande interrupts the story of his father's dying to dwell on the nature of remembering. He cites Daniel Kahneman's distinction, in his 2011 book *Thinking, Fast and Slow*, between the "experiencing self" and the "remembering self." In the chapter aptly called "Life as a Story," Kahneman, an Israeli-American psychologist and economist who won the Nobel Prize in 2002, argues that we remember endings, the "peak-end effect," and tend to forget or minimize the middle of a story, the "duration effect." A story is about "significant events and memorable moments, not about time passing" (387). "Odd as it may seem," Kahneman writes, "I am my remembering self, and the experiencing self, who does my living, is like a stranger to me" (390). Gawande puts this paradoxical knowledge to good use in *Being Mortal*. He ends his vignette on Lou Sanders with the nonagenarian's statement that he doesn't worry about the future now because he is in the right place. "I know my time is limited. And so, what? I've had a good shot at it" (147). And Gawande ends his book with a brief epilogue in which, a few months after his father's death, the family travels to India to cast his cremated remains in the Ganges River, sacred to Hindus. The ritual reminds us of Atmaram Gawande's spiritual beliefs that his son honors. Gawande was not his father's primary caregiver, but he casts the story of his father's death as a spiritual experience, one that the writer witnessed, interpreted, and recorded.

The ritual is not without its challenges. Before drinking three spoonfuls of the water from the polluted river, Gawande took an antibiotic to ward off dangerous bacteria, but he developed a *Giardia* infection. He completed the ritual, however, fulfilling his father's last wish. What we remember the most about Atmaram Gawande's story is not his lengthy suffering or his arguments with his family but his peaceful death. The last paragraph of *Being Mortal* depicts the death as a life-affirming experience, part of a rebirth cycle. "After spreading my father's ashes, we floated silently for a while, letting the current take us. As the sun burned away the mist, it began warming our bones. Then we gave a signal to the boatman, and he picked up his oars. We headed back toward the shore" (263).

## Swimming in a Sea of Death

To avoid the twin mistakes of needlessly prolonging suffering or shortening valued life, Gawande urges physicians, the dying, and their caregivers to have honest and open conversations about end-of-life care. How often do these conversations occur? Seldom, if one is to judge from memoirs. These conversations never occurred when Susan Sontag, one of the country's leading intellectuals, the "Dark Lady of American Letters," was dying. As her son, David Rieff, reveals in his 2008 memoir *Swimming in a Sea of Death*, Sontag was diagnosed with metastatic breast cancer in 1975, at the age of forty-two. She beat the odds despite being given only a 10 percent chance of survival. In the late 1990s, she developed uterine sarcoma and again survived. In 2004, she developed myelodysplastic syndrome, a blood disease that is a precursor to leukemia. According to her son, she allowed no one to speak to her about the possibility of death. Despite a bone marrow transplant, Sontag died in 2004, two weeks short of her seventy-second birthday.

The loved one's dilemma confronts Rieff throughout his memoir, as I suggest in *Dying in Character*. "Should he have told his mother what she wanted to hear, namely, that she was not dying of cancer, or what she did not want to hear—that death was imminent? He tortures himself over the choice he made, and he asks his readers what they would do in his situation" (135). Rieff quotes a paradoxical Jewish saying: "just as it is an obligation to tell someone what is acceptable, it is an obligation not to say what is not acceptable" (104)—a proverb that may be more helpful in theory than in practice. Sontag's faith in medical science approached "religiosity" (31), Rieff reports in his memoir, becoming a "scientism" (94) that contradicted her otherwise intellectually skeptical view of reality. "Almost until the moment she died," Rieff writes, "we talked of her survival, of her struggle with cancer, never about her dying. I was not going to raise the subject unless she did. It was her death, not mine.

And she did not raise it" (17). Rieff implies that his mother's medical situation did not serve her well. He leaves little doubt that her denial to the end of life did not serve *him* well. He characterizes their relationship at the end as folie à deux (73, 113), madness shared by two people. He became her "accomplice" in denial, "albeit with the guiltiest of consciences" (43).

## *Midstream*

The absence of candid end-of-life caregiving conversations can also be seen in Le Anne Schreiber's 1990 memoir *Midstream*, a harrowing story of her mother's death. The first female editor of the *New York Times* sports section and then deputy editor of the *New York Times Book Review*, Schreiber had just turned forty in 1985 when she received news from her brother, Mike, a diagnostic radiologist, that their mother was diagnosed with pancreatic cancer and was given two to six months to live. Schreiber, who had recently bought an old house in rural Columbia County, two hours north of New York City, flew regularly for the next fifteen months to visit her parents in Minneapolis. She also began a journal that became the basis for her memoir.

There are noteworthy similarities between *Midstream* and *Being Mortal*, beginning with the refusal of Bea Schreiber's physicians to have candid discussions with her about the seriousness of her illness. All of the physicians minimized the debilitating side effects she experienced from radiation therapy and chemotherapy. "Last week Mike said to me, 'The medical center doctors aren't interested in Mom. They're interested in her disease. She's just the host for the tumor.' He sounded bitter, vengeful, and said he planned to write a damning letter to the ethics committee at the medical center about their handling of Mom's case." Ironically, Schreiber recalls a time, several years earlier, when Mike himself, enchanted with the latest radiation technology, had once referred to patients as "just hosts for beautiful tumors." "That mentality," she adds ruefully, "seems to prevail among doctors, at least fancy doctors, and Mike has certainly been party to it" (218).

Partly as a result of the absence of frank end-of-life discussions, Bea remains in denial to the end, along with her husband, who is eager to order unnecessary medical tests and procedures that only add to her suffering. He blames himself for not having encouraged his wife to accept her approaching death, but he is part of a culture of denial. His fixation on a miraculous cure for his wife, such as buying her a Fleet enema, "brandishing his purchase like a warrior with a new weapon," further depletes her body and spirit, as well as awakens his daughter's rage: "he acted irrationally, cruelly, heedless of everything but his own fear of death. As if death could be controlled by a dutiful wife and daughter" (235–6).

Gawande would characterize Bea Schreiber's physicians as functioning in the informative, if not patriarchal, mode, certainly not the interpretive or deliberative mode. Mike doesn't share his medical knowledge with the family, which only deepens their denial. Mike was the only one in the family who knew that his mother's chance of recovery had been virtually nonexistent and that the five-week radiation therapy she received, resulting in unnecessary suffering, was doomed from the beginning. "'They succeeded in killing the mother tumor, but the daughters are flourishing,' he concluded" (263). Schreiber understands only at the end of the story why her brother had been hoping that their mother would have a pulmonary embolism, a merciful end of her suffering. Throughout her ordeal Bea Schreiber has been given far less morphine medication than she needed; her doctors feared addiction—as if addiction is problematic in a patient close to death. She often cries out in pain, pleading for more morphine, like Kate Gulden in *One True Thing* and Atmaram Gawande in *Being Mortal*. Schreiber's father was so exhausted by his caregiving responsibilities that he began to lose the ability to make sound judgments. Schreiber tried to help her mother worry less about her body so that she could "tend more to her spirit" (251), but these conversations never occurred.

Family tensions are sharper in *Midstream* than in *Being Mortal*. Schreiber is furious with her brother for wishing to hasten their mother's death, and after her death the daughter is bereft. And yet like *Being Mortal*, *Midstream* ends hopefully, demonstrating that endings matter. Schreiber describes a family visit to Italy in 1987 where she met her father's new companion, Alice, also a widow with children. We never learn about Sushila Gawande's life after her husband's death, a subject that her son may have felt unnecessary to include in a vignette focusing mainly on end-of-life care.

There is one more crucial connection between *Being Mortal* and *Midstream*, the value of writing about death. During the last month of her mother's life, Schreiber observes at the beginning of her memoir, writing a journal was a lifeline. "In part it gave me a saving distance, reminded me that I was a witness to dying, not the one dying. The journal was also my weapon against denial, my way of looking in the presence of so many averted eyes, my way of remembering in the face of so much forgetting" (10–11). Amid her journal entries are occasional doubts about the value of her writing. She worries near the end of the memoir whether her journal has become an "obscenity," an invasion of her family's privacy. "Do I violate my mother by recording what I've recorded here? Would she wish it buried with her? Must my communication always be to myself?" (285). Notwithstanding these anxieties, she never doubts the value of writing the memoir, believing, with Gawande, in the role of storytelling particularly in end-of-life care.

Schreiber continues her storytelling about finitude in her lyrical 1996 memoir *Light Years* in which she laments the three deaths that occurred within five years, those of her mother, father, and brother. She recalls her mother fighting death "tooth and nail, as if it were the angel of hell on earth." Using the same civil war figure as Gawande does in *Being Mortal*, she compares her father's death two years later as a "graceful surrender, like Lee at Appomattox." Three years later, her fifty-year-old brother, "a doctor to his last breath, met death as if reluctantly bowing to his new chief of staff" (143). The three deaths left her numb, but over time she found comfort in "those landscapes whose open horizons induce a larger perspective" (148). She ends the memoir by gazing at the vast horizons light years away—a vision that Gawande offers in *Being Mortal*.

## Changing Our Attitudes toward Dying, Death, and Caregiving

If the central theme of *Being Mortal* is the need to have difficult conversations about dying, death, and caregiving, is this a Sisyphean task, never to be solved? This was Alex Hutchinson's initial impression of *Being Mortal* as he expressed in his review published in the Toronto *Globe and Mail*. Yet upon further thought, Hutchinson realizes that his conclusion might be too pessimistic. He then cites a 1999 physicians' campaign in La Crosse, Wisconsin, to encourage people of all ages to discuss their end-of-life preferences with loved ones. "Within a few years, 85 per cent of residents had filled out an advanced-care directive, up from 15 per cent." The larger story of the La Crosse campaign appears in *Being Mortal*. Hutchinson's new conclusion is that widespread and permanent change in our attitudes toward dying, death, and, presumably, caregiving, is possible. "Maybe Gawande, who wields outsized cultural influence, can trigger it."

Gawande offers, at the end of *Better*, his book on surgical performance, five suggestions for becoming a "positive deviant," that is, making a contribution to society. The one he has taken most to heart is, not surprisingly, to "write something." Although he did not begin writing until he became a physician, writing allows him to step back and think through a problem. Writing also links him to the larger community. "The published word is a declaration of membership in that community and also of a willingness to contribute something meaningful to it" (256). Choose your audience, he advises, and then write something. Not all physicians follow their own advice, but Gawande has, and his patients—and readers—are the beneficiaries.

# Conclusion

## Caregiving—A Beautiful Story?

"Love means not ever having to say you're sorry," declaims Jennifer Cavalieri in Erich Segal's bestselling 1970 novel *Love Story*. The line, which the bereft hero repeats on the last page of the novel, after his 25-year-old wife dies from leukemia, can be applied to Nicholas Sparks's bestselling 1996 novel *The Notebook*. For Sparks, caregiving means not having to say you're sorry—and never feeling distressed, saddened, isolated, or burdened by caring for a person who has lost her memory. No novel portrays caregiving and care-receiving more sentimentally. It is instructive to see why readers and filmgoers are drawn to a story in which the caregiver appears as a romantic hero whose undying love and commitment to a spouse never waver—and why despite its popularity the story is profoundly disappointing.

Sparks has two goals in *The Notebook*, creating the greatest love story ever told, followed by the greatest caregiving story. Noah Calhoun and Allie Nelson fall in love at first sight as North Carolina teenagers in 1932, but class differences in the South threaten to doom their relationship. He is the poetic son of working-class parents; she is the artistic daughter of wealthy aristocratic parents. In an effort to end the relationship, her socialite mother intercepts Noah's heartsick letters to Allie. During a fourteen-year separation, his love remains pure and constant, but she becomes engaged to an ambitious lawyer and contemplates a future devoid of desire. "Passion would fade in time, and things like companionship and compatibility would take its place" (107). Three weeks before the wedding, the ambivalent fiancé seeks out her true love. Destiny is not thwarted. Sparks skips over the next half century, informing us in empurpled prose that the two lovers never settled for mere companionship. The adversary in the novel is not time, a controlling mother, class differences, or the inevitable losses of life, but Alzheimer's disease, a thief that threatens to steal Allie from Noah.

"Who are you?" the demented Allie asks her husband shortly before their forty-ninth wedding anniversary. It is a fair question, but as it turns out, she has lost only her memory, not her cognitive or linguistic skills. When he reads to her from his eponymous notebook containing their love letters to each other during their long marriage, she responds in the way that Sparks wants readers of *The Notebook* to respond: "That was a beautiful story" (158). It doesn't matter, Sparks implies, that Allie fails to recognize Noah is describing their *own* story. Sparks never allows us to forget his enthralling tale of love that can never be lost or forgotten. Everything about their relationship is perfect, even after the thief's arrival. "She stares at the hardened knots that deform my fingers and caresses them gently. Her hands are still those of an angel" (165). Noah reminds us incessantly, lest we forget, that "romance and passion are possible at any age" (170). The married couple may now reside in separate rooms at the Creekside Extended Care facility, but not even severe rheumatoid arthritis, not to mention the inhospitable rules of the nursing home, can prevent him from sneaking into her room at night to gaze at her. She triumphantly remembers his name on the last page of the story. "'Oh, Noah . . . I've missed you.' Another miracle—the greatest of all!" (214). She then begins unbuttoning his shirt, eager for one more act of passionate lovemaking.

The problem with *The Notebook* is not that Sparks lacks an understanding of the reality of Alzheimer's disease. He informs us, for example, about the phenomenon of sundowning, the late-day confusion, murk, and agitation surrounding dementia. He also gives us accurate symptoms of the disease. Rather, the problem is Sparks's refusal to acknowledge the turbulent emotions experienced by the caregiver and care-receiver amid the ravages of dementia. We never see the caregiver's exhaustion in caring for a loved one, nor the stress and frustration of caregiving, nor burn-out or compassion fatigue. "I am not bitter," Noah proclaims twice, the first time about the apparent end of their star-crossed teenage infatuation, (152), the second time about the apparent end of her memory of their marriage (166). Readers familiar with Alzheimer's disease know that Sparks protests too much. Indeed, it is difficult to find *any* caregiving novel, film, memoir, or extended clinical vignette where a caregiver does not feel dark emotions such as anger or bitterness. Though Allie may momentarily experience Alzheimer's demons, haunted by unseen enemies and hallucinations, she is present enough to console him. The nursing home doctors are mystified by Noah's devotion to Allie, but others know the explanation. "Even though the doctors don't understand it, we nurses do. It's love, it's as simple as that. It's the most incredible thing I've ever seen" (210–11).

Made into a popular 2004 film directed by Nick Cassavetes, starring Ryan Gosling and Rachel McAdams and their older counterparts, James Garner and Gena Rowlands, *The Notebook* sugarcoats both aging and Alzheimer's disease. The demented Allie is stylishly dressed, impeccably coiffed, and wears an expensive necklace and earrings. Unlike the equally elegant Julie Christie in *Away from Her*, she never does anything to awaken our curiosity. Though Allie displays a flash of fury and violence at her husband near the end of the film, she quickly regains her composure. Allie listens attentively to the story of her life, as narrated by Noah, appreciating every detail: teachers can only hope that their students will be such good listeners. In the film, which is even more sentimental than the novel, Allie and Noah die peacefully in bed in the nursing home, contentedly holding hands, as a flock of birds soars away, symbolizing, no doubt, the couple's spirit ascending.

"The romantics would call this a love story," the octogenarian Noah tells us in the beginning of the novel, "the cynics would call it a tragedy. In my mind it's a little of both" (2). Cynics would *not* call Sparks's fantasy a tragedy; they would call it the most teary-eyed caregiving story to date, awash in platitudes and bathos. One recalls Oscar Wilde's quip about Little Nell's death in Dickens's *Old Curiosity Shop*: one would need a heart of stone not to laugh. Readers admittedly may feel guilty disliking a story that claims to admire poetry as much as *The Notebook* does. Though he is no poet himself, Noah never tires of quoting his favorite poets, Whitman, Tennyson, Browning, Eliot, and Thomas. During the Second World War, he is holding a copy of *Leaves of Grass* when it takes a bullet for him—saved by literature! Sparks shares Allie's belief that poetry "wasn't written to be analyzed; it was meant to inspire without reason, to touch without understanding" (74). True, a poetry teacher may respond, but critical analysis helps us to understand and appreciate poetry, separating good poems from poor ones. The best poems combine emotion and reason, heart and head. Literature can comfort and console, as Sparks realizes, but it can also shock and disturb, leading us to insights we may not have gleaned elsewhere. These insights never appear in *The Notebook*. At the end of the novel, we learn that Allie has become one of the best southern painters of the twentieth century—a meaningless assertion without elaboration.

## Sentimentalism

As M. H. Abrams has noted, sentimentalism has not always been a pejorative term. "Since what constitutes excess or overindulgence is relative both to the judgment of the individual and to large-scale changes in culture and in literary fashion, what to the common reader of one age is a normal expression of humane feeling may seem sentimental to many later readers" (175). Late eighteenth-century novels like Richardson's *Pamela*, Sterne's *Tristram Shandy*, and Goethe's *The Sorrows of Young Werther*, which all contain virtuous characters who express emotional intensity, were among the greatest novels of their age. But as Abrams points out, "Readers now find both the *drama* and *novel of sensibility* of the eighteenth century ludicrously sentimental, and also respond with jeers instead of tears to once celebrated episodes of pathos" (175).

Sparks's literary pretension leads him astray, as when, in an effort to be eloquent, he begins a sentence, indeed, several sentences, with a preposition: "Of this she knows nothing" (155); "On this there is agreement" (186); "Of this I'm sure" (190). Few caregivers walk into a nursing home thinking, "I am an epic adventure now when I travel the halls" (201). Sometimes Sparks's dependence on a thesaurus betrays him: "I did not know what to say as she sobbed on my bosom" (168). Why not the simpler word *chest*? Other times he uses a word with the wrong connotations, as when Allie writes to Noah, "I find your love for our children very sensual and exciting" (206). Is the novel's hero or heroine a pedophile?

Who would not like to believe in Sparks's fantasy of caregiving? Noah is a selfless caregiver to Allie and to the others in the nursing home. He reads to her every morning, as well as to the other residents, all of whom regard him as a friend. "'I'm so glad you've come,' they say, and then they ask about my wife" (156). Has a caregiver had so many grateful care-receivers? One can only admire Noah for taking the time to read comforting poetry to the residents—"I sit with them and read to lessen their fears" (157). Because a large majority of residents in most nursing homes suffer from dementia, we can only wonder at what Noah's audience is thinking when they express gratitude for his stories. Who would not like to believe that poetry has miraculous healing powers? After his mother died, the five-year-old Noah stopped speaking, and when he resumed, developed a stutter that his father cured by reading poetry to him. One can only wish that bibliotherapy is as effective as Sparks implies, both to children with speech impediments and residents living in typical nursing homes, which are not, as Atul Gawande implies in *Being Mortal*, the most congenial of settings.

"Is it a true story?" Allie asks Noah after he has finished reading from his notebook. Yes, he replies, but we can help Sparks write a truer story by raising questions explored by the other caregiver authors in our study. Noah is an idealized caregiver, as is Tolstoy's Gerasim, but would Noah rise to the challenge if his wife undergoes the physical, mental, and spiritual agonies of an Ivan Ilych? What if Noah fell out of love with his wife, was attracted to another woman, with whom he intended to end his life, and then, surviving a failed suicide pact, found himself and his paramour cared for by his spiteful wife? This might remind us of

*Ethan Frome*, which ends with caregivers and care-receivers living together with no escape, prisoners for life. Given Noah's closeness with Allie, their inseparability, was he susceptible to emotional contagion, as we see in Bergman's *Persona*, where caregiver and care-receiver exchange roles and identities and become bitter enemies? "I think I have an admirer" (183), Allie enthuses, but what if she falls in love with another man in the nursing home? Is Noah so devoted to Allie that he would be willing to become a matchmaker and encourage her romance with another man, as Grant does in Alice Munro's "The Bear Came Over the Mountain"?

Noah admits that he knows what it's like to be with Allie day and night, "always together, forever apart" (177), reminding us of the marriage between John Bayley and Iris Murdoch, when they were moving "closer and closer apart" early in their marriage. Would Noah be able to live with Allie if she were totally dependent on him, as Murdoch became dependent on her husband? Would Noah develop Bayley's survival skills to care for a demented wife? If wife and husband did not conveniently die at the same time, and if Allie pleads with Noah to end her suffering, would he contemplate killing her, as Ellen Gulden considers matricide in Quindlen's *One True Thing*? Would he actually strangle his beloved wife and then take his own life, as Georges does in Haneke's *Amour*?

Would Noah become so angry at Allie's parents for attempting to prevent his marriage to their daughter that he exposes them to public ridicule, as Mary Gordon excoriates her relatives in *Circling My Mother*? Could Sparks learn from Walter Mosley how to write a convincing caregiving story that transcends the generic constraints of a murder mystery or a romance novel? Could Sparks recreate the rhetoric of dementia, as Mosley does? Sparks might not be interested in Margaret Morganroth Gullette's distinction between progress and decline narratives, but could he learn from her how to write about caregiving without indulging in cloying sentimentality? Could Sparks pull back the veil of caregiving to show, as Atul Gawande does in *Being Mortal*, the anguished conversations necessary for end-of-life care? Caregiving does not come across as "beautiful" in these novels, films, memoirs, or clinical vignettes, at least not in the way Sparks attempts to evoke beauty, but they all contain an aesthetic beauty and psychological complexity that make them memorable. Of this we can be sure.

## Beautiful or Cruel Optimism?

Hopefulness is essential not only to well-being but also to life itself. "[P]eople without hope not only don't write novels," remarked Flannery O'Connor, "but what is more to the point, they don't read them" (79). At what point, however, does hope, or beautiful optimism, become cruel? When do our attachments to dreams and fantasies become self-sabotaging? When must optimism be tempered with reality? When must fiction, film, and memoir honor both the pleasure principle and the reality principle?

Lauren Berlant, a professor of English at the University of Chicago, raises these thorny questions in her 2011 book *Cruel Optimism*. Berlant defines cruel optimism as a "relation of attachment to compromised conditions of possibility whose realization is discovered either to be impossible, sheer fantasy, or *too* possible, and toxic" (24). The attachments are cruel, Berlant insists, rather than merely inconvenient or tragic, because subjects cannot endure the loss of their objects of desire. The affective structure of cruel attachments involves emotions that can no longer be sustained. "Why do people stay attached to conventional good-life fantasies—say, of enduring reciprocity in couples, families, political systems, institutions, markets, and at work—when the evidence of their instability, fragility, and dear cost abounds?" (2). Berlant does not discuss caregiving, but her criticisms of cruel optimism apply to sentimental fiction like *The Notebook* that appeals to emotion divorced from reason. "Feeling good" in sentimental literature prevents us from raising the hard questions about what is arguably the most challenging role in life: caring for another person. The best caregiving stories, films, and memoirs explore these hard questions in depth, allowing us to see the consequences of caregiving decisions.

## Caregiving Stories

Caregiving is a story that must be told, and for that reason, it's surprising that there have not yet been book-length studies of the caregiver in fiction, film, memoir, and clinical vignette. There will be, we can predict, a growing number of caregiving stories in the future, perhaps enough to constitute a subgenre of literature. As I noted in the introduction, perhaps the main reason for the scholarly neglect of caregiving as a literary and cultural phenomenon is the resistance to the idea of sickness, dependency, and mortality. The thought of caregiving and care-receiving is deeply threatening, especially since most caregiving stories take place near the end of a care-receiver's life. Caregiving stories take us to places we don't wish to visit, places that reveal decline and death, and for this reason these stories are often unspeakable.

Nevertheless, many of these fraught journeys are, paradoxically, life-transforming and sometimes authentically heartwarming. Caregiving stories have much to teach us about life and death. The best stories provide us with a deep source of pleasure—pleasure that is neither syrupy nor oversweet. As the baby boomer generation ages, there will be more and more caregiving stories. It's likely that the most authentic caregiving stories will be penned by caregivers themselves. Organizations and blogs like *AARP*, the American Society on Aging, *Eldercarelink* Blog, *A Place for Mom*, *Next Avenue*, *Caring Village*, and *Caring.Com* offer their list of the best caregiving memoirs of the year, but my favorites include, to give only three example, Brenda Webster's 2014 novel *After Auschwitz: A Love Story*, Cathie Borrie's 2010 memoir *The Long Hello*, and Emma Healey's riveting 2015 debut novel *Elizabeth Is Missing*. Unlike Sparks's first-person narrator, who proclaims that he is telling us a beautiful story, these authors allow us to see the unvarnished truth of caregiving. I believe that all of the stories, films, and memoirs I have discussed convey the experience of caregiving and care-receiving, including sorrow, frustration, conflict, loneliness, suffering, and, yes, beauty.

# Works Cited

Abel, Emily K. *Hearts of Wisdom: American Women Caring for Kin, 1845–1940.* Cambridge, MA: Harvard University Press, 2000.

Abel, Emily K. *The Inevitable Hour: A History of Caring for Dying Patients in America.* Baltimore: Johns Hopkins University Press, 2013.

Abel, Emily K. *Living in Death's Shadow: Family Experiences of Terminal Care and Irreplaceable Loss.* Baltimore: Johns Hopkins University Press, 2017.

Abrams, M. H. *A Glossary of Literary Terms*, 4th ed. New York: Holt, Rinehart and Winston, 1981.

Adams, Annmarie and Sally Chivers. "Architecture and Aging: The Depiction of Home in Sarah Polley's *Away from Her*." http://ageculturehumanities.org/WP/architecture-and-aging-the-depiction-of.... Issue 2, 2015. Accessed July 1, 2018.

Adams, Kathryn Betts. "What the Film *Amour* Tells Us About Aging and Caregiving." *Psychology Today*, January 23, 2013. https://www.psychologytoday.com/us/blog/mid-life-what-crisis/201301/what-the-film-amour-tells-us-about aging-and-caregiving. Accessed June 13, 2018.

Albom, Mitch. *Tuesdays with Morrie: An Old Man, a Young Man, and Life's Greatest Lesson.* New York: Broadway, 1997.

Almeida, Joyce. "*Amour*." *RCPsych*. https://www.recpsych.ac.uk./discoverpsychiatry/mindsonfilmblog/amour.aspx. Accessed June 13, 2018.

Alterra, Aaron. *The Caregiver: A Life with Alzheimer's*. South Royalton, VT: Steerforth Press, 1999.

Anyar, Uma. "Film Views: *Amour*: An Existential Drama." *Inspired-Bali*. http://www.inspired-bali.com/wp1/film-views-amour-an-existential-drama. Accessed June 13, 2018.

Aries, Philippe. *The Hour of Our Death*, translated by Helen Weaver. New York: Knopf, 1981.

Astrow, Alan. "Thoughts on Euthanasia and Physician-Assisted Suicide." In *Facing Death: Where Culture, Religion, and Medicine Meet*, edited by Howard Spiro, Mary McCrea Curnen, and Lee Palmer Wandel. New Haven: Yale University Press, 1996, 44–51.

Auchincloss, Louis. *Pioneers & Caretakers: A Study of American Women Novelists.* Minneapolis: University of Minnesota Press, 1965.

Barthes, Roland. *Mourning Diary: October 26, 1977-September 5, 1979*, translated by Richard Howard. New York: Hill & Wang, 2010.

Bartlett, Rosamund. *Tolstoy: A Russian Life*. Boston, MA: Houghton Mifflin, 2011.

Battin, Margaret Pabst. *The Least Worst Death*. New York: Oxford University Press, 1994.
Bayley, John. *Elegy for Iris*. New York: Picador, 1999.
Bayley, John. *Iris and Her Friends: A Memoir of Memory and Desire*. New York: Norton, 2000.
Bayley, John. *Leo Tolstoy*. Plymouth: Northcote, 1997.
Bayley, John. *The Power of Delight: A Lifetime in Literature: Essays 1962–2002*, selected by Leo Carey. New York: Norton, 2005.
Bayley, John. *Selected Essays*. Cambridge: Cambridge University Press, 1984.
Bayley, John. *Widower's House: A Study in Bereavement, or How Margot and Mella Forced Me to Flee My Home*. New York: Norton, 2001.
Bennett, Alma. "Conversations with Mary Gordon." *South Carolina Review* 28 (1995): 3–36.
Benstock, Shari. *Women of the Left Bank: Paris, 1900–1940*. Austin: University of Texas Press, 1986.
Bergman, Ingmar. *Bergman on Bergman*. Interviews with Ingmar Bergman by Stig Bjsrkman, Torsten Manns, and Jonas Sima, translated by Paul Britten. Austin; London: Secker & Warburg, 1973.
Bergman, Ingmar. *Face to Face*, translated by Alan Blair. New York: Pantheon, 1997.
Bergman, Ingmar. *Four Screenplays of Ingmar Bergman*, translated by Lars Malmstrom and David Kushner. New York: Simon and Schuster, 1969.
Bergman, Ingmar. *Images: My Life in Film*, translated by Marianne Ruuth. Introduction by Woody Allen. New York: Arcade, 2011.
Bergman, Ingmar. *The Magic Lantern: An Autobiography*, translated by Joan Tate. New York: Viking, 1988.
Bergman, Ingmar. *Persona and Shame: The Screenplays of Ingmar Bergman*, translated by Keith Bradfield. London: Marion Boyars, 2002.
Berlant, Lauren. *Cruel Optimism*. Durham, NC: Duke University Press, 2011.
Berman, Jeffrey. *Companionship in Grief: Love and Loss in the Memoirs of C. S. Lewis, John Bayley, Donald Hall, Joan Didion, and Calvin Trillin*. Amherst: University of Massachusetts Press, 2010.
Berman, Jeffrey. "The Death and Dying of Ivan Ilych." In *Advances in Thanatology*. New York: Arno Press, 1980, 51–60.
Berman, Jeffrey. *Diaries to an English Professor: Pain and Growth in the Classroom*. Amherst: University of Massachusetts Press, 1994.
Berman, Jeffrey. *Dying in Character: Memoirs on the End of Life*. Amherst: University of Massachusetts Press, 2012.
Berman, Jeffrey. *Dying to Teach: A Memoir of Love, Loss, and Learning*. Albany, NY: State University of New York Press, 2007.
Berman, Jeffrey. *Mad Muse: The Mental Illness Memoir in a Writer's Life and Work*. Bingley: Emerald, 2019.
Berman, Jeffrey. *Surviving Literary Suicide*. Amherst, MA: University of Massachusetts Press, 1999.

Berman, Jeffrey. *Writing Widowhood: The Landscapes of Bereavement*. Albany, NY: State University of New York Press, 2015.

Berthin-Scaillet, Agnes. "A Reading of *Away from Her*, Sarah Polley's Adaptation of Alice Munro's Short Story, 'The Bear Came Over the Mountain.'" *Journal of the Short Story in English* 55 (2010). https://journals.openedition.org/jsse. Accessed July 1, 2018.

Bezzubova, Elena. "Depersonalization in the *DSM-5*." *Psychology Today*, June 13, 2014. https://www.psychologytodat.com/us/blog/the-search-self/201406/deperson.... Accessed March 13, 2019.

Borrie, Cathie. *The Long Hello: The Other Side of Alzheimer's*. Nightwing Press, 2010; rpt. *The Long Hello: Memory, My Mother, and Me*. New York: Arcade Publishing, 2016.

Bradshaw, Peter. "Review of *Away from Her*." *The Guardian*, April 27, 2007. https://www.theguardian.com/film/2007/apr/27/drama. Accessed July 7, 2018.

Brock, Dan. "Physician-Assisted Suicide as a Last-Resort Option at the End of Life." In *Physician -Assisted Dying*, edited by Timothy Quill and Margaret Battin. Baltimore: Johns Hopkins University Press, 2004, 130–49.

Brody, Richard. "Michael Haneke's Sterile *Amour*." *The New Yorker*. https://newyorker.com/culture/richard-brody/michael-hanekes-sterile-amour. Accessed June 13, 2018.

Bruckner, D.J.R. "Mystery Stories Are Novelist's Route to Moral Questions." *New York Times*, September 4, 1990.

Brungardt, Gerard. "Teaching *The Death of Ivan Ilych*: A Guide to Introducing Tolstoy's Classic." *Journal of Palliative Medicine* 12 (2009): 679–82.

Butler, Katy. "What Broke My Father's Heart." *New York Times Magazine*, June 18, 2010.

Butler, Robert N. "Age-ism: Another Form of Bigotry." *The Gerontologist* 9 (1969): 243–6.

Butler, Robert N. *Why Survive: Being Older in America*. New York: Harper & Row, 1975.

Byock, Ira. *Dying Well: Peace and Possibilities at the End of Life*. New York: Riverhead, 1997.

Calhoun, Dave. "Michael Haneke Interview." *TimeOut, London*. https://www.timeout.com/london/film/michaelhaneke-interview. Accessed June 13, 2018.

Camus, Albert. *The Myth of Sisyphus and Other Essays*, translated by Justin O'Brien. New York: Vintage, 1955.

Carey, Benedict. "In Month After '13 Reasons Why' Debut on Netflix, Study Finds Teen Suicide Grew." *New York Times*, April 29, 2019.

Carter, Rosalynn. *Helping Yourself Help Others: A Book for Caregivers*. With Susan K. Golant. New York: Times Book, 1994.

Casado-Gual, Nuria. "Unexpected Turns in Lifelong Sentimental Journeys: Redefining Love, Memory and Old Age Through Alice Munro's 'The Bear Came Over the Mountain' and Its Film Adaptation, *Away from Her*." *Aging & Society* 35 (2015): 389–404.

Cassavetes, Nick, dir. *The Notebook*. 2004.

Charon, Rita. *Narrative Medicine: Honoring the Stories of Illness*. New York: Oxford University Press, 2006.

Chivers, Sally. *The Silvering Screen: Old Age and Disability in Cinema*. Toronto: University of Toronto Press, 2011.

Chodorow, Nancy. *The Reproduction of Motherhood: Psychoanalysis and the Sociology of Gender*. Berkeley, CA: University of California, 1978.

Clay, George R. "Tolstoy in the Twentieth Century." In *The Cambridge Companion to Tolstoy*, edited by Donna Tussing Orwin. Cambridge: Cambridge University Press, 2002, 206–21.

Cohen, Hubert I. *Ingmar Bergman: The Art of Confession*. New York: Twayne, 1993.

Coles, Joanna. "The Joanna Coles Interview: Duet in Perfect Harmony." In *From a Tiny Corner in the House of Fiction*, edited by Gillian Dooley. Columbia: University of South Carolina Press, 2003, 245–50.

Conrad, Peter. "Interview: Michael Haneke: There's No Easy Way to Say This." *The Guardian*, November 3, 2012. https:/www.Theguardian.com/film/2012/nov/04/Michael-haneke -amour-director. Accessed June 13, 2018.

Conradi, Peter J. *Iris Murdoch: A Life*. New York: Norton, 2001.

Conradi, Peter J. *The Saint and the Artist: A Study of the Fiction of Iris Murdoch*. 1989, 2nd ed. New York: HarperCollins, 2001.

Couser, G. Thomas. *Vulnerable Subjects: Ethics and Life Writing*. Ithaca: Cornell University Press, 2004.

Cowie, Peter. *Ingmar Bergman: A Critical Biography*. New York: Scribner's, 1982.

Csikszentmihalyi, Mihaly. *Creativity*. New York: HarperCollins, 1996.

Danaher, David S. "Tolstoy's Use of Light and Dark Imagery in *The Death of Ivan Ilych*." *Slavic and East European Journal* 39 (1995): 227–40.

Dargis, Manohla. "Étude on Aging, Its Graces, Its Indignities: Review of *Amour*." *New York Times*, December 18, 2012.

DeBaggio, Thomas. *Losing My Mind: An Intimate Look at Life with Alzheimer's*. New York: Free Press, 2003.

DeBaggio, Thomas. *When It Gets Dark: An Enlightened Reflection on Life with Alzheimer's*. Waterville, ME: Thorndike Press, 2004.

De Beauvoir, Simone. *A Very Easy Death*, translated by Patrick O'Brian. New York: Pantheon, 1985.

DiGiulio, Robert C. *Beyond Widowhood: From Bereavement to Emergence and Hope*. New York: Free Press, 1989.

Dodson, Samuel Fisher. "Frozen Hell: Edith Wharton's Tragic Offering." In *Ethan Frome and Summer: Complete Texts with Introduction, Historical Contexts, and Critical Essays*, edited by Denise D. Knight. Boston, MA: Houghton Mifflin, 2004, 251–7.

Dolby, Sandra K. *Self-Help Books: Why Americans Keep Reading Them*. Urbana, IL: University of Illinois Press, 2005.

Dowbiggin, Ian. *A Merciful End: The Euthanasia Movement in Modern America*. New York: Oxford University Press, 2003.

Ebert, Roger. "Review of *Amour*." January 9, 2013. https://www.rogerebert.com/reviews/amour-2013. Accessed June 13, 2018.

Ebert, Roger. "Review of *Away from Her*." October 11, 2007. https://www.rogerebert.com/reviews/away-from-her. Accessed July 9, 2018.

Ebert, Roger. "Review of *Persona*, 1967." https://www.rogerebert.com/reviews/great-movie-persona-1966. Accessed March 15, 2019.

Edelman, Hope. *Motherless Daughters: The Legacy of Loss*. New York: Delta, 1995.

Eliot, George. *Middlemarch*. London: Zodiac Press, 1967.

Eliot, T. S. *The Complete Poems and Plays, 1909–1950*. New York: Harcourt, Brace & World, 1952.

Emanuel, Ezekiel J. and Linda L. Emanuel. "Four Models of the Physician-Patient Relationship." *Journal of the American Medical Association* 267 (1992): 2221–6.

Erikson, Erik H. *Young Man Luther*. 1958; rpt. New York: Norton, 1962.

Erlich, Gloria C. *The Sexual Education of Edith Wharton*. Berkeley, CA: University of California Press, 1992.

Ernaux, Annie. *I Remain in Darkness*, translated by Tanya Leslie. New York: Seven Stories Press, 1999.

Eyre, Richard, dir. *Iris*. 2001.

*Family Caregiver Basics: A Practical Guide*. https://www.caring.com/caregivers/family-caregivers. Accessed March 25, 2019.

Farwell, Tricia M. *Love and Death in Edith Wharton's Fiction*. New York: Peter Lang, 2006.

Faulkner, William. *Requiem for a Nun*. New York: Random House, 1951.

Feinberg, Cara. "Bringing Life to Life." *The Atlantic*, December 2001. https://www.theatlantic.com/magazine/archive/2001/12/bringing-life-tolife. Accessed July 1, 2018.

Fink, Sheri. "Atul Gawande's *Being Mortal*." *New York Times*, November 6, 2014.

Fitzgerald, F. Scott. *The Crack-Up*, edited by Edmund Wilson. New York: New Directions, 1945.

Forster, John. *The Life of Charles Dickens*. 2 vols. London: Chapman and Hall, 1872; rpt. 1899.

Foster, Gwendolyn Audrey. "Feminist Theory and the Performance of Lesbian Desire in *Persona*." In *Ingmar Bergman's Persona*, edited by Lloyd Michaels. Cambridge: Cambridge University Press, 2000, 130–46.

Franklin, Carl, dir. *One True Thing*. 1998.

Franklin, Ruth. "Assent and Lamentation." *The New Republic*, February 25, 2002. https://newrepublic.com/article/66146/assent-and-lamentation. Accessed July 7, 2018.

Franzen, Jonathan. "My Father's Brain." In *How to Be Alone: Essays*. New York: Farrar, Straus and Giroux, 2001.

Franzen, Jonathan. "'Runaway: Alice's Wonderland.'" *New York Times*, November 14, 2004.

Freud, Sigmund. "Analysis of a Phobia in a Five-Year-Old Boy (1909)." In *Standard Edition of the Complete Psychological Works of Sigmund Freud*, vol. 10, translated and edited by James Strachey. London: Hogarth Press, 1955.

Freud, Sigmund. "Fragment of an Analysis of a Case of Hysteria (1905)." In *Standard Edition of the Complete Psychological Works of Sigmund Freud*, vol. 7, translated and edited by James Strachey. London: Hogarth Press, 1953.

Freud, Sigmund. "Mourning and Melancholia." In *Standard Edition of the Complete Psychological Works of Sigmund Freud* (1917), vol. 14, translated and edited by James Strachey. London: The Hogarth Press, 1957.

Freud, Sigmund. "The Psychopathology of Everyday Life (1901)." In *Standard Edition of the Complete Psychological Works of Sigmund Freud*, vol. 6, translated and edited by James Strachey. London: Hogarth Press, 1960.

Freud, Sigmund. "Recommendations to Physicians Practicing Psycho-Analysis (1912)." In *Standard Edition of the Complete Psychological Works of Sigmund Freud*, vol. 12, translated and edited by James Strachey. London: Hogarth Press, 1958.

Fry, Sara T. "The Role of Caring in a Theory of Nursing Ethics." In *Feminist Perspectives in Medical Ethics*, edited by Helen Bequaert Holmes and Laura M. Purdy. Bloomington, IN: Indiana University Press, 1992, 93–106.

Gailey, Elizabeth Atwood. *Write to Death: News Framing of the Right to Die Conflict, from Quinlan's Coma to Kevorkian's Conviction*. Westport, CT: Praeger, 2003.

Gawande, Atul. *Being Mortal: Medicine and What Matters in the End*. New York: Metropolitan Books, 2014; Picador, 2017.

Gawande, Atul. *Better: A Surgeon's Notes on Performance*. New York: Metropolitan Books, 2007.

Gawande, Atul. *Complications: A Surgeon's Notes on an Imperfect Science*. New York: Metropolitan Books, 2002.

Gawande, Atul. "How Do We Heal Medicine?" *TED Talk*, 2012. https://www.ted.com/talks/atul_gawande_how:do_we_heal_medicine/trans. Accessed January 21, 2019.

Genova, Lisa. *Still Alice*. New York: Pocket Books, 2014.

Gilbert, Sandra M. *Death's Door: Modern Dying and the Ways We Grieve*. New York: Norton, 2006.

Gilbert, Sandra M. *Wrongful Death: A Memoir*. New York: Norton, 1995.

Gilligan, Carol. *In a Different Voice: Psychological Theory and Women's Development*. Cambridge: Harvard University Press, 1982.

Glick, Ira, Robert Weiss, and Colin Murray Parkes. *The First Year of Bereavement*. New York: Wiley, 1974.

Gogröf, Andrea. "Endgame, Conflict, and Interest in Michael Haneke's *Amour*." *Excavatio* 26 (2015). https://sites.ualberta.ca/aizen/excavatio/articles/v26/gogrof.pdf. Accessed June 21, 2018.

Goldfield, Hannah. "Surviving *Amour*." *The New Yorker*, February 26, 2013.

Goldman, Marlene and Sarah Powell. "Alzheimer's, Ambiguity, and Irony." *Canadian Literature* 225 (Summer 2015): 82–99.

Gonzalez-Ramos, Gladys. "The Courage of Caring." In *Always on Call: When Illness Turns Families into Caregivers*, edited by Carol Levine. New York: United Hospital Fund of New York, 2000, 57–70.

Goodman, Susan. *Edith Wharton's Women: Friends & Rivals*. Hanover, NH: University Press of New England, 1990.
Gordon, Mary. "Anger." In *Deadly Sins*. New York: Morrow, 1993.
Gordon, Mary. *Circling My Mother*. New York: Pantheon, 2007.
Gordon, Mary. *Conversations with Mary Gordon*, edited by Alma Bennett. Jackson, MS: University Press of Mississippi, 2002.
Gordon, Mary. *Final Payments*. New York: Random House, 1978.
Gordon, Mary. *Good Boys and Dead Girls and Other Essays*. New York: Viking, 1991.
Gordon, Mary. *Joan of Arc*. New York: Viking, 2000.
Gordon, Mary. *Men and Angels*. New York: Random House, 1985.
Gordon, Mary. *Reading Jesus: A Writer's Encounter with the Gospels*. New York: Pantheon, 2009.
Gordon, Mary. *Seeing Through Places: Reflections on Geography and Identity*. New York: Scribner, 2000.
Gordon, Mary. *The Shadow Man: A Daughter's Search for Her Father*. New York: Random House, 1996.
Gordon, Mary. *Spending: A Utopian Divertimento*. New York: Scribner, 1998.
Gorer, Geoffrey. *Death, Grief, and Mourning in Contemporary Britain*. 1965; reprint, Salem, NH: Ayer, 1987.
Greenberg, Gary. "What if the Placebo Effect Isn't a Trick?" *New York Times Magazine*, November 7, 2018.
Greenwood, E. B. *Tolstoy: The Comprehensive Vision*. New York: St. Martin's Press, 1975.
Gross, Terry. "Interview with Walter Mosley." *Fresh Air*, NPR, December 6, 2010. https://www.npr.org/templates/transcript/transcript.php?storyId=131848211. Accessed February 9, 2018.
Grundmann, Roy. "Love, Death, Truth—*Amour*." *Senses of Cinema*, December 2012. https://sensesofcinema.com/2012/feature-articles/love-death-truth-amour. Accessed June 13, 2018.
Gullette, Margaret Morganroth. *Aged by Culture*. Chicago: University of Chicago Press, 2004.
Gullette, Margaret Morganroth. *Agewise: Fighting the New Ageism in America*. Chicago: University of Chicago Press, 2011.
Gullette, Margaret Morganroth. "*Amour*: How Can We Embrace a Film That Is So Clearly an Advert for Euthanasia?" *The Guardian*, February 28, 2013. https://theguardian.com/film/filmblog/2013/feb/28/amour-advert-for-euthanasia. Accessed June 13, 2018.
Gullette, Margaret Morganroth. *Declining to Decline: Cultural Combat and the Politics of the Midlife*. Charlottesville, VA: University Press of Virginia, 1997.
Gullette, Margaret Morganroth. *Ending Ageism, or How Not to Shoot Old People*. New Brunswick, NJ: Rutgers University Press, 2017.
Gullette, Margaret Morganroth. *Safe at Last in the Middle Years: The Invention of the Midlife Progress Novel: Saul Bellow, Margaret Drabble, Anne Tyler, and John Updike*. Berkeley, CA: University of California Press, 1988.

Gullette, Margaret Morganroth. "When My Mother Wanted to Die." *Tikkun*, July 20, 2018. https://www.tikkun.org/nextgen/when-my-mother-wanted to die. Accessed November 6, 2018.

Gutis, Philip S. "Accepting Alzheimer's, One Lost Memory at a Time." *New York Times*, December 4, 2018.

Haag, Matthew. "Sandra Day O'Connor, First Woman on Supreme Court, Reveals Dementia Diagnosis." *New York Times*, October 23, 2018.

Hall, Donald. *The Best Day the Worst Day: Life with Jane Kenyon*. Boston, MA: Houghton Mifflin, 2005.

Haneke, Michael, dir. *Amour*. 2012. (The DVD includes "The Making of *Amour*.")

Haneke, Michael, dir. *Benny's Video*. 1992.

Haneke, Michael, dir. *Funny Games*. 1997.

Hardy, Thomas. *The Complete Poems of Thomas Hardy*, edited by James Gibson. London: Macmillan, 1976.

Hatfield, Elaine, John T. Cacioppo, and Richard Rapson. *Emotional Contagion*. Cambridge: Cambridge University Press, 1994.

Healey, Emma. *Elizabeth Is Missing*. New York: Harper Perennial, 2015.

Hemingway, Ernest. *The Paris Review Interviews*, vol. 1. New York: Picador, 2006.

Henig, Robin Marantz. "The Last Day of Her Life." *New York Times Magazine*, May 14, 2015. https://www.nytimes.com/2015/05/17/magazine/the-last-day-of-her-life.html. Accessed October 30, 2018.

Hepburn, Janet. "The Freedom of Alzheimer's." *Literary Review of Canada*, May 2015. https://reviewcanada.ca/magazine/2015/05/the-freedom-of-alzhaimers. Accessed April 25, 1919.

Heusel, Barbara Stevens. "Interview with Iris Murdoch." In *From a Tiny Corner in the House of Fiction*, edited by Gillian Dooley. Columbia: University of South Carolina Press, 2003, 194–208.

Hogan, Patrick Colm. "Affect Studies and Literary Criticism." In *Oxford Research Encyclopedia of Literature*. August 2016. DOI: 10.1093/acrefore/9780190201098.013.105.

Holden, Stephen. "Film Review: An Exploration (He Explains) of Reactions to Torture." *New York Times*, March 11, 1998.

Holland, Norman N. *Meeting Movies*. Madison, NJ: Fairleigh Dickinson University Press, 2006.

Holland, Norman N. "Sarah Polley: *Away from Her*, 2006." *A Sharper Focus: Essays on Film*. http://www.asharperfocus.com/Awayf.html. Accessed July 1, 2018.

Howe, Irving. "Introduction to *The Death of Ivan Ilych*." In *Classics of Modern Fiction: Eight Short Novels*. New York: Harcourt, Brace & World, 1968.

Howells, Coral Ann. *Contemporary Canadian Women's Fiction: Reconfiguring Identities*. New York: Palgrave Macmillan, 2003.

Hutchinson, Alex. "Being Mortal's Central Message Is that We Need to Talk, Early and Often, about End-of-Life." *The Globe and Mail*, November 7, 2014. https://www.the

globeandmail.com/arts/books-and-media/book-reviews, being mortal.... Accessed January 25, 2019.

"Informal Caregiving." May 1, 1999. https://www.commonwealthfund.org/publications/publication/1999/may/info.... Accessed April 8, 2019.

Jacobs, Barry J. "From Sadness to Pride: Seven Common Emotional Experience of Caregiving." In *Always on Call: When Illness Turns Families into Caregivers*, edited by Carol Levine. New York: United Hospital Fund of New York, 2000, 83–99.

Jahn, Gary R. *The Death of Ivan Ilich: An Interpretation*. New York: Twayne, 1993.

Jahn, Gary R. *Tolstoy's the Death of Ivan Il'ich: A Critical Companion*. Evanston, IL: Northwestern University Press, 1999.

Jones, G. William, editor. *Talking with Ingmar Bergman*. Foreword by Eugene Bonelli. Preface by Charles Champlin. Dallas, TX: SMU Press, 1983.

Jurecic, Ann. *Illness as Narrative*. Pittsburgh: University of Pittsburgh Press, 2012.

Jusdanis, Gregory. "Anatomy of a Bestseller: Atul Gawande's *Being Mortal*." *Arcade: Literature, the Humanities, & the World*, April 4, 2016. https://Arcade.stanford.edu/blogs/anatomy-bestseller-atul-gawandes-being-mortal. Accessed January 23, 2019.

Kafka, Franz. *Letters to Friends, Family, and Editors*, translated by Richard Winston and Clara Winston. New York: Schocken, 1977.

Kahneman, Daniel. *Thinking, Fast and Slow*. New York: Farrar, Straus and Giroux, 2011.

Kaptchuk, Ted J. and Franklin Miller. "Open Label Placebo: Can Honestly Prescribed Placebos Evoke Meaningful Therapeutic Benefits?" *BMJ*, October 1, 2018. http://www.bmj.com. Accessed December 12, 2018.

Kauffmann, Stanley. "Stanley Kauffmann on Films: Ages Apart." *The New Republic*, December 21, 2012. https://newrepublic.com/article/111241/ages-apart.

Kawin, Bruce F. *Mindscreen: Bergman, Goddard, and First-Person Film*. Princeton: Princeton University Press, 1978.

Kirsch, Irving. *The Emperor's New Drugs: Exploding the Antidepressant Myth*. New York: Basic Books, 2010.

Kitwood, Tom. *Dementia Reconsidered: The Person Comes First*. Maidenhead: Open University Press, 1997.

Klass, Dennis, Phyllis R. Silverman, and Steven L. Nickman, eds. *Continuing Bonds: New Understandings of Grief*. Washington, DC: Taylor and Francis, 1996.

Klein, Julia M. "Interview with Margaret Morganroth Gullette on the New Ageism." *AARP Bulletin*, March 31, 2011. https://www.aarp.org/entertainment/books/info-03-2011/author-speaks-mar.... Accessed November 6, 2018.

Kleinman, Arthur. *The Illness Narratives: Suffering, Healing, and the Human Condition*. New York: Basic Books, 1988.

Knights, Pamela. *The Cambridge Introduction to Edith Wharton*. Cambridge: Cambridge University Press, 2009.

Kusturica, Nina and Eva Testor. *24 Realities per Second: Michael Haneke Documentary*. http://filmslie.com/24-realities-per-second-michael-haneke documentary. Accessed June 13, 2018.

Laditka, Sarah B. and Maria Pappas-Rogich. "Anticipatory Caregiving Anxiety Among Older Women and Men." *Journal of Women & Aging* 13 (2001): 3–18.

Lane, Anthony. "Love Hurts." *The New Yorker*, January 7, 2013. https://www.newyorker.com/magazine/2013/01/07/love-hurts. Accessed June 13, 2018.

Larocco, Steve. "Empathy as Orientation Rather than Feeling: Why Empathy Is Ethically Complex." In *Exploring Empathy: Its Propagations, Perimeters, and Potentialities*, edited by Rebeccah J. Nelems and L. J. Theo. Leiden/Boston: Brill/Rodopi, 2018, 3–13.

Larson, Jennifer. *Understanding Walter Mosley*. Columbia: University Press of Mississippi, 2016.

Leavitt, Sarah. *Tangles: A Story about Alzheimer's, My Mother, and Me*. New York: Skyhorse, 2012.

Lee, Hermione. *Edith Wharton*. New York: Knopf, 2007.

Levine, Carol, editor. *Always on Call: When Illness Turns Families into Caregivers*. New York: United Hospital Fund of New York, 2000.

Levy, B. R., L. Ferrucci, A. B. Zonderman, M. D. Slade, J. Troncoso, and S. M. Resnick. "A Culture-Brain Link: Negative Age Stereotypes Predict Alzheimer's Disease Biomarkers." *Psychology and Aging* 31 (2016): 82–8.

Levy, B. R., C. Pilver, P. H. Chung, and M. D. Slade. "Subliminal Strengthening: Improving Older Individuals' Physical Function Over Time with an Implicit-Age-Stereotype Intervention." *Psychological Science* 25 (2014): 2127–35.

Levy, B. R., C. Pilver, and R. H. Pietrzak. "Lower Prevalence of Psychiatric Conditions When Negative Age Stereotypes Are Resisted." *Social Science & Medicine* 119 (2014): 170–4.

Levy, B. R., M. D. Slade, T. E. Murphy, and T. M. Gill. "Association Between Positive Age Stereotypes and Recovery from Disability in Older Persons." *Journal of the American Medical Association* 308 (2012): 1972–3.

Lewis, C. S. *A Grief Observed*. 1963; reprint, San Francisco: Harper San Francisco, 1994.

Lewis, R.W.B. *Ethan Wharton: A Biography*. New York: Harper & Row, 1975.

Loewald, Hans W. "On the Therapeutic Action of Psycho-Analysis." *International Journal of Psychoanalysis* 4 (1960): 16–33.

Mace, Nancy L. and Peter V. Rabins. *The 36-Hour Day: A Family Guide to Caring for People with Alzheimer Disease, Other Dementias, and Memory Loss in Later Life*. Baltimore: Johns Hopkins University Press, 1981; 4th ed., 2006.

Madden, John, dir. *Ethan Frome*. 1993.

"Making of *Amour*," dir. Yves Montmayeur, 2012. In *Amour*, dir. Michael Haneke, 2012.

Malcolm, Janet. *The Journalist and the Murderer*. New York: Knopf, 1990.

Marriott, Hugh. *The Selfish Pig's Guide to Caring: How to Cope with the Emotional and Practical Aspects of Caring for Someone*. Illustrations by David Lock. London: Piatkus, 2003; rpt. 2012.

Marsh, Calum. "*Amour*." *Slant*, October 2, 2012. https://www.slantmagazine.com/film/review/amour. Accessed June 13, 2018.

Marshall, Karol. "Treating Mourning—Knowing Loss." *Contemporary Psychoanalysis* 44 (2008): 219–33.

McGill, Robert. "No Nation but Adaptation: 'The Bear Came Over the Mountain,' *Away from Her*, and What It Means to Be Faithful." *Canadian Literature* 197 (2008): 98–113.

Merkin, Daphne. "Northern Exposures." *New York Times Magazine*, October 24, 2004.

Michaels, Lloyd, editor. *Ingmar Bergman's Persona*. Cambridge: Cambridge University Press, 1999.

Miller, Sue. *The Distinguished Guest*. New York: HarperCollins, 1995.

Miller, Sue. *The Story of My Father*. New York: Knopf, large print edition, 2003.

Mitchell, David. "Do You Know Who I Am?" *AAFP News*, October 27, 2014. https://www.aafp.org/news/2014-cod-assembly/20141027quindless address. Accessed December 25, 2018.

Moller, David Wendell. *Confronting Death: Values, Institutions, and Human Mortality*. New York: Oxford University Press, 1996.

Montmayeur, Yves. *Michael H.—Profession: Director*. 2013.

Morgenstern, Naomi. *Wild Child: Intensive Parenting and Posthumanist Ethics*. Minneapolis: University of Minnesota Press, 2018.

Mosley, Walter. *Conversations with Walter Mosley*, edited by Owen E. Brady. Jackson: University Press of Mississippi, 2011.

Mosley, Walter. "Giving Back." In *Black Genius: Africa American Solutions to African American Problems*, edited by Walter Mosley, Manthia Diawara, and Regina Austin. With an Introduction by Walter Mosley. New York: Norton, 1999.

Mosley, Walter. *The Last Days of Ptolemy Gray*. New York: Riverhead Books, 2010.

Mosley, Walter. *Twelve Steps Toward Political Revelation: The Potential for an American Epiphany Under the Rough Blanket of Capitalism*. New York: Nation Books, 2011.

Mosley, Walter. *What Next: A Memoir Toward World Peace*. Baltimore, MD: Black Classic Press, 2003.

Moss, Bob. "*Amour* (2012): An Example of Detailed Analysis." *Vibes from the Screen*, August 28, 2015. http://www.vibesfromthescreen.com/2015/08/1011. Accessed June 13, 2018.

Mottram, James. "The Curzon Interview: Michael Haneke." November 13, 2012. https://homemcr.org./article/article-the-curzon-interview-michael-haneke. Accessed June 14, 2018.

Munro, Alice. "The Bear Came Over the Mountain." In *Hateship, Friendship, Courtship, Loveship, Marriage*. New York: Knopf, 2001. Reprinted as *Away from Her*. New York: Vintage, 2007.

Munro, Alice. *Hateship, Friendship, Courtship, Loveship, Marriage*. New York: Knopf, 2001.

Munro, Alice. *Lives of Girls and Women*. New York: Vintage, 1971; rpt. New York: Vintage, 2001.

Munro, Sheila. *Lives of Mothers & Daughters: Growing Up with Alice Munro*. New York: Union Square Press, 2008.

Murdoch, Iris. *Jackson's Dilemma*. New York: Viking, 1996.

Murdoch, Iris. *The Sea, The Sea*. London: Chatto and Windus, 1978.

Nelems, Rebeccah J. "What Is This Thing Called Empathy?" In *Exploring Empathy: Its Propagations, Perimeters, and Potentialities*, edited by Rebeccah J. Nelems and L. J. Theo. Leiden/Boston: Brill/Rodopi, 2018, 17–38.

Nietzsche, Friedrich. *Beyond Good and Evil*, translated by R. J. Hollingdale, with an Introduction by Michael Tanner. New York: Penguin, 1990.

Nietzsche, Friedrich. "Thus Spake Zarathustra." In *The Philosophy of Nietzsche*. New York: Modern Library, 1954.

Nietzsche, Friedrich. *Twilight of the Gods*. In *The Portable Nietzsche*, selected and translated with an Introduction, Prefaces, and Notes by Walter Kaufmann. New York: Penguin, 1959.

Noddings, Nel. *Caring: A Relational Approach to Ethics and Moral Education*, 2nd ed. Berkeley, CA: University of California Press, updated, 2013.

Nuland, Sherwin. *How We Die*. New York: Vintage, 1993.

Nussbaum, Martha C. "Love and Vision: Iris Murdoch on Eros and the Individual." In *Iris Murdoch and the Search for Human Goodness*, edited by Maria Antonaccio and William Schweiker. Chicago: University of Chicago Press, 1996.

O'Connor, Flannery. *Mystery and Manners*, edited by Sally Fitzgerald and Robert Fitzgerald. New York: Farrar, Straus and Giroux, 1969.

Ogden, Jenni. "The Long Goodbye: Alzheimer's Disease." *Psychology Today*, March 17, 2012. https://www.psychologytoday.com/us/blog/trouble-in-mind/the-long/goodbye. Accessed July 1, 2018.

O'Hehir, Andrew. "Beyond the Multiplex." *Salon*, May 3, 2007. https://www.salom.com/2007/05/03btm_tribeca. Accessed July 9, 2018.

Ohlin, Peter. *Wordless Secrets: Ingmar Bergman's Persona: Modernist Crisis & Canonical Status*. Cornwall: Welsh Academic Press, 2011.

O'Sullivan, Suzanne. "When the Body Speaks." *Psychology Today*, January 3, 2017. https://www.psychologytoday. Com/us/articles/2017/when-the-body-speaks. Accessed May 5, 2018.

Overstreet, Jeffrey. "In Defense of 'Amour.'" http://www.patheoos.com/blogs/lookingcloser/2013/02/in-defense-of-amour. Accessed June 13, 2018.

Ovid. *The Metamorphoses*, 2nd ed., translated by Anthony S. Kline. CreateSpace Independent Publishing Platform, 2014.

Parkes, Colin Murray. *Bereavement: Studies of Grief in Adult Life*, 3rd ed. Madison, CT: International Universities Press, 1998.

Parkes, Colin Murray. "'What Becomes of Redundant World Models?' A Contribution to the Study of Adaptation to Change?" *British Journal of Medical Psychology* 48 (1975): 131–7.

Perl, Jed. "Complicated Bliss." *The New Republic*, April 1, 2009. https://newrepublic.com/article/63142/complicated-bliss.

Pevear, Richard. Introduction to *The Death of Ivan Ilyich and Other Stories*. New York: Knopf, 2009.

Phillips, David. "The Influence of Suggestion on Suicide: Substantive and Theoretical Implications of the Werther Effect." *American Sociological Review* 39 (1974): 340–54. Rpt. in *Essential Papers on Suicide*, edited by John Maltsberger and Mark Goldblatt. New York: New York University Press, 1996, 290–313.

Pickering, George. *Creative Malady: Illness in the Lives and Minds of Charles Darwin, Florence Nightingale, Mary Baker Eddy, Sigmund Freud, Marcel Proust, Elizabeth Barrett Browning*. New York: Delta, 1976.

Pipher, Mary. *Another Country: Navigating the Emotional Terrain of Our Elders*. New York: Riverhead Books, 1999.

Polley, Sarah, dir. *Away from Her*. 2006.

Polley, Sarah, dir. "Preface." *Away from Her*, by Alice Munro. New York: Vintage, 2007.

Porton, Richard. "Michael Haneke's *Amour* Explores Euthanasia and the Purity of Love." *The Daily Beast*. https://www.thedailybeast.com/michael-haneke-film-amour-expl ores -euthanasia. Accessed June 13, 2018.

Prose, Francine. "A Masterpiece You Might Not Want to See." *New York Review of Books*, January 7, 2013.

Quindlen, Anna. "Anna Quindlen's Commencement Address at Villanova." http://www.cs.oswego.edu/~wender/quindlen.html.

Quindlen, Anna. *Blessings*. New York: Random House, 2002.

Quindlen, Anna. "Her Father Was Always Prepared, Even at the End." *Good Housekeeping*, February 7, 2014. https://www.goodhousekeeping.com/life/parenting/tips/a 19302/anna-quindlen . . . . Accessed December 25, 2018.

Quindlen, Anna. *How Reading Changed My Life*. New York: Ballantine, 1998.

Quindlen, Anna. *Imagined London: A Tour of the World's Greatest Fictional City*. Washington, DC: National Geographic, 2004.

Quindlen, Anna. *Living Out Loud*. New York: Random House, 1988; Ballantine, 1994.

Quindlen, Anna. *Lots of Candles, Plenty of Cake*. New York: Random House, 2012.

Quindlen, Anna. *Loud and Clear*. New York: Random House, 2004.

Quindlen, Anna. *Miller's Valley*. New York: Random House, 2016.

Quindlen, Anna. *One True Thing*. New York: Random House, 1994; Dell, 1995.

Quindlen, Anna. "Public & Private; Life After Death." *New York Times*, May 4, 1994.

Quindlen, Anna. *A Short Guide to a Happy Life*. New York: Random House, 2000.

Quindlen, Anna. *Still Life with Crumbs*. New York: Random House, 2013.

Quindlen, Anna. *Thinking Out Loud: On the Personal, the Political, the Public, and the Private*. New York: Random House, 1993; Ballantine, 1994.

Rank, Otto. *The Double: A Psychoanalytic Study*, translated and edited, with an Introduction by Harry Tucker, Jr. New York: New American Library, 1979.

Raphael, Lev. *Edith Wharton's Prisoners of Shame: A New Perspective on Her Neglected Fiction*. New York: St. Martin's Press, 1991.

Renzenbrink, Irene. "Relentless Self-Care." In *Living with Dying: A Handbook for End-of-Life Healthcare Practitioners*, edited by Joan Berzoff and Phyllis R. Silverman. New York: Columbia University Press, 2004, 848–67.

Rich, Adrienne. *Of Woman Born*. New York: Norton, 1976.

Rieff, David. *Swimming in a Sea of Death: A Son's Memoir*. New York: Simon & Schuster, 2008.

Ringstrom, Philip A. "Review of the Movie *Amour*." *International Journal of Psychoanalytic Self Psychology* 9 (2014): 157–61.

Rogers, Carl. *A Way of Being*. Boston: Houghton Mifflin, 1980.

Rohter, Larry. "Words of Love from a Severe Director." *New York Times*, November 2, 2012.

Rose, Hilary and Steven Rose. "Grow Old with Me." *The Lancet* 380 (2012): 2012.

Ross, Catherine Sheldrick. *Alice Munro: A Double Life*. Toronto: ECW Press, 1992.

Roth, Philip. *Everyman*. Boston: Houghton Mifflin, 2006.

Roth, Philip. *Patrimony: A True Story*. 1991. New York: Vintage, 1996.

Routledge, Clay. "Suicides Have Increased. Is This an Existential Crisis?" *New York Times*, June 23, 2018.

Rozin, Paul, Jonathan Haidt, and Clark R. McCauley. "Disgust." In *Handbook of Emotions*, edited by Michael Lewis and Jeannette M. Haviland-Jones, 2nd ed. New York: Guilford Press, 2000, 637–53.

Scharnhorst, Gary. "The Two Faces of Mattie Silver." In *Ethan Frome and Summer: Complete Texts with Introduction, Historical Contexts, and Critical Essays*, edited by Denise D. Knight. Boston: Houghton Mifflin, 2004, 262–71.

Schefski, Harold K. "Tolstoj's Case against Doctors." *Slavic and East European Journal* 22 (1978): 569–73.

Scheidt, Rick J., Jim Vanden Bosch, and Helen Q. Kivnick. "Amour Killing?" *The Gerontologist* 53 (June 2013): 518–19. https://academic.oup.com/gerontologist/article/53/3/518/838903. Accessed June 13, 2018.

Schreiber, Le Anne. *Midstream*. New York: Viking, 1990.

Schreiber, Le Anne. *Light Years*. New York: Lyons & Buford, 1996.

Schulz, Richard and Scott Beach. "Caregiving as a Risk Factor for Mortality: The Caregiver Health Effects Study." *Journal of the American Medical Association* 282 (1999): 2215–19. https://www.ncbi.nlm.nih.gov/pubmed/10605972. Accessed April 7, 2019.

Schwartz, Lynn Sharon. "A Domestic Angel's Messy Death: Review of *One True Thing*." *New York Times*, September 14, 1994.

Scurr, Ruth. "The Darkness of Alice Munro." *Times Literary Supplement*, October 4, 2011. https://www.the-tls.co.uk/articles/public/the-darkness-of-alice-munro. Accessed July 1, 2018.

Segal, Erich. *Love Story*. Cutchogue, NY: Buccaneer Books, 1970.

Sehgal, Parul. "#MeToo Is All Too Real. But to Better Understand It, Turn to Fiction." *New York Times*, May 1, 2019.

Seligman, Martin. *Learned Optimism*. New York: Knopf, 1991.
Shapiro, Arthur K. and Elaine Shapiro. *The Powerful Placebo: From Ancient Priest to Modern Physician*. Baltimore: Johns Hopkins University Press, 1997.
Showalter, Elaine. "Introduction." *Ethan Frome*. Oxford: Oxford World's Classics, 1996.
Shulman, Alix Kates. *A Good Enough Daughter*. New York: Schocken, 1999.
Siegel, Lee. "Sweet and Low." *The New Republic*, March 22, 1999. https://newrepublic.com/article/70931/sweet-and-low.
Slattery, Dennis Patrick. *The Wounded Body: Remembering the Markings of Flesh*. Albany: State University of New York Press, 2000.
Smith, Garrett. *Death Sentences: Styles of Dying in British Fiction*. Cambridge: Harvard University Press, 1984.
Snelling, Sherri. *A Cast of Characters: Celebrity Stories to Help You Prepare to Care*. Bloomington, IN: Balboa Press, 2013.
Snelling, Sherri. "Rosalynn Carter: A Pioneering Caregiving Advocate Says More Must Be Done." *Next Avenue*, August 6, 2012. https://www.nextavenue.org/rosalynn-carter-pioneering-caregiving-advocate... Accessed March 23, 2019.
Solomon, Andrew. *The Noonday Demon: An Atlas of Depression*. New York: Simon & Schuster, 2002.
Solomon, Andrew. *A Stone Boat*. London: Faber and Faber, 1994.
Solomon, Robert C. *True to Our Feelings: What Our Emotions Are Really Telling Us*. Oxford: Oxford University Press, 2007.
Sontag, Susan. *Illness as Metaphor*. New York: Vintage, 1979.
Sontag, Susan. "Ingmar Bergman's *Persona*." In *Styles of Radical Will*. New York: Farrar, Straus and Giroux, 1969. Reprinted in *Ingmar Bergman's Persona*, edited by Lloyd Michaels. Cambridge: Cambridge University Press, 2000, 62–85.
Sorfa, David. "Uneasy Domesticity in the Films of Michael Haneke." *Studies in European Cinema* 3 (2006): 93–104.
Span, Paula. "Ageism: A 'Prevalent and Insidious Health Threat.'" *New York Times*, April 26, 2019.
Span, Paula. "Dementia Is Getting Some Very Public Faces." *New York Times*, November 9, 2018.
Sparks, Nicholas. *The Notebook*. New York: Warner, 1996.
Speck, Oliver C. *Funny Frames: The Filmic Concepts of Michael Haneke*. New York: Continuum, 2010.
Spiro, Howard. "Facing Death." In *Facing Death: Where Culture, Religion, and Medicine Meet*, edited by Howard Spiro, Mary McCrea Curnen, and Lee Palmer Wandel. New Haven: Yale University Press, 1996, xv–xx.
Sprengnether, Madelon. *Mourning Freud*. New York: Bloomsbury Academic, 2018.
Stearns, Ann Kaiser. *Living Through Personal Crisis*. New York: Ballantine, 1985.
Steinbock, Bonnie. "Introduction." In *Killing and Letting Die*, edited by Bonnie Steinbock. Englewood Cliffs, NJ: Prentice Hall, 1980, 1–19.

Steiner, Edward A. *Tolstoy the Man*. First published, 1904. Foreword by A.N. Wilson. Lincoln: University of Nebraska Press, 2005.

Stewart, Garrett. *Death Sentences: Styles of Dying in British Literature*. Cambridge: Harvard University Press, 1984.

Stone, Alan. "Review of *Away from Her.*" *Psychiatric Times* 25 (March 1, 2008). https://www.psychiatrictimes.com/dependent-personality-disorder/away-her. Accessed July 1, 2018.

"The Story of *The 36-Hour Day.*" https://jhupbooks.jhu.edu/story-36-hour-day. Accessed July 9, 2018.

Tan, Amy. *The Bonesetter's Daughter*. New York: Putnam's, 2001.

Taylor, Susan L. "The Gerasim Model of Caregiving: Reflections on Tolstoy's Novella, *The Death of Ivan Ilych.*" *Death Studies* 21 (1997): 299–304.

Thompson, Anne. "*Amour* Auteur Michael Haneke Talks Riva and Trintignant, Death of 35 mm." *IndieWire*, February 15, 2013. http://www.indiewire.com/2013/02/amour-auteur-michael-haneke-talks-riva-trintignant-death-of-35mm. Accessed June 13, 2018.

Thomson, David. "The Best Movie of the Year: Michael Haneke's *Amour.*" *The New Republic*, December 12, 2012. https://newrepublic.com/article/110998/the-best-movie-of-the-year-michael-hanekes-amour. Accessed June 13, 2018.

Titze, Anne-Katrin. "Watching Haneke." https://www.eyeforfilm.co.uk/feature/2013-04-26-interview-with-yves-montmayeur. Accessed June 17, 2018.

Tolstoy, Leo. *Anna Karenina*, translated by Louise and Aylmer Maude, Introduction and Notes by W. Gareth Jones. Oxford: Oxford University Press, 1998.

Tolstoy, Leo. *The Death of Ivan Ilych and Other Stories*, translated by Louise Maude and Aylmer Maude. San Bernardino, CA. Accessed February 11, 2018.

Törnqvist, Egil. *Between Stage and Screen: Ingmar Berman Directs*. Amsterdam: Amsterdam University Press, 1995.

Toth, Susan Allen. *No Saints Around Here: A Caregiver's Days*. Minneapolis: University of Minneapolis Press, 2014.

Trilling, Diana. "The House of Mirth Revisited." *Harper's Bazaar* 81 (1974). Rpt. in *Edith Wharton: A Collection of Essays*. Edited by Irving Howe. Englewood Cliffs, NJ: Prentice Hall, 1962, 103–18.

Trilling, Lionel. "Commentary to *The Death of Ivan Ilych.*" In *The Experience of Literature*, edited by Lionel Trilling. New York: Holt, Rinehart and Winston, 1967.

Troyat, Henri. *Tolstoy*, translated by Nancy Amphoux. Garde City, NY: Doubleday, 1967.

Vladeck, Bruce C. *Unloving Care: The Nursing Home Tragedy*. New York: Basic Books, 1980.

Walker, Elsie. *Hearing Haneke: The Sound Tracks of a Radical Auteur*. Oxford: Oxford University Press, 2017.

Walter, Tony. *On Bereavement: The Culture of Grief*. London: McGraw-Hill Education, 1999.

Webster, Brenda. *After Auschwitz: A Love Story*. San Antonio, TX: Wings Press, 2014.

Weil, Robert. "Memories of Iris." In *From a Tiny Corner in the House of Fiction*, edited by Gillian Dooley. Columbia: University of South Carolina Press, 2003, 251–5.

Weir, Robert, editor. *Death in Literature*. New York: Columbia University Press, 1980.

Weisse, Carol, Bernadette Sapienza, and Sophia Foster. "Opportunities for Direct Patient Care in Residential Homes for the Dying: Learning How to Provide Direct Care When There Is No Cure." *The Advisor* (June 2018): 9–19.

Wharton, Edith. *A Backward Glance*. New York: Scribner's, 1964.

Wharton, Edith. *Ethan Frome* (1911). Foreword by Anita Shreve; Afterword by Susanna Moore. New York: Signet, 2009.

Wharton, Edith. *The Fruit of the Tree* (1907). Amherst: Prometheus Books, 2004.

Wharton, Edith. *The Writing of Fiction*. New York: Touchstone, 1997.

Wheatley, Catherine. "Review of *Amour*." *Sight-Sound*, December 2012. https://www.bfi.uk/news/opinion/sight-sound-magazine/reviews-recommendations. Accessed June 13, 2018.

White, Barbara A. "Wharton's New England." In *Ethan Frome and Summer: Complete Texts with Introduction, Historical Contexts, and Critical Essays*, edited by Denise D. Knight. Boston: Houghton Mifflin, 2004, 225–32.

Wilson, Edmund. *The Wound and the Bow: Seven Studies in Literature*. New York: Oxford University Press, 1947; rpt., 1965.

Wogrin, Carol. "Professional Issues and Thanatology." In *Handbook of Thanatology: The Essential Body of Knowledge for the Study of Death, Dying, and Bereavement*, edited by David Balk. New York: Routledge, 2007, 371–86.

Wolff, Cynthia Griffin. *A Feast of Words: The Triumph of Edith Wharton*. Oxford: Oxford University Press, 1978.

Woodward, Kathleen. *Aging and Its Discontents: Freud and Other Fictions*. Bloomington: Indiana University Press, 1991.

Woolf, Virginia. *Moments of Being: Unpublished Autobiographical Writings*, edited with an Introduction and Notes by Jeane Schulkind. New York: Harcourt Brace Jovanovich, 1976.

Wray, John. "Minister of Fear." *New York Times Magazine*, September 23, 2007.

Wurmser, Leon. "Shame: The Veiled Companion of Narcissism." In *The Many Faces of Shame*, edited by Donald L. Nathanson. New York: Guilford Press, 1967, 64–92.

Zarit, Steven H. "The History of Caregiving in Dementia." In *Supporting the Caregiver in Dementia: A Guide for Health Care Professionals*, edited by Sheila M. LoboPrabhu, Victor A. Molinari, and James W. Lomax. Baltimore: Johns Hopkins University Press, 2006, 3–22.

Zernike, Kate. "Love in the Time of Dementia." *New York Times*, November 18, 2007.

Zielinski, Luisa. "Michael Haneke, the Art of Screenwriting." *Paris Review*, Winter 2014. https://www.theparisreview.org/interviews/6354/michael-haneke-the-art-of-the-interview. Accessed June 13, 2018.

# Index

Abel, Emily K.   2–3, 8–9, 40, 201, 226, 234–5
Abrams, M. H.   257–8
Adams, Annmarie   91
Adams, Kathryn Betts   174–5, 187
Adkins, Janet   125
ageism   207, 214, 226–7
Albom, Mitch   210
Almeida, Joyce   186
Alterra, Aaron (E. S. Goldman)   104–5
Anderson, Robert   7
Andersson, Bibi   53, 57, 70
anorexia   168
Antigone complex   168
Anyar, Uma   177
Ariès, Philippe   17
assumptive world   5
Astrow, Alan   137–8
Auchincloss, Louis   35
Auden, W. H.   89, 116
Austen, Jane   105, 128, 215

Barthes, Roland   11
Bartlett, Rosamund   25–6
Battin, Margaret Pabst   136
Bayley, John   1, 7, 11, 14, 22, 26, 95–122, 164, 184, 259
  *Elegy for Iris*   1, 14, 95–112, 117, 122, 198
  *Iris and Her Friends*   14, 95, 98, 108–18, 121–2, 184
  *Leo Tolstoy*   26
  *The Power of Delight*   122
  *Selected Essays*   116
  *Widower's House*   14, 95, 96, 118–22
Beckett, Samuel   27, 209
Bellow, Saul   73, 208
Bem, Sandra L.   211, 228–30
Bennett, Alma   147–8, 156, 159
Benstock, Shari   51
Benzel, Edward   245
Bergman, Ingmar   13, 53–72, 79, 80, 103, 188, 259

*Bergman on Bergman*   54, 60, 69
*Face to Face*   70
*Four Screenplays of Ingmar Bergman*   56, 64
*Images: My Life in Film*   55, 58, 68, 71
*The Magic Lantern*   55–6, 65, 68
*Persona*   13, 53–72, 103, 107, 184, 187, 259
Berlant, Lauren   260
Berthin-Scaillet, Agnès   90
Bezzubova, Elena   38
Bloom, Harold   96
Bonnard, Pierre   167, 170
Borrie, Cathie   261
Bourdain, Anthony   190
Bowlby, John   24
Bradshaw, Peter   87
Broadbent, Jim   108
Brock, Dan   137
Brody, Richard   174, 175, 185
Brontë, Emily   136, 144
Browning, Elizabeth Barrett   49, 146
Bruckner, D. J. R.   205
Buber, Martin   236
Butler, Katy   4
Butler, Robert N.   207
Byock, Ira   136–8

Camus, Albert   98
Canetti, Elias   100
caregiving
  and Alzheimer's disease   1, 4–7, 14, 22, 74, 76, 86–9, 93–5, 98–120, 125, 147, 195, 203–4, 207, 216, 221–31, 243, 255–7
  and anticipatory caregiving anxiety   129, 220
  and assisted living facilities   242–4
  and attachment theory   11, 24–5
  and boundary loss   13, 54, 64
  and burn-out   4, 10, 21, 72, 256
  and challenges of   6, 11, 49, 114, 130, 133, 198

and chronic health issues  4, 77
  and community-run comfort care homes  244
  and compassion fatigue  4, 10, 21, 72, 107, 256
  as a dangerous activity  3–4, 12, 16, 41, 53, 64
  and depression  2, 25, 41, 188, 239
  and emotional contagion  10, 64–6, 68, 71–2, 99, 107–8, 141, 159, 172, 190, 259
  emotional cost of  3
  and empathy  10, 23, 26, 63–4, 68, 102, 107, 127, 130, 135, 144, 181, 191, 224, 228
  and end-of-life issues  2, 5, 16, 21, 28, 87, 124, 136, 159, 181, 213, 222, 230, 233–9, 249–53
  and ethics of care  23, 71–2, 98
  and euthanasia  14, 15, 32, 117, 124–5, 131–3, 136–8, 171, 175, 184–9
  and exhaustion  2, 10, 226, 256
  and fantasies of martyrdom  13, 15, 46, 148, 151, 168–9
  and gender differences  4
  and "Gerasim model of caregiving"  12, 23, 43
  and gratitude  24, 104, 105, 122, 206
  and high morbidity risks  4
  and homicidal/suicidal feelings  10, 15, 27, 134, 141, 184
  and honest communication  23, 43, 253
  and hospice  5, 107, 186, 227, 234–5, 238, 246–7
  and how-to books  1, 13–14, 16, 27, 71, 105
  and incontinence  22, 114–15, 164, 182–3
  intergenerational nature of  33, 140, 186
  and lack of social recognition  3
  and long-term residential care  91
  and losing independence  3, 198, 220
  and matchmaking  14, 82–3
  and narcissistic conflicts  13, 61–3, 80
  and National Alliance for Caregiving  1, 4
  and pain management  17, 129, 140, 186, 234
  and palliative care  14, 137, 185, 234–5, 238, 245
  and physician-assisted suicide  33, 138, 185, 229, 235
  as a progress or decline narrative  16, 207–31, 259
  and psychosomatic illness  13, 16, 40, 49–50
  and reinvention of elder care  244
  and the right-to-die movement  124–5, 142, 229
  and self-care  3, 71, 110
  and self-help books  9–13, 22, 105, 133, 225–6
  stigma of  87, 120, 187
  and survival strategies  14, 104–7, 109–11, 122
  and transference and countertransference  66–7, 168
  and vulnerable subjects  6, 116
  and "writing/righting wrong"  15, 158, 160, 163
Carey, Benedict  190
Carter, Roslyn  1–4
Casado-Gual, Núria  85
Cassavetes, Nick  87, 256
Cavett, Dick  70
Charon, Rita  28, 249
Chekhov, Anton  73, 81, 175, 211
Chivers, Sally  89, 91
Chodorow, Nancy  66, 67
Christie, Julie  1, 87, 88, 93, 173
Clay, George R.  27
Clinton, Bill  193, 234
Cohen, Hubert J.  56, 70
Coles, Joanna  102
*Commonwealth Fund 1998 Survey of Women's Health*  4
Conrad, Joseph  54, 209
Conrad, Peter  173, 182
Conradi, Peter J.  95, 96, 112
continuing bonds  7, 14
copycat suicide  190
Couser, G. Thomas  116
Cowie, Peter  53, 63, 69
creative malady  49
"cruel optimism"  259–60

Cruzan, Nancy   125
Csikszentmihalyi, Mihaly   5

Danaher, David S.   29
Dargis, Manohla   173, 182
Darwin, Charles   49
DeBaggio, Thomas   195
de Beauvoir, Simone   140, 212–13
Dench, Judi   108
depersonalization/derealization
    disorder   38
"devouring mother"   86
*Diagnostic and Statistical Manual of
    Mental Disorders (DSM)*   38
Dickens, Charles   56, 126–7, 149, 257
DiGiulio, Robert C.   17
Dodson, Samuel Fisher   46
Dolby, Sandra K.   225
double effect   135–7
Dowbiggin, Ian   136–7
Drabble, Margaret   208
Dreyfus, Alfred   158
Duffy, Charles   228
Dukakis, Olympia   87

Ebert, Roger   66, 87, 142, 192
Eddy, Mary Baker   49
Edelman, Hope   144–5
*Electra*   13, 53, 58, 66, 68
Eliot, George   26, 45, 95, 144
Eliot, T. S.   54, 257
Emanuel, Ezekiel J. and Linda L.
    Emanuel   236–7
Erikson, Erik   181, 189
Erlich, Gloria C.   44
Ernaux, Annie   166, 239, 243
Eyre, Richard   87, 108, 182

*Family Caregiver Basics: A Practical
    Guide*   2
Farwell, Tricia M.   40
Faulkner, William   194, 209
Feinberg, Cara   85
filial memoir   212–15, 221–2, 226
Fink, Sheri   235
Fitzgerald, F. Scott   12, 245
Flaubert, Gustave   189
Fletcher, John   96
"flow"   5
Forster, John   149

Foster, Gwendolyn Audrey   66
Frankel, Eduard   117
Franklin, Carl   142
Franklin, Ruth   81
Franzen, Jonathan   73, 86
Freud, Sigmund   7, 39–40, 49, 62–3, 85
Fry, Sara T.   23
Fullerton, Morton   80
Fulton, Robert   3

Gailey, Elizabeth Atwood   124
Galsworthy, John   139
Gawande, Atul   16, 233–54, 258, 259
    *Being Mortal*   16, 233–54
    *Better*   234, 253
    *Complications*   234, 237–8
    "How Do We Heal Medicine?"   235
Genova, Lisa   230
Gilbert, Sandra M.   15, 27, 111, 158
Gilligan, Carol   23
Gilman, Charlotte Perkins   48
Glick, Ira   121
Goethe, Johann Wolfgang von   190, 258
Gogröf, Andrea   180, 185
Goldfield, Hannah   174
Goldman, Marlene   86
González-Ramos, Gladys   191
"good death"   28
Goodman, Susan   44
Gordon, Mary   14–15, 40, 74, 147–70, 239, 259
    *Circling My Mother*   15, 147, 149, 152, 155, 157–70, 185, 198, 259
    *Conversations with Mary
        Gordon*   147, 149
    "The Deadly Sins/Anger"   161
    *Final Payments*   148–55, 159, 160, 168–9
    *Good Boys and Dead Girls and Other
        Essays*   40
    *Joan of Arc*   169
    *Men and Angels*   153
    *Reading Jesus*   156
    *Seeing Through Places*   148, 156
    *The Shadow Man*   149, 152–7, 160, 163, 168–9
    *Spending*   169
Gorer, Geoffrey   119
Greenberg, Gary   217

Greenwood, E. B.   31
Gross, Terry   203–4
Grundmann, Roy   185
Gullette, Margaret Morganroth   16, 89, 186, 207–31, 240, 259
  *Aged by Culture*   214–15
  *Agewise*   215–20, 225
  *Declining to Decline*   209–214, 218, 219, 231
  *Ending Ageism*   226–7
  *Safe at Last in the Middle Years*   208–10
  "When My Mother Wanted to Die"   227
Gutis, Philip S.   76

Hall, Donald   11
Haneke, Michael   12, 15, 118, 171–92, 259
  *Amour*   12, 15, 118, 171–92, 198, 242, 259
  *Benny's Video*   175–6, 184
  *Funny Games*   176
Hardy, Thomas   114, 120–1, 215
Hatfield, Elaine   65
Healey, Emma   261
Heilbrun, Carolyn   211, 215
Hemingway, Ernest   130, 132
Henig, Robin Marantz   228–30
Hogan, Patrick Colm   10
Holden, Stephen   176
Holland, Norman N.   72, 93
Hope, A. D.   14, 97
Howe, Irving   29
Hughes, Ted   190
Humphrey, Derek   228
Huppert, Isabelle   172, 189
Hurt, William   142
Hutchinson, Alex   253

irremediable pain   14, 129

Jacobs, Barry J.   37
Jahn, Gary R.   20, 24, 27
Jamison, Kay Redfield   11
Janov, Arthur   70
Jelinek, Elfriede   176
Joyce, James   91
Jurecic, Ann   9
Jusdanis, Gregory   235

Kafka, Franz   27, 69, 144, 209
Kahneman, Daniel   249
Kaptchuk, Ted J.   217
Kauffman, Stanley   179
Kawin, Bruce   57
Kenyon, Jane   11
Kevorkian, Jack   117, 125–6, 131
Kirsch, Irving   216
Kitwood, Tom   224–5
Klass, Dennis   7
Klein, Julia M.   216
Kleinman, Arthur   27
Koestler, Arthur   118

Lacan, Jacques   187
Laditka, Sarah B.   220
Lane, Anthony   173
Larocco, Steve   64
Larson, Jennifer   201
Lawrence, D. H.   122
Lean, David   88
Leavitt, Sarah   6–7
Lee, Hermione   47
Lentricchia, Frank   211
Lermontov, Mikhail   55
Levy, Becca R.   207–8
Lewis, C. S.   11, 98
Lewis, R. W. B.   47–50
Loewald, Hans   157

Mace, Nancy L.   88, 225
McGill, Robert   89, 93
McHugh, Paul R.   225
MacLeod, Alistair   89
Madden, John   45
Malcolm, Janet   115
Mann, Thomas   27
Marriott, Hugh   9, 113
Marsh, Calum   185
Marshall, Karol   7
maternal loss   123–4, 135, 143–5
matrophobia   211
Melville, Herman   58
Merkin, Daphne   74
Miller, Nancy K.   212
Miller, Sue   16, 222–4
Mitchell, S. Weir   48–9
models of physician-patient relationship   236–8
Moller, David Wendell   28

Montaigne 236
Montmayeur, Yves 189
Moore, Julianne 1
Morgenstern, Naomi 11
Mosley, Walter 15, 193–206, 259
   *Black Genius* 206
   *Conversations with Walter Mosley* 203
   *The Last Days of Ptolemy Gray* 15, 193–206
   *Twelve Steps Toward Political Revelation* 204
   *What Next* 203
Munro, Alice 13–14, 73–94, 99, 114, 147, 259
   "The Bear Came Over the Mountain" 13–14, 73–94, 114, 198, 259
   *Hateship, Friendship, Courtship, Loveship, Marriage* 73, 81
   *Lives of Girls and Women* 73, 84
Munro, Sheila 74, 92
Murdoch, Iris 1, 22, 95–122
   *Jackson's Dilemma* 106
   *The Sea, The Sea* 95–6

Nabokov, Vladimir 114
Narcissus 79–82
narrative medicine 28
Nelems, Rebeccah J. 64
Nietzsche, Friedrich 46–7, 53, 72, 119, 192, 214, 230–1
Nightingale, Florence 49
Nitschke, Philip 228
Noddings, Nel 23–4, 43, 180, 198
Nouwen, Henri 3
Nuland, Sherwin 137
Nussbaum, Martha 96
Nykvist, Sven 57

Obama, Barack 234
obsessional review 121–2
O'Connor, Flannery 259–60
O'Connor, Sandra Day 93–4, 105
Ogden, Jenni 92–3
O'Hehir, Andrew 87, 91
Ohlin, Peter 54
O'Neill, Eugene 209
O'Sullivan, Suzanne 49
Overstreet, Jeffrey 185

Ovid 106, 171
Ozick, Cynthia 73, 81

Parkes, Colin Murray 5, 119, 121
PEP-Web 7
Pevear, Richard 27
Pickering, George 49
Pillemer, Karl 208
Pinsent, Gordon 87
Pipher, Mary 211–12
placebo 216–17
Plath, Sylvia 190, 209
Polley, Sarah 14, 73, 86–93, 225
positive psychology movement 209
projective identification 165
Prose, Francine 172, 192
Proust, Marcel 27, 49, 109, 153

Quindlen, Anna 1, 14, 74–5, 123–45, 147, 182, 259
   "Anna Quindlen's Commencement Address at Villanova" 139
   *Blessings* 142
   *How Reading Changed My Life* 137, 138, 143
   *Imagined London* 144
   *Living Out Loud* 123, 124, 129, 130
   *Lots of Candles, Plenty of Cake* 138, 140
   *Loud and Clear* 133, 139
   *Miller's Valley* 143
   *One True Thing* 1, 14, 75, 123–45, 182, 224, 242, 252, 259
   "Public & Private; Life After Death" 133
   *A Short Guide to a Happy Life* 123
   *Still Life with Crumbs* 143
   *Thinking Out Loud* 125
Quindlen, Prudence 123, 138, 140
Quindlen, Robert 139

Rabins, Peter V. 88, 225
Rank, Otto 61–2
Raphael, Lev 39
Renzenbrink, Irene 3
"rest cure" 48, 77
Rich, Adrienne 211
Rieff, David 250–1
Ringstrom, Philip A. 186–8

Riva, Emmanuelle   171–2, 182
Rogers, Carl   26, 64
Rohter, Larry   179
Rose, Hilary and Steven Rose   185–6
Ross, Catherine Sheldrick   76
Ross, Elisabeth-Kübler   27–8, 92
Roth, Philip   22, 115, 209, 213, 240
Rozin, Paul   115, 164
Russo, Mary   2

Sartre, Jean Paul   47, 95
schadenfreude   46
Scharnhorst, Gary   46
Schefski, Harold K.   22–3
Scheidt, Rick J.   186
Schreiber, Le Anne   251–3
Schulz, Richard   4
Schwartz, Lynn Sharon   129
Schwartz, Morrie   210
Scurr, Ruth   86
Segal, Erich   255
Sehgal, Parul   17
Seligman, Martin   209
sentimentalism   257–8
Shakespeare, William   66, 117, 179
shame   10, 21, 39, 43, 68, 76, 96, 130, 149, 155–6, 162–4, 187, 192, 213
Shapiro, Arthur K. and Elaine Shapiro   216
Shelley, Mary   144
Showalter, Elaine   42
Shulman, Alix Kates   16, 220–2, 225
Siegel, Lee   135
Simon, John   53, 61
simulation   10
Siskel, Gene   142
Slattery, Dennis Patrick   24, 29
Smith, Sydney   105, 107
Snelling, Sherri   1–4
Solomon, Andrew   141–2
Solomon, Robert C.   23, 165
Sontag, Susan   19, 66, 250
Sorfa, David   183
Spade, Kate   190
Span, Paula   207–8, 216
Sparks, Nicholas   16, 255–61
Spiro, Howard   119–20
Sprengnether, Madelon   7
stage theory of dying   27–8, 92

Stearns, Ann Kaiser   180
Stein, Gertrude   144
Steinbock, Bonnie   137
Steiner, Edward A.   30
Stephen, Leslie   220
Stewart, Garrett   119
Stone, Alan   87
Stowe, Harriet Beecher   144
Streep, Meryl   142, 182
Syme, Rodney   229

Tan, Amy   243
Taylor, Ella   173
Taylor, Susan L.   23, 43
Terence   110
"textual resurrection"   111
Tharaud, Alexandre   177
*13 Reasons Why*   190
Thomas, Dylan   125, 185, 257
Thompson, Anne   172
Timson, Judith   76
Tolstoy, Leo   12–13, 16, 19–30, 79, 96, 122, 233–4, 241, 243–4, 258
   *Anna Karenina*   29, 117, 128
   *The Death of Ivan Ilych*   12–13, 16, 19–30, 37, 44, 64, 79, 143, 177, 192, 233, 238, 249
Törnqvist, Egil   54, 57
Toth, Susan Allen   5, 9, 214
Trilling, Diana   47
Trilling, Lionel   27
Trintignant, Jean-Louis   171–2, 179, 189
Troyat, Henri   27
Tylor, Anne   208

Ullmann, Liv   53, 57
Updike, John   208

Villers, Audhild   122
Vladeck, Bruce C.   239

Walker, Elsie   175, 178, 185
Walter, Tony   17
Washington, Denzel   193
Webster, Brenda   261
Weevil, Assia   190
Weil, Robert   96
Weir, Robert   27
Weisse, Carol   244

Wharton, Edith   13, 31–51, 79
  *A Backward Glance*   47, 51
  *Ethan Frome*   13, 31–51, 53, 64, 184, 259
  *The Fruit of the Tree*   32–3, 45
  *The Writing of Fiction*   46
Wharton, Edward Robbins   47–8, 50
Wheatley, Catherine   185
White, Barbara A.   37
Wilde, Oscar   257
Wilson, Karen Brown   242
Winslet, Kate   108
Wogrin, Carol   107
Wolff, Cynthia Griffin   48, 50

Woodward, Kathleen   2, 212
Woolf, Virginia   144, 220
Wordsworth, Dorothy   144
Wray, John   175
writer's block   102
Wurmser, Leon   156
Wyatt, Richard   11

Zarit, Steven H.   77
Zellweger, Renée   142
Zernike, Kate   93–4
Zielinski, Luisa   177
Zola, Emile   158

www.ingramcontent.com/pod-product-compliance
Lightning Source LLC
Chambersburg PA
CBHW072127290426
44111CB00012B/1802